Duncan Barrett is a writer and editor specialising in biography and memoir. He grew up in London and studied English at Jesus College, Cambridge. In 2010 he edited the First World War memoirs of pacifist saboteur Ronald Skirth, published as *The Reluctant Tommy*. He is co-author, with Nuala Calvi, of a trio of *Sunday Times* Top 10 bestsellers: *The Sugar Girls*, which was ranked second in the history bestsellers of 2012; *GI Brides*, which was also a *New York Times* bestseller in America; and *The Girls Who Went to War*, which was described by Dame Vera Lynn as 'an important and inspiring book'. In 2014 his first solo title, *Men of Letters: The Post Office Heroes Who Fought the Great War*, was nominated for the People's Book Prize.

WHEN THE GERMANS CAME

*True Stories of Life Under
Occupation in the Channel Islands*

DUNCAN BARRETT

SIMON &
SCHUSTER

London · New York · Sydney · Toronto · New Delhi

First published in Great Britain by Simon & Schuster UK Ltd, 2018,
with the title *Hitler's British Isles*
This edition published in Great Britain by Simon & Schuster UK Ltd, 2019

5 7 9 10 8 6 4

Simon & Schuster UK Ltd
1st Floor
222 Gray's Inn Road
London WC1X 8HB

www.simonandschuster.co.uk
www.simonandschuster.com.au
www.simonandschuster.co.in

Simon & Schuster Australia, Sydney
Simon & Schuster India, New Delhi

A CIP catalogue record for this book
is available from the British Library

Paperback ISBN: 978-1-4711-4816-3
eBook ISBN: 978-1-4711-4819-4

Typeset in Sabon by M Rules
Printed and bound by CPI Group (UK) Ltd, Croydon, CR0 4YY

For Nuala

CONTENTS

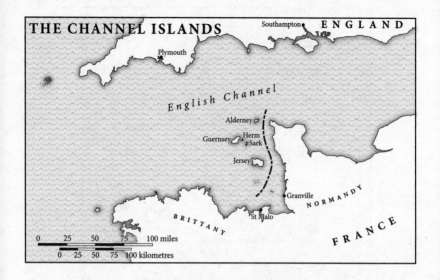

THE CHANNEL ISLANDS

ENGLAND

Plymouth

Southampton

English Channel

Alderney

Guernsey
Herm
Sark

Jersey

Granville

NORMANDY

BRITTANY

St Malo

FRANCE

| 0 | 25 | 50 | 75 | 100 miles |
| 0 | 25 | 50 | 75 | 100 kilometres |

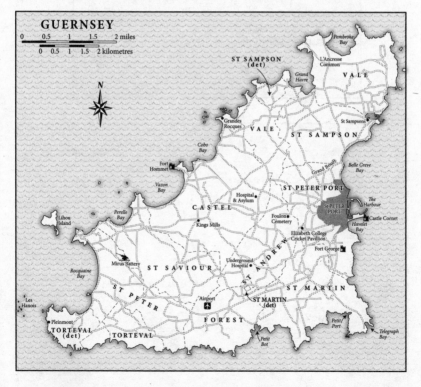

GUERNSEY

| 0 | 0.5 | 1 | 1.5 | 2 miles |
| 0 | 0.5 | 1 | 1.5 | 2 kilometres |

N

Pembroke
Bay

ST SAMPSON
(det)

L'Ancresse
Common

VALE

Grand
Havre

Grandes
Rocques

VALE

ST SAMPSON

St Sampsons

Cobo
Bay

Fort
Hommet

Grand Bouet

Belle Greve
Bay

Vazon
Bay

ST PETER PORT

Lihou
Island

Perelle
Bay

CASTEL

Hospital
& Asylum

ST PETER
PORT

The
Harbour

Kings Mills

Foulon
Cemetery

Castle Cornet

Havelet
Bay

Elizabeth College
Cricket Pavillion

Rocquaine
Bay

Mirus Battery

ST SAVIOUR

Underground
Hospital

Fort George

ST ANDREW

ST MARTIN

Les
Hanois

ST PETER

Airport

ST MARTIN
(det)

Petit
Port

Pleinmont

FOREST

Telegraph
Bay

TORTEVAL
(det)

TORTEVAL

Petit
Bot

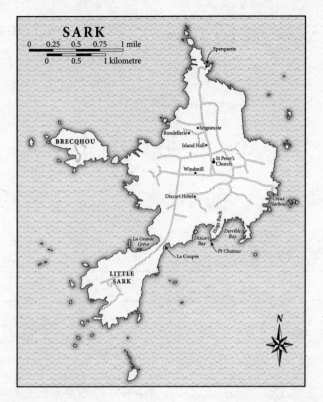

SARK

0   0.25   0.5   0.75   1 mile

0   0.5   1 kilometre

BRECQHOU

Rondellerie •   • Seigneurie

Island Hall •

St Peter's Church •

Windmill •

Dixcart Hotel •

Creux Harbour

Hog's Back

Derrible Bay

Dixcart Bay

La Grande Grève

Pt Chateau

La Coupée

LITTLE SARK

Eperquerie

N

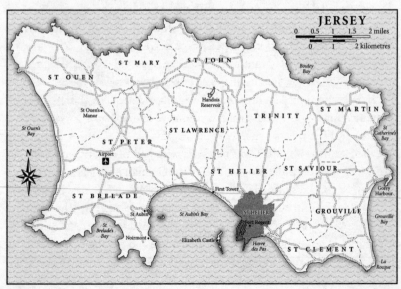

JERSEY

0   0.5   1   1.5   2 miles

0   1   2 kilometres

ST OUEN

ST MARY

ST JOHN

Bouley Bay

St Ouen's Manor

Handois Reservoir

TRINITY

ST MARTIN

St Ouen's Bay

ST LAWRENCE

St Catherine's Bay

ST PETER

Airport

N

ST HELIER

ST SAVIOUR

Gorey Harbour

ST BRELADE

First Tower

St Aubin

St Aubin's Bay

ST HELIER

Fort Regent

GROUVILLE

Grouville Bay

St Brelade's Bay

Noirmont

Elizabeth Castle

Havre des Pas

ST CLEMENT

La Rocque

INTRODUCTION

CUT OFF FROM THE MAIN

'Repugnant!'

The prime minister spat out the word, glowering at the small group of men seated around him. Give up British territory to the enemy without a fight? It was unthinkable.

After just over a month in the top job, Churchill had grown accustomed to fierce arguments with the members of his war cabinet. Only three weeks earlier, he had seen off an attempt by his foreign secretary, Lord Halifax, to open peace negotiations with Germany using Mussolini as an intermediary. Then, a combination of dogged determination, inspired oratory and wily political manoeuvring – the PM had summoned an impromptu meeting of his entire, twenty-five-man cabinet to provide a more responsive audience for a typically barnstorming speech – had carried the day.

This time it was the Chiefs of Staff who had brought Churchill a distinctly unappealing proposal. With the German Army now occupying the coast of France, the time had come, they believed, to withdraw their forces from the Channel Islands, an archipelago off the coast of Normandy that was home to more than ninety thousand British subjects. The islands were, they concluded, 'not of major strategic importance', and defending them was more trouble than it was worth.

Churchill was horrified. The Channel Islands had been dependencies of the Crown for the better part of a thousand years. Whatever their strategic value – or lack of it – as far as he was concerned, holding onto them was a matter of principle. After all, wasn't he the man who had promised to fight on the beaches and never surrender? The prospect of German jackboots falling on British soil – and without a single shot being fired – hardly chimed with that impassioned pledge.

Before becoming prime minister, Churchill had spent five years as First Lord of the Admiralty. Surely, he declared, the Royal Navy ought to be able to defend the islands from the enemy. 'If there is a chance of offering a successful resistance,' he argued, 'we ought not to avoid giving him battle there.'

But the response from the vice-chief of Naval Staff was not encouraging. The islands were too far away from the British mainland, and too near to enemy bases at Brest and Cherbourg, for naval forces to adequately protect them, he explained. Added to which, the necessary material simply wasn't available – if anti-aircraft guns and fighter aircraft were deployed to the islands in the numbers required, it would leave the coast of England vulnerable to attack. To put it bluntly, the Channel Islands could only be defended at grave risk to the security of the mainland.

Put that way, there was really no choice. Whether the islands were expendable or not was no longer the issue. They simply weren't worth losing the war over.

That summer, losing the war was looking like a very real possibility. The blitzkrieg, or 'lightning war', unleashed on France, Belgium and the Low Countries had more than lived up to its name. In six blistering weeks, the Wehrmacht had swept through Europe, bringing nation after nation to its knees. Only two days before the war cabinet meeting on the Channel Islands, France had joined Belgium, Holland and Denmark in requesting an armistice, well aware that this would mean long-term occupation by the Germans.

With every one of her former allies now under the Nazi yoke, Britain alone remained in the fight against Germany – and the odds were not in her favour. She had an army less than a third the size of the enemy's, and a population only half as large from which to draw new recruits. There was no doubt that an invasion of Britain was already in Hitler's sights, and short of outright surrender, there seemed little chance of avoiding it.

Since the British Expeditionary Force's scramble to safety from the beaches of Dunkirk a fortnight earlier, the British public had caught their first glimpse of what a German invasion might mean. In the wake of the exhausted, demoralised and bedraggled soldiers who stepped off the little ships came a stream of pitiful refugees – tens of thousands of ordinary civilians whose homes had been overrun by the German Army, and whose lives had already been destroyed thanks to the apparently invincible war machine. Many of those who saw them couldn't help wondering if the wretched state of the new arrivals was a premonition of what was to come when the Germans finally landed on their own soil.

On both sides, preparations for the expected invasion were beginning to get underway. The German Army, Navy and Air Force had been discussing possible strategies since the previous December. Now, following the fall of France, the German High Command began to draw up more definite plans, under the code name Operation Sea Lion. 'I have decided to prepare for an invasion,' Hitler wrote in his Directive No. 16, 'intended to eliminate England as a base for carrying on the war against Germany and, should it be required, completely to occupy it.' Once the RAF had been pummelled into submission by the Luftwaffe, the plan was for over a quarter of a million men to be landed in a matter of days – enough to seize the country for the Führer, and put an end to the war once and for all.

In Britain, ordinary people were readying themselves for the expected onslaught. Almost half a million men aged from seventeen to sixty-five had already enrolled as Local Defence Volunteers (not yet rebranded as the Home Guard) and were practising making Molotov cocktails to hurl at German tanks. Up and down the country, temporary roadblocks had been prepared using tree trunks, abandoned cars and carts full of builder's rubble, and fields where enemy aircraft might land had been peppered with obstacles too. The Petroleum Warfare Department was looking into ways of repelling an enemy fleet by setting the sea itself on fire.

The day before the war cabinet meeting on the Channel Islands, Churchill had told the British people to prepare themselves to face 'the whole fury and might of the enemy', and to brace themselves for a battle that would be remembered for a millennium as the nation's finest hour. As the prime minister delivered his speech in Parliament, government printing presses were rattling off 1.5 million copies of a leaflet entitled 'If the Invader Comes', to be distributed up and down the country over the next few days. 'Think always of your country before you think of yourself,' it declared firmly.

Privately, many civilians were starting to wonder how they would cope if the Germans came knocking on their door. Some resolved to commit suicide, ideally taking a few of the invaders down with them – a wealthy lady in Buckinghamshire planned to invite a group of officers in for champagne laced with weed killer. Others felt they could do their bit by depriving them of valuable supplies. The government had advised homeowners to hide maps, bicycles, petrol, even food. At a Dorset branch of the Women's Institute, there was a spirited debate about how to prevent their large stock of home-made jam from falling into enemy hands. Some members felt that every jar should be smashed to smithereens, others that merely hiding them under the floorboards was sufficient.

The government leaflet didn't mention the possibility of long-term occupation, but many of those who read it must have had that thought at the back of their minds. They had seen the nations of Europe collapse one by one under the weight of the German advance, and the result in every case had been the same. For all Churchill's impassioned rhetoric, there was no guarantee that the great fight to repel the invaders would succeed. And assuming it failed, what then? What would a German occupation of Britain look like?

Of course, they – and we – never had to find out. Three months later, in September 1940, after the Luftwaffe unexpectedly failed to cripple the RAF in the Battle of Britain, Hitler reluctantly shelved Operation Sea Lion. A German invasion, and occupation, was no longer on the cards.

But for more than seventy-five years, the spectre of what might have been has haunted us: there, but for the grace of God, went we. Our collective nightmares have been realised in a variety of chillingly realistic fictions, beginning with the 1942 propaganda movie *Went the Day Well?*, in which a platoon of disguised German paratroopers take over a small English village. The prospect of a Britain under occupation has proved irresistibly fascinating in novels such as Len Deighton's *SSGB* (in which the Germans successfully invaded) and C. J. Sampson's *Dominion* (in which the British, under Prime Minister Halifax, surrendered), in films including *It Happened Here* and *Resistance*, and in Noël Coward's 1946 play *Peace in Our Time*.

These counterfactual occupations continue to fascinate audiences today, even those who were not alive during the war itself and thus have never known first-hand the dreadful tension of that summer in 1940, when fate could easily have taken us in a different direction. In 2015, Amazon Studios' adaptation of Philip K. Dick's novel *The Man in the High Castle*, set in a distinctly *dis*united states carved up between German and Japanese occupiers, scored the highest viewing figures of any original series on their streaming service.

These fictions allow us to ask what might have been had the pendulum of history swung against us. How would those plucky men and women who endured the blitz have fared under German occupation? Would we have suffered the same brutality and humiliations as were heaped on the citizens of Europe? What kind of accommodation would we have come to in order to survive, and what efforts would we have made to push back?

Except here there is no need for fiction – because for five years during the Second World War, almost seventy thousand British subjects faced just such an existence. The only English-speaking people to feel the full force of the German yoke, the Channel Islanders' experiences show us what so nearly came to pass for the rest of Britain. Their stories – of resilience, of desperation, of a complex mixture of compromise and defiance – offer a glimpse into our own alternate history.

For too long, the Occupation of the Channel Islands has been treated as little more than a historical footnote. But for anyone willing to scratch the surface and look beneath the Churchillian rhetoric that has encouraged us to believe that Britain's victory in the Second World War was a matter of destiny, these stories are far more important than that. The Occupation represents a crucial, if neglected, facet of the history of the war, and one that deserves serious, and measured, consideration.

'Repugnant' it might have been, but the decision was ultimately taken, around a table in Whitehall, on that warm summer's day in 1940. For once, the famously pugnacious prime minister found himself exercising the better part of valour. On Churchill's orders, the two thousand-odd British troops stationed in the Channel Islands were instructed to evacuate as soon as possible, clearing the way for the Germans to walk in and seize them without facing any military resistance.

The same day the war cabinet reached its decision, an envoy was despatched to take the news to those who would have to live with the consequences. The bailiffs (presiding officers) of the legislatures of the two largest Channel Islands, Jersey and Guernsey – the latter was part of a 'Bailiwick' containing the smaller islands of Sark, Herm and Alderney as well – had been begging Whitehall for a decision for days. Now that it had been made, the response was swift.

Edgar Dorey, a jurat (elected lay judge and legislator) in the Royal Courts of Jersey who had been sent to London to sound out the government position, returned to the islands bearing a letter from Sir Alexander Maxwell, permanent under-secretary at the Home Office. In it, Maxwell explained that since demilitarisation of the islands would mean the recall of their lieutenant-governors – the official representatives of the British Crown, and their de facto heads of state – the bailiffs would be expected to formally take their place. The islands' ancient system of government was effectively being rescinded.

The Jersey bailiff Alexander Coutanche, an accomplished lawyer with a good grasp of constitutional niceties, called Maxwell in London to protest at a flaw in the plan. 'I'm quite prepared to take the oath of lieutenant-governor,' he explained, 'but I cannot promise before God in the Royal Court that I will defend the island against all incursions of the enemy when I shall have in my pocket your order to surrender everything to the Germans as soon as they put their noses in.'

By this point, however, Maxwell had bigger fish to fry. 'Cut out anything that seems to you, in your special position, to be wrong,' he told Coutanche. The exact terms of the oath were of little interest to him now. In a matter of days, the Channel Islands would no longer be his government's concern.

The message from London was clear: from now on, the islanders were on their own.

CHAPTER ONE

RABBITS AND RATS

On the ground, the war cabinet's decision didn't go down well. Later that day, the Channel Islanders picked up their evening papers to find some alarming headlines splashed across the front pages. 'EVACUATION,' boomed the *Star* in Guernsey. 'ALL CHILDREN TO BE SENT TO MAINLAND TOMORROW. WHOLE BAILIWICK TO BE DEMILITARISED.'

The rival *Guernsey Evening Press* was a little more measured. 'Arrangements are being made for the evacuation of (1) children of school age and (2) children under school age to reception centres in the United Kingdom,' the paper announced, adding – in bold type – the words, 'if parents desire it'.

That 'if' represented a terrible dilemma. Across the islands, mothers and fathers wrestled with their consciences, trying to decide what was best for their children. Should they send them away across the sea to England, a country many had never even visited before and where they would have to rely on the kindness of strangers? Or keep their families united and face the arrival of the Germans together, along with whatever horrors they might bring?

There was little time to make up their minds. In Guernsey the first boats were scheduled to arrive at 2.30 the following morning. Ambrose Sherwill, the island's attorney general, had persuaded the Home Office to delay boarding until 6 a.m. so that the children could at least get a good night's sleep before the voyage, but even so the registration process had to be well underway within hours of the announcement being published. The thousands of parents who were suddenly faced with the most fateful decision of their lives would need to think quickly.

That evening, registration centres sprang up in every island parish. Volunteers worked into the night gathering the names of children, their mothers (those whose offspring were under school age were entitled to accompany them), and young men who planned to sign up for the forces on arrival in Britain.

By 5 a.m. almost two thousand children had already arrived at the White Rock, as Guernsey's main harbour was known. Every one of them was equipped with some spare clothes, a ration book, a gas mask, and some sandwiches to eat on the journey, hurriedly prepared by a small army of volunteers in the kitchens of the nearby Royal Hotel.

Hasty, tearful goodbyes were whispered in the dead of night, as the young passengers were handed over to the care of teachers and guardians. In the interests of public safety, parents were not allowed to approach the harbour themselves, so they were at least spared the sight of their little ones piling onto the boats and disappearing off to sea.

It had been a difficult, restless night, with plenty of tossing and turning for those already beginning to doubt their decisions. When one Guernsey couple, Alfred and Eunice Mahy, went to wake their nine-year-old daughter Lucille for the journey to England, they found they simply couldn't go through with it. 'What are we *doing*?' Alfred whispered, as they stood over the sleeping girl's bed. She had never spent so much as a night away from them before.

In the end, Lucille's parents left her to slumber until morning, and the boat carrying her classmates sailed without her. But she was far from the only child left behind on the islands. Many other mothers and fathers found it equally impossible to send their children off alone into the unknown.

That morning, as the young evacuees continued to file onto the waiting ships, the last of the military personnel stationed in the islands departed as well. At 8 a.m. the SS *Biarritz* left Guernsey, carrying a thousand troops. Some of the soldiers fled in such a rush that they left half-eaten plates of food strewn around their base in Castle Cornet. Around the same time, their counterparts in Jersey departed on the SS *Malines*.

That left only the islands' volunteer part-time soldiers. The Guernsey Militia had already been disbanded, but now their weapons and equipment were shipped off to England along with the departing troops of the regular army. At the same time, the two hundred-odd members of the Jersey Militia departed en masse to join the Hampshire Regiment, setting sail on the only boat available at such short notice, a potato-export vessel called the *Hodder*.

By mid-afternoon, the islands were officially defenceless. With less than a day's notice, the power that had protected them for almost a millennium had abandoned them.

Along with instructions on evacuating children, the *Jersey Evening Post* had offered some advice to readers who were understandably alarmed by the 'grave decision' to demilitarise the islands. 'We believe there to be no reason at all for panic,' the paper had declared. 'Keep calm, obey the regulations issued by the authorities and carry on, as far as it is possible, with one's ordinary business.'

It was easier said than done. The hurried evacuation of children had sent a message that the islands were no longer considered safe, and as the new day dawned many islanders were in the grip of barely disguised panic. The town hall in Jersey's capital, St Helier, had been besieged since the early hours by long queues of tense, silent people hoping to register to leave as quickly as possible. Once they had the necessary permits, their next concern was securing sufficient funds for a new life in England. That morning there was a run on the banks as thousands of islanders attempted to draw out their savings, queuing for hours and facing terrifying, surging crowds – only to be told that withdrawals had been capped at £5 per person.

At the harbours, the scenes were even more chaotic. Thousands of people were anxiously waiting behind barriers that blocked entry to the piers. Whole families sat together on the ground, their bags and belongings piled up around them as they sweltered in the blazing June sun.

The rush to evacuate had left a trail of chaos. Once-prized vehicles were abandoned by the roadside as their owners raced to board the departing ships – in some cases stopping just long enough to press the keys into the hand of a lucky passer-by – and the hedgerows and ditches along the roads leading into the island capitals, St Helier and St Peter Port, were soon littered with discarded bicycles.

Cats and dogs, meanwhile, were being put down in their thousands. When the vets' supplies of euthanasia chemicals ran out, many owners resorted to killing their pets themselves. Others had the decision made for them. A Jewish couple who lived on Sark, Mr and Mrs Abrams, hopped on the first boat for England, leaving a pair of pet monkeys behind. Their housekeeper had agreed to look after the property while they were gone, but the exotic animals were a step too far for her, so she arranged for a neighbouring farmer to come and shoot them.

In Jersey, roughly half the population – a total of twenty-three thousand people – had soon registered to leave. But evacuation on such a massive scale presented a number of problems beyond the basic logistical challenge of transporting them all. If too many people left, it might be impossible for those who stayed behind to keep the day-to-day life of the islands going. Equally, they would be placing a heavy burden on the British government. Taken together, the population of the Channel Islands was not far short of a hundred thousand people. That number of refugees pouring into Weymouth or Southampton was the last thing anyone needed at what was already a time of crisis.

The island's political leaders did their best to restore calm and attempt to stem the tide of evacuees. The bailiff of Jersey, Alexander Coutanche, addressed a large crowd in St Helier's Royal Square, telling them that their only duty was not to panic. 'I will never leave, and my wife will be at my side,' he announced, promising that the rest of his government – the States of Jersey – would remain as well, and then leading his people in a rousing performance of the national anthem.

Inside the parliament building, Edgar Dorey – the man who had been sent as an emissary to London a few days earlier – took a more confrontational stance, denouncing those who planned to evacuate as 'rabbits and rats'. 'I have been filled with disgust,' he declared angrily, in a speech that was reproduced in the following day's newspaper. 'I would like this house to express its utter contempt for what these people are doing. It is the worst characteristic of human nature, cowardice!'

In Guernsey, the attorney general, Ambrose Sherwill, was attempting to prevent a crisis at the harbour, where the long wait for boats was on the verge of spilling over into outright pandemonium. He had instructed the government secretary to hold onto a dozen rifles and bayonets that were supposed to have been shipped off to England, reasoning that if things got really chaotic he could arm the police with them. Since there were no bullets left he felt he was still obeying the spirit of his orders to demilitarise the island, and there was no need for anyone else to know that the guns weren't loaded. The mere sight of them, he hoped, would be enough.

Posters went up all over the islands, imploring those fleeing their homes to reconsider. 'Keep your heads! Don't be yellow!' declared one. 'Why go mad?' asked another. 'There's no place like home. Cheer up!' The moral force of the messages was somewhat undermined, however, when it became known that the man behind several of them had jumped on the next boat to England as soon as he finished putting them up.

'Mad' as the frantic rush to evacuate might have been, it was at least understandable for a population who had always considered themselves reassuringly cut off from international affairs. Although many islanders had served in the First World War, the islands themselves had remained a safe haven. In fact, only a few months earlier they had been promoted in Britain as the ideal wartime holiday resort. 'Happily, our island is far removed from the theatre of war,' the Jersey Tourism Committee had declared cheerfully. 'The bays, with their eternal sands, sea and sunshine, together produce an atmosphere of peaceful tranquillity strangely different from the rest of the world.'

In mid-June the islands were certainly at their most attractive – the long, sandy beaches glistening under cloudless skies – and for their inhabitants, many of them English retirees who had grown used to the old-fashioned, gentle pace of life they offered, it was hard to credit that they could soon become the site of modern warfare.

And yet, that summer, the terror of the German war machine ran deep. The islanders had read and heard about the brutal blitzkrieg that had cut a swathe through Europe, leaving death and destruction in its wake. Only a week earlier, beleaguered French soldiers had been rescued from St Malo by a flotilla of little ships despatched from Jersey's yacht club, stopping off in St Helier on their way to regroup in England. The sight of their bloodied bandages had made a strong impression on the locals. These were men who had gone up against the Germans and lost – they were lucky to have escaped with their lives.

For those whose memories stretched back as far as the last war, there was the lingering memory of propaganda cartoons in which the 'Hun' was depicted as a ferocious beast, intent on raping women and murdering babies. The prospect of these animals arriving, and making the islands their home, scarcely bore thinking about.

As the days wore on, the island authorities continued to do their best to provide reassurance, and gradually the initial panic gave way to uncertainty. Those who had long-established businesses or farms on the islands were loath to give them up for the life of a refugee. In time, thousands of men and women changed their minds about leaving. In Jersey, where Edgar Dorey's furious speech had cast shame on a population gripped by fear, less a third of those who had registered for evacuation – around 6,600 people – ultimately went through with it. In Guernsey, where the official response was more muted, the number of evacuees was much higher, with seventeen thousand eventually leaving.

Some islanders changed their minds at the last moment, getting as far as the harbour and then baulking at the state of the overcrowded vessels, many of which were normally used for transporting food-stuffs, or even coal, rather than passengers. Reports from those who had already made the journey were not encouraging. A letter written by one evacuated islander, and subsequently published in *The Times*, described a voyage on a troop ship, the *Antwerp*, in which two thou-sand people were crammed into a boat intended for seven hundred, chased by a German submarine across the Channel and then left on board in Weymouth for seventeen hours without food or water.

A number of evacuees had arrived in England only to realise that they had made a terrible mistake. After just a couple of days, one woman had convinced herself that she should never have left her husband behind in Guernsey. She managed to secure passage on the next boat back, but soon found that her beloved had also come to the same conclusion. By the time she arrived home he had already left the island intending to meet up with her in England. It would be five long years before the couple saw each other again.

Others were torn between competing claims on their affections. In Guernsey, eighteen-year-old Ruth Leadbeater and her twin sister Mary had cheerfully waved their parents and younger sisters off, promising to join them on the mainland once they had finished packing up the family home. But a few days later, when they arrived at the harbour to board their own evacuation boat, the girls began to have second thoughts. With them were Ruth's fiancé Cliff and Mary's boyfriend Jack, both of whom were of military age and liable to be conscripted in England. The lads were no cowards, but they felt the war wasn't really theirs to fight – and their families needed them on the island. Jack worked as a fisherman, bringing in the daily catch for his parents' chip shop in the Bouet, just outside St Peter Port, while Cliff was a 'grower', tending the tomatoes in the family greenhouses.

Since their boyfriends wouldn't come to England with them, Ruth and Mary decided to stay in Guernsey. But with the German Army about to arrive on the doorstep, two young women keeping house together didn't seem like the safest idea. Fortunately, Jack's parents were able to help, offering the girls a pair of rooms above the chippie, where Mary was already working shifts.

Ruth was thrilled. She might be staying in a poky box room, but at least she could still see her twin sister every day, plus Jack's mother's chips were widely considered the best on the island. She only hoped her parents would forgive her for breaking her promise to follow them to England.

CHAPTER TWO

THE ENSIGNS OF COMMAND

On 21 June, a day after the last British soldiers left the Channel Islands, the lieutenant-governors set sail for home as well and the bailiffs were officially sworn in to replace them.

In Jersey, Alexander Coutanche, the calm, unflappable lawyer who had held the island's top office for five years, was undoubtedly the best man for the job, but in Guernsey the situation was more complicated. The elderly bailiff, Victor Carey, was little more than a placeholder, keeping the seat warm for a man twenty years his junior, Attorney General Ambrose Sherwill, while the latter acquired some much-needed political experience.

Realising that Guernsey would need strong leadership to survive under occupation, the island's civil servants and legislators established a 'Controlling Committee', replacing the laid-back, deliberate processes of the States with what was in effect a war cabinet with executive powers. The role of president was thrust onto a somewhat reluctant Sherwill. Carey would remain as the island's symbolic figurehead, but the attorney general was really in charge.

From the start, Sherwill viewed his new position as a poisoned chalice. In fact, he was struck with such a terrible headache that he could barely focus on the task of appointing the rest of the committee. Nonetheless, he threw himself into the role, doing everything he could to maintain order at an exceptionally volatile time.

An early test of the new president's abilities came on 23 June, a Sunday, when a group of doctors summoned him to an emergency meeting. They had been up since 4.30 that morning debating whether total evacuation of the island might in fact be necessary given the risks from starvation and the lack of medical supplies that could ensue under a lengthy occupation.

During a lull in the debate, Sherwill's own doctor privately asked him whether there was any way of getting his Jewish business partner off the island before the Germans arrived. After racking his brains for a moment, he devised an ingenious solution: the Jewish doctor would be sent on an official mission to the Home Office in London, where he would recommend total evacuation of the island. Sherwill knew full well that the British government would never agree to the policy, but his plan killed two birds with one stone – getting the Jewish man out of danger and keeping the anxious doctors at bay for a few days while they waited for the official refusal.

With tensions running high, strong leadership was invaluable. This was never more clearly demonstrated than by the contrasting fates of the two smaller inhabited islands in the archipelago, Alderney and Sark, both of which fell under the umbrella of the Bailiwick of Guernsey.

Sark, a small island of about 1,000 acres, was old-fashioned even by the standards of its neighbours. Its benign climate supported a traditional rural community whose bucolic way of life had changed little in the past hundred years, with its dusty roads plied by horses and carts rather than cars. The island's six-hundred-odd inhabitants were ruled, according to an ancient feudal system, by 'the Dame', Sybil Hathaway, an imperious woman who commanded instant respect among her people.

That Sunday evening, after church, Dame Sybil addressed an uneasy gathering at the island hall, exhorting them to stay and face the challenges of the future together.

'You, who are thinking of going away, where are you going?' she asked. 'You will be going to towns that will be bombed. No town in England will be safe.' She could see the doubt on her people's faces as they struggled to decide what to do. 'I am not promising you that it will be easy,' she told them. 'We may be hungry but we will always have our cattle and crops, our gardens, a few pigs, our sheep and rabbits.'

Warming to her subject, she told the crowd, 'We are one big family and must live as such. Each must help the other.' Then to rapturous applause she concluded, 'Britain must win! Britain *will* win!'

It was a command performance, and the result was hard to argue with. Although some of the island's English-born residents chose to return to their homeland, not a single native Sarkese packed up and left.

On Alderney, an island about twice the size of Sark and with a much more rugged, windswept aspect, the situation could not have been more different. Less than ten miles from the French coast, the men and women living there had an alarming view of the developments taking place on the Continent. They could see the fires blazing in Cherbourg, and taste the smoke from the burning oil installations.

That Sunday morning, while the Dame of Sark was rehearsing her speech, virtually the entire population of Alderney evacuated to England. In a matter of hours, more than 1,500 men, women and children, including the head of the island, Judge Frederick French, departed, taking all the island's money with them. Only nineteen stout souls decided to stay behind and take their chances.

When news of the hold-outs reached Ambrose Sherwill, he was concerned. Nineteen people was not enough to form a viable, self-sustaining community, and if a German invasion saw Alderney cut off from the other islands in the Bailiwick there was every chance that they would simply be left to starve. Like it or not, they would have to be brought over to Guernsey. Sherwill despatched the cox-swain of the Guernsey lifeboat, Fred Hobbs, with orders to fetch those who had chosen to remain, 'by force if necessary'.

Taking the attorney general at his word, Fred, a broad-shouldered man who had spent ten years as the island's top lifeboatman, armed himself with a Colt revolver and set off on the twenty-mile voyage to the smaller island.

When he arrived, he successfully persuaded seven of the inhabitants to return to Guernsey with him, among them the rector of the island and his wife. The others insisted on remaining, despite the revolver.

A second attempt was made to remove them by members of the St John Ambulance. Unfortunately, caught in the grip of invasion hysteria, several terrified islanders mistook their smart, pseudo-military uniforms for those of the Wehrmacht and thought the Germans had already arrived. One woman locked herself and her children in the house and refused to come to the door, while at another home the volunteers were met with a shotgun pointed in their faces.

Even those residents who were willing to talk could not always be budged. One very old man calmly explained that he had lived in his house for the better part of a century and he was not going to leave, whatever the consequences.

In all, a dozen of the nineteen individuals who had skipped the evacuation boats were successfully brought over to Guernsey. The names of their die-hard neighbours were kept in a file in Sherwill's office.

It wasn't just the human population of Alderney that the attorney general was concerned about. Four hundred cows had been left to their own devices since the departure of the farmers who owned them, along with almost two hundred pigs, twenty horses and innumerable domestic cats and dogs. Although the local butcher had managed to put to death much of the island's canine population on the morning of the evacuation, some had evaded capture and were now wandering the streets in search of their owners, while many of the island's cats, too wily to let themselves be caught, could now be seen mewling pathetically outside their shut-up homes.

With no owners left to feed them, the pets that remained faced almost certain starvation. To Sherwill, a speedy death seemed like a far more humane option, and he soon despatched another party to Alderney to take care of the island's remaining animals. A group of volunteer farmers and farm hands would round up the livestock and transport them to Guernsey, while a trio of experienced marksmen – one of whom had been awarded the Distinguished Conduct Medal for his service in the First World War – shot dead as many domestic pets as they could lay their gunsights on.

The new arrivals landed on the Tuesday morning, forty-eight hours after the island's hasty evacuation. Now all but devoid of human residents, Alderney had a post-apocalyptic feel. Vehicles had been abandoned on the approach to the quay, and the front doors of houses swung open in the wind. Inside the deserted homes, half-packed suitcases spilled over with clothes, and uneaten meals were beginning to turn mouldy. Escaped cows were roaming the streets, their udders swollen after two days without being milked. When the farmers finally relieved them of their painful burden, they found the milk had thickened and soured.

Other animals had been even less fortunate. A number of calves were found dead in the fields – those which had survived were soon put to death by the sharpshooters anyway, since it was only their milk-producing mothers that were worth the trouble of exporting – and the body of a horse was discovered sprawled across the road. It had apparently broken its neck attempting to jump a gate and escape from its field.

Over the next three days, the party of Guernseymen rounded up as many of the farm animals as they could and loaded them onto the waiting boats, before setting sail for home. All, that is, apart from one. As the last boat was readied for departure, one of the marksmen, Alf Martel, decided that he would rather stay behind. 'I'll be the king of Alderney!' he laughed, insisting that the rest of the party go without him.

A few days later, Alf's brothers from Guernsey arrived to bring him home. They found him passed out on a huge bed in one of the island's smartest hotels, surrounded by empty whisky bottles.

The evacuation of the islands had seen many people forced to shoulder unexpected responsibilities – not just those at the very top of the political ladder. Bob Le Sueur, a pimply nineteen-year-old office boy at the Jersey sub-office of the General Accident insurance company, was planning to travel to England and volunteer for the Royal Army Medical Corps. The day after the evacuation notice went in the paper, he cycled to the town hall on his way into work, hoping to register for a boat leaving as soon as possible and then head to the office to ask his boss, Mr Barnes, for permission to quit.

Bob arrived at the town hall to find a huge queue snaking round the block. It would hardly help his case with his employer if he turned up for work several hours late, so he pedalled off in the direction of the office, resolving to return later in the day. But when he arrived at General Accident, Mr Barnes was nowhere to be seen – and nor were the rest of the company's employees. Other than Bob, the only person who had turned up for work that day was a secretary called Phyllis – and the office was already packed with customers anxious to insure high-value items before they made the journey to England. The phones were ringing off the hook, and Phyllis was frantically struggling to take down all the messages.

One by one, Bob began working his way through the waiting customers, patiently explaining that although he could sell them a policy it would only be valid on a licensed passenger vessel, and even then specifically excluded war risk. If their precious belongings sank to the bottom of the Channel there wasn't much anyone could do for them.

As the day wore on, though, the office only got busier, as more and more islanders, having secured their evacuation permits, arrived in search of insurance. Still there was no sign of the rest of the staff. It looked like they all must have already made for the mainland, leaving Bob and Phyllis to face the anxious hordes alone.

Bob spent the rest of the week dealing with enquiries from customers, and still there was no sign of any of his former colleagues. On Monday morning, he decided to contact the branch manager in Southampton, Eric Thorpe, an imposing man with a walrus moustache who was known, thanks to his First World War service, as 'the colonel'.

'Are you drunk, boy?' Thorpe bellowed when Bob told him that the islands had been demilitarised. 'You expect me to believe that the government would abandon British territory without a single shot being fired?' Clearly news of the evacuation had not yet reached home shores. 'Put Mr Barnes on the line at once!' the colonel demanded angrily.

'I'm sorry, sir, but I haven't seen Mr Barnes since Wednesday,' Bob replied. 'I think he must have taken one of the boats for England.'

The colonel sounded far from convinced, but he promised Bob to send Mr Barnes straight back again if he dared to turn up in Southampton. 'You hold the fort until he gets back,' he commanded brusquely.

Bob still hadn't entirely given up hope of leaving Jersey himself, so he booked himself onto the mailboat leaving for England a week later, reasoning that if the colonel was true to his word, there would be plenty of time for him to fill Mr Barnes in before he set sail. After two days in charge of the busy office, he was feeling distinctly stressed, and although the initial panic of evacuation had passed, Jersey remained under a cloud of anxious anticipation. Several times, German reconnaissance planes, with their distinctive black crosses under the wings, had been spotted flying over the islands. Bob had watched them without too much concern. After all, he would be leaving soon enough.

At least the weather was balmy, and – despite the tense atmosphere – the island's famous beaches were as stunning as ever. On Friday, at the end of his first full week as unofficial office manager, Bob decided to unwind with an early-evening dip in the sea. From his parents' home at First Tower, a mile and a half from the centre of St Helier, he walked down to the beach and swam out about a hundred yards into the water.

As he floated in the sea, Bob gradually became aware of the gentle hum of aircraft overhead. He looked up to see three German planes in the sky, flying low over Fort Regent, a remnant of the Napoleonic Wars which stood on the hill overlooking the town.

Treading water for a moment, Bob kept his eyes fixed on the planes. He could have sworn he saw some small, dark objects falling out of them.

A moment later, there was a series of loud explosions from the direction of the harbour, followed by a flash of fire as a timber warehouse went up in flames. This was no reconnaissance mission, Bob realised. The Germans were bombing St Helier.

Frantically, Bob began swimming for the shore, his chest heaving as his skinny arms beat the water. He staggered breathlessly across the beach and up the slipway towards the road, racing to get back to his parents' house. Then he saw something that made his heart stop: the German planes were flying towards him. They were racing along just above the esplanade as they headed west out of town, following the curve of the bay that separated St Helier from the neighbouring village of St Aubin. People were flinging themselves to the ground at the sides of the road, and Bob could see flecks of tarmac ping up into the air as they were hit with machine-gun bullets.

In nothing more than his swimming trunks, Bob felt totally exposed. There was no real cover to make for, only a line of flimsy tamarix bushes that ran along the edge of the esplanade. In desperation, he hurled himself into them, burrowing under their soft pink blooms and pressing his face into the ground.

Bob listened, terrified, as the planes stormed past overhead. The sharp pinging of the bullets hitting the road continued, growing faster and more insistent with every second, until gradually both it and the hum of the engines began to recede into the distance.

His heart pounding, Bob picked himself up, dusted the earth from his bare chest and legs, and made for home. It was clear now that there would be no mailboat taking him to England.

The time for evacuation was over. The German invasion had begun.

CHAPTER THREE

A BOLT FROM THE BLUE

It didn't take long for the planes to find a new target. Just off Noirmont Point, on the far side of St Aubin's Bay, the Guernsey lifeboat was on its way to St Helier, commanded by the burly coxswain Fred Hobbs. The RNLI in England were anxious about their boats falling into the hands of the Germans and had ordered Fred to collect the Jersey boat and then bring the two of them together across the Channel. He had responded with his usual brisk efficiency, raising a crew of seven men – including his own sons Alec and Harold – and setting sail within less than an hour.

As the German planes banked around for a second attack on St Helier, Fred's lifeboat must have presented a very tempting target – despite the large red cross painted on the deck, which was intended to ward off potential attackers. Seeing the three Heinkel bombers dip down low until they were only 100 feet above the water, Fred knew that he and his men were sitting ducks. 'Get down, everyone!' he shouted, making for the shore at full speed.

Moments later, the boat was showered with a hail of bullets, but Fred pressed on, steering a zig-zag course to try to throw off the gunners. Over the roar of the engine he could hear the hull splintering as a number of rounds hit their target.

Fred kept his eye on the shore ahead of him, racing through the onslaught until the ship ran aground in St Aubin's Bay. The men scrambled out onto the beach as the planes zoomed past overhead, making for a second bombing run over St Helier.

As Fred cast his eyes over the line of men standing beside him, he realised that someone was missing. He turned back to the boat, where a large body was slumped on the deck. Fred rushed over to find his son Harold, a strapping thirty-four-year-old man who had a boy of his own back home in Guernsey, lying motionless with a bullet hole in his head.

A couple of miles away in St Helier, the air raid continued. For men and women who worked in the harbour area, it was a terrifying ordeal. In one of the warehouses along New North Quay, a group of young women were busy packing potatoes for export when the whole building was shuddered by the explosion of nearby bombs. The builder's merchants next door sustained serious damage, sending chunks of masonry smashing right through the glass roof above the girls' heads. They fled in panic, screaming as they rushed off home in search of their loved ones.

Meanwhile, on Albert Pier, stevedore Bob Troy was supervising the loading of a ship. When he heard the sound of machine-gun fire, he shouted for his men to take cover. Some hid under lorries, others under large piles of sacking. Bob himself dashed to the foot of a crane, looking on in horror as several of his men were hit by the German bullets. One of them, Mr Tirel, had the toes of one foot blown off completely.

A little way down the pier, Robert Fallis, a fifty-four-year-old former Royal Artilleryman who collected the tolls due from all vessels moored in the harbour, was sheltering by the Southern Railway sheds when a bomb exploded nearby. Bob rushed over to try and help but as he saw the poor man's mangled body – he had sustained a terrible injury from a bomb splinter – he realised that there was nothing anyone could do for him. Instead, the stevedore made a dash for his car, thinking he could take some of the wounded men to hospital. But the car wouldn't start, and nor would any of the lorries lined up along the pier. They had all been put out of action by the Luftwaffe.

Bob began leading the walking wounded up the pier towards the town, but before long they heard the Heinkels approaching again. They lay down and hugged the promenade wall as they heard the bullets whizz by over their heads.

All told, the raid lasted for just under an hour. Bob and his men were lucky to escape with their lives. As well as Mr Fallis, two more men were mortally wounded on Albert Pier – a forty-five-year-old jeweller, Godfrey Coleman, and the forty-year-old Leslie Bryan, an employee at Voisin's department store, who was hit by a bomb splinter while strolling along the promenade with his wife Florence. Both men died within hours of arriving at Jersey's General Hospital. Another, William Moody, who had been injured at the weighbridge, survived until the following day before succumbing to his injuries.

They were by no means the raid's only casualties. In the quiet fishing village of La Rocque, two high-explosive bombs were dropped on the road near the harbour. Fifty-seven-year-old Jack Adams was struggling to get into his house when the blast from one of them knocked him face down onto his doorstep, killing him instantly. Two other villagers, Minnie Farrell and Thomas Pilkington, were shot by the Heinkels' machine-guns as they sat on a bench, and died in hospital.

In the neighbourhood of Mount Bingham, just outside central St Helier, another two bombs fell, badly damaging a number of houses, including that of seventy-eight-year-old retired plumber John Mauger, who was killed on the spot. (His wife Sarah, who was with him at the time, was lucky to survive.) In the town centre, Edward Ferrand, the landlord of the Bunch of Grapes, was hit by a hail of bullets outside his pub. He made it to hospital but died on the operating table. Sixty-four-year-old Arthur Parr, who was shot alongside him, perished four days later.

Overall, Jersey's death toll, including the lifeboatman Harold Hobbs, stood at eleven – a small number compared to the blitz later unleashed on the cities of the British mainland, but enough to shatter the complacency of islanders who had never expected to find themselves military targets. Jersey had not faced a hostile invasion in almost five hundred years, yet now St Helier's harbour was littered with the blasted wrecks of boats and yachts, and the stores in Commercial Buildings were ablaze, with plumes of black smoke slowly rising into the sky. Two of the island's leading hotels, the Pomme d'Or and the Yacht, had sustained bomb damage, and the stained-glass windows of the town church had been smashed to smithereens. Up on the hill at Fort Regent, the furze was on fire, and it would be several days before the blaze was fully extinguished. Along the coast at La Rocque, windows were shattered and doors blown off their hinges. There was no getting around it: this was the reality of war.

It wasn't just Jersey that suffered at the hands of the Luftwaffe that Friday. In fact, in Guernsey, the German air raid was even more devastating.

It came – almost literally – as a bolt from the blue. It was a balmy summer's evening, with not a cloud in the perfect azure sky. A little after six, Ambrose Sherwill appeared on the steps of the *Guernsey Evening Press* offices in St Peter Port to address a large crowd, in what had become a daily ritual for the members of his Controlling Committee. 'Whatever else is wrong,' he told them cheerfully, 'it has been a beautiful day.'

About half an hour later, having answered a number of questions from the crowd, the attorney general returned to his office in Elizabeth College, where he received a call from London. It was Charles Markbreiter, assistant military secretary at the Home Office.

The last week had been the most stressful of Sherwill's career, but he was relieved to be able to tell Markbreiter that finally things seemed to be settling down. The first furious panic of evacuation had largely abated, and most people were doing their best to get on with their lives. The shipping traffic departing from the White Rock was no longer dominated by anxious evacuees – in fact the annual tomato export, which accounted for a sizeable chunk of the island's economy, was now well underway. A queue of lorries almost a mile long was lined up along the seafront, stretching from the weighbridge, where the produce was loaded onto boats bound for England, all the way to the neighbouring parish of St Sampson.

But if Sherwill's conversation with Markbreiter was unusually cheerful, his good humour didn't last long. Just as he was about to hang up, he became aware of the distant sound of aeroplane engines, followed by the sharp stuttering of machine-guns firing, as the Heinkels approached St Peter Port. The attorney general had served in the trenches of the First World War, and he knew exactly what he was hearing. As the noise from the planes grew louder, he held the phone up to his open office window, telling the astonished Markbreiter, 'Here they come!'

Not everyone was as quick to appreciate the situation, however, and it was another ten minutes before the air-raid siren was sounded. By then, the German bombardment was already well underway.

More compact than St Helier, with its high street barely set back from the waterfront, St Peter Port endured an appalling onslaught, with over a hundred fifty-kilogram fragmentation bombs falling in less than an hour. One young man was in the bath when the first bomb went off nearby, shaking the house and sending the water splashing out onto the floor. When he attempted to stand up, a second blast knocked him off his feet and back into the tub. Then a third explosion shattered the windows, covering him in broken glass. Finally, as he stared – by now somewhat stunned – out of the empty space where the bathroom window should have been, a fourth explosion sent a dead seagull flying through the gap in the wall and into his lap.

Although the Channel Islands had been demilitarised for over a week now, this had not been officially communicated to the authorities in Berlin. The raids on Jersey and Guernsey that evening were an exercise in what was known as 'reconnaissance-in-force', an attack intended to test the strength of the islands' military defences by provoking them into opening fire.

In the event, the sum total of resistance was provided by a single Lewis gun on the *Isle of Sark* mailboat, which was moored in St Peter Port Harbour. Those on board were subjected to a terrifying experience as the Heinkels swooped down over the town. One bomb exploded close enough to badly injure a man on board – he collapsed onto the deck, blood gushing from a wound in his groin. The gunner, meanwhile, received an arm injury so serious that it put him out of action. It was a miracle that the boat itself survived the raid more or less intact. While other vessels sank to the bottom of the harbour, smashed to pieces or burned to cinders by the bombs, the mailboat remained afloat, the passengers cowering below decks as they waited for the ordeal to end.

Aside from its official reconnaissance value, the raid did of course have another, perhaps more significant, impact on the people of Guernsey: a show of strength that stunned its victims into submission prior to the arrival of enemy troops. In this, at least, it was extraordinarily effective, bringing death and destruction on a scale never before imagined in the quaint and charming seaside town. Many of the bombs fell on the long line of tomato lorries lined up along the waterfront, which the German bombers apparently mistook for military vehicles. Drivers who had sought shelter from machine-gun bullets under their lorries were crushed or burned to death as the vehicles caught fire and collapsed on top of them.

By now the ground was littered with dead and dying, their blood mingling with the juice from the tomatoes, scorched and smashed to a pulp, which had spilled out all over the roadways. The whole neighbourhood seemed to be ablaze, with buildings and lorries alike consumed by the fires, and plumes of black smoke blanketing the island from coast to coast.

Fortunately, the raid took place at low tide, and a number of islanders managed to shelter from the bombs and bullets by clambering down from the piers and pressing themselves up against the harbour walls. Gradually, as the planes withdrew and the all-clear was sounded, these terrified survivors emerged and made their way back up to the promenade. Their pallid faces registered a mixture of astonishment and horror as they took in the devastation all around them.

Some families were soon mourning more than one victim. Two unmarried sisters who lived together in Glategny Esplanade, Amy and Daisy Robert, died together, while husband and wife Samuel and Lilian De Jausserand were both fatally injured at the White Rock.

But most tragic was the case of Frank Le Page, from King's Mills, a hamlet on the far side of the island. He had arranged for his eldest son, who shared his name, to meet him at the harbour, but when the time came for Frank Jnr to set off, his brother Roy had begged to come along as well, pestering their mother until she finally gave in. The three bodies were found together in the cab of Frank's lorry.

At just fourteen, Roy Le Page was the raid's youngest victim. The eldest was eighty-one-year-old Alice Brehaut, mortally injured in South Esplanade Gardens. But those who rushed to help the stricken also found themselves in the firing line. A popular police constable, thirty-three-year-old Clifford 'Chipper' Bougourd, was attending to a wounded man at the weighbridge when he was hit in the head by a piece of shrapnel from an exploding bomb. His wife Annette and their son Peter, who had both evacuated the week before, received news of his death in England.

St John Ambulanceman Joseph Way, meanwhile, was shot while driving the wounded to hospital. His ambulance hit a tree, and Joseph, a nurse and the five injured people in the back all lost their lives. Just like the Guernsey lifeboat, the ambulance had received no protection from the distinctive red cross painted on its roof. The Germans, it seemed, were proving themselves just as brutal as the most provocative propaganda had suggested.

Although the bombing campaign in Guernsey was focused on the White Rock harbour, people all over the island came under fire from the German machine-guns. Even as far away as Cobo, on the west coast, residents were fleeing from the planes. Sixteen-year-old Gwen Smith had just popped out to the shop on the corner to buy a bag of sweets when one of the Heinkels swooped down low and began chasing her along the road.

Gwen pounded the tarmac furiously, not daring to look around. From the doorway of their parents' hotel on the seafront, her younger sister Pearl watched aghast as the bullets pockmarked the granite beach wall just behind her. As she neared the hotel, the girls' father shot out of the gate, grabbing hold of Gwen and rushing her inside.

The whole family huddled together in the hallway, tears streaming down their faces while they waited for the planes to pass over. Gwen was screaming hysterically, and she didn't stop until well after they had gone.

Ruth Leadbeater, one of the twins who had cancelled their plans to evacuate so that they could stay in Guernsey with their boyfriends, was on the road with her beau Cliff when the raid started. He had spent the afternoon shopping for clothes in town, and had left his racing-green Austin 7 – his most treasured possession – parked up on Les Banques outside the Fruit Export, on the outskirts of St Peter Port. On the passenger seat were a brand-new jacket, shoes and trousers.

Having parked his car, Cliff had set off in a company lorry to pick up some more tomatoes to be packed that evening, stopping off at the chip shop in the Bouet to pick up Ruth, who had decided to come along for the ride. The young couple were driving along the Rohais, the main road leading towards the centre of the island, when the air-raid sirens began to sound.

They abandoned the vehicle and took shelter under a tree, listening anxiously to the thud of the bombs exploding in the harbour area and watching as the plume of black smoke began to rise over the town. They cowered as the planes screamed past overhead, shrapnel falling like stones onto the trees that lined the road, snapping the smaller branches and scorching the leaves.

When it was all over, Cliff drove back into town to pick up his car. Through the thick smoke he couldn't see much of the damage to the White Rock, but he found the Austin easily enough. The chassis had been torn and sheared by the German machine-gun bullets, the stuffing was poking out of holes in the red leather upholstery, and the new clothes on the passenger seat had been ripped to shreds.

Cliff felt crushed – his pride and joy was a write-off, and he knew that his insurance didn't cover war damage. But mingled with his sadness and frustration at the loss of his beloved vehicle was a sobering realisation: if the raid had taken place an hour earlier Cliff would have been in town himself, and it might have been him, not the Austin, that was riddled with bullet holes.

Ruth wasn't the only girl whose boyfriend had a lucky escape that evening. Nellie Prince was picking potatoes in a field in St Sampson when the air-raid sirens sounded, but her fiancé Oswald was down at the White Rock, sitting in the cab of a lorry packed with crates of tomatoes. Fortunately, rather than taking shelter under his vehicle as many of the other drivers did, Oswald made a run for it, dashing up through the narrow streets into the town, and then gradually making his way home on foot.

When the raid was over, Oswald and Nellie walked back down to the harbour area to see what was left of the lorry. She was stunned by the sight that met her eyes. By now, the bodies of the dead and wounded had been removed and the black smoke was beginning to clear, but the White Rock was still a scene of devastation. Burned and blackened tomatoes littered the ground all around. 'Like roasted chestnuts,' Nellie remarked sadly.

That evening, Guernsey's hospitals were deluged with desperate cases, many of them arriving courtesy of hastily unpacked tomato lorries, since the island's limited complement of ambulances was overwhelmed.

Dr Alistair Rose, a balding, easy-going GP in his mid-thirties, had spent a pleasant afternoon on the golf course with his colleague Dr Gibson. Together, they had observed the incoming German planes, peering through a pair of binoculars at the distinctive black crosses beneath the wings. As the Heinkels disappeared out of view towards the harbour, they heard the distant crump of the bombs. Even a couple of miles away, they could feel a slight concussive force with every explosion.

As soon as the all-clear was sounded, the two doctors made for the Castel Hospital, whizzing along the winding country lanes as fast as Dr Gibson's car would carry them. By the time they pulled up outside the imposing granite building, the wounded had already started to arrive and were being prepped for surgery.

The doctors and nurses worked through the night to save as many lives as possible, aided by a small gang of fishermen who had volunteered to carry the injured to and from the wards. The foreheads of those who had been administered morphine were marked clearly with red lipstick, to avoid any accidental overdoses by the exhausted, not to mention overcaffeinated, medical staff.

Dr Rose spent the evening dashing from patient to patient, but many of the cases he saw were already too far gone for help. One old lady's leg had been shattered by a German bomb, leaving little more than a formless fleshy mass. She urgently needed a transfusion, but he could tell just by looking at her that the blood wasn't going to arrive in time. Sure enough, within a few minutes, she was dead.

Then there were the two French lads who had been waiting for passage to England so that they could sign up with the Free French Army. One of them, Paul, had suffered only minor injuries, but the other, nineteen-year-old Marcel, had taken a piece of shrapnel to the femoral artery in his leg. Dr Rose and his colleagues did their best to tie it off with a ligature, and the young lad kept his spirits up with repeated renditions of the Marseillaise, but despite everyone's efforts, he suffered haemorrhage after haemorrhage, until he eventually bled to death.

It was a gruelling shift, the hardest that any of the doctors – apart, perhaps, from those who had served in the First World War – had ever endured, and the sun was already creeping up above the horizon before the hospital's two operating theatres were finally cleared. By then Dr Rose had inhaled so much of the ether used to anaesthetise the patients that he was beginning to feel light-headed himself.

In Guernsey, the raid had led to the loss of thirty-three lives, in addition to the eleven men and women killed in Jersey. The little island of Sark, although not targeted directly, had also sustained one fatality. As the Heinkels passed over the island on their way to Guernsey, one of them let off a volley from its machine-guns. The elderly landlady of the Pavillion public house, Mrs Jane Falle, was so shocked that she collapsed and died on the spot. All over the Channel Islands, those who had witnessed the German attack at close range would bear the scars – both physical and mental – for years to come.

When Dr Rose finally left the hospital at around 10.30 in the morning, he and Dr Gibson decided to visit the White Rock and see for themselves the damage inflicted by the raid. They inspected the little craters that now pock-marked the roads, and noted the chips of granite blasted out of the sea wall.

The fires that had raged the night before had burned themselves out, leaving a line of giant charred wrecks where the tomato lorries had once stood. Most of the bigger shards from the broken windows had been swept up overnight, but everything seemed to be lightly dusted with a mixture of ash and glass powder.

The large clock tower that stood at the entrance to the weigh-bridge bore the scars of the fire that had swept across the whole area. A car parked outside had crumpled in on itself under the flames, leaving only a mangled mess of metal, and the clock's four faces had shattered, along with the glass windows of the adjoining building.

Only the hands of the clock remained, frozen at a few minutes to seven. In this otherworldly landscape, time itself seemed to have come to a standstill.

CHAPTER FOUR

SURRENDER

The next morning, the islanders shook off a fitful night's sleep and rose to face an uncertain future. It was a time to take stock of what had been lost. To inspect the damage wrought on the islands, not in the smoky gloom of the evening, but in the clear light of yet another bright summer's day. A time to take in the smashed windows and the chipped walls, the wrecks, no longer smouldering, of vehicles and buildings smashed and shivered by the bombs.

But more than that, it was a time to contemplate the human cost. The dead might have numbered in the dozens rather than the hundreds, but in these small island communities almost everyone knew somebody affected by the raid. As the news spread from family to family, the islands became a network of nervous whispers and feverish prayers.

And then there was the big question lurking at the back of everyone's mind: what would happen next?

All day long, the people waited anxiously. The thunder of the previous night had been replaced by the islands' typical tranquillity, only now it felt as if perhaps that quiet calm was nothing more than the eye of the storm. Cautiously, the people emerged from their homes and began to go about their business. Children explored the changed landscape where the bombs had fallen, playing amid the craters and rubble and searching for souvenirs.

In the early afternoon, the islanders were alarmed by the sight of more German planes in the skies overhead, but to their relief these ones passed by peacefully. They were reconnaissance aircraft, snatching photographs to assess the damage done the night before. Despite the local people's fears, no more bombs were to fall that day.

In the Channel Islands, all was eerily quiet. But a thousand miles away, at a high-level meeting in Berlin, their fate was the subject of intense discussion. Admiral Karlgeorg Schuster, the senior German naval commander in northern France, was in the process of agreeing an invasion strategy for the islands, known as Operation Green Arrow. The Wehrmacht's 216 Infantry Division, currently based in Cherbourg, would be tasked with carrying out the operation, led by one of their regimental commanders, Major Albrecht Lanz.

The plan was for a second bout of 'armed reconnaissance' on Monday, followed by an amphibious troop landing, with a battalion apiece taking Jersey and Guernsey, and a single company despatched to subdue Alderney. (Since there were now only seven people living on the island, this was, if anything, overkill.) The glory of the momentous event – the first time British territory had ever been seized in the name of the Reich – was to be shared between all three branches of the armed forces, with the Luftwaffe providing Junkers transport planes as well as reconnaissance and bombing aircraft, the Kriegsmarine a specialist Assault Group who would be the first on the ground, and the Heer the bulk of the manpower to bring the operation to a swift and successful conclusion.

In the event, things turned out very differently. The intrepid Luftwaffe pilots, flushed with the success of Friday night's bombing raid, couldn't resist jumping the gun. The first – unscheduled – landing on British soil took place in Guernsey, early on Sunday afternoon. Dr Rose was in his wife's little open-topped car, driving home from his morning surgery at the hospital, when he heard the sound of a plane coming in low overhead. Having witnessed the gruesome aftermath of the previous raid at first hand, he was understandably anxious at the prospect of another air assault on the island – and even more so that he might be caught up in it.

Dr Rose hit the brakes and the car screeched to a halt. Grabbing the keys from the ignition, he leapt out of the vehicle and into the nearest hedgerow. As he crouched low, peering through the foliage at the Dorniers circling up above, he couldn't help thinking how annoyed his wife would be if her beloved car were to suffer a direct hit.

Fortunately for Dr Rose (and his wife) the planes continued circling, making no move to attack. They were, he realised, almost directly above the island's new airport, so perhaps they intended to land. Dr Rose extracted himself from the hedge, scurried back into the driver's seat of the car, and made off for St Peter Port at speed.

The German planes continued to circle, but their hesitation to attempt a landing was not due to a lack of will. The airport runway was currently playing host to the herds of cattle that had been brought over from Alderney, and by flying low overhead the pilots were doing their best to disperse them.

Eventually, the cows got the message and cleared a safe landing strip. Two of the Dorniers touched down, while the third remained in the air to keep a look-out.

For the Germans, it was a fleeting visit, however. No sooner had Captain Reinhard Liebe-Piderit broken down the door to the airport building and begun to have a nose around than a trio of RAF Blenheim bombers arrived on the scene, causing the pilots to hurry back into their planes. In fact, the startled captain departed in such a rush that he left his revolver behind in the terminal building. It was brought to the attorney general Ambrose Sherwill, who decided to hold onto it for safe-keeping. He had a feeling that it wouldn't be long before he had an opportunity to return the gun to its rightful owner.

When the Dorniers arrived back in France that afternoon, they were met by rapturous applause. Field Marshal Göring himself came to congratulate the aircrews who had been a part of the historic, if somewhat brief, occupation of British territory.

That evening, confident that the islanders had no intention of resisting (sorties by the RAF notwithstanding), the Germans returned for good. Ambrose Sherwill and his wife May had just finished putting their two young boys to bed in the hallway, which was considered the safest place in the house in the event of a second air raid, when they were surprised to spot a young man in full flying gear standing on their doorstep. On his head was the unmistakable blue-grey forage cap of a Luftwaffe officer, complete with swastika and Imperial Eagle. In the driveway, Sherwill could see one of his own policemen, Sergeant Harper, who had evidently driven the German over from the airport.

Careful not to wake the sleeping children, Sherwill sneaked out of the side entrance and approached the German visitor. 'Will you please come in by the side door?' he asked, hoping that the airman spoke English.

The German glared at him. 'Why?' he asked suspiciously.

A little awkwardly, the attorney general explained that his children were asleep in the hall.

The officer's demeanour changed completely. 'I would not dream of disturbing your children,' he replied.

This small gesture of politeness made a strong impact on Sherwill. Before long, he was accompanying the young airman to the Royal Hotel, which his commanding officer, Major Hessel, had already taken over in the name of the Reich. On their way to pick up the elderly bailiff, Victor Carey, at his home in St Martin, the young man offered Sherwill a cigarette, which he accepted. He was beginning to feel sick with nerves, and the nicotine calmed him a little.

Arriving at the hotel, Sherwill and Carey found Major Hessel seated in the lounge, surrounded by many of the island's other leading figures. Once all the formal introductions had been made, the major got down to business. 'What arms do you have on the island?' he asked the bailiff.

'None at all,' Carey replied. 'The island is entirely demilitarised.'

With a sudden pang, Sherwill remembered the guns he had ordered the government secretary to hold onto ten days earlier, in case the evacuation panic reached a fever pitch. To his relief, the police had never had cause to use them, and as a result Sherwill hadn't actually got around to informing the bailiff about the order.

In the current circumstances, however, he felt that honesty was probably the best policy. 'We have twelve rifles and bayonets,' he interjected, doing his best to avoid Carey's eye.

At this point the government secretary, who had also been struck by a spasm of honesty, piped up, 'Actually, there aren't any bayonets, sir.'

'Yes, there are,' Sherwill reminded him. 'I instructed you to keep them back along with the rifles.'

Somewhat sheepishly, the government secretary confessed that he had forgotten that part of the order.

Sherwill could only imagine what kind of impression this confused performance was making on Major Hessel. Fortunately, though, the German seemed keen to move on. With the help of an interpreter, he proceeded to dictate a series of orders, instructing Sherwill to put them into good English for the benefit of the local people. There wasn't much scope for negotiation, although the attorney general did score a small victory by persuading the major that a ban on the consumption of spirits should apply only to pubs and restaurants, and not private houses. Thus – for the time being at least – he succeeded in safeguarding the drinks cabinets of himself and his colleagues.

While Sherwill and the German translator wrangled over the right form of words for their official Occupation announcement, the offices of the *Star* were in a state of nervous anticipation. The paper's editor, Bill Taylor, had been instructed to hold the front page of the following day's edition, before being ushered into a police car and driven to the Royal Hotel.

For two hours Taylor's reporters waited, wondering whether they would have anything to print the next day. When he finally returned he looked exhausted and there was a distinct whiff of whisky on his breath. Evidently the new prohibition on spirits didn't extend to the hotel bar.

Wearily, Taylor called one of his writers, Frank Falla, over to see him. He opened a reporter's pad and began talking Frank through the shorthand notes he had made during his visit with the Germans.

He had been ordered to print their official instructions on the front page of the next day's edition, and to ensure it was delivered free of charge all over the island.

The *Star* had never printed a free issue before, but Bill and his team got straight to work. As soon as the shorthand notes had been typed up, they were passed over to the linotype operators, who began to lay out the page. 'They've said we can write what we like in the rest of the paper,' Taylor informed his staff, 'but they want to see it before we go to press.'

The newspapermen worked late into the night preparing the special edition. When the copy was all laid out, a set of proofs was run off and whisked over to the hotel for inspection. The German censors gave it their official seal of approval, and the presses rolled into action once again. By this time, Ambrose Sherwill, feeling more than a little dejected at the end of a difficult evening, had long since retired to bed.

The *Star*'s journalists were careful to steer clear of any copy that might offend German sensibilities. They did, however, allow an unintentionally amusing advertisement to slip through the cracks. It had been paid for by the management of the Royal Hotel, long before the building had been requisitioned as the local headquarters of the Third Reich. The ad drew readers' attention to a special all-inclusive offer for residence with full board, encouraging anyone interested to phone reception – where their call would presumably be answered by a very confused German operator.

On Monday morning, the people of Guernsey sat down to breakfast with a lot more to digest than usual, thanks to the special copy of the *Star* – clearly marked 'GRATIS' – which had appeared on every doorstep across the island. Aside from a couple of adverts for Fison's blood-and-bone fertiliser and Stewarts Tobacco Mixture, almost the entire front page was given over to the new German orders. A curfew was established between 11 p.m. and 6 a.m., the private use of vehicles was forbidden, fishing boats were not allowed to leave the island without an official permit, and all guns, daggers and other weapons were required to be handed in at the Royal Hotel by noon at the latest. Banks and shops, meanwhile, were instructed to open as usual.

In a small sidebar was a short message addressed 'to every islander' on behalf of Sherwill's Controlling Committee. 'No resistance whatever is to be offered to those in military occupation of this island,' it read. 'The public are asked to be calm, to carry on their lives and work in the usual way, and to obey the orders of the German Commandant which are printed on this page.'

The Germans themselves were more forceful. 'We will respect the population in Guernsey,' their own notice declared, 'but should anyone attempt to cause the least trouble serious measures will be taken and the town will be bombed.'

While the people of Guernsey tried to wrap their heads around the slew of official information, their counterparts in Jersey had already received their own special delivery courtesy of the German Air Force. A little before six o'clock that morning, three heavy canvas bags, adorned with bright red streamers, had mysteriously fallen from the skies. One of them landed near the airport, and was brought straightaway to the bailiff, Alexander Coutanche. Opening it, he discovered a message written in German and signed by a Luftwaffe general, Baron Wolfram von Richthofen.

Coutanche knew almost nothing of the German language, but even so a number of words stood out, most notably '*Kapitulation*', which was repeated several times, and – even more alarmingly – '*Bombardierung*'. It was fairly clear that the document was some kind of ultimatum, and it mentioned a date and time – 7 a.m. on 2 July – that was only twenty-four hours away.

Coutanche summoned his attorney general, Charles Duret Aubin, who turned out to be equally linguistically challenged. Duret Aubin did, however, have an idea. He made an urgent phone call to a Jesuit priest in St Helier, who in turn managed to track down a fellow clergyman from Alsace, on the Franco-German border. Later that morning, the bailiff held the translated document in his hands:

1st July, 1940.

To the Chief of the Military and Civil Authorities Jersey (St. Helier).

1. I intend to neutralize military establishments in Jersey by occupation.

2. As evidence that the Island will surrender the military and other establishments without resistance and without destroying them, a large White Cross is to be shown as follows, from 7 a.m. July 2nd, 1940.

   a. In the centre of the Airport in the East of the Island.

   b. On the highest point of the fortifications of the port.

   c. On the square to the North of the Inner Basin of the Harbour.

   Moreover all fortifications, buildings, establishments and houses are to show the White Flag.

3. If these signs of peaceful surrender are not observed by 7 a.m. July 2nd, heavy bombardment will take place.

   a. Against all military objects.

   b. Against all establishments and objects useful for defence.

4. The signs of surrender must remain up to the time of the occupation of the Island by German troops.

5. Representatives of the Authorities must stay at the Airport until the occupation.

6. All Radio traffic and other communications with Authorities outside the Island will be considered hostile actions and will be followed by bombardment.

7. Every hostile action against my representatives will be followed by bombardment.

8. In case of peaceful surrender, the lives, property, and liberty of peaceful inhabitants are solemnly guaranteed.

There was no time to lose. In a matter of hours Coutanche had copies of the ultimatum rolling off the printing presses, to be plastered in prominent locations all over the island. Before long, Jersey was speckled with white from shore to shore as people rushed to put up their flags. Some were forced to improvise – a pair of old knickers on a broomstick stuck out of the window, or an old sheet hanging from a chimney pot on the roof – but one way or another almost everyone complied with General von Richthofen's orders.

For many, it felt like a humiliation, and the sight of a whole street with every house signalling an individual surrender was a depressing one. But after the terror of the previous week's raid most people were willing to do whatever it took to avoid further bloodshed. They knew it was only a matter of time until the enemy soldiers arrived. The best they could do now was follow orders and hope that the rumours and propaganda they had heard about the fearsome German forces were exaggerated.

Bob Le Sueur had recovered from the ordeal of being shot at during his Friday evening swim and was on his way to the insurance office that morning when he noticed a commotion in St Helier's Royal Square, which was now dominated by a giant white cross painted on the ground. The bailiff had called an emergency meeting of the island parliament, the States of Jersey, and members of the public had gathered outside hoping for some news.

Bob's eye was drawn to two housewives who were having an earnest conversation. 'We'd better hurry home and barricade our doors,' one told the other. 'There'll be a lot of women raped before nightfall.' Elsewhere in the crowd, young women were quietly sobbing.

The States Building itself had been cordoned off, and several workmen were standing guard to prevent the crowd from attempting to get inside. Assisting in this endeavour was a local businessman who had served in the Army during the First World War, Captain Benest.

The captain was something of a local character, known for his booming military voice as well as his distinctive dress sense – he always wore a natty suit and a modish pork-pie hat. Right now, he was in his element, issuing orders to the *hoi polloi*. 'Now you *must* stand back!' he bellowed. 'The States is in session and the bailiff will be coming out any minute. Not *there*, madam, on the other side! Now stand in line. *You, boy*, are you deaf? Get out of the way!'

The tirade went on for a good minute or so, until it was brought to a rather abrupt end. This time it was not the Luftwaffe who dropped their load over the town, but a passing pigeon who managed to score a direct hit on the captain's showy headgear just as he was warming up to issue another round of orders. Fuming, Captain Benest removed the soiled hat, shook it angrily, and marched off in the direction of his office.

As soon as he was gone, a muffled titter began to go round the crowd. The captain, it seemed, had done some good after all: the tense atmosphere had given way to a moment of levity.

That afternoon, when a German pilot returned for a brief reconnaissance mission over Jersey, the response to the morning's ultimatum was unambiguous. Everywhere he looked, there were white flags fluttering in the wind. Nonetheless, he touched down at the airport just long enough to ask the man in charge there to confirm the bailiff's intentions.

Coutanche was sitting in his chambers when the call came through. 'My orders are to surrender as soon as anybody capable of accepting the surrender comes along,' he declared.

While the Luftwaffe pilot was on his way back to France to report to his superiors, the bailiff drove down to Fort Regent, where he personally lowered the Union Jack from the flagpole. The task was, he felt, so humiliating that he couldn't possibly ask anyone else to do it.

With this onerous job discharged, Coutanche set off for the airport, where he and his attorney general, Duret Aubin, were met by a Luftwaffe captain, Hans-Günther von Obernitz.

'You realise you are occupied?' von Obernitz demanded, to which Coutanche, uncharacteristically lost for words, replied merely, 'Yes.'

Next, the captain's interpreter, a German civilian who until recently had been working as a waiter in St Helier, read out a proclamation similar to that which the residents of Guernsey had perused in their free copy of the *Star* that morning. A curfew was to be established between 11 p.m. and 6 a.m., a brief amnesty was offered for the surrender of guns and other weapons, spirits were placed under public prohibition, and harsh restrictions were imposed on the use of cars and boats.

With the recitation concluded, Captain von Obernitz indicated that the formalities of occupation were over and Coutanche was free to go. The bailiff offered Duret Aubin some brief instructions on where to billet the new arrivals before setting off for home, feeling distinctly depressed.

On Monday afternoon, Major Lanz, the German officer who had been chosen to carry out the elaborate plans for military invasion of the islands – before the Luftwaffe had stolen his thunder with their own pre-emptive sorties – decided that the time had finally come to make his grand entrance. Just before 3 p.m., his Junkers 52 touched down at Guernsey's airport, narrowly missing the herd of Alderney cattle who were still grazing there.

Major Hessel was there to meet him, beaming from ear to ear – and he hadn't come empty handed. That morning, he had visited Creasey's department store in St Peter Port, where for the princely sum of £3 0s 4d, he had commissioned a very special bespoke item: the first German war flag, based on the Führer's personal design, that had ever been sewn by British hands. Together, the two majors watched as the flag was run up the mast of the terminal building and the heavy black swastika fluttered gently in the wind.

Hessel had just one more duty to perform before returning to France with his squadron: introducing the island's new commandant to the bailiff, Victor Carey. Together, he and Lanz got into a commandeered Guernsey police car, complete with driver, and set off at speed. For Lanz, it was a chance to get a good look at the island that would be his home – and, in a sense, his kingdom – for the foreseeable future. He was struck by the astonishing number of greenhouses that seemed to populate almost every field, and by the network of

narrow, winding lanes. In fact, the major was a little concerned at
how fast their police driver took the corners, and several times – for-
getting that in Guernsey people drove on the left – he was convinced
that an oncoming vehicle was about to plough into his own. 'These
fellows drive like the devil,' he commented.

Eventually, the police car turned off the road and made its way,
a little more sedately, up the driveway that led to the bailiff's house,
'Rozel', where Lanz, Hessel and their interpreter, Dr Maass, were
ushered into Carey's office.

The old man was already on his feet waiting for them. After
Maass had made the formal introductions and explained that Hessel
had come to take his leave, the bailiff stepped forward and with a
gracious bow assured the new commandant that anything he might
need was at his disposal.

Satisfied that Guernsey was secure, Lanz returned to the airport
and boarded another Junkers 52 for the twenty-minute journey to
Jersey, where he once again oversaw the symbolic hoisting of the
German war flag at the terminal building. He appointed one of his
officers, Captain Erich Gussek, as commandant of the island before
returning to Guernsey again. Although it was smaller in size – at just
twenty-four square miles compared to Jersey's forty-five – Guernsey
was closer to the English coast, and therefore, Lanz felt, more strategically significant as a base of operations.

If the commandant's official report is anything to go by, the short
journey home made quite an impression on him: it was, he said, 'an
unforgettable flight in the glorious evening sunshine, under a cloudless sky, the deep blue sea beneath us and on the horizon glowing
red, the jagged cliffs of the rocky Guernsey coast'.

Clearly Lanz was in a very good mood. It had been a long day,
but one laden with historical significance. A day on which two of the
famous British Isles had formally been taken by the Reich.

By the time Alexander Coutanche arrived home from the airport
it was almost dinnertime, but the sun was still high in the sky. He
knew there was only one thing that would lift his spirits on such a

depressing day, so he changed into a pair of grey flannel trousers and a sports jacket and set to work in his garden.

When the bailiff's servant, Coleman, came to announce that the meal was ready, Coutanche couldn't muster the energy to get changed again, and he joined his wife Babs in the dining room still wearing his filthy outdoor clothes. After a particularly vigorous weeding session the flannel trousers now sported a giant rip at the knee, but she either didn't notice or chose not to comment.

As the Coutanches were finishing up their dessert, Coleman, who had been gazing out of the window, suddenly turned and announced with alarm, 'Sir, the drive is full of Jerries. What do we do?'

The bailiff sighed. 'There's only one thing we can do,' he replied. 'Open the door and let them in.'

Coleman went to answer the door, and a few moments later, Duret Aubin appeared in the dining room. 'The head man has insisted on coming here,' he explained apologetically.

'Where are they?' Coutanche asked.

'In your drawing room.'

The bailiff rose from his chair. 'All right,' he said. 'Let's go and meet them.'

Coutanche was not exactly attired for a formal diplomatic engagement, but there was no time to go and get changed now. Duret Aubin sized up the situation and decided they would just have to bluster their way through it. As they walked into the room, past a pair of German sentries who had been posted at the door, he announced theatrically, 'His Excellency, the Governor!'

Coutanche entered to find Gussek – a short, neat-looking man – standing by the unlit fireplace, surrounded by half a dozen of his subordinates. The captain stepped forward to introduce himself, but when he took in Coutanche's appearance he started slightly. Whipping out a monocle and fixing it in place, he looked the bailiff up and down disapprovingly.

Having already surrendered his island, Coutanche had no intention of surrendering his dignity too, not least to a German officer standing in his own drawing room. Fishing around in the pocket of his muddy sports jacket he produced a monocle of his own and pointedly scrutinised Gussek in the same manner.

This bizarre stand-off lasted several seconds. Eventually, Gussek was the first to look away, turning to one of his subordinates and demanding that he hand over a piece of paper. It was a proclamation, pretty much identical to the one that Coutanche had already heard read at the airport, but he listened patiently while an interpreter went through each point one by one. By now, Duret Aubin had discreetly excused himself. Through the open doorway Coutanche spied him in the dining room, knocking back a glass of port.

Once the proclamation had been read in its entirety, Captain Gussek appeared to be satisfied. He gathered his entourage and departed, instructing Coutanche to come and see him at his office the following morning to hammer out some more practical details.

A few moments later the German party pulled away in their commandeered police cars, leaving Coutanche and Duret Aubin to themselves, along with the decanter of port on the dining room table.

On Tuesday morning, while Coutanche and Gussek sat down together at St Helier's town hall – now the headquarters of the German administration in Jersey – Ambrose Sherwill found himself summoned for a meeting with Major Lanz. When he arrived at the Royal Hotel, Lanz was eating in the dining room, so Sherwill waited in the hallway outside.

After a few minutes, he was approached by a German naval captain. 'This is a dreadful war,' the other man remarked sombrely. 'I have so many friends in England.'

Sherwill had been feeling distinctly low himself and the captain's sincere regret caught him off guard. 'I'm dreadfully worried,' he admitted frankly. 'I don't know how I'm going to feed the people once winter comes.'

'My dear fellow,' the German replied reassuringly, 'there's not the slightest reason for you to worry about that. This war will be over in six weeks!'

It wasn't exactly a comforting prediction, but before Sherwill could find himself debating the likelihood of such a swift German victory, Major Lanz himself emerged from the dining room, accompanied by the interpreter Dr Maass.

The new commandant had been working late the night before, and Sherwill was a little surprised at how shabby he looked. His cool, taciturn manner hardly made a favourable impression either. Dr Maass, on the other hand, seemed altogether more approachable. He was a young, handsome man whose excellent command of English had been honed during his training in tropical medicine at the University of Liverpool. As well as functioning as Lanz's translator, he had also assumed the role of public relations chief for the German administration, something that suited his outgoing personality. This was a man, thought Sherwill, with whom it would be possible to do business. If only Dr Maass were the one making the decisions.

Since his encounter with Major Hessel on Sunday evening, Sherwill had been preparing himself mentally for his first official meeting with the island's new German commandant. While he knew that Lanz held all the cards in their negotiations, he was determined to represent the interests of his own people, and to secure whatever concessions he could. Knowing that Lanz had a PhD in law, Sherwill had dressed in his own legal robes, and had even brought some props with him in an attempt to make a strong impression. As they sat down at a little table to discuss the next official proclamation, he reached into his pocket and pulled out the Military Cross he had been awarded after the Battle of Messines in 1917, along with his other war medals. 'Please tell Doctor Lanz that I, too, have been a soldier,' he told Maass, laying the decorations out on the crisp white tablecloth. 'I bitterly regret that I am one no longer.'

Lanz picked up the medals and gave them a rather perfunctory examination before handing them back again. He was not a man to be swayed by such romantic gestures. Then, speaking through Dr Maass, he began to dictate his next set of orders.

This time, Sherwill was determined to push back as much as possible, quibbling, questioning and debating every new rule and regulation. After a long couple of days, Lanz didn't have the energy for a battle of wits, and the attorney general won more concessions than either of them had expected. Freedom of worship was guaranteed by international law, but Sherwill pushed further, requesting that prayers for the Royal Family, and even the British Empire, should be permitted. To his astonishment, the commandant agreed. Furthermore, although it would be forbidden for islanders to play or sing the national anthem in public, Lanz agreed that those tuning in to BBC broadcasts which included it would not be punished for listening. Cinemas, concerts and other forms of entertainment would be allowed to continue as well, as long as such gatherings weren't used as a means of spreading anti-German propaganda.

There were limits to Sherwill's powers of persuasion, however. When he attempted to reopen the subject of the ban on spirits, suggesting that perhaps they could be sold in private members' clubs, he was met with an exasperated 'Nein!'

That evening, the new list of orders was published in the *Guernsey Evening Press*. Although many islanders understandably resented each new imposition – Lanz's insistence that the island's clocks be moved forward an hour to match the time in Berlin left a particularly bad taste in the mouth – Sherwill felt satisfied that he had done his best. He might be living at the whim of the German administration just as much as every man and woman in Guernsey, but he at least had a role to play in lessening the crushing weight of the jackboot.

If Sherwill left his meeting with Major Lanz pleased with the way he had handled him, his performance was nothing compared to the *coup de théâtre* offered by Sybil Hathaway, the redoubtable Dame of Sark, during her own first encounter with the new commandant. On Wednesday morning, Lanz and Dr Maass boarded the Guernsey lifeboat – patched up after its machine-gunning off the coast of Jersey the previous week – for the nine-mile journey across the Roussels, as the stretches of water between the islands were known.

Despite the fine summer weather, it was a rough crossing, and by the time Lanz set foot on dry land two hours later he was feeling a little fragile. The island's tiny harbour was deserted, save for the seneschal (the head of Sark's parliament), who had been sent by the Dame to meet the new arrivals. Unlike Guernsey and Jersey, Sark had no gentle slopes down to the water, but sat 300 feet above sea level, with steep drops on all sides. At one end of the little harbour was a tunnel through the cliff face, which led to the road up to town. 'I'm afraid there are no vehicles on the island,' the seneschal told Major Lanz, with perhaps the tiniest glint in his eye. 'So we'll have to walk up the hill.'

It was true that the little island had no motor vehicles, but there were plenty of horses and wagons. That morning, however, under the glare of the punishing July sun, the three men trudged up the long, steep path on foot. By the time they reached the crossroads at the top of the hill, Lanz and Maass, in their heavy grey uniforms, were dripping with sweat.

The seneschal, who had already stopped off at the pub that morning on his way to greet the new arrivals, was feeling a little the worse for wear himself, but he led the two German officers along the town's dusty high street – curtains twitching in the window of every house – and up to the Seigneurie, where elaborate preparations had been made for their arrival. Keen to make an imposing impression, Dame Sybil had spent the morning rearranging the furniture, placing a pair of high-backed chairs behind a desk at one end of her drawing room so that the officers would have to walk as far as possible to meet her. 'We'll take a leaf out of Mussolini's book,' she had told her husband Bob, as they dragged their makeshift thrones along the floor. She had also instructed her maid Cecile to announce the Germans like ordinary house guests, as though having them call at the Seigneurie was an entirely everyday occurrence.

When the two exhausted officers finally entered the drawing room, the Dame greeted them in the manner of a gracious monarch deigning to grant her subjects an audience, rather than a woman who was about to be subjugated herself. As they came in, Lanz and Maass both raised their right arms in a Nazi salute, but neither quite dared say the words, 'Heil Hitler!'

Dame Sybil knew a little German herself thanks to a brief stint as a librarian at the YMCA in Cologne. When she asked the two men to take a seat in their native tongue, the official interpreter was caught off guard. 'You speak German?' he asked, astonished.

'Badly,' the Dame replied, with uncharacteristic modesty. 'But well enough to understand it.' She looked him in the eye before adding, 'And to make myself understood.'

'You do not appear to be in the least afraid,' Dr Maass observed.

'Is there any reason why I should be afraid of German officers?' Sybil asked him.

Major Lanz emphatically assured her that she had no cause to fear him or his men.

The Dame continued to treat the visit as an ordinary social engagement rather than a military takeover, even inviting the Germans to stay for lunch. The two men, famished from their long and arduous journey, readily agreed.

While they ate, Sybil treated Major Lanz to a potted history of the island, dating back as far as the first Viking settlers, as well as explaining its unusual system of governance. By the time the meal was over, he was feeling distinctly confused. Unsure whether the island had ever technically been at war with Germany, he wrote to the Foreign Office in Berlin to check he had the authority to occupy it after all.

Dame Sybil's sheer force of personality had been enough to bamboozle the new commandant, and although she acceded to the same terms of Occupation that Sherwill and Coutanche had done – a curfew from 11 p.m. at night, all guns to be handed in, the sale of spirits forbidden, and so on – she did it with such an air of insouciance that it felt like no victory at all.

The blitzkrieg of the past few months had shown the German Army to be an unstoppable force, but in the person of Dame Sybil Hathaway, Major Lanz had found his own immovable object. It was no coincidence that the German garrison who arrived the next day to formally occupy the island came to refer to her as '*Königin*' (Queen).

CHAPTER FIVE

FIRST IMPRESSIONS

While the islands' civilian leaders spent the first days of Occupation getting to know the German top brass, most ordinary people were doing their best to avoid the new arrivals. They complained bitterly about the rules and regulations published in the local press – not least the introduction of the German Reichsmark, valued at around eight to the pound. Perhaps most unpopular of all, though, was the imposition of double summer time, which brought the clocks in line with those in Berlin. As one elderly Guernseywoman, Violet Le Bideau, wrote in her diary, 'The wretched summer time is the most irritating of all. The one hour is annoying enough but two hours is purgatorial, nippy chilly mornings and the heat of the day reserved until after teatime. Why cannot people who are so mad on early rising stay up all night but leave their fellow creatures asleep in their beds?'

But however much they might grumble in the privacy of their own homes, when they left their houses to go to the shops or set off for work, the islanders would typically keep their eyes down, hoping to pass by the Germans unnoticed. When they did find themselves forced to interact with them, there was often an undercurrent of hostility. Mabel Green found it hard to suppress her contempt when she and her husband Bill were stopped in the street by a pair of young, blond soldiers who were confused about where exactly they had landed. 'Which way London?' one of them asked uncertainly. 'Over *there*!' Mabel replied, pointing out to sea.

To begin with, the number of Germans on the islands was small, but day by day more troops continued to pour in. Before long, Jersey was playing host to one rifle company, half a machine-gun company, a quarter of an anti-tank company, and a platoon each of engineers and cyclists, in addition to ever-increasing numbers of Kriegsmarine and Luftwaffe personnel.

Although the average soldier on the street bore no direct personal responsibility for the bombing raid the week before, it was hardly surprising that the locals should hold it against them, with many of the dead still yet to be buried. Ambrose Sherwill couldn't resist demanding that the genial Dr Maass explain the attacks on the lifeboat and ambulance, both of which had been clearly marked with red crosses. But the interpreter shrugged off the question. 'There are lunatics in the armed forces of all nations,' he retorted.

Nonetheless, on a personal level, those in authority were doing their best to make reparations. When Mrs Hobbs, whose husband Harold had been shot dead in his father's lifeboat off the coast of Jersey, arrived at the Royal Hotel to beg for his body to be brought back home for burial, she was seen by a deeply apologetic German admiral. 'We're not animals,' he told her, taking Harold's four-year-old son Tony onto his knee and letting the boy play with his Iron Cross. 'Is there anything I can do for you, Mrs Hobbs?'

The young widow thought for a moment. 'Harold was an officer in the naval reserve,' she said. 'Can we have a Union Jack for the coffin?'

'Of course,' the admiral replied. 'We'll even provide a military salute if you wish.'

'No,' Mrs Hobbs told him. 'There've been enough German bullets fired already.'

Little Tony might have been too young to really understand what had happened to his father – or to see the kindly man in the smart blue uniform as in any way connected to his loss – but for many older children living in the Channel Islands, the German soldiers were figures of terror. One of the first pieces of correspondence that Major Lanz received in Guernsey was from a woman whose children, aged seven and five, were so scared that they were unable to sleep at night.

Would the new commandant be willing to come and meet them, she asked, to reassure them that they were in no danger? The major readily agreed, shocked at the extent to which Allied propaganda, as he put it, 'had not even stopped short at the souls of little children, and had poisoned even the tiniest of them'.

Such fears could cast a sinister glow over the most innocent of interactions. In Jersey, ten-year-old Leo Harris and his thirteen-year-old brother Francis were on their way to school one morning when a loud, deep voice bellowed at them from across the road, '*Kommen Sie her!*'

They looked over to see a heavy-set German sergeant, dressed in white fatigues. '*Kommen Sie her!*' the man repeated, gesturing for the boys to come and join him.

Nervously, they crossed the road and approached the sergeant. As they drew near, they were overwhelmed by an unfamiliar smell – the pungent mixture of boot polish, gun oil and eau de cologne that made the German soldiers stand out wherever they went.

The boys looked up in terror at the giant of a man in front of them. 'You are English schoolboys?' he demanded, inspecting their bright blue blazers and leather satchels.

Technically, the Channel Islands were British rather than English, and in any case the Harris family were from Scotland. But this didn't really seem like the right time to get into a geography lesson. The two boys nodded, gulping as they murmured a hasty 'Yes, sir.'

'*Gut!*' the German declared cheerfully, reaching into his breast pocket. The boys' eyes were drawn to the patch stitched onto the uniform just above it: an eagle clutching a swastika in its talons.

The sergeant pulled out a small silver tube. 'Hold out your hands,' he told the boys.

They did as they were told, and from the tube he carefully extracted a pair of fruit gums, placing one into the palm of each outstretched hand.

'Oh, no thank you, sir,' Francis said politely, trying to hide the fear in his voice. He had been brought up never to accept sweets from strangers – let alone Germans.

But the sergeant was not to be contradicted. 'Eat!' he insisted.

Gingerly, the boys brought their hands up to their mouths and placed the sweets onto their tongues.

'*Ist es gut?*' the German asked.

They nodded weakly, and Leo felt a leather-gloved hand pat him gently on the head. 'Go to school!' the sergeant told them kindly.

The two boys turned and left, taking care not to run but desperate to get out of the sergeant's sight as quickly as possible. As soon as they rounded a corner they spat the sweets out onto the ground, convinced they had narrowly avoided being poisoned.

Gradually, fear began to give way to curiosity. In fact, the children of the islands – often disobeying their parents' explicit instructions – soon became a first line of communication with the German soldiers. The men of the Wehrmacht might be technically the 'enemy', but they were exciting and glamorous figures nonetheless, sporting smart military uniforms and carrying exotic weapons. For young boys, in particular, the appeal was hard to resist, and many began following the new arrivals around, even teaching themselves to imitate their characteristic goose-step and trying to piece together the strange-sounding words of their marching songs – 'Aye-ee, Aye-oh, Aye-ah!' went one of the more popular ones – the better to imitate these unlikely role models.

For their part, most of the soldiers appreciated the attention, and they showered the children with chocolate and sweets – even, on occasion, ice creams. Many kids were soon completely won over. 'They're just like us!' one boy in downtown St Helier was overhead telling his parents.

For most adults on the islands, however, it would take much longer for their instinctive hostility and suspicion to subside, however much the soldiers failed to live up to the monsters of the old propaganda cartoons. In the meantime, they continued to keep their heads down and did as their leaders had told them, getting back to work with a minimum of fuss and doing their best to carry on as normal.

For some, this was easier said than done. Having missed his

chance to leave Jersey on the mailboat thanks to the unexpected bombing raid, nineteen-year-old office boy Bob Le Sueur now found himself in charge of the General Accident insurance company. To make matters worse, his only remaining colleague, the typing girl Phyllis, had already handed in her notice.

The easiest thing would have been to simply shut up shop, but Bob couldn't afford to lose his job, and day by day customers continued to turn up with cheques and cash to pay for their policies. He had to somehow keep things ticking over. But running an insurance company was not exactly a one-man job – and certainly not for a man who had never done it before.

During that first week of Occupation, even the most experienced members of the island's insurance community were growing anxious about how they were going to cope under the new regime. A few days after the Germans arrived, a special meeting was organised at the office of Pearl Assurance, and the managers of all the insurance companies on the island were invited. Since Bob was the de facto manager of General Accident, he decided that he should go along too.

He arrived to find a room full of middle-aged men in smart tailored suits, gathered around a large conference table. The youngest of them was in his thirties, and all had been in the insurance trade for years. The seats around the table had all been taken already, but Bob managed to find a chair by the door.

A man from the Prudential stood up to speak. The most urgent problem, as he saw it, was that since the local insurance companies were all branches of English firms, any funds they accumulated – for example, by people paying in their premiums – could be confiscated by the Germans as enemy assets, leaving them unable to pay out when a claim was made. Fortunately, he had a solution. 'We're all cut off from our head offices,' he declared, 'so we're going to have to make decisions for ourselves.' The man looked around the room at the rows of concerned faces. Bob did his best not to blink. 'But perhaps we can make collective ones,' he suggested. 'We could form a kind of loose federation.'

It turned out that the man from the Pru had already been to visit the state treasurer to run this idea past him. The plan was that to avoid any individual firm accruing too much money, the new federation would loan their profits to the States of Jersey at a negligible interest rate. Since the States were now under German supervision, the funds would therefore be safe from confiscation.

A wave of relief swept round the room, and the ingenious proposal was readily accepted. Someone produced a sheet of paper, which everyone was asked to sign to indicate their willingness to join the new organisation.

Eventually the sheet made its way round to Bob. He scanned the list of names and titles on the page. Everyone else was a company manager, or at the very least a deputy, and he felt self-conscious putting down 'office boy' after his name. So he granted himself an on-the-spot promotion: from now on, the pimply teenager sitting in the corner was Bob Le Sueur, 'Acting Resident Secretary' of General Accident. To his relief, no one decided to question his credentials.

By the time Bob left the meeting that afternoon, he was beginning to feel like a genuine Acting Resident Secretary, but he knew he couldn't keep the company running by himself. At the very least, he would need a typist to replace Phyllis, so he placed an advertisement in the *Jersey Evening Post*, announcing that he was looking for someone to start immediately.

Bob expected to receive a handful of applications, but he soon had a stack of almost two hundred CVs on his desk. A lot of the island's businesses had already been forced to close due to the loss of their trading links to the mainland, throwing a large number of highly qualified people out of work. Looking through the vast pile of papers, Bob realised that many of the applicants had decades of experience in senior secretarial roles. They'll run rings around me, he thought.

Bob began to work his way through the CVs, searching for the least qualified candidates. In the end, he offered the job to a girl around his own age called Myra Hunt. She was a rather dumpy young woman and not particularly bright, but she seemed amiable enough, and unlike most of the girls who had applied for the job, Bob didn't feel intimidated by her.

The new typist started work almost immediately, and Bob never had any cause to regret his decision. She was hard working, easy to get along with, and never once questioned his often hastily improvised decisions. As far as Bob was concerned, they made a good team, but despite the fact that the two of them were both no more than teenagers, they maintained a distinctly formal, old-fashioned working relationship. She always referred to him respectfully as Mr Le Sueur, and he responded in kind, addressing her as Miss Hunt.

In any case, the two teenagers weren't alone in the office for long. The next General Accident employee was an older man called Mr Rod, who approached Bob directly looking for work. He was a middle-aged commercial traveller from Bournemouth who had been on one of his annual visits to Jersey when the bombing raid had caught him by surprise. Essentially, he had been marooned on the island, with no income and no way to contact his family.

Bob was more than happy to give Mr Rod a job in the office to help pay the bills. He soon found him to be a model employee – reliable and conscientious, and with decades of experience in dealing with customers that stood him in good stead in his new role as an insurance agent.

There was a touching innocence about Mr Rod, who despite his unfortunate situation, always looked on the bright side of life. In fact, more than once it occurred to Bob that the Englishman had not fully taken on board the gravity of his situation, stranded under enemy occupation for the foreseeable future and totally cut off from everyone he knew. But in those early days of Occupation, the number of German soldiers in St Helier was relatively small, and – busy as they all were with the practicalities of keeping the business going – it was almost possible to forget the momentous change that had occurred.

Finally, though, the penny dropped. One oppressively hot July afternoon, Bob and his employees were working in the office with the window open, when they heard a faint sound coming up the street towards the office. It was music, Bob realised with surprise.

The gentle strains gradually grew louder, until the three of them could make out a marching band. There were voices too, loud, confident and guttural, ringing out over the sound of the instruments. Mr Rod stood from his chair and wandered as if in a daze over to the window. There he stood, slack jawed, as an entire company of German soldiers marched by, their heavy black jackboots hitting the cobbles in perfect time as they goose-stepped right past the office.

'*By Jehoshaphat!*' Mr Rod exclaimed, his face fixed in an expression of stunned horror. The reality of his situation had finally sunk in. *This* was the infamous fighting force that had laid waste to half of Europe, and now had its sights set on his homeland. They were marching right past his office window.

The German Army was here to stay, and Mr Rod was going to have to live alongside them.

CHAPTER SIX

THE SPOILS OF WAR

In many ways, the occupation of the Channel Islands was seen as a dry run for the eventual administration of a conquered Britain, and those in charge were keen to make a positive impression, to prove that they would be fair and measured rulers rather than tyrants. The emphasis was very much on the velvet glove as opposed to the iron fist beneath it.

The restrained approach suited the average German soldier, who was scarcely in the mood for tyranny. To the men who arrived on the islands during that beautiful, drawn-out summer, the posting seemed almost too good to be true. One of them, Werner Grosskopf, had visited England as a schoolboy ten years earlier, and when he landed in St Helier's harbour and saw the perfect white villas set against the blue sky he couldn't help feeling that he had returned for another holiday.

On those long summer days, the islands were certainly looking their best. In Jersey, the row of ancient oak trees that lined the Esplanade leading out of town stood majestically against the twinkling blue of the ocean. In Guernsey, the pretty houses of St Peter Port glimmered in the sun, and the shady country lanes, bordered by hedgerows humming with insects, were at their most bucolic and serene.

The very landscape of the islands seemed to be teeming with new life. It wasn't just Guernsey's tomato crop that was ripe for the picking – strawberries, grapes, figs and melons were all ready to be plucked as well. In the parks and gardens, a dazzling array of brightly coloured flowers was in bloom, and the broad sandy beaches offered temperate, crystal-clear waters to swim in.

Off duty, the Germans and the islanders increasingly began to mingle. Churchill had promised that the British people would fight them on the beaches, and yet here 'they' were, sharing the sand with the locals – and fighting was the last thing on anybody's mind. Stripped of their intimidating grey uniforms, it was even harder to see the new arrivals as anything other than fellow human beings. In a bathing suit everyone looked more or less the same – although the Nazi cult of health and fitness, combined with good old-fashioned Army discipline, ensured that the bronzed bodies on display were not displeasing to the eye.

Many locals couldn't fail to appreciate the attractive young men. Violet Le Bideau, in fact, could barely contain her excitement. 'Half-naked Germans are doing physical exercises in the field opposite,' the old lady confided to her diary. 'They look most beautiful, with well-tanned arms "on which the swelling muscle slopes". When they lie on their back and do the pedalling exercise they are more beautiful still. A Guernsey cow is looking on unmoved.'

Not everyone was impressed, however. On Sark, an English bed-and-breakfast proprietor, Julia Tremaine, also noticed the prevalence of semi-naked Teutonic bodies all around her, but her reaction was one of revulsion. 'They go about the island more or less nude and sunbathe everywhere,' she wrote in her own diary. 'They are a dirty, disgusting lot.'

For the most part the Germans did their best to make a good impression on the locals – in part because they knew that they had scored the cushiest posting imaginable, and had no desire to be transferred to some less desirable theatre of operations. 'The officers behave just as our own would do,' wrote Mrs Le Bideau approvingly. 'They always make way for women in the town, and they open doors and stand back for one in the shops in the most matter-of-fact fashion.' Those who were expecting a reign of brutality and beatings had, she concluded dismissively, been reading too many novels. 'It is quite interesting to reflect that we really are under the Nazis,' she wrote, 'and it is disappointing that we can produce no real good bloodthirsty horrors to illustrate the terror of their regime.'

Nonetheless, although most individual German soldiers treated the islanders they encountered with courtesy, inevitably the Occupation brought with it many unpleasant changes to people's lives. The logistical challenges were enormous, both for the civilians – whose food infrastructure and labour market had suffered crippling blows when the islands were cut off from mainland Britain – and for the rapidly increasing number of German soldiers. Before long there would be several thousand extra men on the islands, all of them requiring hot meals and warm beds.

One of the first problems to be addressed was accommodation. The evacuees had left a large number of empty properties, but even so many families were unceremoniously turfed out of their homes, particularly if they lived in desirable, or strategically significant, locations. Bob Le Sueur and his parents watched sadly as the couple who lived at the end of their row of houses, Mr and Mrs Trigeur, were evicted, with only forty-eight hours to pack up and find a new place to live. But alongside the pity they felt for their neighbours was relief that they had escaped a similar fate.

Some people went to extraordinary lengths to prevent their property being requisitioned. Gladys Finigan knew that her six-bedroom house in St Peter Port, which was only a few minutes' walk from the Royal Hotel, was bound to be high up on the Germans' list, and sure enough they soon came to inspect the property. '*Prima!*' she heard one of them tell another approvingly, as they admired the stunning sea views.

Prime real estate it might have been, but Gladys wasn't going to give it up easily. As she led the Germans back down the stairs, she suddenly collapsed on the floor, groaning in agony. Her nine-year-old daughter Molly rushed over to see what was wrong, but her mother winked at her, before letting out another great moan.

'*Was ist los?*' one of the Germans asked anxiously.

'She's sick,' Molly replied, with the best poker face a nine-year-old could muster.

It was obviously enough to convince the Germans. They apologetically took their leave and never bothered the Finigans again.

Mrs Finigan wasn't the only one to resort to desperate measures to avoid requisitioning. One morning, John Harris, whose boys Leo and Francis had fled in terror from the sergeant who had offered them sweets, saw a German captain eyeing up the old Victorian chapel that stood on his land, abutting his own property. It would be perfect for a drill hall, he realised, and the last thing he wanted was hordes of enemy soldiers marching up and down next door.

Mr Harris decided to go out and see for himself what the officer's intentions were. 'Good morning!' he exclaimed, making an effort to sound friendly.

The captain didn't even turn around. 'You are the owner of this building?' he asked, as he continued to inspect the chapel.

'That's right,' replied Mr Harris.

'I need to see inside.'

There was nothing Mr Harris could do but unlock the door of the chapel and let the captain in. The German nodded approvingly as he squinted up at the high vaulted roof, which was covered in corrugated iron. 'So,' he declared, 'I will come back.' Then he clicked his heels and departed.

The next morning, Leo awoke to find his father up on the roof of the chapel, frantically unscrewing the iron panels. 'What are you doing, Dad?' he asked him.

'I'm taking it apart before they come back and requisition it,' Mr Harris shouted down.

He worked tirelessly all morning and by lunchtime the roof was off, leaving only bare wooden beams exposed to the sky. Next Leo and his elder brother Francis helped dismantle the walls, until all that was left was an empty wooden frame. Eventually, this too was pulled down. Before long, the little chapel had been reduced to nothing more than a pile of timber and several stacks of corrugated iron.

About a week later, the German captain returned to formally requisition the property. Mr Harris told his two sons to stay inside while he went out to greet him. From the kitchen window, Leo and Francis watched anxiously as the officer turned a bright shade of purple, gesticulating wildly and shouting expletives in his native tongue. Mr Harris remained perfectly calm, shrugging his shoulders as he insisted that the building had fallen down of its own accord. He had kept a few bits of rotten timber handy to lend credibility to the story.

The captain was not convinced, and continued ranting and raving. At one point the boys thought he was about to draw his pistol. Eventually, though, faced with Mr Harris's unflappable demeanour, he stormed off. The family never heard from him again.

Not everyone was as daring – or as foolhardy – as Mr Harris, and most simply did as they were told when the Germans came knocking. Dr Alistair Rose was given only a few hours to gather his things and clear out of his home. He ended up moving in with one of the partners at his surgery, who had already taken in three other doctors in the same situation. The men's wives had all evacuated to England, and they weren't used to cooking and cleaning for themselves. They were soon joined by a chemist and his wife, and the poor woman ended up as cook and housekeeper for all six men, although they did at least chip in with the washing up.

Although he missed his wife and children, Dr Rose rather enjoyed the return to bachelor life, sitting up late into the evenings with his colleagues, reading or listening to the wireless. But not everyone relished the prospect of mucking in with their friends. For Violet Le Bideau, the thought was positively appalling. 'The authorities want to know how much room we have in our respective houses,' she wrote in her diary. 'We are also told to make provisional arrangements with our friends for in case we're turned out suddenly. It will be hateful if we do have to go, we seem to have grown into our houses like snails. And then to live with friends or have them to live with us. How ghastly! I believe that I would rather have Fritz pounding up and down my back stairs than have my very dearest friend billeted on me for the duration.'

Before long, Mrs Le Bideau got her wish, when a couple of German soldiers were assigned to stay in her two spare bedrooms. They turned out to be model house guests, creeping down the stairs at six every morning so as not to wake their landlady. 'The Huns have been here a week and are as quiet and considerate as one can desire,' she wrote. 'I don't think either is likely to shed my blood or steal my money.'

In fact, as time went on, Mrs Le Bideau grew rather fond of her German lodgers, inviting them to join her in the living room to read by the fire in the evenings, and taking an interest in their lives back in Germany. One of them, a young man called Oppenberg who had worked as a stable hand before the war, made a particularly good impression. Despite being 'a peasant' – something the old lady apparently found thrilling – he had impeccable manners, always asking permission before he popped his head into the room to check the time on his landlady's wall clock.

Mrs Le Bideau soon grew so used to her friendly German lodgers that she almost forgot they were supposed to be the enemy. But one day she was brought back to reality when a young soldier marched into the house looking for one of them and, without thinking, greeted her in the traditional German fashion. 'The Heil Hitler salute has actually been done in my own sitting room,' she confided to her diary that evening.

Few people were as sanguine about letting the Germans into their homes as Mrs Le Bideau, but everyone knew that orders had to be obeyed. From the large bay window of Les Pieux Hotel on Cobo beachfront, the Smith family looked on anxiously as a busload of German soldiers pulled up outside. The eldest daughter, Gwen, had barely recovered from the shock of being machine-gunned by one of their planes and now a whole platoon had turned up on her doorstep.

A smart young officer marched over to the front door and Mr Smith went out to meet him. The German held out his hand, but after an awkward few seconds in which Mr Smith refused to acknowledge it, he quietly let it fall back to his side.

'I want to look over your hotel,' the officer said, apparently unmoved by the small gesture of defiance. His English accent was flawless. In fact, were it not for the smart grey uniform, you would hardly have known he was German.

'Well,' Mr Smith replied, 'I suppose I can't do anything about it.'

The officer followed him inside. 'You are living here alone with your family?' he asked.

'No, I have my mother and my sister here as well,' Mr Smith retorted. 'They were bombed out when your planes attacked the harbour.'

'I'm sorry to hear that,' the young man replied, 'but that is how things happen in wartime. They must vacate their rooms immediately. I will need them for my men.'

'Now just a minute—' Mr Smith began angrily, but his wife stepped forward and placed a hand on his arm, silencing him. Together, they led the German officer on a tour of the building.

A few minutes later, the busload of soldiers was pouring into the hotel, taking it over room by room. Despite their father's barely supressed rage, Pearl and Gwen couldn't help finding the young men rather fascinating. Perhaps it showed, because that evening, as the family sat up chatting in the kitchen – their dining room and lounge had been commandeered as an officers' mess – Mr Smith warned the girls to be very, very careful around all the young men staying in the building. He had served with the Royal Welch Fusiliers in the First World War, and his daughters knew all too well how much he hated Germans. Pearl had always found his attitude a little ridiculous, but nonetheless she and Gwen made sure to lock their bedroom door that night.

For Mr Smith, however, the humiliations weren't over quite yet. With his hotel largely requisitioned by the enemy, he soon found himself forced to hand over an even more prized possession: his Vauxhall 10. Almost five thousand cars were seized by the German authorities in Guernsey, with only a promissory note given to the owner assuring them that they would be recompensed within six months of the end of hostilities between Britain and Germany. In Jersey, meanwhile, more than twice as many vehicles were appropriated in the same way.

From now on, if people wished to travel beyond their own little patch of their island, they would have to get hold of a bicycle. Soon, nearly everyone had one, and the roads were filled with unlikely cyclists who hadn't ridden in decades, wobbling along awkwardly on clapped-out old bikes. Fifty-two-year-old Guernseywoman Ruth Ozanne described a typical encounter in her diary: 'I was pushing my bike up the hill and was joined by another fat woman pushing hers. We got talking in the matey way one does nowadays and she remarked, "I saw an elderly lady learning to ride the other day. She must have been quite as old as you!"'

Although keeping motor vehicles running against the rules was out of the question – aside from a handful of individuals whose work was impossible without one and who were issued official permits – some people were so sentimentally attached to their cars that they were determined to hold onto them, even if they couldn't be used. Scores of islanders succeeded in hiding their beloved vehicles behind bales of hay or stacks of tomato crates on remote farmland.

In Jersey, Mr Harris managed to conceal a dozen cars in lock-ups and stores all over St Helier, buying up new vehicles and secretly stowing them before they could be requisitioned by the Germans. They would be smuggled in at night, long after the official curfew, and he would make sure to keep them all in good working order, checking up on them every so often to ensure that when the Occupation finally ended they would still be roadworthy.

Most people, however, had nowhere to safely hide their vehicles, and were forced to simply hand over the keys when the Germans demanded them. The majority were shipped off to France and sold, while the more desirable models were repurposed as staff cars.

It was one such vehicle that provided insurance clerk Bob Le Sueur with his first encounter with a member of the Army of Occupation. A bill had arrived at the General Accident office from a local garage, who claimed they had carried out extensive repairs to a Standard Swallow sports car that was covered by one of their policies. The vehicle had apparently been involved in a collision shortly before the Germans arrived, and had been fitted with a new radiator grille, bonnet, offside door and wing mirror, as well as various other accoutrements to replace those damaged in the accident. In total, they were demanding several hundred pounds to cover the parts and labour.

Bob might not have been running an insurance company for long, but he was highly doubtful that, with the island cut off from the mainland, the mechanics would have been able to lay their hands on so many specialist parts. He called the garage and asked to speak to the manager, Mr Bree. 'I've received your bill for repairs to a Standard Swallow,' Bob told him, 'but I'll have to see the vehicle myself before I can authorise payment.'

Mr Bree laughed. 'You'll be lucky, sonny,' he replied. 'The Hun took the car after we'd finished working on it.'

'Why weren't we informed?' Bob asked.

'We thought your office was closed.'

'That's odd,' said Bob, 'because you sent the bill through to us this morning.'

There was a pause before the manager replied angrily, 'Don't you start getting funny with me, boy. We did the work and we expect to be paid.'

There was only one way to resolve the issue. Bob would have to track down the car himself. He cycled down to the office for requisitioned property in Bond Street, where he learned that the vehicle had been taken by a tall German officer who was staying at the Grand Hotel.

It didn't take long for Bob to find the Swallow, parked on a side street around the corner from the hotel's main entrance. He propped his bike up against the wall and began to inspect the vehicle, crouching down to get a closer look at the paintwork and scribbling some notes on a little pad.

It was clear what had happened. The car had indeed been in an accident, but far from replacing the offside door, the garage had simply hand-beaten and repainted it. Nor did the grille or the bonnet look new either. Just as he had suspected, Mr Bree was trying to con him.

Bob was still crouched down writing when he saw a shadow pass over his notepad. Looking up, he was met by a giant of a man in a smart field-grey uniform. 'What are you doing with my car?' the German officer demanded.

'*Entschuldigen Sie!*' Bob exclaimed anxiously, struggling to dredge up his schoolboy German. '*Ich arbeite für—*'

'I speak English,' the officer interrupted impatiently.

'Oh, of course,' Bob replied. 'I'm investigating an insurance claim.' Fumbling in his pocket, he pulled out the dubious repair bill.

'May I see?' the German asked politely.

Bob handed it over. The officer cast his eyes down the itemised list of parts, glancing back now and then to the vehicle. 'So ...' he remarked thoughtfully, 'I see the motor repairers in this island are no more honest than those in Germany.' He climbed into the driver's seat and started the engine, but before driving off he turned to Bob once again. 'And when you return to raise the subject with them,' he told him, 'I wish you the very best of Jersey luck.'

Back at the office, Bob phoned the garage again. To begin with, Mr Bree was even more confrontational than before, reminding him of the longstanding relationship between their two businesses and threatening to write to his superiors. But when Bob mentioned that he had personally inspected the vehicle, the manager's tone changed abruptly. He rang off, promising to investigate and get back to him.

When Mr Bree called back he was conciliatory in the extreme. 'I do apologise for this unfortunate error,' he said. 'It turns out we tried to source new parts but we couldn't get hold of them, so my boys did the best they could in the circumstances.'

'I understand,' Bob replied coolly.

A few days later, a revised bill arrived at the office, for a third of the cost of the original one.

The confiscation of housing and motor vehicles was official German policy, but for the people of the Channel Islands, the practical costs of Occupation went far beyond that. One of the earliest frustrations felt by ordinary islanders was the devastating effect that large numbers of cash-rich soldiers were having on the high street. Vast quantities of Reichsmarks were soon changing hands, as the new arrivals rushed to buy up all the best goods to send to their families back home. Compared to both Germany and occupied France, the Channel Islands – with their strong import–export ties to mainland Britain – were awash with luxuries, everything from perfume and jewellery to fur coats and designer shoes. The only problem was that with the link to the mainland now cut off, the supply of goods was finite, and it didn't take long for the high-street shops to begin boarding up their empty window displays as they ran out of anything to sell.

After less than a fortnight of Occupation, the situation in Jersey was already so serious that the island commandant, Captain Gussek, issued an order severely limiting the purchasing power of his troops. But the damage was already done – before long, many longstanding shops in St Helier and St Peter Port were closing their doors for lack of stock. Some abandoned premises were hastily commandeered by the Germans – Burtons menswear became an army canteen, while a tailor's shop, now all out of material, was repurposed as a propaganda office for the Reich.

The spending spree went beyond strictly luxury goods and affected the basics of everyday life for islanders. Underwear, shoes, candles, even pots and pans were soon virtually impossible to source. The people would just have to make do with what they already had in their houses.

More alarming for the islands' civilian leaders, however, was the food situation. Guernsey, in particular, was virtually a monoculture, with the vast majority of agricultural space on the island given over to greenhouses full of tomato plants. Although about half of the harvest had already been exported to England before the German bombers arrived, there were two thousand tonnes of tomatoes ripening every week, more than the Germans and islanders could possibly consume between them. Nor were there the facilities on the island for preserving them.

On the orders of Major Lanz, half the existing tomato crop was destroyed, making room in the greenhouses for other vegetables to be grown, while a small proportion of those tomatoes that had already been picked were shipped off to France. But despite such efforts there was no way for the island to become self-sufficient in time to avoid starvation. The supply of flour and wheat would last only another five months, and the utilities would begin failing around the same time. By November, the gas was projected to run out, while the island's water would be cut off – for lack of electricity to power the pumps – some time in February, leaving the sewers to lie stagnant, and the crops in the greenhouses to wither and die. In short, the island's infrastructure simply couldn't survive the coming winter.

Ambrose Sherwill and the members of his Controlling Committee worked furiously in an attempt to stretch the island's meagre resources. But it was the Germans who ultimately provided the solution. The officer responsible for agriculture, Dr Reffler, gave permission for a representative from the council to be sent to Occupied France to set up a kind of trading post where the island could barter for supplies. Sherwill gave the job to his agriculture minister, Raymond Falla, a man with great energy and a shrewd eye for a bargain. He was someone, as the attorney general later wrote, who could 'purchase wheat or meat, dead or on the hoof, or flour, or wireless batteries without being had too badly', and he was also not averse to a bit of under-the-counter trading if it meant getting hold of the right goods.

Falla was joined in France by a representative from Jersey, Jean Joualt, and between them they orchestrated the wartime imports and exports of their respective islands. Much of the money to pay for the goods came from the sale of confiscated vehicles, but the Germans laid down some frustrating regulations in regard to currency. The new office, based in Granville, at the base of the Cotentin

Peninsula, was not allowed to open a French bank account, so all their transactions were conducted by means of huge tea chests full of Reichsmarks, and each note had to be laboriously counted by hand.

The Granville office helped keep the wolf from the door, as hundreds of tonnes of flour, sugar and other essentials began pouring into the islands. But the Occupation had brought with it plenty of other food restrictions as well. Under German rule, fishing was massively curtailed. Fishermen were restricted to daylight hours, which meant they couldn't work the tides, banned from setting off altogether in the event of fog or mist, and even when they did go out they were generally accompanied by an armed guard, either sitting in the boat alongside them or following in a patrol vessel. Many of the most prolific fishing spots – the banks off Alderney, home to mackerel, rays and eels, and the waters to the south and west of Guernsey, which teemed with lobsters and crayfish – were marked out of bounds. All in all, the new regulations made the job of the fishermen a distinctly thankless one, and hit their stocks hard.

Then there were the farmers, who were required to hand over a certain proportion of their meat to the German Army. Each farm animal born had to be officially registered, and there were frequent spot checks to ensure that everything stayed on the books. Even the bakers found the Germans poking their noses into their business. At the Perelle Bakery in Guernsey, one day a week the ovens were given over to a German soldier who in peacetime had worked as a confectioner. Unlike the locals, he seemed to have an unlimited supply of sugar, butter, chocolate and more, and the bakers would look on enviously as he assembled row after row of beautiful shortbreads and cakes.

While the islanders struggled to get by, the Germans were living the life of Riley. Their spending sprees might have driven the highstreet shops out of business, but their needs were soon being met in specialist stores. The St Peter Port branch of Woolworths, having closed down for want of stock, reopened as a German-only business. Those islanders like Mrs Le Bideau who had soldiers billeted in their homes suddenly found themselves in a very advantageous position. They had only to beg one of their lodgers to do the shopping for the household and they would have access to a whole raft of supplies that their neighbours could only dream of buying.

Sixteen-year-old Marcelle Le Poidevin was one of a dozen or so local girls who worked behind the counters in the German shop. Her father, who had been gassed in the First World War, didn't like the thought of her spending her days in close proximity with the 'Hun', but the island was facing a labour crisis and for Marcelle, who had only recently left school, any job was a good job. At least, reasoned Mr Le Poidevin, his daughter would be working under the watchful eye of local managers, and in a public shop on the high street – and she would be surrounded by other, older girls who were in the same difficult situation.

The fact was that the Occupation had hit the job market hard. Dozens of shops had been forced to close for lack of stock, and their staff had been laid off. In Guernsey, the Controlling Committee had stepped in to prevent an even bigger problem with the thousands of islanders whose work was connected to the tomato trade. The end of exports to mainland Britain was an unemployment disaster waiting to happen, as growers struggled to pay their bills, let alone their workers. The solution was a voluntary nationalisation of the tomato industry. Those growers who were willing would have their businesses taken over by the Committee, along with their responsibility to their employees. A glasshouse utilisation board (or 'GUB') was formed to allocate the island's considerable agricultural resources, and new public-works programmes saw unemployed workers widening roads, chopping wood and more. In Jersey, meanwhile, a defunct clothing factory was reopened to provide employment for several hundred women.

There was also another, more controversial, new source of employment on offer: working directly for the Germans. Within six weeks of their arrival the authorities were demanding that the States of Guernsey provide them with labour to help with repairs to the airport, which was already being used for raids against mainland Britain. As an inducement, they were willing to pay three times the market rate, plus danger money to cover the possibility of attack by the RAF.

In the end, ninety-odd men were found to carry out the repairs, in what was arguably a violation of the Hague Convention. Much to the occupiers' frustration, however, the work proceeded suspiciously slowly. Whether this was an act of sabotage or simply a means of stretching out some highly lucrative employment was hard to say, but many people were unhappy at the idea of islanders directly helping the German war effort.

There were, however, plenty of jobs available with the new authorities that couldn't really be classified as war work, and at a time of mounting unemployment, these were something of a godsend. Ruth Leadbeater was still living above her future in-laws' chip shop, where she had witnessed the difficulties faced by local fishermen first-hand, when she saw an advert in the paper for a kitchen maid and general dogsbody to work at one of the island's grand houses. Ordinarily, there would be nothing surprising about a girl like Ruth going into service, but in this instance the house in question – an imposing old building on Queens Road, which went by the name of Camblez – had been taken over by the German authorities. It was being used as a billet for the top officials of the Feldkommandantur, the German civil administration of the island.

Based at Grange Lodge, the Guernsey Feldkommandantur was technically a *Nebenstelle* (branch) of FK515, located at Victoria College House in Jersey. It was staffed by civilians in uniform, a mixture of lawyers, civil servants and so on, who though they had been granted military status – not to mention side arms – were really little more than part-time soldiers, attending brief training sessions once a week, along with a week-long refresher course every six months, but otherwise left to their office duties.

After a brief interview at Grange Lodge, Ruth was told she had the job. Apparently, she had been the only applicant. When she arrived at Camblez on her first day, the Germans had already left for work, and she was met by a Swiss couple who had taken over housekeeping duties. Her own role, she learned, would be largely confined to the kitchens, but she would also be responsible for dusting the living areas, sweeping the stairs leading up to the bedrooms, and bringing down the officers' boots for polishing. 'They'll leave them outside the bedroom doors,' the Swiss woman told her. 'You won't ever need to go inside their rooms.'

That evening, Ruth met some of the men who were living at Camblez. There was the agriculture officer, Dr Reffler, his right-hand man, Dr Brosch, who also took on responsibility for censorship, and Prince Eugen Oettingen-Wallerstein, a Bavarian aristocrat whose spotless appearance was matched by impeccable manners. The prince spoke flawless English, and as he chatted affectionately about the wife and children living in his castle back home in Germany, Ruth felt herself warming to him immediately. Dr Reffler, too, was a perfect gentleman – handsome, smart and always polite, even to the servants. He treated Ruth with respect and even took an interest in her own life, asking questions about her family and what it was like growing up on the island.

Dr Brosch, meanwhile, remained stonily silent. He was a morose, unlikeable man, and evidently hard to please. While the prince and Dr Reffler always thanked Ruth for polishing their black jackboots, Dr Brosch felt that her work wasn't up to his standards. More than once he sent the boots back down after she had finished, demanding that she do them again. And then there was the way he spoke her name, barking '*Root!*' whenever he saw her, as if he were issuing orders to a platoon of soldiers.

Nevertheless, Ruth considered herself lucky to have found such a good job, and she welcomed the financial security it gave her. The Occupation was still in its infancy but it had already brought some form of hardship to most Channel Islands families. Some had been turfed out of their homes, most had parted with their beloved motor-cars, and many had been forced to improvise in order to keep themselves gainfully employed. But while out-of-work tomato pickers and domestic servants could look for new opportunities under the new regime, other workers – in particular skilled tradespeople and small-business owners – were staring into the abyss.

Harold Langlois was one of Guernsey's top estate agents, catering largely to the wealthy English retirees who saw the island as the perfect tranquil haven in which to spend their golden years. For decades, his little office in St Peter Port had been a hive of activity, but with the link to the mainland cut off, his telephone suddenly stopped ringing. A hundred miles of water now separated Harold from his customers, and he was facing a bleak future. There was no way his business could survive the change in circumstances. His own smart town house, which he shared with his beloved wife and four children, was mortgaged to the hilt, and he knew that it was only a matter of time before the debt was called in.

The Germans may not have hurt Harold personally, but their arrival cost him his business, his home and ultimately his mind. Only a few weeks into the Occupation he suffered a devastating breakdown and was admitted to the island's mental hospital. He would never go home again.

Harold's wife Louisa fought to keep the rest of the family together. With her beautiful home repossessed, she was lucky to find a much smaller house to rent, swallowing her pride as she leant on her two elder sisters for financial support. She began selling her furniture to help pay the bills, supplementing the children's meagre rations with bones from the local butcher and broken biscuits from the baker's shop. The once prosperous family had been brought unspeakably low.

Louisa felt both wronged and humiliated, and her anger found an obvious target: the Germans. They were the ones who had brought ruin on her family and taken her husband away from her, as surely as if they had stormed into his office and shot him in the head. She forbade her children from so much as talking to a German soldier in the street, and kept her daughters virtual prisoners in the house.

One day, Louisa was out with her youngest child in town when a soldier walked up to the pram, picked up the little girl inside and planted a kiss on her forehead. 'I have a daughter her age in Germany,' he explained. 'I couldn't resist.'

Louisa was furious. She grabbed the baby, put her back in the pram and, without a word, turned away from the soldier, marching home as fast as she could. The German's apologies echoed down the street, but she barely noticed them. As far as Louisa was concerned, there was nothing he could say that would ever atone for what his people had done to her family.

CHAPTER SEVEN

UNDER COVER

The German authorities had good reason to pursue a relatively 'soft' Occupation in the Channel Islands. As one of Hitler's advisers, Professor Karl Pfeffer, put it astutely, 'the islands naturally have an importance for us at present as a trial case for meeting an English population.'

Pfeffer spent over a fortnight on the islands on a fact-finding mission for the Führer, summarising his observations in a lengthy report. All things being equal, he argued, the Occupation was best understood as a public-relations exercise. 'At the moment it is naturally a matter of complete indifference to us what the English think about us,' he conceded. 'If, however, after victory we intend to draw part of the British people over to our side, the prevailing conduct of the German occupation troops can be abundantly employed as propaganda.'

The islanders did have another value that hadn't escaped Pfeffer's notice. 'The inhabitants of the islands represent for us hostages of the British people,' he remarked bluntly. If British forces mistreated German hostages elsewhere, the occupied Channel Islands would provide a useful means of exacting revenge and applying leverage. In the meantime, however, it was best for the velvet glove to remain in place.

Meanwhile, the islands' civilian leaders were keen to keep relations with the Army of Occupation as cordial as possible. After all, the government in Whitehall had decided they were not to be fought over. Their job, as they saw it, was to protect the interests of their own populations by developing a good working relationship with their new overseers. Alexander Coutanche, the bailiff of Jersey, described the carefully cultivated rapport he had developed with his German opposite number: 'We agreed mutually that we were enemies and that there must be no sort of social intercourse between us of any kind whatsoever. Within those limits, however, we could still both behave like gentlemen and that was what we tried to do.'

Coutanche was a shrewd political operator, and he saw his inter-actions with the Germans as an elaborately courteous battle of wits. Whenever they proposed a new policy that threatened the interests of his people, he would do his best to outmanoeuvre them and force them into a volte-face. Sometimes he came out on top, and some-times they did. Either way, the unflappable bailiff always lived on to fight another day.

Coutanche's counterpart in Guernsey, Ambrose Sherwill, shared many of his goals, although his own methods were typically less successful. An honest, upstanding man, he had little time for bluffing or machinations. He lacked the cool inscrutability of his opposite number in Jersey, not to mention his years of political experience. The first summer of Occupation was to prove the greatest challenge of his career.

Sherwill was determined to prove to the Germans that, as long as they were treated fairly, the people of Guernsey would give them no trouble. 'As an old soldier I know how to follow orders,' he told Major Lanz emphatically. But less than a fortnight into the Occupation, his commitment to a policy of good behaviour was undermined by someone with a more rebellious attitude: Winston Churchill.

A month earlier, the prime minister had declared that the battle for France – and, by extension, Europe – was over. And yet he was deeply unwilling to simply let the Germans control such vast swathes of territory unchallenged. A full-scale military assault was out of the question, at least for the time being, but that didn't mean Hitler's authority couldn't be shaken. Churchill ordered the head of his new Special Operations Executive – a spy network designed to operate behind enemy lines – to 'set Europe ablaze'.

The prime minister had never quite got over the humiliating withdrawal from the Channel Islands, and now he saw a chance to make amends. He might not have been able to prevent British territory from falling into German hands, but he could at least make holding onto the islands as troublesome as possible.

Churchill instructed General Ismay, his closest military adviser, to come up with a plan for some 'nuisance raids'. The idea, he explained, was to land men on the islands in the dead of night with orders to kill or capture as many Germans as possible. First, though, the British forces would need more information on the strength of the German garrison – and that meant on-the-ground reconnaissance. The obvious candidates for such a mission were the men from the island militias who were now serving in the Army. They knew the geography and had local contacts who would help them evade capture.

Within a matter of days, 'Operation Anger' – appropriately named, given Churchill's mood on the subject – was in full swing. On Friday 5 July, Lieutenant Hubert Nicolle, a twenty-year-old civil servant from Guernsey who had just completed his officer's training course, was unexpectedly summoned to a top-secret meeting at the Admiralty. By the time he arrived in London from the barracks of the Hampshire Regiment it was already early evening, and the building was all but deserted. Escorted through the long empty corridors to Room 74, Nicolle was surprised to spot a familiar face: his old Guernsey Militia captain Harry Cantan was standing at a conference table with a large map of the island spread out in front of him.

Cantan introduced Nicolle to an officer from Combined Operations, Major Warren, who outlined the mission they had in mind for him. The plan was to land an operative in Guernsey for three days, during which he would gather as much intelligence as possible on the German forces. When his time was up, he would be picked up again and returned to London.

The mission went far beyond what could reasonably be expected of a young officer. Operating out of uniform, Nicolle would be more spy than soldier. 'If you do this and are caught, we don't want to know you,' Major Warren warned him. 'You will be shot and that will be the end of it. Go away and think about it. If you say no, you don't want to go, you will go back to your unit.'

Nicolle didn't need any time to make up his mind. 'I'm happy to do it,' he told Warren. The truth was that, aside from wanting to do his bit for king and country, he was desperate to find out how his family and friends back home were getting on.

Once Nicolle had officially volunteered, the planning began in earnest. Warren asked him to suggest a good spot for a landing by canoe – he would be brought close to the coast of the island by a British submarine – and, after a quick look at the map, Nicolle suggested Le Jaonnet, a small cove on the south coast of the island where he had often gone swimming as a boy. Next there was the question of his outfit. The only clothes Nicolle had with him in London, aside from his Army uniform, were a white shirt and a 'Guernsey', as his countrymen stubbornly referred to the knitted sweaters produced on their own island. Fortunately, he was able to borrow a pair of grey flannel trousers from a junior naval officer who was about his size.

With the evening closing in, Major Warren sent Nicolle off to find a bed for the night. He checked into the Garrick Hotel, grabbed a quick bite to eat, and even took in a show at the Hippodrome before returning to his room for a restless, sleepless night. At one point in the small hours of the morning he was struck by a sudden worry that his shirt and borrowed trousers might stand out as too clean and immaculate, so he hastily screwed them up and bundled them under the covers, tossing and turning on top of them until they were well and truly crumpled.

The next morning, Nicolle was so nervous about the impending mission that he forgot to retrieve his outfit from underneath the tangle of sheets. He was already halfway down Charing Cross Road when he remembered, and had to dash back and beg the maid who was cleaning the room to let him root around under the bedclothes.

Nicolle arrived at the Admiralty at 9.30, ready for another long day of intently poring over maps. In the afternoon, Major Warren suggested he nip out and buy a bottle of brandy for the mission. Meanwhile, a porter was despatched to Gamages department store in Holborn to purchase the canoe – some assembly required – that would be used for the landing. He arrived with it carefully wrapped in brown paper, just in time to bundle both it and Nicolle into a taxi that was waiting to take them to Paddington Station, ready to catch the train to Plymouth. With a swift handshake and a 'Best of luck!' from Major Warren, Nicolle set off on his journey.

That evening, shortly after 9 p.m., he was on board HMS *H43*, a 400-ton First World War submarine with a crew of twenty-two, heading into the Channel. It was a rough voyage, and in the cramped confines below decks, Nicolle soon began to feel queasy. He clambered up inside the conning tower and hurled his guts up over the edge. Shortly afterwards, the hatch to the tower was closed, and the vessel gently dived under the waves.

It would be almost a full day before the *H43* resurfaced off the coast of Guernsey. Nicolle spent another fitful night on a bunk in the cramped officers' quarters, before waking at around 9 a.m. to a cold breakfast. His day beneath the waves was spent going over the plan for the landing with Sub-lieutenant Leitch, a navigator who would be joining him in the canoe for the short trip to shore before paddling it back to the submarine. Three nights later, Leitch would return to the same spot and pick him up.

It was a good job they had time to prepare since the canoe, once assembled, turned out to be too wide to pass through the fore-hatch of the submarine. A resourceful sailor set about making some last-minute modifications and by the time the *H43* finally surfaced a little before midnight the jury-rigged vessel was ready for action. Nicolle and Leitch clambered up on deck, and at 00.17 hours on Monday morning they slipped into the waiting canoe and began gently paddling towards the shore. It was a brilliant moonlit night and the hulking cliffs of the island were unmissable against the inky blue sky.

Gazing up at the stars as he paddled, Nicolle had time to dwell on the dangers that lay ahead of him. If he had turned Major Warren down, he realised, he would be safely tucked up in his bunk at the Hampshire Regiment barracks right now, instead of embarking on a dangerous mission behind enemy lines. A mission in which any small mistake – or even simple bad luck – could see him shot as a spy without trial. Had he been a fool to accept such a risky assignment, he wondered. Was his first operation as an officer in His Majesty's Army also going be his last?

Nicolle was still lost in such reveries when, only about twenty yards away from the shore, the canoe suddenly swung around into the waves, tipping him and Leitch into the water. Lucky, they were just about in their depth, so they grabbed hold of the vessel and dragged it up onto the beach, tipping it upside down to let the water out. Then they hauled it back into the water and Nicolle gave it a hearty push, wishing Leitch a safe passage back to the submarine and promising he would see him again in three days' time.

It was a little after 2 a.m. by the time Sub-lieutenant Leitch was finally hauled back on board the *H43* for the twenty-four-hour journey back to Plymouth. Meanwhile, Lieutenant Nicolle was still on the beach at Le Jaonnet, doing his best to dry out his clothes – if he was unfortunate enough to run into a German patrol in the middle of the night, his drenched outfit would be something of a giveaway. He stripped naked and began furiously wringing out his garments, draping them over a rock in the hopes that the water would evaporate in the sea breeze. Then, to keep himself from freezing in the cool night air, he took a few swigs from his brandy bottle and began hopping around the beach. Fortunately, there were no German soldiers around to witness this bizarre nude performance. If there had been, they might easily have taken him for a lunatic.

Nicolle knew he needed to be safely hidden away before dawn, which in Guernsey in July could be as early as three or four in the morning. So shortly after two o'clock he forced his cold limbs into his still-sodden clothes and began the steep climb up the path that led up to the cliffs. Every so often as he dislodged a stone or disturbed a rabbit in the undergrowth, the still silence of the night would be punctured, and Nicolle would freeze to the spot. But time and again, these little disturbances appeared to go unnoticed by the Germans. There was no sign of any human beings as far as Nicolle could see or hear – only the occasional lowing of a Guernsey cow.

At the top of the cliff path, Nicolle clambered through the hedge into a field, and made for a nearby copse of trees, resolving to stay there until sunrise. His damp clothes were still clinging to his body, as he lay there waiting for the island to come to life.

A few hours later, he emerged – at last almost dry – to find a friendly face among the cows in the field. It was Roy Thoume, a lad with whom Nicolle had served in the Militia, out on his early morning milking round. As Nicolle approached, Roy stared at him as if he had seen a ghost. 'What the hell are you doing here?' he exclaimed.

Nicolle briefly filled Roy in on his top-secret mission, before asking him if there was anything he needed to know in order to survive on the island undercover.

'Well, curfew's between eleven at night and six in the morning,' Roy told him. 'Other than that, you should be able to get around without any trouble. Oh, and the clocks are an hour ahead. We're on Berlin time now.'

'Thanks, Roy!' Nicolle replied, adjusting his watch. 'Now, you mustn't tell anyone I was here this morning.'

His old friend nodded. 'I'll forget I saw you, eh?'

Nicolle made off in the direction of the airport. He knew Major Warren was particularly interested in intelligence on the Luftwaffe's presence on the island – at this point, Air Force personnel in Guernsey actually outnumbered the Army – and he was hoping that some friends whose fields abutted the airfield, the Mansells, might be able to provide him with information.

As he began the kilometre-long walk along the Forest Road, Nicolle was surprised by the sound of a motorcycle engine approaching from behind. His heart leapt into his throat, but he didn't dare look round. He was just an ordinary local man, going about his business, he told himself. There was no reason for anybody to stop him.

A few seconds later, the motorbike whizzed past, complete with sidecar. Nicolle could make out the blurry form of three German soldiers in their distinctive field-grey uniforms. This was the enemy that he had been trained to fight – now, though, he would have to let them go in peace. As they passed into the distance without so much as a second glance in his direction, Nicolle breathed a deep sigh of relief.

Arriving at his friends' house, Nicolle made his way round the back, where a rather astonished Viv Mansell opened the door to him. Hurriedly ushering him inside, she set about preparing some breakfast. Before long her brothers Tom and Dick had joined them at the table, asking what they could do to help. 'Keep an eye on the airport for me,' Nicolle told them. 'I'll be back before I leave the island on Thursday, and you can tell me how many planes have landed and taken off in the meantime.'

Next, Nicolle borrowed Tom's bike for the twenty-minute ride to his parents' house in St Peter Port. On the way, he passed several more German soldiers, although he did his best to stick to the back streets and avoid the area around the Grange, where many of the top brass had their offices.

When he arrived home, Nicolle wheeled the bike out of sight down the side passage and slipped in through the unlocked back door. He found his mother in the kitchen. She was shocked to see him, but did her best to maintain a calm demeanour as she telephoned her husband Emile at work. 'I'm not feeling very well,' she told him. 'Can you come home?'

Emile rushed back as fast as he could, expecting to find that his wife had injured herself using their new electric washing machine, but when he burst into the kitchen and found his son sitting at the table, his alarm only increased. 'What the bloody hell are you doing here?' he asked.

The young man looked up and replied, 'I'm a spy.'

Nicolle's parents listened attentively while he explained his mission. They were both deeply worried, but his father at least understood why he had volunteered for it. A veteran of the First World

War, he knew what it meant to risk your life for king and country, and he could hardly begrudge his son's bravery.

He did, however, have a plan to increase Nicolle's chances of concluding his assignment in one piece. 'It's too dangerous for you to be out and about in town,' he told him. 'Anyone could see you. You can stay here for the next few days, and I'll make sure the information you need comes to you.' Mr Nicolle was a senior civil servant, the secretary to Ambrose Sherwill's Controlling Committee. He had the connections to find out what his son needed to know without attracting too much attention.

Over the course of his three days in Guernsey, Nicolle gathered an impressive amount of intelligence. His uncle Frank, who was the island's assistant harbour master, brought news of shipping movements. The Mansells provided him with details of the Luftwaffe's activities, and from various other sources he was able to learn the location of no fewer than seventeen machine-gun posts and three anti-aircraft sites dotted around the island. He was even able to deduce the size of the German garrison thanks to his parents' neighbour, Mr Collins, an elderly gentleman who was the managing director of Guernsey's largest grocery store, Le Riches, which had been supplying provisions for the troops. There were, he told Nicolle confidently, 469 of them now living on the island.

On Thursday afternoon, having committed all that he had learned to memory, Nicolle set off to return his borrowed bike to the Mansells and make his way back down to the little cove at Le Jaonnet. Checking that nobody was watching, he vaulted over the hedge that abutted the cliff path, and then lay hidden behind it for several hours, waiting patiently for darkness to fall. Then he began carefully scrambling back down the cliff path to the beach.

The rendezvous had been scheduled for 00.30 hrs, but the appointed time came and went with no sign of Sub-lieutenant Leitch's canoe. Nicolle waited anxiously, scanning the horizon again and again, but still there was no sign of the little vessel. Then suddenly, a dinghy carrying three people appeared in the distance, heading for the shore.

Nicolle was sure it must be the Germans coming to capture him. Someone must have told them where he would be. He turned and began to make for the cliff path once again, when he heard voices coming from the dinghy. They were speaking English.

A few minutes later, the little boat reached the shore, swamped with water from the difficult approach. Out hopped Leitch, along with a couple of men Nicolle recognised as fellow Guernsey lads serving in the British Army, Desmond Mulholland and Philip Martel. 'These two are staying for a few days,' Leitch told him, as the four of them righted the dinghy for the return journey to the submarine.

Before they pushed off, Nicolle quickly imparted a few tips to the men who would be taking over from him as Churchill's eyes and ears on the island. Then he wished them good luck and clambered aboard the little boat, setting off for open water as fast as he and Leitch could paddle.

On their first attempt, the dinghy was swamped by the breakers again, sinking in about five feet of water. Nicolle and Leitch dragged it back to shore, signalling to Mulholland and Martel – who were already halfway up the cliff path – to come back and help them relaunch it. This time, the two men made it out of the bay, but somewhere along the way the boat had sprung a leak. It was rapidly filling with water.

Nicolle bailed furiously and Leitch paddled as fast as he could. He knew that their window to make it back to the submarine was rapidly shrinking. The operation had been planned to take place during the turning of the tide, when the waves were at their least choppy. In a matter of minutes, the wind would be blowing up a nasty lop more than capable of sinking the compromised vessel.

Fortunately, the two men made it just in time, pulling up alongside the hulking form of the *H43* a little after 2 a.m. The crew hauled them, bedraggled and exhausted, up onto the deck and got them inside.

Within moments, the submarine was moving again. The scuttled dinghy was towed a safe distance from the shore before being cut free to sink to the bottom of the Channel. Then the submarine dived down too, 60 feet beneath the waves, for the day-long journey back to Plymouth.

In the vessel's tiny officers' quarters, Nicolle found Major Warren, ready to debrief him en route. Together, they began working on the detailed report that the young lieutenant would submit to the Admiralty.

On Friday morning, a week after he had been summoned to London, Nicolle returned to be greeted with a hero's welcome, at least within the cloistered confines of Whitehall. The amount of intelligence he had gathered in just three days was truly impressive – and almost all of it without leaving his parents' house. When he had completed his official report to the military top brass, someone came up and murmured in his ear, 'You'd better go and clean yourself up. The PM wants to see you.'

CHAPTER EIGHT

TROUBLE AT THE TOP

Everyone in London agreed that the undercover mission had been a great success, but in Guernsey it was a very different story. When Ambrose Sherwill learned that Emile Nicolle's son had returned to the island as a spy he was deeply alarmed. Had the young lad been caught, he was certain the Germans would have executed him – and that would hardly have helped the fragile accord that he was so desperately trying to establish.

There was a personal reason for Sherwill's concern as well. His own son John was also serving in the British forces and had stronger local connections than Hubert Nicolle. If the British continued landing former Guernseymen to gather intelligence, he could easily be next.

Sherwill could only hope that Nicolle's visit was a one-off, and not the start of some new strategy cooked up in London. But it didn't take long for his worst fears to be confirmed. Two days later, Guernsey experienced its first 'nuisance raid' courtesy of the newly formed British Commandos.

The raid certainly caused a lot of nuisance, although not to the Germans. The plan was for a multi-pronged assault, with one group landing two boats, at Moye Point and Petit Bot respectively, before meeting up to attack the airport. A second, smaller unit was to make a diversionary raid at Petit Port, attacking a machine-gun post there and killing or capturing its crew. The two local lads Nicolle had met at Le Jaonnet, Desmond Mulholland and Philip Martel, had been sent ahead to scope out the lie of the land and meet the commandos when they arrived. All in all, 140 men were involved in the operation.

In reality, only one of the three groups made it to shore. One boat missed the island altogether thanks to a problem with their compass, landing briefly on either Sark or Herm – in the dark, they weren't sure – before realising their mistake and heading back to their destroyer, HMS *Scimitar*. Another, spotting Mulholland and Martel's flashing torches at Le Jaonnet, mistook them for a German patrol, decided they must have been seen, and also turned back. Only the diversionary party, a forty-strong group led by Lieutenant-Colonel John Durnford-Slater, actually succeeded in making landfall, but on their approach into Telegraph Bay they ran their boats aground on the rocks and were forced to bail out. By the time they had waded ashore and trudged up the steep 250-foot cliff path, weighed down by their sodden uniforms, most of them were already done in.

Despite their exhaustion, Durnford-Slater and his men led a bold assault on the German machine-gun post – only to find it unoccupied. In fact, aside from rousing a few dogs, the only living being they encountered was an old man who lived in a nearby cottage, and who was so terrified at the sight of the landing party that they couldn't get any information out of him. They had just enough time to put together an improvised roadblock – ransacking a local garden for materials before realising they had left their barbed wire down on the beach – and cut a few low-hanging telephone wires – since they had no climbing irons, the majority were out of reach – before the time came to return for their pick-up.

In their two hours in Guernsey, the commandos had killed no Germans, taken no prisoners, and got nowhere near their primary objective, the airport. Cutting through a few phone lines was hardly a great military achievement – as Durnford-Slater himself admitted, 'A youth in his teens could have done the same.'

But the farce had only just begun. On the way back down the cliff path, Durnford-Slater lost his footing and his cocked revolver went off in his hand. The gunshot echoed off the cliffs all around, attracting the attention of a German machine-gun on the far side of the cove. Fortunately for the landing party, the Germans hadn't actually seen them and began firing blindly out to sea, assuming that the shot had come from a boat.

Despite the gunfire, a dinghy was sent to shore to collect the men, but in the rough conditions it was soon smashed to pieces on the rocks, with one man on board presumed drowned. For those still waiting on the beach, there was nothing for it but to swim out to the waiting boats. They began stripping off and plunging naked into the chilly water.

There was just one problem: only now did three of the forty-strong party admit that they couldn't swim.

Durnford-Slater was furious, but there wasn't much he could do. 'You chaps hide up,' he told them, hoping he could persuade his superiors in London to send a rescue party.

'Thank you, sir,' replied one of the men sheepishly. 'Sorry to be such a nuisance.'

The commandos returned to England with their tails between their legs. Unsurprisingly, Churchill was deeply unimpressed, describing the operation as a 'silly fiasco'. But his reaction was nothing to that of Ambrose Sherwill in Guernsey.

The first the attorney general knew of the raid was when Dr Maass arrived in his office the following morning looking uncharacteristically sombre. His men had found the stone roadblock and the cut telephone wires, along with a magazine from a Bren light machine-gun. He insisted that Sherwill find and punish whoever had caused the damage immediately. Otherwise, he would order his own troops to begin making arrests.

Sherwill wasn't sure whether or not the German guessed the true story behind the morning's discoveries, but it seemed pretty obvious to him that they had nothing to do with the local people. 'Will you give me a few hours to make some enquiries?' he asked.

'Of course,' agreed Dr Maass.

Sherwill phoned his chief of police, William Sculpher, instructing him to investigate the matter – but to take his time about it. If there had been a landing, it was possible that some of the men were still on the island. Every minute he bought them before the search parties were sent out could prove vital.

Gradually, the Guernsey police pieced together what had happened. On the beach at Telegraph Bay, they found rifles, steel helmets, the remains of a dinghy, and even several British Army uniforms, among them Lieutenant-Colonel Durnford-Slater's. There was no escaping the conclusion that a military operation, however ineffective, had taken place there.

As soon as the Germans were informed, they began combing the island. Within twenty-four hours, Durnford-Slater's non-swimmers were rounded up, along with the man presumed drowned, who had miraculously found his way to shore. Fortunately, all four were still in their Army uniforms so they were classified as enemy combatants. After a fruitless interrogation – they refused to divulge any details of the operation, or even the names of the ships involved – they were despatched to a POW camp in Germany.

The Germans took the whole business remarkably well, perhaps encouraged by the raid's evident ineptitude. Sherwill, however, was furious. Not only had it been a disaster militarily, it was also a huge potential obstacle to his attempts to establish a working relationship with his German counterparts.

Exasperated, the attorney general penned a letter to Charles Markbreiter at the Home Office, handing it to a visiting German officer in the hope that it might be dropped over London. 'I do not know what the object of the landing was but to us it seemed senseless,' he wrote. 'The object of this letter is to ask that you will make the strongest representations in the proper quarter to the effect that, it having been decided by the British Government, in the interests of the people of the Channel Islands, to demilitarise them, military activities of the kind referred to above are most unwelcome to us and are likely to result in loss of life among the civilian population and generally to make our position much more unpleasant.'

Sherwill had no idea whether the letter ever made it to London, but writing it made him feel a little better. At least, he reasoned, with the non-swimmers from Durnford-Slater's raid rounded up as POWs, the Army were done causing trouble in Guernsey for the time being.

But there were still two British soldiers on the island that neither Sherwill nor the Germans knew about: Desmond Mulholland and Philip Martel. In the chaos of the commando raid, the two men had never been picked up. Now, without uniforms to mark them out as soldiers, their lives depended on not being discovered.

It was easier said than done. The lads had landed in Guernsey expecting a visit of only a few days and were not prepared for a longer stay. For a start, they had no means of shaving, or washing their clothes, and the more shaggy and dishevelled they looked the more likely they were to attract attention. Nor were they well equipped for travelling by night, after curfew. Mulholland had brought a pair of rubber-soled shoes, but Martel was forced to go barefoot outside daylight hours, and his feet were soon bloodied and painful.

The longer they spent on the island, the more chance encounters they had with local people. Their fellow islanders would always turn a blind eye to the two young men camping out in an empty barn, or raiding an abandoned house for supplies, but they knew that every person who saw them was potentially exposing themselves to danger by not reporting it. In the long term, it was simply unsustainable.

In desperation, the young soldiers turned to the one person they thought might be able to help them: Ambrose Sherwill. One late-July morning, the attorney general was up early to stoke the boiler at the back of his house when he found them waiting outside his back door.

As soon as he saw the two lads, Sherwill's heart sank. Desmond Mulholland was a friend of his daughter's and he knew that he had left Guernsey to join the Army. He realised at once what the nature of their mission must have been, and that something had gone terribly wrong.

This was exactly the sort of situation Sherwill had feared, and now he was personally implicated. For all he knew, offering assistance to British spies was a capital offence in itself. A veteran of the

First World War, he wasn't afraid of risking his own neck, but he had other responsibilities to consider. 'Wait here for a moment,' he told the two men. 'I need to speak to my wife.'

Sherwill rushed inside and up to his wife May's room, where he rapidly explained the situation. 'I didn't think it was right to let them into the house without speaking to you,' he told her. 'It could be very dangerous for us as well.'

But for Mrs Sherwill the idea of turning away two lads in need of help was unthinkable. 'I'd better get them some breakfast,' she replied, making for the kitchen.

While Martel and Mulholland wolfed down their first hot meal in days, Sherwill was contemplating a plan that he hoped might save their lives. The soldiers from Durnford-Slater's landing party had been treated well by the Germans. If Major Lanz could be persuaded that these two lads were part of the military raid and not undercover operatives, they would be able to live out the rest of the war in a POW camp. The only problem was that they had left their uniforms behind in England.

After their meal, Mulholland and Martel were led up to a bedroom in the attic, where they soon fell into a much-needed sleep. Sherwill, meanwhile, hopped in his wife's little Fiat, one of the few vehicles on the island that hadn't been confiscated, and set off to see his friend Don Bisset, a builder who had keys to half the doors on the island. 'We're going burgling,' Sherwill announced cheerfully, before telling him exactly what he needed.

Bisset was a former captain in the Guernsey Militia and, as Sherwill had hoped, he knew exactly where to look. At the Town Arsenal, he dug out an old chest filled with service uniforms from the First World War. Sherwill selected a couple that looked about the right size, carefully snipping off the twenty-year-old ribbons and smudging the unfaded fabric beneath with a bit of dirt from the floor. He then enlisted the help of Mrs Dawes, the wife of the Arsenal caretaker, to swap the Guernsey Militia buttons for some British Army ones.

When this was done, he raced back home and roused the two men from their slumber, instructing them to put on the new outfits. As it turned out, they were a reasonably good fit, although Sherwill had to lend Martel a pair of braces to stop his trousers falling down.

Once the lads were ready, Sherwill telephoned German head-quarters and asked to speak to Dr Maass. He didn't like the thought of lying to him, but the situation called for a convincing performance. 'Two British officers have just surrendered to me,' he announced, hoping he sounded more composed than he felt.

'Two officers?' Dr Maass replied, surprised.

'Yes.'

'When?'

'I won't lie,' Sherwill lied. 'It was two or three hours ago. They were in a pretty bad way, so I gave them a chance of some food and a rest before telephoning you.' That bit at least was true, although he was aware that it sounded dangerously close to sheltering fugitives from the law. He just hoped that by admitting to a smaller crime he might deflect attention from a larger one.

'Are they in uniform?' asked Dr Maass suspiciously.

'Yes.'

'At your house?'

'Yes.'

'You mean,' the German officer asked smoothly, 'they were able to walk through the streets in British uniform without being seen?'

Suddenly, Sherwill saw the flaw in his story. 'Of course not!' he blustered, stalling for time. 'Do you think they're mad?' Then the answer came to him: 'They landed in uniform, but they had some civilian clothes to come here.' He added, as nonchalantly as he could, 'I've kept the clothes to show you.'

'Very well,' Maass replied. 'Bring them in now.'

There was a click as the call was disconnected.

Had it worked? Was it going to work? Sherwill couldn't be sure. Dr Maass was no fool, and had already almost trapped him once. As they drove down to German headquarters, he told the two lads, 'Give them your name, rank and number – nothing else. Otherwise you'll be shot, and I'll be shot too.' Sherwill might have developed a good working rapport with the Germans, but he was under no illusions about how much danger he was in.

They pulled up outside the Channel Islands Hotel, which was now home to the German Kommandantur, and Sherwill led the nervous young men up to the door, telling the guards outside, who were bristling at the sight of their uniforms, that he had an appointment with Dr Maass.

Inside, Maass was as genial as ever, offering Martel and Mulholland a warm handshake before asking them, in the most relaxed conversational way, when exactly they had arrived on the island.

Disarmed, the young men began filling him in on the details of their visit. Sherwill was horrified. As they were led away to the guardroom, he begged Dr Maass for another moment alone with them. 'Do you mind?' he asked. 'I meant to give them some cigarettes and forgot.'

Maass smiled obligingly, and Sherwill raced off after the soldiers, handing over a couple of smokes with a fake smile plastered across his face, and whispering urgently as he did so, 'You bloody fools – nothing but name, rank and number!' Then he left them with the German guards, bid Dr Maass a hasty adieu and returned home.

The next few days were an agony of anxious waiting for Sherwill, as Martel and Mulholland were flown to Dinard for a rigorous interrogation. He felt sure that sooner or later one of them would say something incriminating, and then he too would also fall under suspicion.

In the end, unable to bear the suspense, he asked Dr Maass, with feigned indifference, 'By the way, have you heard anything about how those two young officers are getting on?'

'They'll be all right,' the German doctor told him reassuringly. Then he added, '*If* their story holds.'

As it turned out, the young men did better than Sherwill expected. Despite many hours of determined interrogation, they never betrayed the true nature of their mission. In time they were sent off to Germany as prisoners of war. The attorney general's bold bluff had undoubtedly saved their lives.

After less than a month of Occupation, Sherwill was already finding the delicate balancing act that his position demanded almost too much to bear. The next crisis came courtesy of Mr Collins, the elderly managing director of Le Riches Stores who had provided Hubert Nicolle with figures for the number of German soldiers on the island.

Le Riches was popular with the Occupation forces, and Mr Collins was fortunate that one of the assistants he employed was fluent in German. But the man had a habit of abruptly breaking off from serving local customers whenever a soldier walked through the door. As far as Mr Collins was concerned, this was plain rude – Occupation or no Occupation. But when he threatened to discipline the offending assistant, he found himself reported to the German authorities for the crime of 'propaganda against the German Army'.

The first Sherwill knew of the affair was when he arrived at the Channel Islands Hotel for one of his regular meetings with Dr Maass and was told that he was on his way to arrest Mr Collins. Sure enough, the old man was soon locked up in a gaol cell. His crime may not have been as serious as Martel and Mulholland's, but Sherwill feared a custodial sentence could be dangerous for a man whose health was far from robust. He begged Dr Maass for permission to post bail so that Mr Collins could at least await his trial at home. Maass put the request to Major Lanz but it was denied. As far as the commandant was concerned, Sherwill's word wasn't enough for him to release a man accused of such a serious crime.

The major was willing to grant one concession. Given the circumstances, he was content for Mr Collins to be tried in the Royal Court of Guernsey rather than by a military tribunal. There was just one problem: there was no crime under Guernsey law that he could plausibly be charged with.

When Sherwill tried to explain this to Lanz's adjutant, Lieutenant Mittelmüller, he received a frosty reply. If he didn't find a way to bring Mr Collins to trial, the lieutenant warned him, the Germans would be forced to bring their own system of justice to bear.

Sherwill racked his brains for a workaround. When he finally came up with a solution, it was one that offended every fibre of his professional being, both as a lawyer and as a politician. With the commandant's approval, he told Mittelmüller, he could push a new law through the States that would make it an offence for any islander to cause a deterioration in relations between the locals and the occupying forces. But since the alleged crime had already taken place, the legislation would need to be retrospective, backdated to the start of the Occupation.

Mittelmüller was a law graduate himself, and knew that *ex-post-facto* legislation was generally frowned upon, but he assured Sherwill that Major Lanz would not object if it allowed Mr Collins to be brought to trial. Lanz was as keen as Sherwill that the matter be brought to a speedy conclusion – the longer the elderly gentleman spent locked up in a gaol cell, the more strained relations between the two sides were likely to become.

At a private session of the Royal Court the following morning, Sherwill persuaded his colleagues to pass the new legislation. They all knew Mr Collins and were more than happy to do what they could to help him. Less than four hours later, the first trial of the Occupation was underway. To begin with, the disgruntled shop assistant claimed that Mr Collins had forbidden him to speak to the German customers at all, but under cross-examination he grew less confident, admitting that perhaps he had misunderstood him. An English-German dictionary that Mr Collins had purchased for the shop was brought into evidence as proof of his willingness to serve the German customers.

Before long, the magistrate threw out the case and Mr Collins was free to go. Sherwill was hugely relieved, but oddly the Germans didn't seem all that disappointed either. When Sherwill passed on the news to Mittelmüller, the adjutant replied nonchalantly, 'I expected as much.' The only person who was obviously unsatisfied with the outcome was the shop assistant, who was now out of a job.

Sherwill couldn't help feeling pleased with himself. For the second time in a week, he had rescued his people from rough justice at the hands of the Germans. But one lingering question hung over the whole affair: had the attorney general been a little too quick to pass legislation requiring the islanders to both put up and shut up with their new masters? Now that damaging relations with the occupiers had been formally recognised as a crime, it was unlikely that the next person charged with the offence would get off as lightly as Mr Collins.

Well-intentioned but politically inexperienced, Sherwill took it for granted that his amiable German counterparts were as honourable and straight-backed as he was. At 11 a.m. on 1 August, the morning after Mr Collins was acquitted, he arrived for his daily meeting with Dr Maass to learn that arrangements had been made for him to produce a short recording to reassure the island's evacuees that all was well at home.

It's hard to imagine that Jersey's shrewd bailiff, Alexander Coutanche, would ever have agreed to such an obvious propaganda set-up, but Sherwill, blinded by his own sense of fair play, saw no reason to refuse. After all, compared to the reign of terror that he and his compatriots had been expecting, the new regime *had* proved remarkably civil. The thousands of men, women and children now living in England – members of his own family among them – would surely be relieved to hear that their fears were unfounded. Having secured a promise from Dr Maass that his statement wouldn't be edited, Sherwill set off to pen his hundred-word message.

He began by acknowledging that some listeners might question his credibility. 'Some will fear, I imagine, that I am making this record with a revolver pointed at my head and speaking from a transcript thrust into my hand by a German officer,' he wrote. 'The actual case is very different.' To prove that he had written the message himself, he included a number of personal details, sending love not only to his own children but to a family friend, Diana Raffles, who was serving with his daughter Mary in the WAAF.

Satisfied that he had established that the message was authentic, and not made under duress, Sherwill set about describing the Occupation in what can only be described as glowing terms. The

States were still functioning, he declared, and banks, shops and churches were open as well. Unemployment figures were much lower than might be expected given the circumstances, and public-relief schemes were taking care of those in desperate need.

But most significant was Sherwill's next assertion. 'The conduct of the German troops is exemplary,' he declared. 'We have been in German occupation for four and a half weeks and I am proud of the way my fellow islanders have behaved, and grateful for the correct and kindly attitude towards them of the German soldiers.' The message ended with an entreaty to the BBC and the British papers to circulate this news as widely as possible on the mainland.

In seeking to reassure those islanders now living as refugees on the other side of the Channel, Sherwill was acting out of genuine kindness. But the recording was spectacularly naïve. As he spoke, the Battle of Britain was raging over the skies of England, in a last-ditch attempt to prevent Hitler from launching his planned invasion. The last thing those brave men of the RAF needed to hear was that occupation by the Nazis wouldn't be so bad after all.

Predictably, Churchill was furious. To the war cabinet in London – who had little idea of the challenges Sherwill faced on a day-to-day basis – the only possible conclusion was that Guernsey was being led by a quisling. They did their best to suppress the offensive recording, ensuring that the BBC never transmitted it. It did, however, go out on Radio Bremen, home to the infamous propaganda broadcasts of 'Lord Haw-Haw' – which if anything only added to the impression that it was the work of a shameless collaborator.

Sherwill was utterly oblivious to the damage he had done. The following week, in a speech to the first session of the States of Guernsey since the arrival of the Germans, he reiterated his rose-tinted view of the Occupation. Under the penetrating gaze of Major Lanz, who had taken the chair beneath the royal coat of arms which was normally reserved for the island's lieutenant-governor, he told his colleagues, 'My relations with the commandant and his staff are of the best, and throughout I have been treated with the greatest courtesy.'

The attorney general went on to set out what he expected from the people of Guernsey, as well as their new masters. 'May this occupation be a model to the world,' he declared. 'On the one hand tolerance on the part of the military authority and courtesy and correctness on the part of the occupying forces, and on the other dignity and courtesy and exemplary behaviour on the part of the civilian population.' Sherwill fervently believed that such a 'model occupation' was possible. 'When it is over,' he continued, 'I hope that occupying force and occupied population may each be able to say: "Of different nations, having differing outlooks, we lived together with tolerance and mutual respect."'

It was a stirring, idealistic vision, but Sherwill ended his speech on a more modest note. 'I have frequently during the past six weeks been perplexed and baffled by the problems which have arisen,' he admitted. 'Many a time since the twenty-first of June have I wished that I might have been doing the type of work to which I was accustomed, and where I more or less knew my way about.'

Honest to a fault, the leader of the Guernsey people concluded with a startling confession, made in the presence not only of the assembled States officials but also the German commandant himself: 'I certainly never realised', he admitted, 'how little I knew about anything.'

They were words that would come back to haunt him.

CHAPTER NINE

FRENEMIES

It was the perfect day for a white wedding. The summer sun beat down on the parish of St Sampson, shining through the high vaulted windows of the Capelles Church and dazzling the congregation inside. Nellie Prince and Oswald Falla were only the second Guernsey couple to get married under Occupation, but they were determined to make the most of their big day, Germans or no Germans. They had a traditional cake, a stunning bouquet of carnations, and a handmade wedding dress of the finest silk Creasey's had to offer.

The happy couple and their guests made their way out of the church for the short walk to the reception. Before they got there, however, the gentle sounds of birdsong and the hum of insects were drowned out by an insistent mechanical whine. Looking up, they saw the source of the ugly noise: dozens of planes passing overhead. On the underside of the wings they could make out the distinctive black crosses of the Luftwaffe.

The guests hurried down the road away from the church, shouting over the noise of the planes and trying not to think too hard about where they were going. After all, this was supposed to be a joyous occasion. No one wanted to dwell on what those planes intended to do on the other side of the Channel.

It was two days since the Germans had launched Operation Adlerangriff ('Eagle Attack'), an all-out assault on British airfields that signalled the start of the most intense phase of the Battle of

Britain. The goal was to bring the RAF to its knees, eliminating the most powerful line of defence that stood in the way of Operation Sea Lion, the seaborne invasion of the South Coast of England. If German air power prevailed, it wouldn't be long before the Channel Islands weren't the only British isles in German hands.

The day of Nellie and Oswald's wedding, 15 August 1940, soon became known as Black Thursday – a day when the Luftwaffe flew a record-breaking two thousand sorties over England. Although most of the bombers took off from German-occupied territories on the Continent, the Channel Islands played a part in the ongoing operations too. Guernsey provided the Messerschmitt fighters that engaged the British Spitfires and Hurricanes in the aerial dogfighting which came to define the campaign, while the state-of-the-art airport in Jersey played host to a long-range reconnaisance unit, Fernaufklärungsgruppe 123.

Three days later, on Sunday afternoon, Ambrose Sherwill looked up, appalled, as scores of planes gathered in the skies above him. 'The entire sky – or so it seemed to me – was black with German bombers,' he wrote, 'and, as I watched them, the fighters to escort them took off from our airport. I counted no less than sixty of these as they soared into the air above my head.'

The people of Guernsey could only stand by and watch as the polite young men they had grown used to seeing on the streets of St Peter Port or sunbathing on the island's beaches set off across the Channel, wave after wave of aircraft flying over on their way to wreak havoc on the mainland. For those with friends or relatives living in England – among them the tens of thousands of Channel Islands evacuees – it was a deeply uncomfortable experience.

The daily carnage of the Battle of Britain was a timely reminder that, good manners notwithstanding, the Germans were still the enemy. Three weeks later, with the start of the London blitz, that fact became even more inescapable. The BBC broadcasts tried to put a positive spin on the bombing campaign, focusing, at the prime minister's insistence, on the reconstruction efforts and stories of Londoners pulling together. But the bare facts spoke for themselves.

Night by night, German bombers were raining down hell on innocent civilians – men, women and children no different from those they lived side by side with in the Channel Islands.

With the Battle of Britain raging in the skies over England by day, and the German bombers dropping devastation by night, the authorities in the Channel Islands were waging a campaign of their own: a battle for the hearts and minds of the islanders. They were determined to prove that they were decent, reasonable men – and that while their people might be fighting on opposite sides in the war, *they* didn't see the Channel Islanders as their enemies. But they were also respectful of those who understandably felt otherwise. When Jerseyman Joe Miere explained that he couldn't shake an officer's hand because his brothers were serving in the Royal Air Force, the German accepted his reasoning without question.

Many soldiers seemed determined to prove themselves good neighbours. Guernsey farmer Harold Burton was busy delivering a calf when a young German soldier called Franz Werner arrived on the doorstep, clutching a German-English dictionary and begging to speak with the homeowner. 'He's in the yard,' Harold's wife replied, gesturing in the appropriate direction. When the young man arrived on the scene, he immediately took off his Wehrmacht tunic, rolled up his sleeves and began to lend a hand. In broken English he explained that he himself was a smallholder in Germany and had plenty of experience birthing cattle. Mr Burton was a little surprised at this new, unexpected assistant, but he wasn't about to turn down some help, and from then on Franz became a regular visitor to the farm. A few miles away, the Trubuil family became friendly with a soldier called William Kettner, who was a talented watercolourist and spent most of his free time painting the stunning island landscape. He gave them several of his pictures to hang in their house, and when he saw that their living room walls were looking a bit tired and faded he turned up with a bucket of paint and a sponge and redecorated the whole room for them.

Soldiers who were missing their own children would often shower gifts on other people's. At the Baker farm on Sark, a German man assigned to keep an eye on the milking of the cows greeted the arrival of a new baby in the family with delight, presenting the little boy with a beautiful hand-carved gift. It was a tiny wooden dachshund, carefully crafted in three segments, with strips of leather between them so that it would wiggle along when he pulled on its string. The family called the toy dog Fritz, although they didn't tell the German. In Guernsey, Esme Ingrouille mentioned to a soldier billeted in the house next door that her eleventh birthday was coming up. Soon after, he went on leave to Germany, and when he returned he brought with him a magnificent chocolate cake that his wife had baked especially for Esme, complete with little edible mice.

Even when they encountered outright hostility from the islanders, some soldiers would respond with humour rather than aggression. One afternoon, Jersey housewife Emma Ginns was walking her dog with a rather formidable elderly lady called Mrs Joy when they saw a couple of German soldiers erecting a barbed-wire fence around the local golf course. Mrs Joy marched straight up to the soldiers and demanded angrily, 'What do you men think you're doing?' One of the Germans turned to her and smiled. 'Madame,' he said smoothly, 'we are building a second Siegfried Line, on which you will no doubt wish to hang your washing.' The joke left Mrs Joy momentarily speechless, and Emma did her best to stifle a laugh.

Of course, not all interactions between soldiers and civilians were quite so amiable. The German authorities were keen for the Army of Occupation to behave in the 'model' fashion Ambrose Sherwill had proposed, and in the two months since they had first arrived, the polite, smartly dressed young men had done much to dispel the caricatured image of them depicted in Allied propaganda. But now and then, individual German soldiers would fall far short of this ideal, much to the irritation of their superiors. To an extent, abuses of power were almost inevitable in a situation where soldiers and civilians – especially women – were living on top of each other, but such unpleasant incidents represented yet another obstacle to the German authorities winning the trust of the local people.

Working as a maid for the top brass of the Feldkommandantur, Ruth Leadbeater typically saw the Germans at their best: polite, friendly and sympathetic. One of the officers billeted at Camblez, a man by the name of Peltzer, even suggested she start inviting her fiancé Cliff to come and visit her at the grand house. The two men shared a love of music – Cliff was a keen accordionist, while Peltzer loved nothing better than spending his evenings tinkling away on the beautiful grand piano in the drawing room, and was more than happy to oblige him with an impromptu performance of some of his favourite German tunes.

But working in such proximity to the Army of Occupation, it was only a matter of time before Ruth began to see glimpses of a darker side. The men she encountered at work were nearly always of the officer class, but one day she was sent to clean the bathroom in a little bungalow down the drive, where some of the rank and file were billeted. She was just rinsing out the basin when she heard footsteps entering the room behind her, and before she could turn around a pair of strong arms had locked themselves around her waist.

Ruth squirmed round on the spot, finding herself in the embrace of a tall German soldier. Lost for words, she pushed hard on his chest, trying to break his hold on her.

The man obviously wasn't interested in a fight. Ruth felt his arms loosen as he stepped back and hurriedly disappeared out of the bathroom.

It wasn't her only frightening encounter with a German soldier. When the officers at Camblez hosted their friends for dinner, Ruth would be expected to stay on late and wash up afterwards, although she would always leave the house in time to make it back to the fish-and-chip shop just before curfew. One evening, she was walking along La Vrangue, a road that led down into the Bouet, when she became aware of the sound of footsteps behind her. The tread was heavy and irregular but they were moving fast – in a few moments, whoever it was would catch up with her.

Ruth looked around, but in the gloaming she couldn't make out another figure as far as she could see. She began to walk a little faster, listening for the sound of the heavy jackboots. After a few steps, she felt certain they had increased their pace too.

Ruth quickened into a run, her feet pounding the pavement as she shot down the hill. Her heart was racing now, and in between frantic gasps for air she could hear the jackbooted figure behind her had started running as well. The heavy thud of each foot hitting the pavement sent a chill through her as she forced herself onwards, rounding the corner and racing as fast as she could in the direction of the chip shop. She only hoped that the side door to the building, which led to the living quarters, was open and she wouldn't have to fumble for her key.

Ruth raced up to the door and was relieved when the handle turned in her grasp. But before she could lock it behind her, her pursuer was already in the house too. For the first time, she got a good look at the soldier who had chased her all the way home. He was a tall, heavy-set man, and his tight grey uniform was stained with sweat from his exertions. In the dim light, Ruth thought his eyes looked a little bloodshot, and as he staggered unsteadily towards her she could smell alcohol on his breath.

Ruth froze to the spot in terror, but before the German could reach out a hand towards her, she heard a noise from inside the house. They both turned to see the dining room door swing open as Ernie Downes – the brother of her sister's boyfriend Jack – stepped into the hallway.

Ernie didn't speak a word of German, and the soldier didn't appear to know any English, but in a few seconds of wordless communication Ruth's fate was decided between them. Ernie held the other man's stare until the German, looking a little sheepish and embarrassed, finally backed down, stumbling out of the hallway and into the street.

As Ernie came over to put an arm around her, Ruth was still struggling to catch her breath. It had been a narrow escape, and one she hoped never to experience again. The good impression she had previously formed of the German soldiers had been sorely shaken.

Ruth never reported either incident to the authorities, but in fact the German forces took allegations of sexual misconduct very seriously. One Sunday evening in the autumn of 1940, Guernsey doctor Richard Sutcliffe was called out to the home of two elderly sisters who had suffered a terrifying ordeal. A drunk German soldier had forced his way into their house, robbed them both at gunpoint and then raped one of them. By the time Dr Sutcliffe arrived, Ambrose Sherwill was already on the scene, along with Dr Maass and Major Lanz's adjutant, Lieutenant Mittelmüller. The soldier had left his pistol behind so there was no question that the robbery had taken place, but Dr Maass was more sceptical about the rape allegation, remarking that he found it improbable given that the supposed victim was in her seventies.

Dr Sutcliffe examined the patient and informed Maass that he had no doubt she was telling the truth about the rape. Duly corrected, he appeared to take the news in his stride, but Lieutenant Mittelmüller was furious. In fact, Dr Sutcliffe had never seen a man in the grip of such barely contained rage.

The two German officers promptly left to track down the guilty party, which, thanks to the pistol, took only a couple of hours. At 9 a.m. the following day, a court martial was convened in a small requisitioned cottage on the edge of the airport. Dr Sutcliffe was summoned to give evidence and, once again, Sherwill was present as well.

The whole matter was handled with great delicacy. Rather than have to face her attacker directly, the victim was allowed to give her testimony to a female clerk in a separate room. Clearly it was a matter of honour for the Germans that the trial be compassionate as well as just.

It didn't take long for the young man to be found guilty. 'He will be shot,' one of the Germans told Sherwill. 'Would you like to witness the execution?'

The attorney general declined the invitation, as did the rather stunned Dr Sutcliffe.

In one sense, the Channel Islanders and their occupiers weren't entirely on opposite sides. Those, like the farmer Harold Burton, who had allowed themselves to become friendly with some of them invariably made a distinction between 'Germans' and 'Nazis'. Although there were a number of card-carrying National Socialists among the troops, the bulk of the men were ordinary soldiers, many of them conscripts, with little interest in Hitler's ideology.

Occasionally, individual members of the Army of Occupation could be quite outspoken on the subject of the Führer, especially when talking to local people who were unlikely to report them for their views. After his parents' back yard was requisitioned as a bicycle park, Jersey schoolboy Harry Aubin overheard a surprising conversation between his father and one of the Germans. When Mr Aubin remarked that Hitler had at least succeeded in resolving his country's unemployment crisis, the other man replied bitterly, 'Hitler will be the undertaker of Germany.'

Those at the head of the administration, meanwhile, had even less time for the cult of the Führer. The upper ranks were typically staffed by old-school aristocrats who sneered at Hitler's humble origins. Baron von Aufsess of the Jersey Feldkommandantur – the owner of a splendid ninth-century castle in Bavaria – wrote scathingly in his journal about the 'little upstart, World War One corporal and house-painter'. 'I am inclined to think that Hitler will not be of much attraction to the biographer,' he declared. 'He has no complexity of character or breadth of appeal; on the contrary, he is crude, unintellectual, and bigoted in disposition, forged by a single-minded drive for power into a narrow, stereotyped figure.' Needless to say, however, von Aufsess took care to keep his journal hidden from his colleagues.

Of course, however much they might have in common, many islanders were still determined to give the Germans the cold shoulder. Some simply did their best to avoid running into them, and for those living in remote, rural parishes, it was possible to go for weeks – or even months – without spotting a member of the Army of Occupation. But others, who were unable to avoid them altogether, found their encounters tinged with uncertainty as they wrestled with a thousand small daily dilemmas. What level of interaction was acceptable? How should they respond when a soldier acknowledged them in the street, or stopped to ask directions?

Bob Le Sueur's mother Lizzie arrived home one afternoon in a terrible state of agitation. She had been carrying a lot of heavy shopping and when she got on the bus a young German soldier had offered her his seat. The poor woman had been thrown into a paroxysm of indecision. If she accepted it, would it seem unpatriotic? Might she even be accused of fraternisation? On the other hand, the soldier didn't seem to speak any English and might not understand her reason for refusing. His own mother had clearly brought him up well, and as a mother herself, Lizzie felt it was almost her duty to reward his polite behaviour. Eventually she had decided to sit down, murmuring a barely audible 'Thank you.' But she had spent the rest of the bus journey turning the incident over in her head, convinced she could feel the eyes of the other passengers boring into her.

Predictably, those least willing to forget that the Germans were their enemies were the men who had served in the trenches of the First World War. But even so the hardest of hearts was capable of melting a little in the face of respectful young soldiers. At the Smith family's hotel on Cobo beachfront, a young Wehrmacht lieutenant, Ulrich Dryer, was celebrating his twenty-first birthday. 'Oolie', as he was known to his friends, was a popular lad who had walked with a limp ever since he broke his leg in a motorcycling accident. When Mrs Smith learned that it was his birthday, she was struck by a sudden rush of generosity. 'I made a carrot cake today,' she told her husband. 'How about if I take it in for Oolie to eat with his friends?'

'Absolutely not!' exclaimed Mr Smith, who had fought on the Western Front. As far as he was concerned, it was bad enough having Germans in his hotel, without his wife baking for them.

But Mrs Smith was determined. 'Just imagine if we had a son, and he was celebrating his twenty-first birthday miles away from home,' she protested.

'We haven't got a son,' said Mr Smith. 'Only two daughters who need every crumb we can give them.' But he could see the strength of feeling in his wife's eyes, and he had no wish to fight with her. 'All right then,' he agreed with resignation.

Mrs Smith pulled her best plate out of the cupboard, and even managed to find an old half-burned candle in one of the kitchen drawers. Lighting it, she carried the cake into the lounge, where the group of noisy young men suddenly fell silent.

Oolie looked up at her with tears in his eyes, deeply touched by the friendly gesture. 'You will never know how much I appreciate this,' he said, awkwardly shaking Mrs Smith's hand. 'For as long as I live, I will not forget your kindness.'

His words turned out to be prophetic. The next day the island was buffeted by a heavy summer storm, with giant waves crashing over the Cobo sea wall. Oolie was out driving with a friend when they skidded on the slippery road. He never recovered from his injuries.

When the news of Oolie's death reached the hotel, even Mr Smith was glad that he had given in to his wife's request to show a little kindness to the enemy.

In Jersey, another hardened First World War veteran, John Harris, was forced to confront his own prejudice where the Germans were concerned. One day he was visiting a farmer friend, Ken Richardson, who lived in North Lynn, when a sergeant pulled up on his bicycle to collect the quota of oats that had been earmarked for the Wehrmacht's horses.

'*Guten Morgen!*' the German called cheerfully, offering Ken a warm handshake. They had got to know each other a little thanks to his repeated visits to the farm. 'Tell me, who is your friend?'

Ken made the introductions, and the German turned to Mr Harris, extending his hand with a smile. But Mr Harris kept his own arm pinned to his side.

'You don't like me?' the sergeant remarked. 'You were in the first war?'

Mr Harris nodded.

'You would like to shoot me then, if you had the chance?' the German challenged him.

'Yes,' Mr Harris replied. 'I would.'

'Ha!' the German laughed. 'You would no more shoot me than I would shoot you.' He drew the pistol from his holster and cocked it, offering the weapon to Mr Harris. 'So,' he declared, opening his arms wide in a gesture of surrender, 'shoot!'

Mr Harris hesitated for a moment. Then, with a sigh, he handed the gun back to its owner.

'You see,' the German told him. 'You do not want to shoot me, and I do not want to shoot you.' He returned the gun to his holster and once again offered his hand to Mr Harris. 'I don't want to be here,' he told him. 'I'm a farmer, like your friend. I would much rather be back on my own land than here in Jersey.'

This time, Mr Harris accepted the handshake, and when the sergeant remarked, 'So, we are friends now?' he didn't say anything to contradict him.

Mr Harris's sons Leo and Francis also took a hard line as far as the 'enemy' were concerned. One day, the two boys were walking along the beach at Havre des Pas when a German nurse came over to them and offered Francis a box of dates. He shoved it back at her angrily and walked on, telling her, 'We don't take things from Germans!'

The young woman looked crestfallen. She probably had brothers back in Germany the same age as the Harris boys and was only trying to show them a little kindness. In any case, she had good cause to be shocked by Francis' reaction, since typically children – and particularly young boys – were on friendlier terms with the Germans than their parents were. It didn't hurt that the troops tended to shower them with treats – one high-ranking officer kept a pocket full of sweets at all times to hand out to any passing children, and chocolate, ice cream and other luxuries could all be had for the asking if you found the right soldier in a generous mood.

But more than that, a number of boys had begun to idolise the smart young men in their stylish grey uniforms. Their leather boots, their guns, even their goose-stepping, inspired not so much terror as awe for lads who had in many cases never seen any British soldiers, and knew about war almost exclusively from the cinema. Several of them sought out grey jackets that resembled the uniforms of the Wehrmacht, and begged their mothers to stitch on military-looking shoulder tabs and insignia.

Many islanders were concerned at such behaviour, fearing that in their excitement at the glamour of the German Army the children might forget whose side they were supposed to be on. On Sark, Julia Tremaine wrote in her diary, 'It is sad that the schoolboys are all practising and playing at soldiers, doing the German drills, the goose-step and marching four abreast, bowing from the waist, heel clicking and glorifying it.' The danger, as she saw it, was that through simple imitation a home-grown Hitler Youth was springing up on the island. 'Our island boys are drilling and copying them at every opportunity,' she wrote. 'Big black-eyed Tom Baker is sergeant master and he gives the orders and commands in a regular German hard voice, just like Hitler addressing his youth campaign.'

Much as these stories alarmed the islanders, to the Germans they were a real propaganda coup, and those in charge were not always above bending the truth in order to tell a good story. One day during that long glorious summer of 1940, Jersey's schoolchildren were summoned to a rally in downtown St Helier. There were bands playing, and a stage had been erected outside the town hall, from which a German officer, speaking perfect English, addressed the crowds of excited children. After a few brief remarks about the German Army liberating Europe from the scourge of Bolshevism, he declared, 'Hands up all the children who would like to have a bar of German milk chocolate!'

Hundreds of hands shot up in the air – just in time for the German cameramen who were filming the entire thing. By the time the footage was edited for the official newsreels, the meaning of the moment was clear: the German Army had so comprehensively won over their enemy's children that the little boys and girls were enthusiastically hailing the Führer.

CHAPTER TEN

THE SHOW MUST GO ON

A model to the world it may have been, but despite the best efforts of all concerned, the Occupation couldn't help bringing a deterioration in the quality of life of most Channel Islanders. As the novelty of the new regime – and its new rules and regulations – wore off, perhaps the most keenly felt symptom of the general Occupation malaise was a surprisingly mundane one: boredom. Previously, with good transport links to both France and mainland Britain, the local people had never really felt cut off from the outside world, but now they began to truly understand the limitations of living on a small island. Even the regular boat services between Jersey and Guernsey were suspended for all but the most essential travel, which required a permit from German Army HQ. A quiet night at the pub wasn't what it used to be either, thanks to the combination of a strict curfew every evening – the exact hours varied, but it sometimes started as early as 9 p.m. – and rumours of plain-clothes Gestapo operatives mingling among the local population, hoping to overhear stray snatches of incriminating gossip.

The creeping ennui that characterised daily life under Occupation soon acquired a name: 'mental blackout'. For most people, the best chance of escape was a trip to the movies. The reels of film held by the islands' cinemas had been seized by the German Army soon after they arrived, and taken away for careful inspection. In Guernsey, the job of censoring entertainment fell under the authority of Dr

Brosch, the gruff officer who had sent his boots back down for Ruth Leadbeater to polish a second time. Those films deemed politically inoffensive eventually found their way back into circulation. By mid-August, Guernsey civil servant Ken Lewis was able to record in his diary a trip to see the Hollywood musical *Sing, Baby, Sing*, which was paired with a Disney cartoon featuring Donald Duck as a hapless plumber, as well as a short German newsreel.

Predictably, the final part of the bill was the most problematic, and trips to the cinema soon became an opportunity for mild acts of rebellion. In the dark of the auditorium, it was very tempting to boo the German soldiers marching across the screen, and soon the newsreels had to be screened with the house lights up so trouble-makers could be identified and ejected. Bill Finigan was so amused by the outlandish claims of military prowess in one German reel that he spontaneously burst out laughing. A soldier standing guard by the door hauled him out of his seat and issued an on-the-spot fine of ten Reichsmarks.

As time went on, the limited supply of English-language films was eclipsed by an influx of German movies. Starved of entertainment, bored islanders continued to visit the cinemas, although not in the same numbers as before. A rope was placed down the middle of the auditorium to separate the Germans from the locals. Typically, the German half was full – it didn't hurt that their tickets were provided free of charge – with only a handful of islanders dotted around on the other side of the barrier.

For those who did make the trip, there was no escaping the onslaught of propaganda, and it started even before the newsreels began playing. In the foyer of the Gaumont in St Peter Port a portrait of Adolf Hitler loomed over the cinema-goers, local and German alike. And then there were the films themselves – propaganda pieces such as *The Rothschilds*, with its chilling final shot of a Star of David burning over a map of Europe, and *Bismarck*, in which the heroic Prussian nationalist succeeds in unifying Germany despite an assas-sination attempt from a sinister English Jew.

Some islanders chose to boycott the cinemas altogether, even when what was showing was relatively harmless. In Jersey, Leo and Francis Harris attended a screening of *Münchhausen*, an escapist fantasy shot in glorious Agfacolor that was intended as Germany's answer to *The Wizard of Oz*. Their parents allowed them to go, but made it clear they felt it was unpatriotic.

In Guernsey, there was at least one way of watching movies without submitting to insidious German propaganda. Herbert Pritchard, a garage mechanic known as 'Ginger' for his shock of bright red hair, was one of the men who had been sent over to Alderney to salvage the island's livestock and perishable goods. While he was there he made the most of the opportunity to ransack the little cinema, returning home with a projector and as many reels of film as he could carry. Before long, Ginger had set himself up as a travelling projectionist, bringing his stock of cartoons to primary-school classes, and his Ealing comedies to adult gatherings, all over the island.

One evening, Ginger had been booked for a private party at Grandes Rocques, on the west coast. It was an all-night affair, a popular way of avoiding the curfew restrictions by letting guests kip on the floor. For the most part, such quasi-legal gatherings escaped the notice of the German authorities, but unfortunately the uproarious laughter of several dozen islanders watching George Formby's caper *Keep Your Seats, Please* was enough to attract the attention of a passing patrol. Midway through Formby's performance of 'When I'm Cleaning Windows', the door to the house burst open and in charged the Germans. The cheery banjo strumming came to an abrupt end, the film equipment was confiscated, and Ginger was hauled away to prison.

After five days in the cells, Ginger was released without charge, but when he asked the military police to return his equipment they refused. Enraged, he stormed off to German Army HQ, refusing to leave until he was granted an interview with the commandant. He had promised to bring his stash of cartoons to a children's party the following week, he explained, and he couldn't bear to let them down. A little bemused, the commandant relented and – after satisfying himself that Ginger's film collection was politically harmless – granted him a permit to carry on screening them without fear of interference.

While cinema attendance dropped during the Occupation, live performance saw an explosion in popularity, with record numbers of people volunteering to take part. At one point around five hundred men and women in Guernsey (more than two per cent of the total population) were involved in the burgeoning entertainment industry. For amateur performers, taking part in a collective creative activity was an antidote to the depressing passivity of life under German rule. They might not be in a position to do anything meaningful for the war effort, but they could at least bring a bit of joy to their fellow islanders.

The shows were typically escapist, light-hearted fare – troupes of chorus-line dancers in sparkling costumes such as Dorothy Langlois' Co-optimists and Joyce Ferguson's Regalettes, who set out from their base in St Peter Port to perform in church halls all over the island. Amateur-dramatics companies were also forced to raise their game, with Guernsey's Regal Players offering a broad repertoire including spy thriller *The Ghost Train*, spooky melodrama *A Murder Has Been Arranged* and comedies such as *Charley's Aunt* and the recent West End smash *The Wind and the Rain*. At St Peter Port's Little Theatre, the attorney general's wife May Sherwill was even found treading the boards, starring as the imposing matriarch Lady Madehurst in the frothy society comedy *Family Affairs*.

The Candie Gardens auditorium, set in a large Victorian flower garden with spectacular views of the sea, offered a varied repertoire of concerts, ranging from operatic arias with full orchestral accompaniment to popular songs such as 'Tea for Two' and Charles Trenet's 'Boum!'. Even the Germans got in on the action, providing their own 'Militär-Konzert', featuring a mixture of Strauss classics and German romantic music, including the overture to Hitler's favourite operetta, *The Merry Widow*. Since arriving on the islands, many soldiers had taken the opportunity to indulge in their favourite artistic exploits, whether joining the regimental band, penning romantic poetry, or attempting to capture the stunning landscape on canvas. In fact, so many of them turned their hand to painting that before long an exhibition was mounted in St Peter Port, with well-heeled locals encouraged to splash out on Wehrmacht originals. 'Art, as we have been told before, has no frontiers,' Mrs Le Bideau commented wryly in her diary.

The jewels in the crown of Guernsey's wartime entertainment were the new variety companies, and among them none was more beloved than the Lyric No. 1 Company, established by Eric Snelling, a dapper young man with slicked-back hair and a pencil moustache who managed the Regal and Lyric cinemas. Snelling was quick to turn the dearth of wartime movie reels into an opportunity, applying to the German authorities for permission to use his picture-houses for theatrical performances. Soon the Lyric was providing the island with a weekly repertory programme, each company performing every fourth week, and spending the following three preparing their next show.

The No. 1 Company attracted the most talented performers. Snelling, along with his business partner Peter Campbell, a middle-aged man with large round glasses who also took on the role of master of ceremonies, had drawn on a number of established acts: an elderly gent called Wilf Shirvell who brought his music-hall roots with him, the rubber-faced comic Cyd Gardner, and talented young dancers Jessie Mariette and Douglas Luckie. But the two men also saw themselves as talent scouts, scouring the island in search of new faces to add to the line-up.

At a charity concert in the parish of St Sampson, Campbell spotted two sisters, Daphne and Frieda Brache. They weren't officially performing that evening – their father Frederick was playing the piano and they had come along to sell programmes – but during the group singalong after the end of the concert proper, their performance of 'Pack Up Your Troubles' was enough to catch his attention. The next morning, he was knocking at their door in Vale parish, asking Mr Brache if he would be willing for his daughters to audition for the company. In the end, Campbell ended up taking on all three of them – the two girls to sing and perform comedy sketches, and their father to write their material and accompany them on the piano.

Sister acts were particularly desirable at the time, thanks in part to the success of the Andrews Sisters, a trio of American siblings whose close-harmony renditions had seen them catapulted to worldwide fame. So when Gwen Smith, from Les Pieux Hotel on Cobo beachfront, was invited to join the Lyric company, it didn't take Snelling and Campbell long to realise that she had a younger sister, and Pearl was summoned to an audition.

Together, Pearl, Gwen and their mother cycled into town from Cobo, a journey of just under five kilometres, which, on their old rickety bikes, took them about half an hour. When they arrived at the cinema, Gwen led Pearl up to the stage, where a single microphone stood waiting for her. Then, after a whispered 'Good luck!' she descended into the orchestra pit to provide the accompaniment.

Gwen was a talented pianist, and could play almost anything by ear, but Pearl had the better voice. It certainly made an impression on Eric Snelling. As she launched into her audition piece, 'That Lovely Weekend' – a rather grown-up song for a girl just coming into her teens – Pearl spotted the manager lean over and whisper something in her mother's ear. Mrs Smith nodded appreciatively, and gave Pearl an encouraging smile.

No sooner had Pearl reached the end of the song than Mr Snelling was on his feet, applauding. 'That was *marvellous*!' he declared. 'I'd be delighted to have you in the company.' And with that, a second sister act was added to the Lyric line-up.

On the bumpy ride back to Cobo, Pearl asked her mother what the manager had whispered during her audition. Mrs Smith looked over at her with a mixture of pride and embarrassment. 'He said you were a second Vera Lynn!' she replied.

Pearl almost fell off her bike. As far as she was concerned, there was no greater praise.

The Lyric company's performances were always based on a particular theme, which the individual variety acts would reference in their costuming and song choices. Pearl's first show was one of the stalwarts, *Café Continental*. The stage was set as a Parisian street café, with all the performers onstage throughout, whether as customers, waiters, the chef, or a newspaper boy holding up the front page of *Paris Soir* bearing the optimistic headline, 'Des Jours Heureux Seront Bientôt De Retour' ('Happy Days Will Soon Return'). The French flavour of the show was enhanced by performances of Maurice Chevalier's 'Sous les toits de Paris' and the ever-popular 'Boum!'

Pearl herself was to perform a handful of numbers, including a reprise of her audition piece and a couple of routines with her sister. Fortunately, she and Gwen were well equipped for rehearsals. In the back yard of their parents' hotel was a row of wooden huts that were used as overflow accommodation during the busy summer seasons. One of them boasted a piano and mirrors along an entire wall – the perfect dance studio for a pair of aspiring performers.

In one routine, Pearl sang with her hands clasped behind her back and Gwen, standing behind her, performed operatic gestures with her own arms. In another, set to the tune of the 1935 hit 'Dancing with my Shadow', they wore complementary monochrome dresses – Pearl in brilliant white, and her sister (the shadow) in black. Finding outfits for the shows was the performer's own responsibility, and Mrs Smith soon found her old lace tablecloths and curtains appropriated for refashioning as frilly French skirts and glamorous ballroom dresses.

With their own routines rehearsed to perfection, Pearl and Gwen were both eager to see what the other acts had come up with. On the day of the dress rehearsal they arrived at the Lyric, where Pearl was finally introduced to the rest of the company: old Wilf Shirvell, the gangly comic Cyd Gardner, the Brache sisters (plus their father Frederick on the piano), dancers Jessie Mariette and Douglas Luckie, who also sang baritone, plus a couple of younger singers, Gertie Duquemin and Rex Priaulx. The latter was an awkward, lanky boy with a pair of heavy specs that did little to disguise his cross-eyes, but he made up for his appearance with a beautiful tenor voice. In addition to the onstage performers, there was a ten-strong variety orchestra in the pit, under the command of conductor Fred Collette.

One by one, the members of the company took to the stage, running through their acts not only for Peter Campbell and Eric Snelling, but for a very important guest. In the front row of the auditorium sat the stern-faced German censor, scrutinising every line spoken or sung for anything offensive to the Reich. Fortunately, Cyd Gardner steered clear of any topical material, falling back on his repertoire of mother-in-law jokes and physical comedy, which often involved a set of false teeth. The Brache sisters sang a couple of songs penned by their father – 'Underneath the Counter' (about the island's growing black-market trade) and 'Rumours!' (on tall tales overheard while queuing for food) – but the gentle humour was far from subversive, and the censor merely nodded to indicate his comprehension before passing them fit for public consumption.

After the stony reception at the dress rehearsal, Pearl was taken aback at the rapturous response the show received on opening night, when a packed audience of local people filled the five hundred-odd seats of the Lyric auditorium. Every act garnered fulsome applause, and the merest hint of a joke had them rolling in the aisles. Worn down by the crippling tedium of Occupation, this audience had come to be entertained, and they were going to make the most of the opportunity.

In fact, it wasn't only the locals who appreciated the shows. Back at the hotel, Pearl noticed the German officers looking at her differently and realised they must have been in the audience too. Suddenly she was no longer just the youngest daughter of the house – she was a star of the stage. The young men began finding opportunities to sidle up to her and compliment her on her singing voice. Pearl learned to accept the tributes politely, before abruptly finding an excuse to leave the room. She knew her father would never forgive her if she gave them any more than the time of day.

Over the next few months, Pearl grew familiar with the Lyric company's revolving repertoire of shows. The next offering, *Anchors Aweigh*, was set on a cruise liner and featured a spirited rendition by the Brache sisters of 'The Sailor with the Navy Blue Eyes', as well as a Hawaiian-style dance by Pearl, Gwen and Jessie Mariette, all of whom sported grass skirts and coconut bras, along with colourful garlands of paper flowers. Then there was *Texas Trail*, set in a Wild West saloon. Sourcing the costumes for this show was more of a headache than usual. Daphne Brache resorted to asking a woman she met milking a herd of goats out on L'Ancresse Common if she could borrow a pair of britches, only realising once she got them home that they absolutely reeked of stale milk. The show featured a new song by her father Frederick on the recently introduced tobacco tax, along with 'Deep in the Heart of Texas' and – appropriately for an island under occupation – 'Don't Fence Me In'.

The more time Pearl spent with the other members of the company, the more she liked them. Soon they were meeting up in between performance weeks, taking turns to host increasingly raucous parties, after which everyone would end up sleeping on a couch or curling up on the floor in order to beat the curfew. There wasn't much alcohol to spare, but the dregs of any nearly empty bottles would be carefully drained and mixed together to produce a truly revolting cocktail that was passed around the room for everyone to swig, and the singing and dancing would go on until the early hours of the morning.

One time, Gwen and Pearl hosted a party in the lounge of Les Pieux. It was late, and the bottle of spirits had already made its way around the company several times, when the girls decided it was time for an impromptu performance. There was a grand piano in the hotel's bay window, and as one of their castmates picked out the accompaniment they began singing the popular anti-German anthem 'We're Going to Hang Out the Washing on the Siegfried Line', goose-stepping up and down the room holding one finger up to their top lips in imitation of the Führer's moustache, while they performed the Hitler salute with their other arm.

The girls had already done a couple of lengths of the room when they realised that the door to the lounge was wide open. Just beyond the threshold stood a trio of young German soldiers, watching the performance intently. Pearl's arm fell limply to her side as the pianist abruptly stopped playing. Everyone looked anxiously to the men in the doorway.

After a few tense moments, though, a smile passed over the face of one of the Germans. 'Please, will you do it again?' he asked. 'We want to see.'

The look on the girls' faces must have registered their alarm. 'No trouble,' the officer reassured them. 'I promise you, no trouble.'

The pianist took up the tune again, a little more quietly this time, and Pearl and Gwen awkwardly resumed their parade up and down the room. But they only made it once through the chorus before bringing the song to an early end, desperate to know how the German would respond.

The soldier was still smiling, and as they finished he burst into applause. 'Will you write out the music and bring it to me tomorrow?' he asked.

Pearl nodded silently, and the Germans turned to go. As the door shut behind them, everyone breathed a sigh of relief.

The next day, as promised, Pearl delivered a handwritten score to the German officer's room, still not entirely sure that it wasn't all an elaborate trap. Perhaps he was simply gathering evidence so he could charge her and her friends with insulting the Reich. But the days passed by with no sign of impending arrest.

One night the following week, Pearl and Gwen were sitting up in bed late one evening when they heard the faint sound of piano music coming from the lounge, accompanied by the noise of goose-stepping jackboots hitting the floor.

There was no mistaking the tune, or what was going on downstairs. It seemed the Smith sisters weren't the only budding performers at the hotel.

Increasingly, Les Pieux became something of a home away from home for other members of the Lyric company. The makeshift dance studio out back was an ideal rehearsal venue, and Jessie Mariette and Douglas Luckie would often come there to practise their routines. They were a talented pair with a sparkling onstage chemistry, but as soon as the music came to an end the romantic air suddenly evaporated and they seemed more like siblings. In any case, Jessie was already spoken for. Her long-time boyfriend was none other than

Hubert Nicolle, the young man who had spent three days undercover gathering intelligence on the German forces.

During rehearsals for a revival of *Café Continental*, Jessie and Douglas had perfected a particularly impressive routine in the hotel's dance studio. They would start off sipping their drinks at separate tables on opposite sides of the stage, then he would cross over and ask her to dance. As the music swelled, they transitioned from staid ballroom fare to something altogether more adventurous, until, in a dramatic finale, he held her aloft by just a wrist and an ankle as he whirled around on the spot.

It was a marvellous routine, and Pearl loved watching them practise it. When the time came for the first performance at the Lyric, she went up to the balcony to see how it looked under the stage lights, safe in the knowledge that her next song was several acts down the bill. The dance went magnificently and the audience were thrilled, but as Douglas swept Jessie up in the air and began twirling her around, Pearl could tell from the look on his face that something wasn't quite right. Under the heat of the lights his hands had grown sweaty, and he was struggling to maintain his grip.

Pearl watched in horror as Douglas stumbled backwards and Jessie flew out of his hands, crashing into the wings. After a few seconds, the safety curtain came down and an announcement sounded over the Tannoy: 'Is there a doctor in the house?'

Pearl raced backstage to find out what had happened. When she arrived, Jessie was still out cold, having hit her head on some scenery when she landed. Douglas was beside himself, pacing anxiously as a doctor tended to her injuries. After a few minutes she came round and was lucid enough to reassure him that she didn't blame him for the accident, before the doctor ordered her home to rest.

Before long, the safety curtain had been raised and the Café Continental was buzzing once again. Everyone knew that no matter what happened, the show still had to go on.

Since joining the Lyric company, Pearl had developed a soft spot for all her fellow performers – even the pompous young tenor Rex

Priaulx, whose know-it-all attitude frequently saw him rub colleagues up the wrong way. But in particular she had grown fond of Douglas and Jessie, and the three of them had become firm friends.

Jessie was a few years older than Pearl, around the same age as her sister Gwen, but she had always treated her as an equal. One day, she took her into her confidence on a very secret matter. 'Hubert's back in Guernsey,' she announced, with a mixture of excitement and anxiety.

Hubert Nicolle was indeed back on the island, along with another local lad now serving in the Hampshire Regiment, James Symes. The two had known each other at Elizabeth College, where they were both on the athletics team. When Nicolle had returned from his previous undercover mission, Symes had come to see him, extracting a promise that if he was ever ordered back to Guernsey the two of them would go together.

The two young officers had landed at Petit Port in the early hours of the morning and scrambled up a little-used cliff path, avoiding the main steps that led up from the beach, and swigging liberally from a bottle of brandy as they went, hoping to keep both the cold and their nerves at bay. By morning, they had made their way to the house of Nicolle's uncle Frank, where they were met by the usual astonishment, followed by the best cooked breakfast that rations allowed.

The plan was for another three-day mission, during which they would once again gather as much intelligence as possible, before being picked up by a motor torpedo boat. It was a dangerous assignment, since – like Mulholland and Martel before them – they ran the risk of being treated as enemy spies rather than soldiers if they were captured. But despite the risks, there was one major consolation – they would get to see their girlfriends again.

Jessie had no telephone at home, so she began spending more time than ever at Les Pieux, so she could use the phone there to stay in contact with Symes' girlfriend Mary. Fearful that their calls might be intercepted by the Germans, the two girls developed a code to tell each other that they were planning a romantic visit. 'Are you wearing silk stockings tonight?' one would ask the other. If the answer was, 'Yes,' that meant she was going to see the boys.

Although Jessie couldn't help worrying about Hubert's safety, she was thrilled to be able to spend time with him again, and she went around with a new spring in her step just knowing that he was so close to her. But on the fourth day after her boyfriend's arrival in Guernsey, she arrived at the hotel looking ashen-faced. 'The boat didn't come,' she told Pearl weakly. 'They went down to the beach and signalled, but it never showed up.'

The following evening, the lads returned to Petit Port and flashed their torch out to sea once again, signalling the letter 'R' in Morse code, as they had been instructed in their briefing. But again, there was no sign of the vessel that was supposed to pick them up from the shore.

After a third attempt, including another fruitless trek down to the beach, they were forced to accept the awful truth: something must have gone wrong, and the Navy weren't coming back for them.

CHAPTER ELEVEN

AMNESTY

It didn't take long for news of the young soldiers' predicament to reach Ambrose Sherwill. When Nicolle's father Emile turned up at his office in Elizabeth College and revealed that his son was under-cover in Guernsey for a second time, the attorney general struggled to disguise his annoyance. Yet again, it seemed, the British government were determined to send young Guernseymen into danger, threaten-ing the delicate rapport he had worked so hard to build with the Germans – and yet again, they had somehow bungled the operation.

Sherwill knew that his successful resolution of the Mulholland and Martel affair had been a close-run thing, and he was reluctant to push his luck by trying something similar again. 'Of course I fully understand that you are compelled to shelter your son,' he told Emile, 'but I must refrain from having any part in it.' If it were discovered that he had been assisting British spies, the consequences – both for him and for his people – could be disastrous. It would be all the excuse the Germans needed to sweep aside the Controlling Committee altogether and impose a much harsher military regime.

In any case, Sherwill was having enough difficulty dealing with troublemakers among his own population. Only a few days before, a group of eight men had taken a fishing boat and set off across the Channel, successfully reaching the coast of Ireland after a long and arduous voyage. The German response was a drastic clampdown on the island's fishermen, who had already been forced to adapt themselves to stringent limitations placed on their hours and territory. From now on, all fishing sorties would have to depart from St Peter Port – the other small harbours dotted around the island were effectively closed for business. Over the ensuing days, boats from all over the island were brought to the White Rock, where the harbour master could keep a close eye on them.

It was a crushing blow to the island's fishermen, and Sherwill certainly felt for them, but he was in no doubt as to where the blame should fall. Far from criticising the Germans for their heavy-handed response, he sent a notice to the *Star* newspaper explaining that the damage done to their livelihoods – and thus to the plates of all who relied on them for their meals – was a 'direct result' of the escape attempt. 'Any persons who manage to get away do so at the expense of those left behind,' he wrote. 'In these circumstances, to get away, or attempt to get away, is a crime against the local population, quite apart from the fact that the German authorities will deal very severely with persons who are caught making the attempt.'

In his dealings with the Germans, Sherwill continued to tread carefully. His relations with them were, in fact, so good that one morning in early September he received a rather extraordinary letter from Dr Brosch at the Feldkommandantur. Since the States of Guernsey had never formally issued a declaration of war against Germany, Brosch wondered, was it possible that the island could in fact be regarded as neutral rather than enemy territory?

As an accomplished lawyer, Sherwill could probably have constructed an argument supporting this interpretation, and there was a strong temptation to do so, since neutral countries were entitled to better supplies. But there was a limit to how far he was willing to go for the sake of good relations, so he wrote back to the Feldkommandantur politely explaining that regardless of any action by the States, a declaration of war by the king of England was indisputably binding on Guernsey.

Less than a week later, on 15 September, the German military suffered their first real defeat of the war. Over a thousand Luftwaffe aircraft flew across the Channel to bomb targets in London, Southampton and Portland, but the RAF were more than ready for them. Tens of thousands of people witnessed the furious dogfights that took place in the skies. At the end of the day, the Germans had lost twice as many planes as the British. It was a decisive defeat for the Luftwaffe, and although the sorties continued for another month or so, it marked the beginning of the end of the Battle of Britain.

Two days later, Hitler's plans for an invasion of England, Operation Sea Lion, were placed on hold indefinitely. Subtly, the status of the Channel Islands had shifted – they were no longer mere staging posts on the way to the real prize. There was no more talk of the war being over in a matter of weeks either. The German soldiers on the islands knew they were settling in for the long haul.

Not all of the old guard would be remaining, however. The commander-in-chief of the islands, Major Albrecht Lanz, arrived at Sherwill's house at eleven o'clock one Sunday morning to bid him farewell. He was smartly dressed, in a new lieutenant colonel's uniform, complete with his shining Knight's Cross medal. Sherwill, who had never much liked Lanz, wasn't particularly sorry to see him go, but he did his best to make friendly conversation through the commandant's interpreter, Dr Maass. 'I have done all in my power to avoid any difficulties between the occupying forces and the civilian population,' he told him. 'But I hope you appreciate that this was not through lack of loyalty to my own country but in order to secure the greatest possible measure of liberty and normality for my people.' Dr Lanz replied politely that he had never doubted Sherwill's loyalty, or that he had acted at all times in the best interests of his own people.

The new *Befehlshaber* (commander) of the Channel Islands was Colonel Rudolf von Schmettow, who arrived, along with two new battalions of troops, and set up his headquarters in Jersey. Von Schmettow was a Silesian aristocrat and a career soldier, with a reputation for being strict but fair. Guernsey, meanwhile, was placed under the command of the more affable Major Fritz Bandelow, a man whose remarkable good temper made an immediate impression on Sherwill. During their first meeting it soon became apparent that the major's new interpreter had dramatically overstated his linguistic skills, but instead of losing his temper at the young man's incompetence, Bandelow was patient and sympathetic. It boded well, thought Sherwill, for the kind of regime they could expect from him.

It wasn't long before Sherwill had reason to rely on the major's good nature. At the end of September, more than three weeks overdue, the Royal Navy finally arrived to pick up Nicolle and Symes. Having missed their initial rendezvous, they had been forced to wait for the next new moon, and sure enough, on the evening of 30 September, Captain John Parker of the Lancashire Fusiliers rowed ashore at Corbière, intending to track down the two lads and bring them home.

Parker's rescue attempt, however, didn't exactly go as planned. Scrambling up the cliff path on his elbows, as he had been instructed to do in London, he soon found his uniform ripped and his arms bleeding from the prickly undergrowth. Cautiously, he rose to his feet and proceeded as quietly as he could, but in the still night every gorse-pod he trampled underfoot seemed to let out an almighty pop.

Finally, after what seemed like an interminable ascent, Parker reached the top of the cliff – whereupon he immediately lost his footing and stumbled head first into a German trench.

A bright light was shone in the captain's face and half a dozen guns were raised in his direction. He heard a German voice remark cheerfully, 'For you, the war is over!'

At least Parker had landed in uniform rather than plain clothes, so he was safe from being shot as a spy, but the Germans were understandably curious about why he had come to Guernsey. He was taken to a prison in Cherbourg for questioning but managed to avoid giving away the real purpose of his mission, insisting – despite his interrogators' scepticism – that he had been sent to observe the airfield. The Germans soon brought a second prisoner to share his cell with him – supposedly a Jerseyman who had been caught with a wireless transmitter, although his stilted English gave Parker cause for doubt. His suspicions were confirmed when he discovered a microphone hidden in the ceiling of the room, and he resolved to tell his new cellmate nothing. Eventually, he was classed as an ordinary prisoner of war and transferred to a camp in Germany.

In Guernsey, meanwhile, the authorities remained unsatisfied. Major Bandelow thought it highly unlikely that Parker was the only British soldier on the island, and telephoned von Schmettow in Jersey to ask permission to begin a house-to-house search. But von Schmettow, reluctant to commit the entire battalion necessary for such an involved undertaking, and concerned about the potential impact it might have on relations with the civilian population, suggested an amnesty instead. Bandelow thought this was an excellent idea, and asked Sherwill to come and see him at home the following Sunday to discuss the details.

When the attorney general arrived at 11 a.m., he was informed by the commandant's adjutant, Lieutenant Schnadt, that Bandelow was still asleep, having spent most of the previous night touring the island's sentry posts. Schnadt, however, was more than willing to bring Sherwill up to speed on the plan. 'If your soldiers give themselves up by the appointed day,' he explained, 'they will be treated as prisoners of war and nobody who has harboured them will be punished.' Then he added, almost as an afterthought, 'If, however, members of the armed forces are discovered later, we will select twenty prominent civilians and shoot them.'

Sherwill was horrified. 'And one of those will be me?' he asked.

'Oh *no*, Mr Sherwill,' the adjutant insisted soothingly.

But Sherwill was far from reassured. 'If you do this,' he told Schnadt, 'the British will never forgive you.'

The adjutant reached into his pocket, drew out his cigarette case and offered it to Sherwill. 'Let us talk of more pleasant things,' he said with a smile.

Sherwill accepted a cigarette and did his best to make polite chit-chat for a few minutes. Then he excused himself and headed straight to his office at Elizabeth College, where the rest of the Controlling Committee was waiting to find out what had happened. He talked them through his conversation with Schnadt, including the threat to execute a score of leading citizens. Then, for some reason, a mischievous impulse came over him. The island's medical officer, Dr Symons, was one of twenty men serving on the Central Douzaine, as the local council for St Peter Port was known. Sherwill fixed his eyes on the doctor's. 'I had obviously to make a gesture,' he remarked breezily, 'so I offered Schnadt the Central Douzaine.'

For several seconds, Dr Symons remained frozen in shock before Sherwill put him out of his misery. 'Not on your life, I didn't!' he laughed.

The following week, Sherwill went again to see Bandelow to finalise the details of the amnesty. This time, the commandant was awake and in good spirits, having just returned from a rabbit shoot on the tiny uninhabited island of Herm, three miles off the coast of Guernsey. Unlike his adjutant, Bandelow made no mention of threats or penalties, merely declaring that he had a feeling there might be some British soldiers hiding out on the island and he would like to clear the matter up as soon as possible.

Sherwill kept his cards close to his chest, acknowledging the possibility that British troops could be lying low in Guernsey without giving away any specifics. The idea of an amnesty suited him since he dearly wished to get back to business as usual, without the constant niggling anxiety that a diplomatic crisis could blow up at any minute.

Rather than simply publishing a proclamation – which, coming from a new and unknown commandant, might not inspire sufficient trust for the soldiers to risk their lives on it – Sherwill suggested that Bandelow write a letter to him personally, laying out the terms of the amnesty. He would then write back to confirm he was happy with them, and the two letters could be printed side by side in the newspaper. In fact, he proposed, in order to strike just the right tone, perhaps it would be best if Bandelow allowed him to write both letters, which the commandant would of course be free to amend as he wished. It was an extraordinary proposal, but Sherwill knew that two men's lives hung in the balance. Emile Nicolle had already told him that he doubted the Germans were trustworthy. If the two lads were to be persuaded to hand themselves in, the correspondence would need to convince them that Bandelow was a man they could trust.

Remarkably, the commandant agreed to the suggestion and Sherwill set to work crafting the two letters – one supposedly penned by Bandelow, which he wrote in intentionally stilted English, and then his own more fluent reply. It was a strange position for the island's civilian leader to be placed in, playing the role of draughtsman to the Germans and deliberately deceiving his own people. Nonetheless, Sherwill's conscience was untroubled. As he saw it, he was working to protect the best interests of the islanders, both those in the British armed forces whom he hoped once again to save from the firing squad, and their families and friends who by helping them had already made themselves accessories to espionage. It can't have escaped his attention that he was dangerously close to the latter category himself – not only had he helped Mulholland and Martel avoid execution, he had also known about Nicolle and Symes for several weeks now and held his tongue.

When the letters were finished, Sherwill had them sent to the Kommandantur for Bandelow's approval. Then they were taken to the *Guernsey Evening Press*, with instructions to publish them immediately.

A few days later, Bandelow went on leave, so it was left to Dr Brosch to provide the final piece of the puzzle, an official notice setting the date and time by which all British forces must surrender: 6 p.m., Monday 21 October 1940.

Nicolle and Symes, meanwhile, had been hiding out in a cricket pavilion at their old school's sports field, whiling away the hours devising a series of increasingly outlandish plans for escape. The wildest involved Symes, who spoke a smattering of German, impersonating Major Bandelow and stealing the commandant's personal motor boat. Now it seemed that such improbable heroics might not be called for after all. After six long weeks in hiding, an opportunity had presented itself to end their ordeal.

The idea of surrender didn't come easily to the young lads, but the advice they received from family and friends was unanimous: they no longer had any other choice. Sherwill offered the same view to Emile

Nicolle, reassuring him that he believed Major Bandelow could be trusted and promising to do everything within his own power to ensure the two men were treated fairly.

There remained one stumbling block, however. Like Mulholland and Martel before them, the lads would need a pair of Army uniforms to convince the Germans that they were soldiers and not spies. Fortunately, Nicolle's uncle Frank, the deputy harbour master, was able to find some in a shed on the White Rock, where he dug out a long-forgotten stash of Army battledress that had been brought over from Alderney after the evacuation.

On Sunday night, the two lads held a farewell party at the Nicolle family home, cracking open some old bottles of champagne to toast those who had helped them during their time undercover. The next day they rose and dressed in their new uniforms. At five-thirty that afternoon, half an hour before the deadline, Ambrose Sherwill was at a meeting of parish constables when a telephone call came through for him, informing him that two British officers had just turned themselves in. His reaction of feigned astonishment was apparently convincing enough to fool everyone present. No one suspected the powerful wave of relief that the attorney general felt washing over him at the thought that the stressful and trying business was finally being brought to a close.

Nicolle and Symes spent the night in a cell at the island police station, but they certainly weren't treated as common criminals. Mr Travers, the landlord of the Prince of Wales pub across the road, brought them a generous hot dinner, and their gaoler slipped them a lemon gin to wash it down. It wasn't quite the final meal of the condemned, but there was no doubt that despite Major Bandelow's assurances, their situation remained precarious. That afternoon, the island's chief policeman, William Sculpher, had brought the two lads up to his office and given them some advice. 'Whatever they ask you, just give your name, rank and number,' he told them. 'Nothing more.'

When the interrogations began at Fort George the following morning, it was clear that the Germans were not going to be satisfied with that. Convinced that the two men had been sent to Guernsey to kickstart a resistance movement, the Geheime Feldpolizei – plain-clothes military police who were so feared on the islands that most people believed they were the Gestapo – grilled them relentlessly, day after day. During one gruelling session, the questioning continued without a break for fourteen hours.

Meanwhile, Major Bandelow's promise that the families and friends of British soldiers who handed themselves in would be left alone didn't appear to be worth the paper it had been printed on. One by one, the lads' parents, friends, even the groundskeeper of the cricket pavilion where they had sought refuge, were arrested and called in for questioning. One evening the cast of the Lyric No. 1 Company arrived at a rehearsal to find that Jessie Mariette would not be joining them as planned – the Germans had learned that she and Nicolle were sweethearts and had summoned her for interrogation as well.

For Sherwill, it was an alarming turn of events. As the days went by, his confidence that the situation would be brought to a satisfactory conclusion was diminishing. But there was work to be done, and distracted as he was by the latest worrying developments, official matters of state demanded his attention. On 23 October, just two days after the lads had turned themselves in, the Royal Court was asked to register a law concerning the Jewish populations in German-occupied territory. The new statute required all Jews to wear a yellow Star of David on their person, and Jewish businesses to be clearly marked as such in English, French and German.

Instinctively, Sherwill recoiled at the idea of such clearly racist legislation, but having made a few enquiries, he satisfied himself – wrongly, as it later turned out – that the handful of Jews who had been resident in Guernsey before the Occupation had all boarded the evacuation boats for England. Thus, as far as the attorney general was concerned, the new law could do no practical harm. Anxious as he was to preserve a good working relationship with the Germans while the Nicolle and Symes affair remained unresolved, it could scarcely have been a worse moment to stage a protest on a matter of principle.

At a private meeting with the bailiff and jurats before the official deliberations began, Sherwill explained his reasoning and strongly encouraged his fellow legislators to allow the German law a free and speedy passage through the court. When it came to it, only one man defied him: the States controller, Sir Abraham Lainé, who not only refused to give his assent to the new law but spoke eloquently about his deep-seated moral objections to it. Listening to his colleague's words, Sherwill felt a prick of conscience – he knew that Sir Abraham was right. Nonetheless, the law passed and was duly registered on the Guernsey statute book.

As the days went on, Sherwill became increasingly concerned that the carefully managed surrender of Nicolle and Symes was leading to something more sinister. On the Saturday morning, he went to see Dr Brosch at the Feldkommandantur, hoping to smooth matters over. But the administrative staff there, who had always treated him with friendly courtesy, were suddenly cold and unhelpful, and Dr Brosch himself was even more sour-faced than usual. Ushered into Brosch's room, Sherwill got the distinct impression than he was weighed down by something deeply troubling.

Nonetheless, he decided to proceed as planned. 'Dr Brosch,' he announced formally, 'before he went on leave, the commandant gave me his word of honour that any members of the British armed forces who surrendered by a given date would be treated as prisoners of war, and that no one who had helped them would be harmed. They surrendered by the due date and since then you have been making a whole series of arrests.' He looked the other man straight in the eye and asked, 'Are you going to keep your word?'

Dr Brosch cast his own eyes down to the ground. 'We *must* keep our word, but it is going to be very difficult,' he said quietly. Then he added, 'Only the Führer can decide.'

Sherwill felt his blood run cold. If the Nicolle and Symes affair was being referred all the way to Berlin then the Germans were obviously taking it even more seriously than he had feared. Bandelow might have given him his own word of honour, but there was nothing to stop him being overruled by someone higher up the chain of command.

Sherwill thought about the unusually cold reception he had received from the office staff, and the fact that Dr Brosch was still refusing to meet his eyes. This was it, then, he realised. The Germans must have learned about his discussions with Emile Nicolle. Perhaps they even knew about him helping Mulholland and Martel three months earlier.

That afternoon, Sherwill ran into an old friend, Jack Falla. 'How's it going?' Jack asked him.

'Very, very badly,' the attorney general replied. 'I give myself a week.'

Meanwhile, Nicolle and Symes were also growing increasingly despondent. Under the incessant questioning of the lead German interrogator – a short, fat man who always sat with his legs resting on an upside-down waste-paper basket – discrepancies were beginning to appear in the stories told by their various family members and friends. Like Mulholland and Martel, the lads had surrendered with their civilian clothes wrapped up in brown paper, claiming that they had landed in their Army uniforms and then been given the civvies on arrival. The grey flannel trousers Nicolle had handed in were, he said, an old pair belonging to his uncle Frank. Frank corroborated this story, but when he was questioned in more detail about the trousers – were they old or new, patched or unpatched, and so on – it was clear that he didn't have a clue. The German interrogator kicked his waste-paper basket across the room triumphantly.

Nicolle soon found himself hauled before a court martial. Under questioning, he stuck to the story he had maintained throughout his interrogation, hoping that the German judge would believe him. But before the verdict could be handed down, the proceedings were suddenly interrupted by the German interrogator bursting into the room. 'You have been to Guernsey before!' he shouted. 'Why didn't you tell us?'

'You didn't ask,' Nicolle replied laconically, wondering which of his friends or relatives had broken under interrogation. Now that the Germans knew about his previous undercover mission, he felt sure that his number was up.

A second court martial was convened two days later to consider the new evidence. This time it took up the better part of the morning. When the judge was satisfied that he had heard all he needed to, he looked directly at Nicolle and told him, through an interpreter, 'You are a dirty common-or-garden spy. You will be shot.'

That afternoon, from his bedroom window, Nicolle saw Symes walking in the garden below. 'It's the end, Jim,' he called down to him, drawing a finger across his throat.

Sure enough, Symes too was found guilty of espionage and sentenced to death.

As Sherwill had predicted, it wasn't long before the investigators came looking for him too. He and his wife May had just finished their Sunday lunch when he spotted a couple of German soldiers walking up the front drive. 'This is it,' he told May sombrely.

Sherwill let the men in and accompanied them into the drawing room, where he was held while they waited for a plain-clothes policeman to arrive. When he did, Sherwill told him defiantly, 'I am saying absolutely nothing.'

The other man looked astonished. 'Do you not realise the terribly dangerous position you are in?' he asked.

Again, Sherwill insisted that he intended to hold his tongue.

The interrogator looked disappointed. 'We never expected this of you,' he said. 'We thought you were our man.'

His words were enough to break Sherwill's vow of silence. 'That's not true!' he exploded. 'I was never your man and you know it!'

May, who had been listening at the door, suddenly burst into the room. 'How dare you treat my husband like this!' she yelled.

Sherwill had never seen her look so angry, and the interrogator was taken aback too. 'Please, tell her we haven't been treating you unfairly,' he asked.

Sherwill did his best to calm his wife down. 'May, if you go on like this you'll only be doing me harm,' he told her.

'Your husband did not tell us the truth,' the interrogator chipped in. 'We've got it all down in black and white.'

'I don't care if you've got it down in blue and purple!' Mrs Sherwill cried. 'I know my husband. He never told a lie in his life!'

Eventually, she was persuaded to retire to her bedroom, while her husband sat up in the drawing room, guarded by two men with revolvers. More than ever, he was convinced that his days on earth were numbered. That night, neither he nor his wife got a wink of sleep.

In the morning another officer arrived. 'I suppose I am going to be shot?' Sherwill asked him.

'No, we don't shoot people as easily as that,' the German replied. 'You will be tried first.'

Sherwill was flown to Paris, where he spent a night, rather incongruously, at the luxurious Hôtel des Ambassadeurs on Boulevard Haussmann – in recognition, presumably, of the exalted position he hadn't yet been stripped of – before being transferred to Cherche-Midi prison, where Nicolle, Symes and a dozen or so of their family and friends were already incarcerated. The accommodation couldn't have presented more of a contrast – in place of a palatial room with en-suite bath, he would have to make do with a cell measuring ten feet by five and a bucket on the floor. The only light came from a little window too high to see out of, and apart from a few moments of snatched conversation when the prisoners were allowed out into the yard to empty their buckets, the experience was an entirely solitary one.

In an attempt to preserve his sanity over the ensuing weeks, Sherwill did his best to keep busy. Much of his time was spent scrubbing the walls of his cell with a nailbrush to rid them of graffiti. He also began keeping a diary, although more often than not each day's entry was the same: 'Nothing happened.'

In Guernsey, the treatment of Nicolle and Symes and their families – not to mention the loss of the island's civilian leader – sent shockwaves through the population. Major Bandelow's promises had, it seemed, been hollow ones, and all Sherwill's efforts to remain on good terms with the Germans had done him little good in the end.

The relationship between the local people and the authorities had never been more strained. One man was asked by a high-ranking German official what the islanders thought about the handling of the Nicolle and Symes affair. His response certainly captured the mood of the moment. 'They knew they couldn't trust the word of the Germans,' he said, 'and this proves it.'

CHAPTER TWELVE

THE HONEYMOON IS OVER

With Ambrose Sherwill languishing in a French gaol cell, the presidency of the island's Controlling Committee passed to the Reverend John Leale, a clear-headed Methodist minister who had previously been responsible for economic matters. It remained to be seen whether Leale's working relationship with his opposite numbers would be as cordial as Sherwill's, but after less than a week in his new job he was informed of a worrying new development in German policy: as a punishment for the 'favouring of espionage' by certain members of the island population, all wireless sets were to be confiscated.

It was a deeply unpopular move. Under the stifling boredom of Occupation, radios offered a major boost to morale, as well as a way of keeping informed about the progress of the war. 'Oh, day of mourning!' Sark's Julia Tremaine wrote in her diary. 'They have taken our wirelesses away and we are cut off from everything.' Without access to the BBC, the only source of news available on the islands was the deeply unreliable German war reports published by the local newspapers. 'It is miserable to be cut off from all news from home and not to know how the war is going on,' Mrs Tremaine continued. 'The propaganda in their news makes you think *they* are on the winning side and that makes me very down-hearted at times.'

Others, though, chose to put a different spin on the situation. When one Guernseyman was asked by a German soldier how his fellow islanders had taken the loss of their wirelesses, he replied defiantly, 'They were rather pleased. They felt the news must be so good you didn't want them to hear it.'

Either way, the confiscation of radios signalled a watershed in how the German authorities intended to treat the islanders. The closure of rural fishing ports following the boat escape to Ireland had been unpopular, but it had at least seemed like a practical response to the events that led up to it. The confiscation of radios felt very different: a punishment imposed on the whole population for the crimes of a handful of individuals. It didn't quite match the threat to round up twenty people and shoot them, but it was still an expression of arbitrary authoritarian power that couldn't fail to breed both resentment and fear.

As the leaves fell from the trees during the autumn of 1940, memories of those long summer days in which Germans and locals had swum side by side in the sea were starting to fade. In fact, ever since mid-September, when the climax of the Battle of Britain had brought expectations of a swift march on London to a sudden and unexpected end, there had been a subtle shift in the mood of soldiers and civilians alike. Old anxieties and distrust had surfaced once again as the cracks began to show in the model occupation.

Such was the lack of trust in the authorities that wild stories about the latest rules and regulations were greeted with increasing credulity. 'We don't know what to believe,' lamented Julia Tremaine. 'What we hear one day is denied the next.' Hot on the heels of the confiscation of radios came a rumour that all pet cats and dogs were to be put to death. In Guernsey, Ruth Ozanne was beside herself with worry about her beloved highland terrier. 'It is making me so miserable,' she wrote in her diary. 'I would willingly go on half rations to feed Gary if shortage of food is the reason.' Those without animals of their own found such devotion hard to understand. 'If women were asked to sacrifice their dogs instead of their sons,' Mrs Le Bideau observed wryly, 'war would perhaps lose its popularity.'

In fact, the German authorities had no intention of summarily executing the canine populations of the islands, although they did warn that any dogs found off the leash in a public space were liable to be seized, and in some cases destroyed, with their owners fined up to £10. Mrs Le Bideau, however, having seen the soldiers billeted near her own home petting the neighbourhood strays, doubted even this policy would ever be implemented. 'Fritz is often seen playing with local mongrels,' she wrote. 'They fawn on him for food and he loves them. If he finds himself obliged to shoot some friendly Rover or Rosie who has fed out of his hand, I have a shrewd suspicion that he will miss his aim.'

Nonetheless, not all Germans were animal lovers and a number of dogs experienced close shaves. Bonzo, a spaniel-terrier cross in Guernsey, had developed a dangerous habit of chasing German soldiers. One day, while he and his owner, schoolboy Michael Trubuil, were playing outside, a Wehrmacht officer walked past. Bonzo's reputation must have preceded him because as soon as he saw the dog, the soldier drew his pistol, keeping it levelled at Bonzo's head as he made his way along the road. '*Stay*, Bonzo!' Michael hissed, praying that for once the dog would do as he was told. Somehow Bonzo seemed to understand the gravity of the situation, remaining rooted to the spot as the German soldier went on his way.

Some animals seemed to positively delight in provoking the Germans. Leo Harris watched with rapt attention as his neighbour's Alsatian ran up to a group of soldiers sunbathing on the beach and cocked his leg against one of them. As the warm liquid trickled down his back, the young man suddenly leapt to his feet. Disgusted, he dashed into the sea to wash himself off. By the time he returned, the dog was long gone.

The panic over a non-existent pet cull might have been groundless, but bit by bit the German regime was showing hints of a darker kind of occupation. In October, Dr Brosch of the Guernsey Feldkommandantur, whose responsibilities included press censorship, issued a new set of guidelines for the editors of the island newspapers. From now on, every issue was to bear the name of the 'responsible editor' who had overseen it, and pseudonymous bylines were forbidden. Anonymous letters to the editor would still be permitted, but only if their content was unambiguously 'non-political'.

More sinister still was the desire of the German authorities to establish if any Jews had remained in Guernsey after the evacuation. Acting on Dr Brosch's orders, Police Inspector Sculpher began interviewing anyone suspected of having Jewish blood in their family. By the end of November, he had identified a handful of Jewish women. The new president of the Controlling Committee, Reverend Leale, passed their names on to the Feldkommandantur.

Even children, who had previously got on well with the German soldiers, were beginning to see them in a new light. Guernsey schoolgirl Betty Jagou was walking along the road one morning when she stumbled upon some troops taking part in a mock battle. One of the soldiers turned to look right at her, raising his rifle and pointing it directly at her head as his lips curled into a smile. Betty was convinced that she was about to be shot, but instead he merely whispered, 'Pop! Pop! Pop!' For a moment she stood frozen to the spot. Then she bolted, racing down the road as fast as her legs would carry her. She could hear the German's laughter echoing across the fields behind her.

Like any army, the Occupation force contained a few bad apples, and some of the German soldiers just couldn't resist throwing their weight around. Another Guernsey schoolgirl, Molly Finigan, spent much of her free time out and about with her sister, searching for food to bring home to their mother. Between them they could generally gather a basket full of potatoes by following the local boys who transported them from the docks on their backs, and scavenging any stray ones that fell to the ground. Most of the Germans who supervised the distribution were inclined to look the other way, but one very large, angry-looking soldier known as Otto, who had already earned a reputation for brutality after kicking an elderly man, showed no such mercy. One day, when he caught Molly picking up a couple of spuds from the side of the road, he landed such a powerful kick on her backside that she burst into tears.

Molly rushed home and told her parents what had happened. Her father, who was already bitterly depressed at having to sit out the war under Occupation rather than join the fight, was so furious that his wife had to physically restrain him from rushing out in search of Otto then and there. He vowed that when the day finally came that the islands were liberated, he would find the German brute and kill him.

Molly wasn't the only member of the family to experience an unnerving encounter with one of the Germans. One night, shortly before curfew, Mrs Finigan was walking home through St Peter Port after a whist drive when she saw a group of soldiers coming up the high street towards her who had clearly spent the best part of the evening in the pub. They were joking loudly with each other as they staggered along the road, and Mrs Finigan was careful to keep her eyes averted. But as they came closer, one of the group sidled up to her, drew his revolver and pushed it hard into her chest. She froze in terror, not daring to say a word, or even to draw breath. After a tense few moments, the soldier reholstered his weapon and stumbled off to rejoin his friends. Deeply shaken, Mrs Finigan practically ran the rest of the way home.

As the nights continued to draw in, the mood on the islands grew more and more miserable. Operating on Berlin time, it was dark until well after ten o'clock in the mornings, and the poor fishermen couldn't set out for the day until eleven, further limiting the size of the average catch. Gradually, though, the thoughts of both islanders and Germans began to turn to their first Occupation Christmas. The atmosphere was far from festive, with the islands buffeted by fierce winter storms that left the sentries shivering in their sodden boots. The bare shopfronts of St Helier and St Peter Port offered little in the way of presents, but the locals weren't deterred, crafting their own gifts for family and friends, or wrapping up old toys so that their children would at least have something to open. Some had been planning for the big day for months, diligently hoarding a few chocolates or even a bottle of champagne, along with other luxuries that were now almost impossible to get hold of.

In Guernsey, the festive season saw the arrival of some unexpected guests. On 13 December, a group of young Frenchmen who had stolen a boat in Brittany landed on the beach at Vazon Bay. Inspired by General de Gaulle's BBC radio broadcasts, they planned to travel to London and sign up for his Free French Army. Sadly, their navigational skills didn't quite match their enthusiasm and when they sighted the northern coast of Guernsey they were convinced that they had reached the Isle of Wight. Marching up the beach proudly singing the Marseillaise, the young lads were immediately captured by German sentries and, after a brief interrogation, sent off to Jersey for trial. Under the laws of Vichy France, they stood accused of a capital offence: treason.

While the Frenchmen waited to hear their fate, the people of Guernsey were more concerned with their fellow islanders still banged up in Cherche-Midi prison over the Nicolle and Symes affair. The two soldiers had been found guilty of espionage, their friends and family of high treason, and Sherwill of 'acting against his appointed duty' in failing to inform the authorities as soon as he learned that the lads were on the island. The latter charge carried a penalty of up to a year in prison, while the others could all lead to a firing squad.

There was, though, still the matter of Major Bandelow's amnesty agreement. The Guernsey commandant was deeply unhappy at the thought that those higher up the chain of command might force him to break his word. He told his immediate superior, Count von Schmettow, that if it came to it, he was willing to resign his commission rather than carry out such dishonourable orders. As a matter of principle, von Schmettow was inclined to agree with him, but he was also aware of a more pragmatic consideration: if the Germans went back on Bandelow's promise it could damage relations with the islanders for good.

Von Schmettow flew to France to discuss the matter with his own superior officer, General von Brockdorff, who in turn sent a member of his staff all the way to Berlin for final adjudication. The matter didn't quite get as far as the Führer himself, but it did make it to the desk of Field Marshal von Reichenau, one of the generals who had spearheaded the invasion of France and Belgium six months earlier. As a career soldier, he placed a premium on military honour. 'When one gives his word, one gives his word,' he declared gnomically.

While their lives were being weighed in the balance at the highest echelons of the German Army, Guernsey's prisoners in France were growing more and more miserable. Living in cold, dark cells, surviving on a diet of soup, bread and cheese, and denied more than the briefest of contact with other human beings, it was no surprise that many of them fell prey to depression. 'We live almost like animals,' Sherwill wrote in his diary. 'Never had I been in touch with so much misery at the same time.' On 23 December, Symes' father Louis was found dead in his cell with his wrists slashed.

The next day, Christmas Eve, all of Guernsey was abuzz as the islanders pored over the latest issue of the *Star*, which contained a proclamation from Colonel Schumacher of the Feldkommandantur in Jersey. Although the guilt of the prisoners had been established beyond doubt, he declared, their sentences had all been commuted. Nicolle and Symes would be taken to a POW camp, and the others would be sent home to Guernsey. The wireless sets confiscated five weeks earlier would also be returned to their owners.

For Sherwill, the relief of seeing his wife and children again was tinged with disappointment and regret. On the express orders of Dr Brosch at the Feldkommandantur, he was forbidden from ever holding public office again. His time in prison had given him a chance to reflect on the decisions he had made during his four months as the island's de facto president, and he had come to some damning conclusions. He had seen himself, he later wrote, as a 'buffer' between the Germans and the islanders, protecting his people from abuse at the hands of the authorities by attempting, as he put it, to run the Occupation for them. With the benefit of hindsight, however, he had concluded that this idea was 'fatuous'. Now, having swapped the frantic affairs of state for permanent gardening leave – he spent his days carefully tending his vegetable patch and looking after a small herd of goats – Sherwill had plenty of time to dwell on his mistakes.

Hubert Nicolle's father Emile was also barred from returning to the civil service, and his uncle Frank was forced to give up his job as assistant harbour master. Jessie Mariette, meanwhile, returned to the Lyric No. 1 Company, but her fellow performers couldn't help noticing a change in her. The spirited, carefree young dancer they remembered had been replaced by someone more serious and thoughtful. She had only been gone for a couple of months but somehow she seemed a lot older.

And then there was the Symes family, who returned to Guernsey missing not only a son but a father. They refused to believe that Louis had killed himself, convinced that the Germans had murdered him in his cell and then doctored the crime scene to make it look like suicide. But whatever the truth of the matter, Louis Symes was never coming home again.

The first major confrontation between the islanders and the German authorities had ended, appropriately enough on Christmas Eve, with an expression of forbearance and mercy. But the proclamation from the Feldkommandantur concluded with an ominous warning. 'All the above measures have been taken in the expectation and under the condition of a perfect loyalty on the part of the Island Authorities and population in the future,' Colonel Schumacher wrote. 'Any disloyal or illegal behaviour will result in immediate counter-measures. The whole community would bear the consequences of individual misconduct.'

That evening, curfew regulations were relaxed to allow the islanders to attend midnight mass. In Jersey, ten-year-old Leo Harris was an altar boy at the local Catholic church, St Mary and St Peter. Over the last few months he had grown used to the sight of a handful of Germans sitting at the back during services. When they came up and knelt at the altar rail to take the communion wafer, his instinctive hostility always faltered a little. On Christmas Eve, though, the Germans arrived in force. In the dim light of the candles set up on the altar, Leo could make out their smart grey uniforms dotted all around the church.

The Germans sat respectfully as Canon Arscott conducted the service in English, remaining politely tight-lipped when he offered the usual prayers for the king and the rest of the Royal Family. Then, unexpectedly, a number of them rose from their pews and walked slowly up to the front, turning to face the congregation. Without accompaniment, they began a beautiful performance of 'Silent Night', in the original German. As they sang, the flickering candle-light played across faces struggling to hold in their emotions. For the first time Leo felt a kind of sympathy for them, far away from home and facing an uncertain future.

The next day, the islanders received a very welcome Christmas present as the radios confiscated over the Nicolle and Symes affair began to be returned to their owners. Ruth Ozanne was thrilled to hear a knock on the door just before lunchtime and rushed out to take delivery of her precious wireless set.

That afternoon, the whole family gathered in Ruth's mother's room, where a temporary aerial had been set up, to listen to the king's speech.

'The future will be hard,' King George announced sombrely, 'but our feet are planted on the path of victory, and with the help of God we shall make our way to justice and to peace.'

CHAPTER THIRTEEN

MAKING DO

As the new year dawned, it brought with it a slow and crushing realisation. Hardly anyone, other than perhaps the most optimistic of German soldiers, had really expected the war to be over by Christmas, but now the Occupation seemed to stretch on into an indefinite, never-ending future. Cut off from Britain, with only the BBC broadcasts as a tenuous link to the world outside, the islands felt more removed and isolated than ever. It was six months since the evacuation ships had left, tearing many families apart, and in all that time not a word had come back from those struggling to make a life for themselves on the mainland. At times, for those suffering from the pangs of separation and loneliness, those six months could feel like six years.

The strange unreality of the Occupation found its perfect emblem in the Weighbridge clock of St Peter Port Harbour. Badly damaged in the initial German air raid six months earlier, the exterior of the clock had since been cleaned up, but the mechanism inside had proved irreparable. The hour and minute hands, which had been stopped by the blast of one of the first German bombs, had since been removed, leaving only four empty faces. 'I feel glad that it is not mended as its blank expressionless dial so well represents our feelings,' wrote Mrs Le Bideau. 'It merely records No Time, the time which it always seems to be nowadays. No food, no cars, no amusements, no tea parties, no cocktails, no fun, and to cap it all it is always No Time by the wounded clock.'

Many islanders had already fallen prey to listless depression. 'Most people blame the inadequate diet for their troubles,' wrote Dr Alistair Rose, 'but I am not so sure. I think it is more probably due to mental stagnation and the monotony which has become such an integral part of our daily life. In fact, we might say that we are almost losing our individuality, and becoming exceedingly like the cabbages which we consume in such vast quantities – we have to suffer the monotony of diet, monotony of conversation ... monotony of faces and monotony of scene.'

Monotony of diet was certainly a major problem, thanks to heavy rationing and the limited supplies available from the trading post that had been set up in France. By January 1941, butter was rationed to 2 ounces (around 50g) per week, bacon and eggs were both all but unobtainable, and a shortage of white flour meant that the only bread available was dark and stodgy.

The islanders did their best to adapt, making do with whatever ingredients they could get their hands on. The traditional Guernsey bean jar, a slow-cooked stew whose flavour derived from a pig's trotter left in the pot overnight, suddenly became – horror of horrors – a vegetarian option, while the ubiquitous potato-peel pie replaced the meatier staples of the pre-war diet. When supplies of imported sugar ran low, those with a sweet tooth began growing their own sugar beet, boiling it down into a dark, musty syrup that, with a bit of imagination, wasn't too far removed from Lyle's finest. A bit of potato flour mixed with water, meanwhile, was a serviceable alternative to custard.

Carrageen moss, a soggy, reddish-brown seaweed that could be harvested in abundance at low tide, was used in a number of recipes, most frequently as the core ingredient of a traditional Irish blancmange. Pearl and Gwen Smith would scour the beach at Cobo, hauling back as much moss as they could carry to the kitchen at Les Pieux and doing their best to wash the sand off, although never entirely successfully. Then they would take it out into the garden and lay it out on a low table with a wire mesh across the top, leaving it to bake and bleach in the sun. Their mother would place the moss in a muslin bag, along with some milk and a little bit of sugar or syrup, and bring it to the boil on the stove. The resulting dessert bore a passing resemblance to a genuine blancmange, although however much Mrs Smith sweetened the mixture, it always tasted vaguely of saltwater. Nonetheless, carrageen moss puddings soon became an Occupation staple, and for those who couldn't harvest the seaweed themselves, Cumber's, the chemist on the high street in St Peter Port, began stocking a pre-made carrageen jelly.

For heavy smokers, the weekly ounce of tobacco permitted under rationing was far from sufficient, and a variety of alternatives were tried, including rose petals and watercress leaves. Ersatz tea, meanwhile, was brewed using everything from bramble leaves and dried clover heads to parsnips. One popular option was cubes of baked sugar beet, which made for a rather sweet, refreshing drink with the addition of boiling water.

Unsurprisingly, the new diet didn't always sit well in the stomach. At one time or another, almost everyone was struck down with a bad case of diarrhoea, known colloquially as 'Occupation Disease'. There were various theories as to the cause. Some blamed the new bread, others the large quantities of fibrous vegetables. Either way, there wasn't much they could do other than let the illness run its course.

The shortage of supplies brought about a curious inversion of the traditional class structure, with wealthy town-dwellers suddenly worse off than the cash-poor farmers who had the space and resources to grow their own food. At his school in St Helier, Leo Harris and his fellow townie friends resented the fat, well-fed farmers' sons who always had the largest sandwiches in their lunchboxes.

Leo's father John was lucky that his farmer friends were very generous, offering him the odd hunk of meat or slab of butter whenever they had some to spare. Other town-dwellers began moonlighting as casual labourers, and were happy to be paid in kind. Stanley Ruez worked for the Midland Bank in St Helier, but since the majority of their business was concerned with accounts on the mainland there was very little for him and his colleagues to do. Every day after lunch, Stanley would leave the office, roll up his shirtsleeves and cycle over to one of the nearby farms, offering to milk the cows or muck out the pigs in exchange for a bottle of milk or a few vegetables to take home to his family.

It wasn't only foodstuffs that were running short. In February, the supply of soap ran out and islanders were encouraged to wash their hands with wood ashes or sand instead. In time, a replacement product was imported from France but it was far from popular – it failed to lather when mixed with the Channel Island water, and left an unpleasant slimy residue on the hands. By April, there was no leather for soling shoes, and cobblers began using wood instead. This didn't do much for comfort, but children appreciated the cheerful clacking noise they made, especially since it added extra authenticity to their attempts to mimic the marching of the German soldiers in their hobnailed jackboots.

More than ever, younger siblings were dressed and shod in hand-me-downs, and a number of boys were sent off to school in their mother's old flat-heeled shoes, desperately hoping that none of their peers would notice. When one girl grew out of a pair of shoes, her parents simply cut off the toes, leaving her feet to protrude over the front of the soles. Many children's clothes were patched with non-matching fabric, and when woollen garments were outgrown they would be carefully unravelled and then reknitted into something else.

Keeping a kitchen operational could be a challenge when broken crockery and cooking implements were virtually impossible to replace. After extensive use, enamel saucepans would eventually burn through, and the holes had to be plugged using little disks of cork, held in place by a tiny nut and bolt, which were imported from France. Often, though, it was a case of making do with what you could find around the house. Six-year-old Christine Du Feu was forced to give up the little wooden spade she took to the beach in the summer when her mother's final cooking spoon split in half. One of their neighbours, meanwhile, had recently broken the last of their cups, so they drank their bramble tea out of a jam pot.

Such everyday struggles made domestic life a stressful business for the wives and mothers who were expected to keep putting food on the table, and clean sheets on the beds, despite increasingly difficult conditions. But the islanders could see the funny side too. During one of the Lyric No. 1 Company's performances, the Brache sisters sang a defiantly cheery song that their father had composed on the subject.

> Nothing's going right at all, the home is gone to rack
> For we cannot find a cup or dish without a crack!
> Father's hair is whiter, he's got two stone lighter,
> Still he whistles every day.
> Mother cannot do her washing 'cause she's got no soap,
> All she's been able to do is put it all to soak!
> Still we're happy all the day, we never get the blues,
> Singing on our way.

The island newspapers turned out to be the saving grace of many families when they opened 'Exchange and Mart' columns. When Joan Blake began planning her forthcoming wedding in Guernsey she was determined to make the cake herself, but try as she might she just couldn't get hold of enough flour. In the end, she placed a notice in the *Guernsey Evening Press*, asking if anyone could help her. A few days later, she received a little envelope marked 'Wedding'. Inside was a handwritten note signed by a Mr G. Symons in St Sampson, who was willing to offer a 10-pound bag of flour in exchange for some packets of cigarettes. Joan wrote back at once to arrange the trade.

Sometimes the pairings of items sought and offered were distinctly incongruous: 'a goat for a bicycle; a dozen eggs for a pair of shoes; salt for a tennis racket or perhaps a fowl for a couple of packets of razor-blades,' as Jerseyman Arthur Kent commented wryly. In fact, the 'Exchange and Mart' columns soon became a much-loved feature of the daily papers, in large part due to their entertainment value. 'Someone wants a kitten and offers a tin of sardines in exchange,' wrote Mrs Le Bideau. 'The kitten would appreciate this.'

Once again, Frederick Brache had his finger on the pulse when he composed the popular 'Barter Song', sung by his daughters during a performance of *Anchors Aweigh* at the Lyric.

> Some folks never buy or sell,
> But they get things just as well.
> 'How is it done?' you'll say.
> Look up your press to-day.
> They're you'll find it's swop, swop, swop,
> For things we haven't got.
> Everybody wants to swop,
> Swopity-swopity swop!

Although rationed goods were not technically allowed to be bartered, there was an easy workaround for those desperate to get hold of them. By adding the words 'or what' to the end of the list of items they would accept as payment, an advertiser could be fairly certain that they would receive at least a handful of offers that were not strictly in accordance with the regulations.

If all else failed, there was always the black market, where almost anything could be purchased if you could afford the outrageously inflated prices. Mrs Le Bideau recounted an amusing, and almost certainly apocryphal, story in her diary: 'An old country woman staggered into the town on foot. Once arrived there she went up to the policeman. "Please, can you tell me the way to the market?" "Which market?" "The black market." And, alas for the honour of our local police, they know far more about that much-frequented place of merchandise than they should.'

Joking aside, few islanders were really so innocent and naïve about the existence of black-market trading. Those who abstained altogether, whether out of principle or simple lack of funds, were probably in the minority. Nonetheless, resentment remained towards those wealthy, well-connected people who seemed to be able to get anything they wanted. One of the Brache sisters' most popular songs was a cheerful ditty called 'Underneath the Counter', which described a cornucopia of exotic delights – rhubarb, peaches, raspberries, melons and cream – followed by the refrain, 'but not for you or me'.

The prevalence of under-the-counter trading meant that normally law-abiding islanders suddenly found themselves embroiled in acts of criminal deception as they attempted to avoid discovery by the German authorities. Those with small children learned that their prams could be adapted to include a secret compartment underneath. Once the Germans cottoned onto this, they began stopping women in the street and demanding they rouse their sleeping babies so that they could search for contraband goods.

One woman was cycling home with a packet of illegal butter in the basket of her bike when a friendly neighbour warned her there was a German patrol doing spot checks a little further along the road. In desperation, she shoved it into her knickers, hoping that the elastic would hold it in place. Fortunately, the Germans only checked her basket and didn't notice the trickle of melted butter oozing down to her ankle, but by the time she got home at least half of it had been lost.

Baron Hans von Aufsess, the administrative head of the Jersey Feldkommandantur, saw it as his duty to discourage black-market trading. When a large haul of contraband was seized from a French doctor – including ham, beef, flour, sugar, and more than 1,000 kilos of potatoes – he commandeered an empty shop window and put the goods on public display, along with a placard marked 'Help Defeat the Black Marketeers'. But the sight of crowds of desperate islanders staring at the vast array of goods clearly pricked his conscience. 'In the sleepless watches of the night the hungry faces of all those poor people gazing so longingly at the unimaginable piles of foodstuffs again passed before me,' he wrote in his diary.

The deprivations of Occupation were emotional as well as practical, and for many people loneliness was the hardest thing to bear. For over six months now, islanders like Ruth Leadbeater whose families had evacuated to England had been totally cut off from their loved ones. But early in 1941, thanks to the efforts of the International Red Cross, a special postal service was established whereby short messages could be transmitted to and from the mainland via Switzerland.

Fifteen-year-old Margaret Chalker had recently left school when she got a job working as a typist in the Guernsey Red Cross Bureau. The little office on Market Square, in the heart of St Peter Port, was always a hive of activity – the more striking because of the empty, boarded-up shops all around it.

Islanders would be allocated their messages alphabetically, typically once every six months, with a notice placed in the local papers – as well as in the office window – indicating who was entitled to send one the next day. Margaret was one of a dozen typists responsible for taking the people's handwritten messages, checking that they contained no more than twenty-five words, and then copying them onto the official Red Cross stationery.

The messages were supposed to stick strictly to personal subjects, although occasionally people managed to get around this by the use of coded phrases – 'Mother Hubbard is sick', for example, to indicate that they were running out of food. The typing girls would of course see through such ploys but they generally let the messages pass, as long as the hidden meanings weren't too obvious.

At the end of the week, one of the girls would be charged with the task of delivering the pile of slips to Grange Lodge, for censorship by the German authorities. Margaret dreaded the days when this responsibility fell to her, and would always hand over the tray of papers and rush back down the stairs as quickly as possible, doing her best to avoid the flirtatious overtures of the young soldiers who attempted to engage her in conversation.

When the replies came back from the mainland, little cards would be despatched alerting islanders that a message awaited them, and advising them to call at the office to receive it at a specific time. One of the girls in the office would always read it first so they knew what kind of a reaction to expect. In among the friendly greetings and expressions of familial love were messages announcing the death of a loved one in a bombing raid or while serving overseas. The girls always felt awkward prying into these private expressions of grief and sorrow, especially when the recipient was someone they knew.

The Red Cross bureaus were supposed to be for family communications only, but Jersey teenager Bob Le Sueur managed to get a message out to his bosses in England. Ever since the evacuation crisis, he had been running his branch of the General Accident insurance company without any contact with his superiors, and he had no way of letting them know how he was getting on. But since the Southampton office was based at an ordinary street address, Bob gambled that the German censors would assume it was a residential property. He began composing a message to his branch manager, Eric Thorpe, that he hoped would pass for family business. 'Dear Uncle Eric,' he wrote, 'Health good. Still the same job. Quite busy. New staff.'

When Bob finally received a reply – in equally guarded code – it was clear that the manager was not sure how to interpret his message, in particular the reference to 'new staff'. He must have thought, Bob deduced, that the Germans had taken over the business. Fortunately, Bob was able to set him right, and by virtue of this rather stilted back-and-forth communication, to reassure him that the office was in good hands.

The Red Cross message service brought back a fragile connection with the quarter of the Channel Islands population who had evacuated before the Occupation started, as well as – by extension – to some of the ten thousand young men from the islands who were serving with the British forces. But while these occasional brief messages were extremely welcome, they were a poor substitute for real human company. No one knew how long the war might last, and in the meantime life would have to go on.

The islands had been all but denuded of men of military age, presenting something of a dilemma for young women, who at some point or other were invariably subjected to the advances of a smart German soldier. The majority did their best to keep the enemy troops at arm's length, fearful of breaking a deeply held taboo concerning fraternisation with the enemy – something which, as far as many islanders were concerned, was unpatriotic and tantamount to treason. Confident young women would toss their hair defiantly when they were assailed by appreciative whistles, as if to say, 'Not a chance!' Others would simply walk on, staring straight ahead, seemingly oblivious to the unwanted attention. The Germans called them *Gespenster* (ghosts). And then there were the women – just how many remains a matter of debate – who, as Mrs Le Bideau euphemistically put it, went 'over the border' with the Germans.

Some simply fell in love, innocent Juliets to their equally besotted German Romeos. Others were, perhaps, a little more calculating. Despite intense social opprobrium, the girlfriend of a German officer could find her quality of life enhanced significantly, being wined and dined in style while her neighbours struggled to get by on meagre wartime rations. When their lovers went on leave to Paris, they could fetch luxuries such as lipstick and silk stockings – not to mention real soap – that were all but unobtainable on the islands.

It was women such as these who earned themselves a new nickname that was soon being whispered on every street corner: 'Jerrybag'. The level of hostility directed at them was extreme, outstripping even the venom directed at suspected collaborators and quislings. But censure wasn't reserved only for those who were seen as deliberately working the Occupation to their advantage by selling their bodies to the enemy. Even naïve love-struck teenagers were subjected to harsh criticism. 'Some of the Sark girls are walking out with the German soldiers,' wrote hotelier Julia Tremaine in disgust. 'Silly little asses, I feel I would like to shake them.'

In Jersey, Leo and Francis Harris took a very dim view of Jerrybags. If they ever saw a local girl walking arm-in-arm with a German soldier, or sunbathing with one on the beach, they would stare at her angrily. When a new boy arrived in Leo's class at school whose mother was known to 'fraternise' with the German officers, the entire year group shunned him, refusing to speak to the poor lad and mocking him whenever he made a mistake in class. The bullying eventually got bad enough that the boy told his mother about it. She in turn told her German friends, who paid the school's headmaster a visit. At the next morning's assembly, the head told the boys to treat the new arrival more kindly, well aware that if the bullying continued the whole school could be closed down.

One Jerseywoman – the aptly named Gloria Love – became such a social pariah that she was eventually forced to quit the island altogether. She made no secret of her relationship with Colonel von Schmettow's adjutant Walter Zepernick, alias 'Zep', and delighted in riding about town in the bright red convertible Peugeot coupé that he had requisitioned from the island's inspector of motor traffic. Their boozy parties at Grey Gables, a grand house situated on the hill above the charming St Aubin's Bay, often carried on into the small hours of the morning, fuelled by a mixture of champagne, chartreuse, cognac and red wine.

When Zepernick was killed on his way home from France by a bomb hitting his train, Gloria took up with von Schmettow's chief of staff, Hans von Helldorf, instead. As far as her fellow islanders were concerned she was the worst kind of Jerrybag – unprincipled, self-serving and unashamed, the perfect target for their resentment and righteous indignation. One local club refused to allow her in – von Helldorf promptly had it shut down – and when she took to the stage in a local cabaret show the audience rose from their seats and walked out in protest. Clearly, Gloria was never going to be accepted by society again. Eventually, she decided to cut her losses and move to Guernsey.

In the face of such opprobrium, it was a wonder that any girl dared to go out with a German, but the young men could be very persistent. On Sark, the tea room of the Mermaid Pub had been turned into a schoolroom where local children were taught by Hazel Hamon, the beautiful eighteen-year-old daughter of one of the local fishermen. The boys in the class found Hazel utterly entrancing, and they weren't the only ones. At the end of the day, off-duty German soldiers would gather outside, offering to do the lads' maths homework if they would provide an introduction to their teacher. Unfortunately for the troops, she always gave them the cold shoulder.

Some girls found themselves fending off the advances of distinctly powerful admirers. Baron von Aufsess was devoted to his wife back home in Germany, but that didn't stop him embarking on a string of dalliances while he was away from her. 'The Englishwoman is astoundingly simple, effortless and swift in her lovemaking,' he wrote approvingly in his diary. 'While the French woman involves herself totally in the game, which she likes to be conducted along intellectual lines, for the Englishwoman it is a surprisingly straight-forward, physical matter.'

Rich, handsome and still on the right side of forty, von Aufsess was a man who was used to getting what he wanted. Nonetheless, not all his intended conquests were happy to play along. During a visit to the Le Cuirot farm in Jersey, the baron took a shine to the farmer's daughter Madeleine, but when he invited her to accompany him to a German party, she politely declined and left the room. A few weeks later, von Aufsess returned to the farm, greeting Madeleine warmly and extending his hand to her. She shook it a little awk-wardly, but then immediately went to the sink and began washing her hands. 'Is it myself or my uniform that you dislike?' the baron asked. Madeleine replied simply, 'You're the enemy.' Her father, in an attempt to defuse a potentially dangerous situation, suggested that if the baron had a sister who was approached by a British officer, perhaps she would react in the same way. This seemed to satisfy von Aufsess, and he soon moved on to the next girl.

In many cases, it was not really their own moral principles or a fear of society's judgement that stopped girls from getting involved with the Germans, so much as an awareness of what such a relation-ship would do to their fathers. Marcelle Le Poidevin worked behind the counter of the German shop in St Peter Port, one of about a dozen local girls who spent their days serving the troops. Two of her colleagues had already acquired German boyfriends and Marcelle certainly got her fair share of offers. A few times she allowed one of the handsome young men to walk her home at the end of the day, but it never went any further than that. Marcelle's father had been gassed in the First World War and she knew it would break his heart if she were to get involved with one of the soldiers.

Unsurprisingly, women who decided to embark on affairs with the Germans often did so with great trepidation, and tried as much as possible to keep their assignations a secret. One night at Camblez, Dr Reffler informed Ruth Leadbeater that he had a 'special friend' coming to see him. 'When the bell rings, would you go to the front door and show her into the lounge?' he asked.

'Of course,' Ruth replied, not thinking much of the request.

At around half past seven, the bell duly rang, and Ruth went to answer the door. Standing on the step was her old maths teacher from school, who turned a bright shade of beetroot as soon as she saw Ruth.

In fact, the two women were both so embarrassed that neither of them felt able to acknowledge that they knew one another. 'This way, madam,' Ruth said politely, leading the guest into the lounge as if she were a perfect stranger.

The next morning, Ruth was up early – in time to see her former teacher attempt to discreetly show herself out. She smiled to show there were no hard feelings between them, but the other woman still looked acutely embarrassed. It was the last time Ruth saw her at Camblez. If Dr Reffler invited her back, she must have turned him down.

Ruth was far from the only islander to discover that someone they knew was a Jerrybag. At fifteen, Pearl Smith had recently started a new job at Grut's, a photographic studio on St Peter Port's main thorough-fare, Le Pollet. The owner, Norman Grut, was the son of a very famous Guernsey photographer, although these days his own work was largely confined to taking the little pictures required for the identity cards that were now mandatory for all islanders, along with the occasional formal portrait of a recently arrived German officer in his smart new uniform. But many of the Germans were keen photographers themselves, and would bring their own reels of film into the shop to be developed. Working in the darkroom, Pearl was astonished to see a number of women she knew in the pictures who had obviously been fraternising with the soldiers. In time it became a kind of game between the girls in the shop to see who could identify the most Jerrybags.

Pearl had already seen plenty of local women consorting with the officers billeted at her parents' hotel. Mr and Mrs Smith did their best to hide their disapproval as long as the guests remained downstairs in the lounge and never ventured up to the bedrooms. Some were classic Jerrybags, dressed up to the nines and positively caked in make-up, reeking of a mixture of alcohol and cheap perfume. Others were more innocent, naïve girls who didn't know what they were letting themselves in for.

One of the latter, Susie, was a sweet girl barely out of school, and was totally besotted with the batman of one of the officers based at Les Pieux. One day she arrived at the door and announced excitedly, 'Peter and I are engaged!'

'Oh, that's nice,' said Pearl, not entirely convincingly. She suspected that Peter might already have a wife in Germany. But when Susie flashed her engagement ring, her opinion of the young man only dropped further. It was a signet ring that her mother had given her for her birthday, and which had gone missing a few weeks earlier. It even had Pearl's initials – P.S. – engraved on it.

'For Peter and Susie,' the other girl explained, when she saw Pearl scrutinising the inscription.

Pearl didn't say anything, but once Susie had gone she rushed off to speak to her mother, begging her to get the ring back for her. Mrs Smith, however, knew better than to interfere in a German love affair. 'Let her have the ring,' she said. 'I'll buy you another one when this wicked war is over.' She took her daughter's hands in her own as she told her, 'The best thing you can do is to forget you ever had it.'

Whether or not Susie's dishonest boyfriend ever made an honest woman of her, a handful of over-the-border relationships did go the distance, blossoming into lifelong unions. It was technically illegal for two people to marry while their countries were at war, but one couple defied this prohibition, at least on their own terms. Dorothy Edwards was only seventeen when she met Willi Joanknecht and fell head over heels in love with him. Dating an enemy soldier brought with it certain challenges – when they went to the cinema they would have to sit either side of the rope dividing the German half of the auditorium from the local half, holding hands across the divide. But Willi treated Dorothy better than any Guernsey boy ever had, and before long she felt sure she wanted to spend the rest of her life with him.

The young couple sought the advice of a local Quaker lady, who told them they could marry in the eyes of God by simply saying, 'We love one another, and we are now man and wife,' in front of an altar. In lieu of a traditional gold band, Willi placed a curtain ring on Dorothy's finger.

It was a union that was to last more than seventy years, until Willi's death in 2015.

CHAPTER FOURTEEN

TROUBLEMAKERS

On 17 March 1941, at Jersey's Grand Hotel, François Scornet waited patiently while Father Maré performed the last rites. The 22-year-old Frenchman had been identified by the German authorities as the ring-leader of the group of young men who had sailed away from Brittany hoping to join General de Gaulle's Free French Army in London. Since their capture in Guernsey the previous December, they had been interrogated at length, and then tried in the Old Committee Room of the Jersey States Building. Now the time had come to make an example of one of them.

When the priest had finished his ministrations, Scornet was allowed to pen a brief message to his parents, who had been brought over from France to witness the execution. 'I will die for France, bravely facing the enemy,' he told them. 'Be assured that I will die a good Christian.'

A lorry arrived to take Scornet, Father Maré and a simple wooden coffin to St Ouen's Manor, a fifteenth-century mock castle, complete with round corner turrets and a moat, that was being used as a German barracks. There the young Frenchman was led through the grounds and tied to the trunk of a giant ash tree. At 8.20 a.m., his final words – 'Vive Dieu! Vive La France!' – were drowned out by the fusillade of bullets from the twelve-man firing squad.

Scornet's death was widely publicised in the Channel Islands, with public notices on behalf of the German War Court explaining that he had been killed for 'favouring the actions of the enemy by wilfully supporting England in the war against the German Empire'. It was a carefully calculated move, shocking enough to scare the population into submission, and yet carried out against a foreigner rather than a local person. Nonetheless, the transition to ruling by fear was an admission that Sherwill's 'model occupation' had most definitely broken down.

The longer the Army of Occupation remained on the islands, the more hostility and resentment towards them grew. 'The Germans still continue to eat all our stores, great fat ugly dissipated hounds,' wrote Sark hotelier Julia Tremaine. At a time when local people were increasingly struggling for food, the inequality was hard to ignore.

On 20 April, just over a month after François Scornet's execution, the islanders were introduced to a new ritual that would in time become depressingly familiar: the celebration of Adolf Hitler's birthday. The military bands performed more bombastically than ever, parades of wagons decorated with Nazi regalia filled the streets, and the cinemas, draped in giant swastika flags, screened an epic two-hour documentary, *Sieg im Westen* (Victory in the West).

For those islanders who insisted that all the soldiers *they* knew were 'Germans' rather than 'Nazis', the annual celebrations were an uncomfortable reminder that they really were living under the Third Reich. The number of card-carrying National Socialists in the Occupation forces might have been small, but, emboldened by the festive atmosphere and fortified by plenty of alcohol, they certainly managed to make their presence felt.

Compared to most islanders, Mrs Le Bideau was on remarkably good terms with the Germans, and in particular with the two young soldiers billeted in her house. But there were limits to how far even she was willing to go to accommodate the Führer's birthday. When a tipsy *Unteroffizier* barged into her garden that evening, demanding that his driver, who was married to Mrs Le Bideau's housekeeper, take him back to his barracks, she found herself drawn into a conversation on the merits of French cognac. The officer had spent the last few hours toasting Hitler's health with every variety of booze he could lay his hands on, and now, he explained, it was the one thing he craved more than anything.

'I only take it when I'm ill,' the old lady told him tersely. Fortunately, the driver soon appeared and the drunken soldier was carted off home.

A little while later, however, after Mrs Le Bideau had retired to bed, she was startled by a commotion coming from the kitchen downstairs. Before long, there was a knock on her door and the housekeeper entered, looking distinctly embarrassed. She and her husband had been sitting by the fire with a couple of friends, she explained, when the German officer had unexpectedly returned bearing a large wooden box containing a bottle of cognac. He had demanded that they all join him in drinking a toast to the Führer – and that the lady of the house should not be exempted from the general invitation.

By now, Mrs Le Bideau's patience was wearing thin. 'Tell him I'm ill,' she protested. 'Or make up some other excuse.'

The housekeeper scurried back down to the kitchen, but a minute or two later she returned, looking more sheepish than ever. 'He insisted you have this,' she told Mrs Le Bideau, forcing a large glass into her hand.

Mrs Le Bideau was not normally one to turn her nose up at a free tipple, but she was damned if she was going to drink to the Führer's health. So she took the cognac and poured it into a little flask for later, before sending the housekeeper back with the empty glass.

There was little chance of getting to sleep now. For the next couple of hours, she lay there listening to the German officer's braying laughter echoing up the stairs, punctuated by the occasional cheer from the party in the kitchen. She couldn't help feeling a little uncomfortable at the thought of Hitler being toasted under her roof.

The next morning, the German soldier appeared again, sober this time. He had brought some kitchen supplies with him to thank the housekeeper and her husband for their hospitality. Mrs Le Bideau was surprised to find him transformed into the model of polite military formality, although they spoke only briefly before he made his excuses and dashed off to another engagement. The spell of the Führer's birthday had been broken, it seemed. Now it was back to business as usual.

Ten days later, the Channel Islands were subjected to the greatest upheaval since the start of the Occupation as military command was transferred to a new infantry division, 319 ID. The complex hand-over process took place gradually, putting more pressure than ever on the islands' limited resources. With troops from two divisions overlapping for several months, extra properties were requisitioned to accommodate the thousands of new arrivals. For the islanders, it was a deeply trying time.

As resentment towards the Germans grew, people looked for small, symbolic ways to register resistance without being hauled away to prison. Some expressed their patriotic sentiments through concealed Union Jacks, which were banned under the rules of the Occupation. One man pulled down a strip of wallpaper in his living room, hung a flag up on the wall and then covered it over again, confident that if the Germans searched his house they wouldn't find anything, and thrilled by the thought that he was flying the king's flag under their noses. Another family kept the toilet used by the German soldiers they were billeting stocked with a mixture of red, white and blue packing paper from their tomato crates – although given the purpose it was being put to, this was a rather ambiguous gesture.

Sometimes, patriotic statements could even be made inadvertently. Dorothy Langlois, the founder of the Co-optimists dance troupe, went on stage one evening without realising that the outfit she had selected was a mixture of red, white and blue fabric. When the audience began hooting and cheering she couldn't work out why, until someone came up to her afterwards and asked how she had got away with such blatant defiance under the nose of the German censors. Over the next few days, Dorothy was repeatedly accosted by strangers in the street, who told her – despite her protests – how much she had inspired them.

Opportunistic pranks offered a popular form of resistance. In Guernsey, teenage girls would comb the beaches for the uniforms of swimming soldiers, moving them closer to the water's edge so that the tide would carry them out to sea. Many cooks and waiters took the opportunity to slyly spit in a German's soup when they were out of sight, but one man, who worked as a delivery driver for a large Guernsey off-licence, went a step further. Knowing that only the Germans were allowed to purchase spirits, whenever it was his turn to fill a crate of bottles with hard liquor, he would always empty his bladder into it first.

Arthur Rabet worked for the Jersey Water Board and had a farm adjacent to Handois Reservoir. The Germans built a pile of marker stones so that they could see how much the water level was rising and falling day by day, but every night after they were gone Arthur would move them so that they sat right at the edge of the water. The confused soldiers couldn't work out why, however much it rained, the reservoir never seemed to get any fuller.

Such minor gestures of defiance were reasonably safe since the chances of discovery were slim. Occasionally, though, islanders were provoked into more outright displays of hostility. One of the more legendary cases was that of Winifred Green, a waitress at the Royal Hotel in Guernsey. When a Swiss chef with Nazi sympathies greeted her with a cheerful 'Heil Hitler!' as he handed her some desserts, she responded memorably, 'To hell with Hitler for a rice pudding!' For this act of resistance, Mrs Green was sentenced to six months in prison in France, where she whiled away the time in her dank little cell embroidering 'Heil Churchill' onto a square of cloth she had ripped off her bedsheet.

Once a source of shame, serving time was now seen as a badge of honour. Before long, the limited number of cells on the islands were full, and guilty parties began being placed in a queue, sometimes waiting up to six months before their sentence could begin. But while the official punishment for low-level troublemaking was rarely more serious than a brief spell behind bars, sometimes matters could get tragically out of hand. John Harris and his wife Anne were friendly with Mr and Mrs Ferrers, an elderly couple who lived at the nearby Ommaroo Hotel. Mr Ferrers was a former High Court judge who had retired to Jersey for the balmy climate. One afternoon his wife was sitting in the hotel lobby admiring the sea view when she was accosted by an irate young officer. 'Madam, would you please remove that badge?' he demanded. 'It is offensive to the German forces.'

Mrs Ferrers looked down at her blouse, where she had unthinkingly pinned a little sapphire-and-ruby brooch in the shape of an RAF pilot's wings. Her son had given it to her after he flew his first solo flight and it was one of her most treasured possessions. 'No!' she replied, uncharacteristically defiant. 'It's my brooch, and I am proud to wear it.'

By this point, Mr Ferrers had joined his wife by the window. The German officer turned his attention to the old man. 'If the lady does not remove this badge now,' he told him, 'I will tear it from her myself.'

Mr Ferrers drew himself up to his full height. 'If you do any such thing,' he boomed, 'I will knock you down where you stand!'

That was all the provocation the officer needed. He whipped out his revolver and held it trained on Mr Ferrers as he violently tore the brooch from Mrs Ferrers' chest. A few minutes later, the feldgendarmerie arrived and the now apoplectic judge was hauled off for questioning.

He was handed a heavy prison sentence, to be served in France, and was allowed only a brief time to gather some clothes from the hotel before he was taken away to the harbour. Mr and Mrs Harris, who had heard about the incident, managed to slip him a tin of home-baked shortbread to take with him on the journey. 'He'll need that where he's going,' Leo's father told him grimly.

Mrs Ferrers, meanwhile, was utterly distraught, and her already frail health declined rapidly. Mrs Harris arranged a room for her at a nearby nursing home and spent many hours every day trying to keep the old lady's spirits up. But unable to get over the shock of the traumatic incident, and heartbroken at the loss of her husband, she never recovered. Within a matter of weeks, she was dead.

Young Leo, meanwhile, was doing his bit to resist the Occupation in his own way. He was an adept prankster, pouring sand into the fuel tanks of parked German cars – sugar would have been better, but it was rationed – and scouring the seats inside for anything worth stealing. With the help of his older brother Francis, who was a verita-ble Artful Dodger himself, Leo also indulged in more serious acts of larceny, grabbing unattended German bicycles off the street and ped-alling them home before their owners even knew they were missing.

Mr Harris, who delighted in any opportunity to frustrate the German troops, was an enthusiastic accomplice to his sons' endeav-ours. With his help, the lads would haul the bikes down into the cellar beneath the kitchen, where the three of them would strip them down for parts that could be traded on the black market. Tyres were particularly sought after, since most islanders had long since resorted to riding around on loops of hosepipe, which produced a distinctly bumpy ride.

With enough stolen bits and pieces filling up the cellar, it was even possible to assemble whole new vehicles. Mr Harris worked diligently, taking a saddle from one bike and a wheel from another, and carefully filing off the German Army's identification markings, then soldering and repainting until the bikes were completely unrec-ognisable. As he commented with satisfaction after one particularly complex job, 'There, its own mother wouldn't know it!'

For Mr Harris, the underground bike garage represented quite a serious risk, since if the authorities ever discovered it, the conse-quences would likely have been severe. His sons, though, were simply channelling their instinctive rebellious tendencies towards a more appealing target than their parents or teachers. Whether driven by patriotic duty or a simple delight in mischief-making, many chil-dren – particularly boys – spent a lot of their time looking for ways to wind up the German soldiers.

On Sark, six-year-old George Guille, along with his sister and a friend, tied a piece of copper wire between their garden gate and a tree on the far side of the road, watching with delight as a German soldier cycled right into it. The man flew over his handlebars and landed with a heavy thud, sending a cloud of dust up into the air. The three children made a run for it, but the angry German gave chase, pistol in hand. In the end, though, all that came of the incident was a severe tongue-lashing from George's parents, interspersed with a few untranslatable words from the soldier.

Such incidents, while relatively harmless, didn't exactly foster good relations with the German Army. Ambrose Sherwill – now no longer the island's leading politician but an amiable gardener frequently spotted in St Peter Port with a wheelbarrow full of home-grown produce – found that even his own boys were not exempt from the widespread troublemaking. A troop of soldiers often paraded on the lawn outside the Sherwill residence, Havelet House, a beautiful Georgian property with a first-floor balcony at the front. It was here that young Rollo Sherwill would stand and hurl gobbets of spit down on them, safe in the knowledge that their strict military discipline would require them to pretend to ignore it. One bald German officer presented a particularly tempting target, and the thrill of a direct hit on his shiny pate was hard to beat.

In Vazon Bay, to the north of the island, ten-year-old Doris Lihou had joined a gang of kids from school who spent their free time 'turfing' the open-topped jeeps that drove along the coast road. As the only girl in the group, Doris played the role of look-out, whistling whenever she saw a likely target. On her signal, the boys would rip up clumps of grass and earth and hurl them into the German vehicles, ready to scarper quickly if the driver decided to slam on the brakes.

In fact, several lads from Doris's school were involved in the first widespread act of resistance against the German authorities. In July 1941, Winston Churchill began adopting the distinctive hand gesture that would become his lasting trademark: the 'V' for victory sign. Across Occupied Europe, BBC broadcasts encouraged those living under the Nazi yoke to signal their spirit of resistance by displaying capital Vs wherever they could, in the hopes that this would boost the morale of civilians and damage that of the German troops. Soon men and women all over the Channel Islands were secretly chalking Vs on doors and walls, wearing V-shaped badges on the inside of their lapels, and even adopting the so-called V-knock when they called to visit friends: a sequence of three short raps followed by one long one, as in the opening notes of Beethoven's Symphony No. 5 – or 'V' in Roman numbering – which was played at the beginning of the BBC's overseas broadcasts.

Some islanders greeted the sight of each new V-sign with exhilaration. Pearl Smith was always thrilled to spot them around Cobo, little suspecting that her own aunt Mabel was one of the illicit graffiti artists. Others, though, feared that the campaign was simply antagonising the Germans. The Guernsey bailiff, Victor Carey, received a couple of sinister letters from the Feldkommandantur, threatening 'severe reprisals' if the perpetrators were not brought to justice. He acted swiftly, offering a £25 reward to the first informant whose tip-off led to a conviction. It was the most controversial act of his career, and proof for some islanders that he had become little more than a collaborator. Shortly afterwards, a satirical cartoon began doing the rounds showing Carey as Judas Iscariot, hanging from a V-shaped tree. The caption read: '£25 reVard'.

A number of islanders were arrested over the V-sign campaign, and among those rounded up for interrogation were seven of Doris's fellow students at the Castel School. Their young wartime headmaster, Peter Girard, spent as much of his time farming as he did teaching classes and frequently conducted assemblies still wearing his Wellington boots. Inexperienced in matters of crime and punishment, let alone politics, he was alarmed to receive a request from John Leale, the new head of the island's Controlling Committee, to hand over his students to the German authorities. Leale promised Girard that no harm would come to the boys, some of whom were as young as six, but warned him that if he refused to comply the Germans were threatening to arrest several prominent islanders as hostages.

Reluctantly, Girard agreed to send the children away for questioning. He was extremely relieved when they returned several hours later, unharmed and in good spirits. Apparently the Germans' main interrogation strategy had been to ply the boys with chocolate until they had solicited confessions of guilt. Their parents received a rather frightening visit from the plain-clothes field police that evening, but beyond that no action was taken.

Adults who were denounced to the authorities, however, couldn't rely on such lenient treatment. A handful of islanders convicted of 'V propaganda' were sent to prison on the Continent for sentences of up to a year, while others served shorter terms in the island gaols. But despite the punishments, the V-signs kept appearing, and tracking down every last vandal seemed impossible. In fact, several members of the Guernsey police force, far from apprehending the culprits, were now spending their late-night patrols chalking V-signs of their own.

Unable to put a stop to the rash of Allied propaganda, the Germans came up with a more ingenious strategy: they adopted the Vs as their own, adding laurel leaves underneath them and insisting that the letter stood for the German word 'Viktoria'. Mrs Le Bideau was impressed. 'Beautifully drawn V's are made on practically every car, house or shed that they are using,' she wrote. 'Good clear mathematically correct V's, evidently drawn with compasses, and neat conventional laurel wreaths finish the design.' If nothing else, the old lady observed, the German Vs proved they took pride in their handiwork, certainly compared to the slapdash efforts of the original local vandals.

Whether troublemaking by the children of the Channel Islands was influenced more by genuine resentment or simple mischievousness, as the Occupation went on they had good cause to dislike the Germans as the impact on their schooling became increasingly acute. From the beginning, education had been a challenge. The majority of professional teachers had departed on the evacuation ships, leaving those with little training or experience to step up to ensure that the children who remained didn't miss out entirely on their learning. The situation was chaotic and improvised – when Doris Lihou first reported to the Castel School, having missed the evacuation boats due to chickenpox, she had joined students from over a dozen other schools dotted around Guernsey.

Resources were limited, and gradually ran out almost completely. The only ink available was distinctly watery, with dark flecks floating around in the bottom of the pot, and with no exercise books, one teacher was reduced to cutting up a roll of wallpaper and threading it with string, encouraging his students to write on both the white and the patterned side. Since large school buildings were frequently requisitioned by the authorities, classes were often forced to relocate to less suitable locations – a tea room, a church, or even, in the case of Doris and her friends, an abandoned greenhouse. One class was moved six times in an eighteen-month period.

Worst of all, though, was the introduction of German language classes. At first these were voluntary but they were later made a compulsory part of the curriculum, with prizes offered to the students who made the best progress. Leo Harris found his instinctive hostility towards the occupiers challenged when a very pretty young nurse in a swastika-marked blouse arrived to teach his class German. She sang beautiful traditional hunting songs during their lessons and always brought apples to give out to the most promising students, but despite his crush Leo dreaded the thought of being singled out for praise by the enemy, so he made sure to pay as little attention as possible.

Another Jersey boy, Pat Troy, took a different approach. He studied hard in his German lessons, ending up as top of the class. As a result, he was summoned to the Feldkommandantur to receive a prize, which he accepted politely. As soon as he had left the grounds, however, he promptly tossed it back over the wall.

Pat was, as it happens, involved in illegal activities of his own as a member of an underground organisation: the 11th Jersey Scout Troop. The Scouts had been banned by the Germans early in 1941 – along with another 'paramilitary' organisation, the Salvation

Army – but a number of troops had continued to meet in secret, forsaking their uniforms and badges but otherwise going on pretty much as usual. They had even found a way of performing the traditional scouting salute without attracting attention: instead of raising three fingers up in front of them, they would discreetly tap them on their thighs.

Pat's troop met every Thursday afternoon at a little hut in the garden of one of their teenaged patrol leaders, John Painter. They kept meticulous logs and registers of every meeting, working their way through the pre-war scouting manuals and making a note of the badges earned by each boy, even though they couldn't actually receive them.

The lads learned about knots and knives, how to find dry wood to start fires, orienteering, tracking, and other traditional scouting activities. They even went on camp – one of their number, Arthur Ruez, had an uncle with a farm in the countryside who let them stay in the hayloft of the barn where he kept his cattle. It was a fairly remote area, so on their daily excursions into the nearby valley they were able to light campfires, sing songs and practise their outdoor skills, and as far as they knew, the Germans were none the wiser.

One day, though, the boys arrived at school to find a worrying rumour doing the rounds. The Painters' house had been raided. John's father Clarence and his elder brother Peter – a troop leader himself – had been arrested after a camera and an antique pistol were found under the floorboards. Fortunately, the authorities hadn't searched the hut in the garden where all the Scout records were kept, listing the names of every boy in the group, along with their flags and other paraphernalia.

The troop decided to lie low for a couple of weeks, but eventually re-formed at a new base: the Victoria College cricket pavilion. Clarence and John Painter, meanwhile, were transferred to Cherche-Midi prison in Paris, and then to a labour camp in Dietzdorf, where they were put to work making aeroplane parts.

In time, the Painters were moved to Gross-Rosen concentration camp in lower Silesia, joining almost a hundred thousand prisoners, most of them Jews. The inmates were forced to labour in a nearby granite quarry, performing back-breaking work in inhuman conditions. After four months at Gross-Rosen, Peter fell prey to pneumonia and died in his father's arms. He was only twenty years old.

Clarence Painter lasted another two and half months after the death of his son. In the end, it was the journey to the concentration camp at Dora-Mittelbau that proved too much for him. Tens of thousands of prisoners from Gross-Rosen were loaded into open-top goods wagons, crammed in a hundred to each. They had no coats or blankets to protect them from the rain and snow, no food or water, not even the space to lie down. When the prisoners died en route, the corpses were piled up at one end of the wagon, stripped naked by others desperate for a little more warmth.

On the third day of the journey, Clarence Painter was added to the pile. When they reached the camp, his body was taken straight to the crematorium.

CHAPTER FIFTEEN

CAUGHT RED-HANDED

Not all crimes against the regime were acts of resistance. Under the rules of the Occupation, farmers were required to allocate a certain percentage of what they produced to the Germans, and inspections were carried out frequently to ensure that the Army was getting its share. But many islanders found ways to cheat the system. At one farm in Jersey, the German inspector would always be greeted with a generous tankard of cider when he came to collect what was due. When he inevitably dozed off in the afternoon, the farmer would quietly unload some of the wheat he had piled into the truck, covering it over with straw before his sozzled visitor roused himself for the return journey.

Many farmers, meanwhile, underreported the number of piglets born when a mother sow gave birth, shuffling the extras off to a neighbour's farm when they knew the inspectors were on their way. Others tried to hide unregistered animals out of sight. Sark farmer Philip Hamon was asked by a German inspector how many swines he owned. 'Oh, no swines,' he replied confidently. But a few minutes later an unmistakable oinking sound began coming from the nearby stables. 'You said no swines!' the German shouted angrily, ready to report Philip for deliberately deceiving the authorities. All Philip could think of was to play dumb. 'That's not a swine,' he said, 'it's a pig.' Remarkably, the inspector didn't take the matter any further.

Even dead animals could land islanders in hot water, as the

discovery of a whole carcass on private property was a pretty sure indication that it had been come by illegally. One Guernseywoman, who had a pig hanging up in the bedroom, was horrified when the police arrived to search her property. She hastily rushed upstairs, threw the carcass in her bed and drew the covers over it, telling the search party that her aunt was very ill and needed to rest. They glanced briefly at the bulging shape before nodding sympathetically and moving on to the next room.

A Jersey farmer, meanwhile, found himself in something of a pickle when a German unit set up camp in his fields. He had an illegal pig ready for slaughter, but didn't see how he could get the animal away for butchering without being discovered. In desperation, he got in touch with a former butcher, Alf Cornish, who told him he would kill the pig himself and then find a means of smuggling the meat away.

A few days later, a horse-drawn wagon pulled up outside the farm, and out got four men in the distinctive black garments of undertakers. 'Where is the deceased?' one of them asked the farmer sombrely. It took him a moment to realise that it was Alf, but once he did he wasted no time. 'This way,' he said, leading the little party through the house to the back yard, where the pig was being kept. They stripped off their formal attire and put on aprons instead, before setting to their gruesome task, killing and butchering the animal in record time. Then they went back to the wagon and fetched an empty coffin, bringing it out to the yard and packing it with the slabs of meat. Soon they were on the road again, where the German guards bowed their heads respectfully and sent them on their way.

Typically, illegal slaughtering would take place in the dead of night. The mischievous water-board worker Arthur Rabet had a pair of illegal pigs concealed in a secret underground sty at the back of his farm. He had dug the hole for the structure himself, walling it with sheets of corrugated iron and then covering the roof with earth. Access was by a trap door in the adjacent stable, which was hidden under a layer of straw.

When the time came for the pigs to be slaughtered, Arthur made an arrangement with a local carpenter, Mr De Caux, who wanted to buy the meat of one of the animals and said he would bring someone with him to kill and butcher them both. Late one night, Arthur's six-year-old son David was surprised to see these two figures tramping over the fields towards the farm – they didn't dare travel by road for fear of encountering a German patrol. When his father came out of the house to meet them, David tagged along too, and the four of them proceeded together to the secret sty. There, David watched with grim fascination as the tall, strong man whom Mr De Caux had brought with him took hold of one of the animals, dragged it roughly out of the sty and slit its throat. The pig squealed as the blood ran out of its body, soaking into the straw that Arthur had laid on the stable floor. In less than a minute it was dead, and the butcher went to fetch the second animal. Little David was still watching, his eyes wide with astonishment.

After Mr De Caux and his burly friend had departed, Arthur salted what was left of the pig he had decided to keep, and stored it in a barrel. Between them, he and his wife made sure to use every last piece of the carcass, mincing the liver into a pâté with some onion and garlic and boiling the head down into brawn, which was served on bread with a little parsley. Mrs Rabet was terrified that the illegal meat would be discovered by the Germans, but somehow they always managed to avoid getting found out. On one occasion, she was just starting to prepare a leg of pork for dinner when a couple of soldiers barged into the house. Fortunately, David's nanny Doreen was a quick thinker. She bundled the joint up in a tea-towel, marched straight out of the scullery door and hid it in a hedge while the Germans began searching the kitchen.

Slaughtering pigs without attracting attention was difficult enough given the noise they made, but it was nothing compared to the effort involved in sourcing black-market beef. Guernsey tomato farmer Stanley Lihou, whose daughter Doris played the role of look-out for the group of kids who enjoyed 'turfing' German vehicles around

Crowds gather in St Helier to register for evacuation. (Société Jersiaise Photographic Archive)

Guernsey families prepare to leave for England. (Occupation Archive)

A white cross is painted in St Helier's Royal Square. (Jersey Heritage)

Bomb-damaged tomato truck in St Peter Port. (Occupation Archive)

The formal surrender at Jersey Airport. (Société Jersiaise Photographic Archive)

Alexander Coutanche.
(Getty Images)

Ambrose Sherwill.
(Guernsey Archives)

Sybil Hathaway.
(Bundesarchiv)

Hubert Nicolle.
(Occupation Archive)

Louisa Gould.
(Jersey Heritage)

Harold Le Druillenec.
(Jersey Heritage)

Bob Le Sueur.
(Jersey Heritage)

Phyllis Baker.
(Courtesy of Chrysta Rang)

Ruth Leadbeater.
(Guernsey Archives)

Leo Harris.
(Jersey Heritage)

Francis Harris.
(Jersey Heritage)

Michael Ginns.
(Author's collection)

Major Lanz and driver. (Imperial War Museum)

Count von Schmettow with some of his troops. (Société Jersiaise Photographic Archive)

Dame Sybil with German guest. (Bundesarchiv)

Baron von Aufsess. (Imperial War Museum)

Werner Rang in Normandy, 1941. (Courtesy of Chrysta Rang)

If upon your friendly face,
I've sometimes raised a smile,
I thank my stars that I was born,
With such a funny dial.

Sincerely Yours,
Cyd Gardner

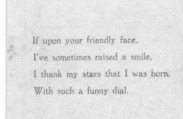

The Lyric Theatre company – Cyd Gardner (centre) and, clockwise: the Brache sisters
and their father, Rex Priaulx; Gwen Smith; Pearl Smith; Wilf Shirvell;
Eric Snelling; Peter Campbell; Jessie Mariette; Douglas Luckie; Gertie Duquemin.
(German Occupation Museum; Island Archives)

A German military band marches through St Peter Port. (Imperial War Museum)

A German soldier cycles in the rain. (Société Jersiaise Photographic Archive)

Jersey's Forum Cinema showing the propaganda film *Sieg im Westen*. (Société Jersiaise Photographic Archive)

A sentry at Guernsey's Castle Cornet. (Getty Images)

Shopping in St Peter Port. (Bundesarchiv)

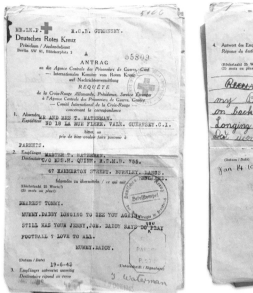

Red Cross message from Mr and Mrs Waterman to their son Tom in England, with his handwritten reply on the reverse. (Courtesy of Tom Waterman)

Letter from escaped OT worker Piotr Bokatenko to the Le Flem family. (Jersey Heritage)

The SS *Vega* docks in Guernsey. (Imperial War Museum)

Unloading the SS *Vega* in St Helier. (International Committee of the Red Cross)

Inspecting the Red Cross parcels in St Helier. (International Committee of the Red Cross)

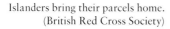

Women and children pick up their parcels at Le Riches Stores. (Imperial War Museum)

Islanders bring their parcels home. (British Red Cross Society)

Liberation Day crowds in St Peter Port.
(Occupation Archive)

Flags and bunting for Liberation Day.
(Imperial War Museum)

The Tommies arrive in Jersey.
(Getty Images)

Local people welcome the
Tommies in St Peter Port.
(German Occupation Museum)

German soldiers depart as
prisoners of war. (Alamy)

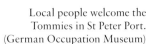

Vazon Bay, was involved in a local gang of his own: a group of men who were called on to assist when one of the farmers was planning an illegal cattle-killing. Stanley's job was to help round up the animals that were to be slaughtered and guide them, in the dead of night, to a remote location where the deed would actually take place. For every killing he participated in he was paid with a proportion of the meat, which he would either feed to his family or trade with friends and neighbours.

In the early autumn of 1941, after one of his late-night excursions, Stanley was rewarded with a generous side of beef, which he hung up behind a curtain on the landing of his house on Rue des Goddards. The whole operation had gone smoothly, and the Germans were none the wiser. But a week or so later, a group of men from the nearby neighbourhood of King's Mills who were involved in the same line of work got themselves into something of a jam. They were leading two young cows and a bull along the road when the heifers turned a corner and the male, losing sight of them, suddenly grew distressed. The men did their best to calm the animal, but for all their efforts he continued to bellow angrily, snorting and lowering his head to the ground as if he was about to charge.

Rather than risk the bull unleashing his fury on them – or worse, attracting the attention of a German patrol – the men decided to slaughter him then and there by the roadside. When the deed was done they bundled the bloody carcass into a tomato truck and drove off to the place they had originally earmarked for the killing, where a butcher was waiting to carve it up for them. In their haste, nobody noticed that the truck was leaking blood all the way, leaving a trail of evidence for the Germans to discover in the morning.

The next day, Doris went to school as normal, but on her way home in the afternoon she found the road blocked off with barbed wire while the local police conducted a house-to-house search. By the time she was allowed through the barricade, the side of beef hanging on the landing had already been discovered.

Doris walked straight through the house to the field out back, where her mother, Amy, was watching anxiously as a local policeman, Sergeant Le Cocq, supervised a thorough search of her husband's greenhouse, ordering his men to dig up every square inch of earth in search of further evidence. A few German Feldpolizei stood by, quietly keeping an eye on proceedings.

When Stanley arrived home from work that evening, he was furious. 'What are you doing to my greenhouse?' he asked the sergeant angrily. 'There's nothing in *there*!'

'I'm sorry, Stan,' Le Cocq replied. 'I'm just doing my job.'

Anyone could tell just by looking at the meat hanging on the landing that it hadn't come from the previous night's killing, but the police – both local and German – thought that Stanley might know who had been involved. They were right, he knew the lads well – but there was no way he was going to give their names to the Germans.

As the sun began to set that evening, the police abandoned their search of the greenhouse, but when they left they took Stanley and Amy Lihou with them. Doris, along with her brothers John and Richard, was entrusted to the care of their elder sister Blanche. To a girl of ten, the sight of her parents being hauled away for questioning was terrifying, and for the next three days, while they underwent a thorough interrogation at the police station, she wouldn't so much as take a bite of the food that Blanche dutifully prepared for her.

When Amy finally returned home, Doris began eating again. That night, she crept into her mother's bed, cuddling up to her and praying that they would never again be separated.

Stanley was sentenced to twenty-one months in prison, and was shipped away to France before Doris could even say goodbye to him. It was a harsh penalty, far in excess of the usual punishment for possession of black-market goods, but by refusing to give up the names of any of his fellow criminals he had been branded an enemy of the Third Reich. Amy was left to look after the children alone, relying on the meagre wages earned by Blanche, a trainee milliner at De La Mare's, and John, an apprentice carpenter, and sometimes selling the family furniture to buy food.

A few months later, John came home from his carpentry workshop complaining of a sore throat. His mother sent him to bed to sleep it off, but he awoke the next morning feeling much worse. He was drowsy, running a high fever, and his neck was badly swollen. There was a thin grey film covering the back of his throat and it was giving off a terrible smell. Amy sent Blanche next door to use the neighbour's phone to call a doctor, waiting anxiously by John's bedside for help to arrive.

It was half past six before the doctor finally turned up at the door and dragged his push bike into the hallway. He had been on the road since early morning and looked to be on the verge of collapse himself. 'Where's the patient?' he asked Amy wearily.

'He's in bed upstairs,' she replied.

The doctor stood on the bottom step with one hand on the banister. He was about to start up the stairs when he stopped and sniffed the air. 'The boy's got quinsy,' he declared.

'Don't you even need to examine him?' Amy asked.

The doctor shook his head. 'I can tell from the smell. Give him plenty of rest and a hot compress around the neck and it'll soon go down.' He took his bike and cycled away.

Amy wanted to stop him, but she felt powerless. If only her husband were here, she thought. She knew Stanley would have insisted on a proper examination.

That night, Amy lit the fire in John's room, and everyone took turns heating wet towels to place around his neck while she prepared dinner in the kitchen downstairs. He wouldn't eat but he did drink some water. When it came time to sleep, Richard gave up his bed in the room he and John shared so that his mother could keep an eye on him. As they all settled in for the night John seemed to have improved a little, and although Amy didn't get any sleep, she felt calmer than she had done all day.

In the early hours of the morning, Doris woke up and crept into the room, anxious to know how her brother was doing. 'He's sleeping,' her mother whispered. 'Here, get in with me.' Doris crawled into the bed with her and they hugged each other close.

A few minutes later, there was a rustling from John's side of the room. Amy looked over anxiously. In the dim light of a flickering candle, his tall figure was clearly visible, rising from the bed.

'It's all right, mum, I'm only going for a pee,' said John, as he leant over and drew the potty out from under the bed. When he had finished, he clambered back under the covers. But after a few seconds of silence he suddenly began coughing and spluttering.

Amy rushed over to find her son gasping for breath. The swelling around his neck had burst, and he was drowning in the fluids that were seeping out of it. She barely had time to cradle his head in her arms before the life drained out of him altogether.

Doris followed her mother over to John's bed, looking down at her brother's lifeless face. Then Amy started to scream. '*Blanche!*' she yelled. '*Richard!*' Soon the whole family was gathered by the bedside.

The first light of dawn was already beginning to creep over the horizon, but until the curfew lifted there was nothing that anybody could do. They couldn't even call the undertaker to arrange for them to come and fetch the body. So instead the family all just sat up together in silence, waiting for the new day. Amy was eerily quiet, but amid her grief a single thought kept going round and round in her mind: if only Stanley had been here, this would never have happened.

Later that morning, Doris was sent to stay with the neighbours while the rest of the family began making arrangements for the funeral. John's body was laid out in the living room so that family and friends could come and pay their respects, and a message was sent over to France informing Stanley about his son's death. Amy, meanwhile, was becoming more and more convinced that the doctor had misdiagnosed John's condition. A number of cases of diphtheria had recently cropped up in the neighbourhood, and the symptoms she heard described sounded distinctly similar to his illness.

Stanley was brought over from France for the funeral, arriving at the house the night before, handcuffed to a policeman. He was only allowed to stay for a few moments – enough time to give his wife a quick hug – before he was taken away to the cells again.

The next day, at Cobo Church, he was uncuffed just long enough to see his son buried, and then he was whisked back to France. Amy and the children returned to a house that was now missing two of its inhabitants. With their mother consumed with grief, Doris and Richard once again looked to their older sister Blanche to hold the family together.

The loss of John's income as an apprentice carpenter only made the household economy even harder, and increasingly the family struggled to find enough food. Doris began going out gleaning in the fields after the official harvest was complete, collecting stray ears of corn in a bucket, and pulling up headless stumps of broccoli.

By the time Christmas came around, Amy had nothing to serve for a festive meal. But one night she was sitting up in the kitchen with the rest of the family when a couple of men appeared outside the window.

'Wait here,' Amy told her children, rising to go and see what they wanted.

A few minutes later she returned, clutching a large plucked goose in her arms.

The men were from the killing gang whose names Stanley had refused to divulge. This was their way of saying thank you.

CHAPTER SIXTEEN

A NEW ARRIVAL

Around the time Stanley Lihou left Guernsey to serve his prison sentence in France, a young Army medic by the name of Werner Rang was travelling in the opposite direction. With German forces now fighting a war on two fronts, following the invasion of Russia ('Operation Barbarossa') in June, Hitler had decided it was only a matter of time before Britain attempted to retake the Channel Islands. On 20 October, he ordered a massive military fortification programme, along with a major new influx of personnel. The goal was to increase the size of the garrison to almost thirty-seven thousand men, making 319 ID the largest infantry division in the entire German Army. Among the troops earmarked for the task was Werner's unit, the 4th Company of Infantry Regiment 583.

At twenty-one, Werner had been in the German Army for a little over two years, and had seen frontline action during the battle for France the previous spring. Newly promoted to lance corporal, he arrived in Guernsey following a six-month tour of duty in Normandy, serving as part of the Army of Occupation there.

Werner had at least heard of the Channel Islands, which was more than could be said for most of his comrades, but until he arrived in St Peter Port on a crisp autumn day in 1941, he had no idea what to expect of them. The sight of the town's fine, clean buildings, shining in the bright afternoon sun, was enough to put a smile on his face. It had been a blissfully calm journey across a clear blue sea, and the young soldiers had been accompanied by a pod of dolphins surfing in their wake. They arrived in good spirits, and toasted their new 'holiday posting' with a tot of whisky at the Channel Islands Hotel. 'I'm going to write and thank the Führer for sending us here!' Werner joked to his best friend, Fritz Imke, a young man from Frankfurt who had served with him throughout his Army career.

Certainly, compared to France, Guernsey was a very cushy posting. The shops might be boarded up, but the town was clean and well kept compared to those in Normandy, which had already descended into squalor. When he wasn't practising on mock casualties at the local German hospital – where regular rehearsals for the anticipated British invasion were held – Werner spent his time with Fritz, strolling the charming cobbled streets, taking in the odd movie at the island's cinemas, and playing their accordions together in the regimental band.

For Werner, the most striking contrast between France and Guernsey was that in his new posting he was able to relax. In France, he had always felt like a soldier in enemy territory, guarding himself against the possibility of a random attack. But resistance in the Channel Islands rarely went beyond the odd bit of subversive graffiti, and relations between occupiers and occupied varied from, at worst, cool politeness to, at best, genuine friendship. As he cycled around the island, with a red cross on his bike to indicate his medical profession, Werner never felt in any danger.

As one of the company medics, it was Werner's responsibility to look after not only the health of the soldiers but those with whom they had intimate physical contact. Both St Helier and St Peter Port were home to officially sanctioned *Freudenhäuser* – 'houses of pleasure' – staffed by French prostitutes shipped into the islands for the express purpose of keeping the troops happy. The Army did their best to look out for the welfare of these women, even having them classed officially as 'heavy labourers' – a fact that was regarded with great amusement by the civilian population – in order to justify granting them enhanced rations.

Once a week, Werner was responsible for visiting a brothel that had recently opened in Hauteville, a smart neighbourhood of St Peter Port. He would arrive at 10 p.m. on the dot, just in time to see the last of the day's clients being turfed out of the building, and examine the women one by one for any signs of venereal disease, before signing them off as fit to carry on working. Despite being surrounded by half a dozen young women in various stages of undress, Werner told himself that he was there in an official capacity, and mercifully his patients conducted themselves with such an air of cool, polite professionalism that the young man was spared any potential embarrassment.

It wasn't long before Werner made his first friends among the islanders. He was billeted in a house called Hazeleigh, in the parish of St Peter, not far from the westernmost tip of the island. A large shed in the garden had been converted into a makeshift kitchen, where a local man called Harold Blondel was employed peeling potatoes and washing the dishes. Harold was a new father and his wife Elaine would often bring their little baby to the house after work. They lived in a small cottage with Elaine's parents and her younger brother Tom, and now – with an extra mouth to feed – they were struggling more than ever.

Werner did his best to help, slipping Harold the odd loaf of bread or some cigarettes that he could trade for supplies. Before long, he was paying Elaine's mother to do his laundry every week. Her husband would pick it up from Hazeleigh on his milk round, and drop it back the following morning. Werner also visited the cottage himself now and then, and he always brought his accordion with him. Accompanied by Elaine on the piano, he would play well past curfew, surrounded by the whole Blondel clan. Far away from home, he felt like he had found a second family.

As the Occupation wore on, many German soldiers started forming real friendships with the locals. Mrs Le Bideau already had two young men billeted in her house when a third arrived asking if she would help him improve his English. The old lady soon became very fond of her new pupil, Lieutenant Kirschner. He was a keen reader, with a passion for the novels of Rudyard Kipling and Robert Louis

Stevenson. While she patiently schooled him in the Latin origins of various English words, he began teaching her German ones.

When Christmas came, Lieutenant Kirschner presented Mrs Le Bideau with a beautiful edition of Grimm's fairy tales, along with a loaf of traditional German bread. 'Prussian or not, I very nearly embraced him,' she wrote in her diary. She was thrilled with the book, and took to walking about town with it, stopping random soldiers in the street and begging their assistance in translating particularly difficult passages. Soon, she was expanding her library, visiting the German bookshop in St Peter Port, a place few islanders had cause to enter. 'It is quite exciting,' she wrote. 'The men simply crowd in and one hears "Heil Hitler!" on all sides.'

With Lieutenant Kirschner, Mrs Le Bideau had entered into a genuine cultural exchange, in which patriotic loyalty gave way in the face of shared humanity. As he commented during one of their lessons, 'We shall all be friends in heaven.' But the friendship wasn't to last. Soon after Christmas, Kirschner was one of a number of Channel Island troops transferred to the Russian Front, as Operation Barbarossa ground to a wintry halt and began swallowing men's lives by the thousands.

That Christmas, while the local people celebrated the entry of the United States into the war, the Germans stationed in the Channel Islands were far more concerned with what was happening in Russia. As much as they tried to enjoy the festivities, the new year that lay ahead of them looked bleak. The war in the East wasn't going well, and it was looking increasingly likely that their idyllic island life wouldn't last for ever. Sooner or later, they were going to be sent out East, to a far less hospitable – and far more dangerous – theatre of operations.

Among the German soldiers, the Eastern Front was a sensitive subject, and at least one Guernseyman found himself in hot water for making light of it. He was pushing an old horse and cart up a hill when a soldier remarked sardonically, 'Your horse is kaput!' 'Yeah,' he laughed, 'just like your army in Russia.' It was a joke that saw him locked up for the rest of the war.

In fact, the threat of the war in the East was so terrifying that it could drive men to distraction. One night, Guernsey couple Bill and Miriam Mahy were roused by a crashing noise coming from their greenhouse. When they got up to investigate they found a young soldier in a state of utter derangement, bellowing in German as he hurled rocks and stones through the panes of glass. They later learned that he had just received a transfer to the Eastern Front and had suffered a breakdown as a result.

When Werner Rang's best friend Fritz Imke was informed of his own imminent departure for Russia, he also took the news badly. Gone was the old, cheerful Fritz who delighted in playing the accordion for the regimental band. Werner watched sadly as his comrade withdrew into himself, forsaking the company of his old friends.

A few days after Christmas, Werner was attending a party in the local school hall at Pleinmont. Fritz had been unable to make it since he was slated for switchboard duty in the guard room. When the celebrations finally began to wind down at the end of the night, Werner returned to his billet and staggered upstairs to the room that he and Fritz shared on the first floor. But as he opened the door to go inside he froze on the spot. Slumped over one of the beds was Fritz, surrounded by a dark pool of blood. In his right hand was his Army-issue pistol.

Werner knelt down to feel for a pulse, but he already knew it was hopeless. Doing his best to shut out his own feelings, he went downstairs and telephoned a medical officer to arrange for the death to be certified. The next day he was summoned to a military court to give evidence into the circumstances surrounding Fritz's suicide.

When all the paperwork was concluded, the body was released for burial. Since he had taken his own life, Fritz wasn't entitled to a military funeral, but his friends did their best to give him a proper send-off. Werner marched alongside the coffin all the way to the cemetery, on the far side of the island, where Lieutenant Karl Schädel, who had been a vicar before the war, drew a little cross out from under his uniform and performed a brief graveside service.

Not long after, Werner received his own transfer orders. He had been expecting the news and was already resigned to his fate, but when he told his superior officer, Dr Pfeiffer, that he was due to leave for Russia, the other man was appalled. 'You can't possibly go!' he exclaimed.

'My name is on the list,' Werner shrugged. 'I don't have any alternative.'

'We'll see about that!' declared Pfeiffer, setting off at once for the Kommandantur. A few hours later he returned in much better spirits. 'Let's celebrate with a drink,' he told Werner. 'You aren't going to the East. Your name has been crossed out!'

Werner thanked the doctor profusely, aware that he had probably saved his life. But his relief was mingled with regret. He couldn't help thinking about Fritz, and wishing that someone had stepped in to save him as well.

While Werner remained in Guernsey, others continued to be sent out East, many of them never to return. In January 1942, Dr Albrecht Lanz, the first German commandant of the Channel Islands, died in Smolensk of injuries sustained on the battlefield. Not long after, Lieutenant Kirschner, the polite young man who had been teaching Mrs Le Bideau German, met the same fate.

When she heard the news, the old lady was deeply upset. 'It makes me feel miserable, he was so nice and kind,' she wrote. 'He was the only son and his mother was a widow.'

Grief was a lingua franca shared by occupiers and occupied alike. When 'Buster' Beaumont, the son of Dame Sybil of Sark, was killed by a German bomb that hit his hotel in Liverpool, the news reached the Channel Islands via the American consulate in Berlin. Colonel von Schmettow travelled to Sark personally to offer his condolences, telling Sybil, 'Mothers of all nations grieve in the same way for their sons.' She never forgot the kind gesture, and later, when von Schmettow's son was killed on the Russian Front, she repaid his thoughtful words with a heartfelt message of her own.

The Germans certainly knew how it felt to fear for the safety of their loved ones. In March 1942, Guernsey schoolgirl Betty Jagou was sitting with her family on the beach at Pembroke Bay when they were approached by a German soldier called Willi. The young man was in a terrible state, having learned that the RAF had begun bombing his home town of Essen, where his mother, wife and two children all lived. Communication had been entirely cut off and for all he knew his whole family might already be dead. Betty's parents told Willi he was more than welcome to sit with them, and in his anxious state he clung to the foreign family like a life raft.

Not that the islanders were safe from air attacks themselves. The RAF would periodically send planes over the islands to target German installations, as well as dropping bombs in the harbours to disrupt shipping. 'British planes have been horribly active this week,' Mrs Le Bideau wrote in her diary one evening. 'Terrible bangs and explosions have occurred two or three times just as the dark was coming on. No human being in possession of his senses could listen to the horrors without feeling afraid.'

Some islanders, indeed, were almost paralysed by fear. Guernsey teenager Margaret Chalker had to cycle past the White Rock on her way to school every morning. She had seen British planes zooming in to bomb the boats that were moored there, and the German anti-aircraft guns opening up their terrifying volley of shells in response. One time, the noise of the explosions was just too much for her. She threw her bike down at the side of the road and ran up to the nearest house, flinging open the front door and cowering in the hallway until the raid was over. For years afterwards, Margaret was so traumatised by her experiences that she couldn't walk down a street that had no houses on it.

The terror of the RAF raids formed a bond of sympathy between the islanders and the German soldiers. After all, when the bombs rained down from the skies, friend and foe were caught up in it together. Jerseywoman Tina Du Feu was taking a bowl of scraps out to the yard to feed her rabbits one day when a piece of shrapnel whizzed down in front of her, passing straight through the bowl and embedding itself in the concrete floor. As she gazed in astonishment at the little hole that had just been blasted through her crockery, she couldn't help thinking that if she had taken one more step forward it would have been her head and not the bowl that was hit. She kept that little bit of shrapnel on her mantelpiece, as a souvenir of her alarmingly close shave.

When Luftwaffe fighters engaged the RAF bombers, the ensuing dogfights fought above the skies of the islands would draw crowds, both local and German. Teenager Esther Hamon lived in Little Sark, a large peninsula at the southernmost tip of the island accessed by a narrow, vertiginous ridge known as La Coupée. One day, she heard a commotion among the troops stationed at a nearby bunker. She could hear them triumphantly shouting, *'Englisch kaput!'* and realised that a plane must have been shot down over the sea. Half an hour later, though, she ran into one of the soldiers, who was wearing a distinctly sour expression. 'You will be happy,' he told her. 'It was a German plane, not an English one.'

'I'm not happy at all,' Esther replied sharply. 'A man's life is gone. He had a mother and a father, and perhaps a wife and children, and they will all be very unhappy.'

From the look on the man's face, she could tell that her words had embarrassed him, especially after the way he and his friends had celebrated when they thought it was one of her countrymen who had died.

CHAPTER SEVENTEEN

'SUBHUMANS'

Hitler's intention was to make the Channel Islands 'an impregnable fortress', the foremost stronghold in a 1,600-mile Atlantic Wall that was to stretch all the way from Norway to Spain. The construction project, which involved digging vast networks of tunnels, as well as building bunkers, observation towers and gun batteries, was on a scale never before seen on the islands. To perform the work, more than ten thousand foreign workers were shipped in under the auspices of the Organisation Todt, an engineering outfit that, following the death of its original eponymous founder, had fallen under the direct control of the Führer's chief architect, Albert Speer.

While the OT was officially a civilian organisation, its supervisors were typically ardent Nazis, wore pseudo-military khaki uniforms with bright red swastika armbands, and had a reputation for brutality bordering on sadism. The workers they employed were a mixture of skilled volunteers, paid conscripts and slaves, taken from all over the conquered nations of Europe, some of them as young as fourteen. Among their number were a significant number of Russian and Ukrainian workers, both civilians and prisoners of war, brought from the Eastern Front. As far as the Nazis were concerned, the Slavic races were '*Untermenschen*' ('subhumans'), and these unfortunate souls were treated accordingly.

Most islanders reacted with astonishment at their first sight of the army of forced labourers, 'brought over like so many head of cattle', as Mrs Le Bideau observed in her diary. One morning the old lady was walking through Hauteville when she encountered a middle-aged Frenchman who was now working for the OT. He told her that he had been plucked off the streets of Paris, with nothing more than the clothes on his back and no way of telling his family what had happened. 'It was almost impossible to believe that such a thing could be true,' the old lady wrote. 'Slaves were carried off in darkest Africa as we all know, but to think of people being carted about the country nowadays as if they were bales of goods is stretching one's power of imagination to the utmost.'

Mrs Le Bideau did her best to cheer the poor man up by pointing out the house that Victor Hugo had lived in during his fifteen-year stay in Guernsey. But not everyone greeted the new arrivals with kindness. 'They are the scum of the continent and it is sad to see Guernsey overrun by such filthy undesirables,' wrote Hauteville resident Ruth Ozanne in her diary. 'It is rather a time of terror over here just now with this big element of the riffraff of Europe, every conceivable race and colour, all looking desperate and hopeless.'

To some islanders, the wretched OT workers were convenient scapegoats. In March 1942, when several of Guernsey's food depots were raided, Mrs Ozanne was convinced it must have been the work of the forced labourers. In fact the culprits were members of the island police force and seventeen of them soon found themselves being tried in front of the Feldkommandantur's Prince Oettingen-Wallerstein. Ambrose Sherwill, who now had plenty of time on his hands, offered to represent them, pleading mitigation on the grounds that at least one of the men was owed money by the German authorities. There was also some question about the legality of their confessions. One man claimed he had been told he would be shot unless he signed a document placed in front of him, which he couldn't read as it was written in German. Nonetheless, the men were found guilty and sent to France to serve out their sentences.

The forced labourers presented a truly pathetic sight, with little more than rags covering their emaciated bodies, and scraps of rubber strapped around their feet in place of shoes. When a group of French and Spanish workers was brought to live in the empty house that adjoined Les Pieux Hotel, Pearl Smith couldn't help feeling sorry for them. She watched every lunchtime as a truck rolled up, and metal rubbish bins filled with watery cabbage soup were lowered to the ground, while the labourers queued with broken old cups to get what sustenance they could. One man was seen drinking his soup from an old bowler hat, a remnant of the old life he had been torn away from.

Pearl was shocked at the way the OT overseers treated the workers, shoving them into line and herding them around as if they were animals. But some islanders witnessed even worse treatment. Jersey teenager Maurice Green was out picking blackberries with his little sister when they stumbled across a German beating a French worker on the head with the butt of his rifle. When the man lay motionless on the ground the German sat down and began to smoke a cigarette, before spotting the two children watching him. 'Come over here,' he shouted cheerfully, gesturing with his hand. Terrified, Maurice and his sister approached the soldier. He took some bread and cheese from his haversack and shared it out between the three of them. The children did their best to accept the food gratefully, trying not to think about the poor Frenchman lying only a few feet away from them.

For the most part, the worst excesses of Nazi brutality took place out of sight. Rumours abounded about secret camps being set up on Alderney, far away from the prying eyes of the locals, but few had any idea what was really going on there. Closer to home, a number of unpleasant stories centred on a house in Guernsey's Vale parish which was used as an OT prison. One local resident wrote to the commandant to complain that she could hear screams coming from the building, which still went by its old name, 'Paradis'. Another was alarmed when he discovered a stash of coffins piled up outside. Once again, though, there was little concrete evidence of what exactly went on behind closed doors.

A few islanders did attempt to bend the ear of the authorities about the treatment of the slave workers. Marie Ozanne wrote to the commandant several times about the sinister goings on at 'Paradis', describing the treatment of the workers as a 'reign of terror'. Her pleas, however, fell on deaf ears. Marie had already been identified as a troublemaker – a major in the Salvation Army, she had continued to wear her uniform with pride even after the organisation was banned, reading the scriptures in public and preaching against the Occupation, as well as penning letters on the German treatment of OT workers and the Jews.

To begin with, the authorities saw Marie as an eccentric, a religious fanatic with more courage than sense. But she was tenacious. After they arrested her and confiscated her uniform, she returned to the streets in mufti, and even taught herself German so that she could speak to the ordinary soldiers.

In the end, Marie was sent to prison for two months. Her time behind bars did nothing to dent her spirit – from her cell, she wrote to the commandant declaring that she wouldn't take back a single word – but it did take a toll on her body. She died only a few months after her release, at the age of just thirty-seven.

In Jersey, the bailiff, Alexander Coutanche, raised his concerns about the treatment of the Todt workers with the newly promoted Major-General von Schmettow. The commandant appeared genuinely sympathetic, but his purview extended only so far as the military forces on the islands. The civilian Organisation Todt, headed by Speer – a man the Führer trusted implicitly – was beyond his reach.

The OT was the most visible emblem of racist Nazi ideology in the Channel Islands. To a political moderate like von Schmettow, the Todt supervisors represented the worst elements of the Third Reich, but there was little he could do about them. His own position was vulnerable from those with more hardline views. He even told Coutanche that he believed he was under surveillance by Nazi agents. Outside his office at the Hotel Metropole was a large balcony, on which a sentry would march up and down on patrol. Sometimes, when the commandant and the bailiff were discussing a delicate matter, von Schmettow would hold a finger up to his lips as the sentry approached, pausing the conversation until the spy had retreated.

It was those islanders who lived near the coast who generally saw the most of the OT workers. Amy Lihou was still struggling to provide for her family, after the death of her son John and her husband's banishment to prison in France. When the tide was out she would send Doris down to Vazon Bay to search for food. As the sea receded from the broad sandy beach, a Martian landscape of craggy red rocks would be revealed, teeming with limpets and winkles. But the already eerie scene was growing more sinister by the day with the addition of a number of concrete fortifications.

From the beach, Doris could see over to the promontory that jutted out between Vazon and Cobo, where the OT labourers were building a huge concrete bunker on the site of an old Martello tower, Fort Hommet, which dated from the Napoleonic Wars. It was one of over three hundred new fortifications across the Channel Islands, requiring more than six hundred thousand cubic metres of concrete between them, a tenth of the amount used in the entire Atlantic Wall. The new emplacements were armed to the teeth, with anti-tank guns capable of piercing metre-thick armour plating. The four giant barrels of Guernsey's Mirus Battery, meanwhile, provided coastal defence with a range of over fifty kilometres. And then there were the tens of thousand of mines dotted on and around the islands. Not for nothing did some advisers in Berlin speak of Hitler's obsession with defending his prized British possessions as an '*Inselwahn*' ('island madness').

It wasn't just the new fortifications that were gradually disfiguring the beautiful coastal landscape. Both Guernsey and Jersey saw the introduction of narrow-gauge railway networks designed to carry materials from St Helier and St Peter Port to the building sites. Often passing through residents' front gardens – and occasionally requiring the demolition of properties that were deemed to be in the way – the railways proved a boon to local children, who found they could hitch a lift on the footplate of a passing train and thus travel a considerable distance without much effort. Once again, though, it was the Organisation Todt who provided the labourers charged with the back-breaking work of laying the tracks.

Many islanders were determined to do what they could to help the poor workers, even if it meant risking punishment themselves. Amy Lihou had precious little food for her own family, but every so often she would boil up some old bones on an open fire in the back yard, tossing in whatever leftover scraps she had to hand. Doris would watch through the misted-up kitchen window as the men from the local OT camp crept across the fields after dark to wolf down her mother's latest offering.

Other children her age were doing their bit to help as well. Jersey girl Joyce Satchwell often chased after the OT lorries on her way to school, lobbing a couple of home-grown apples to the slave workers inside. One day, Leo and Francis Harris were sent by their father to a group of Russians working on the railway line at Havre des Pas, with the pockets of their long blue raincoats bulging with vegetables. The boys released their contraband cargo as subtly as possible, avoiding the supervisor's attention, but as they were leaving one of the men in the trench looked up gratefully. He reached out a hand, taking the hem of Francis' raincoat and bringing it up to his lips. Despite their sympathy for the slave workers, the boys couldn't help feeling a little embarrassed.

Mr Harris saw the treatment of the foreign labourers as a vindication of all his worst suspicions about the Germans. He began watching the routine of their supervisors, making a note of when they would disappear for a cigarette break. As soon as the coast was clear he would signal to the workers, summoning them over to his yard, where he would offer them whatever spare food he could scrape together.

One time, Leo watched in astonishment as a group of labourers fell upon a box of turnips, freshly pulled from the ground and still covered in earth, and began eating them on the spot. The rags hanging from one one man's back were just about recognisable as the remnants of an old suit jacket. Having devoured a couple of the raw vegetables, he approached Mr Harris, fishing around in the tattered lining of what had once been a pocket. He drew out a tiny piece of soap and pressed it into Leo's father's hand, kneeling at his feet as he did so.

The noble gesture was too much for Mr Harris. With tears in his eyes he took the man's hands in his own and gently pushed them away from him, whispering, 'No, no.' A few moments later, the labourers scurried out of the gate again and returned to their work.

The treatment of the Todt workers was a reminder that beneath the civilised veneer of the model occupation lurked the brutal cruelty of the Nazi regime, dormant for the most part but now and then rearing its ugly head. In the spring of 1942, the Guernsey authorities carried out perhaps the most sinister orders of the whole Occupation when they ordered the deportation to camps in Europe of all Jewish people living on the island.

Throughout the Occupation, the civil authorities in both Guernsey and Jersey had complied with the Germans' anti-Semitic orders, shutting down Jewish-owned businesses and imposing punitive curfew restrictions. Two men in Jersey died as a result of the persecution they suffered. Victor Emmanuel, a retired professor from Hamburg, hanged himself in his home and Nathan Davidson, a Romanian national whose grocery shop in St Helier had been forcibly closed, suffered a breakdown and died in the island's mental asylum. The Jersey bailiff, Alexander Coutanche, did protest at plans to introduce yellow Star of David badges, but since they never arrived on the island anyway his arguments were somewhat moot.

In Guernsey, Ambrose Sherwill, distracted by the Nicolle and Symes affair, had pushed through the legislation requiring Jews to be registered, believing – at least so he later claimed – that it was purely hypothetical since no Jews were left on the island after the evacuation. Two months later, with Sherwill in Cherche-Midi prison, Guernsey's chief of police, Inspector Sculpher, had proved otherwise. Acting on orders from Dr Brosch at the Feldkommandantur, Sculpher had launched his own investigation and had managed to identify four Jewish women. In Jersey, meanwhile, the chief aliens officer, Clifford Orange, compiled a list of twelve Jews. In both islands, the names were duly handed over to the Germans.

None of the Jewish women in Guernsey was a native islander, which might explain why Sherwill wasn't familiar with them. Elda Brouard was a middle-aged housekeeper from Italy while the others, Auguste Spitz, Therese Steiner and Elizabet Fink, were young women from Vienna. Since arriving in Guernsey, the three Austrian Jews had become fast friends.

Only a few months before the start of the Occupation, Elizabet had married Pearl and Gwen Smith's uncle, Harry Duquemin, a widower who ran the post office in Cobo. The girls had taken immediately to their new 'Aunt Betty', who had a beautiful singing voice and would often come to the hotel to play on the piano in the lounge. When the evacuation boats arrived, Harry and Betty had intended to leave for England but they kept putting the journey off, until finally the German bombing raid had put paid to their plans.

Betty's family background was known to everyone in the local community, so when the time came to register she saw little point in lying about it. She did, however, have the good sense to put down her religion as 'Christian', and to mention that she was married to a Guernseyman. Her friends Therese and Auguste (or 'Gusti'), meanwhile, were both single, with no real ties to the island. They had little choice but to put 'Jewish'.

Therese had arrived in Guernsey by accident. An attractive young woman with dark wavy hair, she had taken a job as au pair to a family from Kent, and had accompanied them on holiday to Sark in the summer of 1939. It had been an idyllic experience, wandering the lanes of the unspoilt, picture-postcard island with her two little charges, and taking them swimming in the beautiful Dixcart Bay. She had even made a local friend, Phyllis Baker, who was often at the beach with her two younger sisters. While the children all splashed around in the surf together, Therese and Phyllis would sit on the beach and chat.

The blissful holiday had come to an abrupt end when Britain

declared war on Germany. The family Therese was working for had booked themselves on the first boat back to England, but as an Austrian national she had not been permitted to travel with them. Instead, she had been taken to Guernsey and detained there on orders from the Home Office. By the time she was released her employers were long gone, so she had done her best to make a life for herself on the island, getting a job as a nurse at the Castel Hospital, where Gusti was already working as a cleaner.

On 21 April 1942, Gusti and Therese arrived at Betty's house asking to borrow a suitcase. They had been ordered to report to the harbour for deportation to a prison camp on the Continent. Therese in particular was very shaken. When a police sergeant had informed her of the orders she had burst into tears, telling him that she would never be seen again.

For the time being at least, Betty had been spared from being sent away, as had the Italian woman Elda Brouard, who had also listed her religion as Christian. The twelve Jews in Jersey had been left to their own devices too. But in Guernsey the authorities had found one other person to deport, a girl by the name of Marianne Grunfeld, who had, until recently, succeeded in hiding her Jewish blood, helped in part by the fact that with her pale skin and shock of ginger hair she was far from the stereotypical image of a 'Jewess'. Marianne had studied at agricultural college and had come to Guernsey to work on a farm owned by the Ogier family, with whom she soon developed a warm friendship. When the authorities came for her – acting, it was believed, on a tip-off from a neighbour – her employer, Edward Ogier, tried his best to prevent her deportation, but without success. Like Therese and Gusti, Marianne was put on a boat for France. Soon the three women were languishing in an internment camp at Drancy.

Other Jewish islanders managed to avoid deportation thanks to the help of local people. In Guernsey, a woman who went by the name Miriam Jay – her real surname was Jacobs – successfully avoided discovery thanks to her partner, George Ridgway. Ironically, as the island's solicitor general, he was one of those responsible for passing the anti-Jewish laws. On Sark, Annie Wranowsky, a Czech woman who had come to the island in 1934 following her divorce from a German doctor, vehemently denied that she was Jewish, despite the prominent red 'J' stamped on her passport. Dame Sybil counted Annie as a personal friend, but she also served a very useful purpose, helping to prop up the local myth that the Dame was fluent in German by acting as an unofficial translator. Inspector Sculpher was unconvinced by Annie's claim that she was an Aryan, but she insisted that she could trace her family back five generations without encountering a drop of Jewish blood. Finally, after extensive interviews and repeated denials, she was given leave to remain.

Most remarkable was the story of Jersey's Mary Richardson, a Dutch-born Jew who was sheltered for over two years by Albert Bedane, a physiotherapist who operated out of his home in St Helier. While Bedane continued to see clients – among them a number of Germans – in his consulting rooms, she was hiding down beneath them in the cramped cellar. At least one of Bedane's neighbours knew she was there: Hermann Rentsch, a Swiss-German hairdresser who had no love of the Nazis. Every few months, Hermann would call at the house to cut Mrs Richardson's hair, aware that keeping up a respectable appearance helped with the psychological strain of living underground.

With Therese and Gusti whisked away, Betty Duquemin feared that it was only a matter of time before she too would be taken, but as the weeks and months went by the Germans seemed to have forgotten about her. For her friends she could only hope for the best, praying that one day, after the war was over, the three of them would be reunited.

It wasn't to be. On 20 July, Gusti, Therese and Marianne were put on a train at Drancy. Three days later, they arrived at Auschwitz. It's not known whether they survived the initial selection process, but none of them made it through to the end of the war.

Fifty years later, when the full story of the three women's experiences was revealed, Therese's brother Karl came to Guernsey to find out about her time there. The policeman who had given her the deportation orders was guilt-stricken. 'She was a lovely girl,' he told Karl, sobbing. 'If I'd known what was going to happen to her, I would have hidden her in my own house.'

CHAPTER EIGHTEEN

MURDER IN PARADISE

Of all the Channel Islands occupied by the Germans, the loveliest was undoubtedly Sark. 'What ill luck', wrote Baron von Aufsess of the Jersey Feldkommandantur, 'that situated so far to the north, it remained unsung by Homer.' The baron was clearly infatuated with the island. One day, while on a hunting expedition to Herm, midway between Sark and Guernsey, he found himself so mesmerised by its beauty that he forgot what he was doing. 'Sark lay before me,' he wrote, 'like a model of the island of one's dreams, its tall cliffs fissured by deep bays and its upland plateau of lush verdant land etched in tapestry detail. I could hardly tear myself away from the sight and in doing so almost stumbled over and missed two rabbits.'

For the small number of troops stationed on Sark, it was the cushiest posting imaginable. The scenery was spectacular, the way of life relaxed and the people were friendly. Compared to the inhabitants of Jersey and Guernsey, the Sarkese had formed the warmest relationship with the Germans. It was a small community in which everyone knew each other, and the culture of old-fashioned courtesy was automatically extended to the more recent arrivals, enemy or no. In any case, with everyone living on top of one another, it was hard to maintain a frosty air for long.

It didn't hurt that the Occupation had hit the small island less hard than its larger sisters. Compared to Guernsey and Jersey, Sark had a plentiful supply of locally grown food, as well as its trademark creamy milk and butter. And the worst excesses of German brutality had barely touched the island at all: there were no abused Organisation Todt workers to inspire the locals' sympathy, and no Jews had been spirited away to camps on the Continent.

The island's leader, Dame Sybil, was on excellent terms with the senior German officers, in particular Prince Oettingen-Wallerstein at the Guernsey Feldkommandantur, with whom she had many mutual aristocratic friends. In early 1942 she asked for his help with a problem concerning her people. Ever since the evacuation, when Sark's resident English doctor had departed, the island had been subject to distinctly unsatisfactory medical care: first an elderly retired doctor whose eyesight was so poor he could barely see his patients, then a GP from Jersey who unplugged his phone so that he wouldn't be disturbed out of hours, and finally a Guernsey nurse who quit when she fell pregnant with twins.

When Dame Sybil explained the problem to Prince Oettingen-Wallerstein during one of his visits to the Seigneurie, they came up with a radical solution. From now on, the German Army would take responsibility for the medical needs of the islanders.

The Sarkese accepted the plan willingly, and the extra personnel brought over from Guernsey to staff the medical facilities were grateful as well. Among the new arrivals was Lieutenant Karl Schädel, the former vicar who was a friend of Werner Rang and had performed Fritz Imke's unofficial funeral the previous winter. A few years older than Werner, Karl was a tall, thoughtful-looking man and still wore a crucifix hidden beneath his uniform at all times. Arriving in Sark, he must have felt all his prayers had been answered. He wrote to tell Werner that he was living in 'a little paradise'.

Before long, Karl had come up with a scheme to bring his friend to Sark for a visit. The Army required an inventory of the medical supplies on the island, and as far as Karl was concerned, Werner was the only man for the job. 'It'll take at least two days,' he told him enthusiastically.

The journey over was perfect, with calm, crystal-clear waters glistening under the brilliant summer sun. For Werner, it really did feel like he was going on vacation, and the good impression was only enhanced when he got his first sight of the island, soaring up from the sea like some ancient prehistoric landmass, a beguiling mixture of jutting brown rocks and rich greenery.

The little boat pulled into Creux Harbour to the accompaniment of squawking seabirds. Werner disembarked and passed through the tunnel in the sheer rockface, which was marked with one of the few swastikas on the island. It took him about ten minutes to trudge up the hill to the high street, where he was instantly enchanted by the old-fashioned rustic charm of the tiny village.

Over the next two days, Werner saw enough of Sark to realise that Karl had not been exaggerating. It was truly a paradise on earth. The lack of cars lent it a quiet, peaceful air. Every hedgerow teemed with butterflies and a short detour off the ancient dusty roads led to magnificent sea views in every direction.

On Werner's last night, he and Karl sat together outside their bungalow, feasting on freshly caught lobsters and marvelling at their good fortune. Once again, Werner offered his thanks to the Führer for sending him to such a beautiful spot.

'Don't make too big a deal about it when you get back to Guernsey,' Karl told him the next morning as he set off for the harbour. 'The whole German Army will want to come here!'

Werner could well believe it. If he could choose one place to spend the rest of his life, he was pretty sure Sark would be it.

The new medical arrangement in Sark seemed to suit everyone. The doctor in charge of the islanders' health, Lieutenant August Göbel, was a good-looking, affable young man who enjoyed a warm relationship with the locals, and especially the women. In fact, it was hard to find a civilian who had a bad word to say about him – which is why what happened next came as such a shock.

On 29 April, the doctor's batman, Lance Corporal Johann Uhl, burst into Company Headquarters and announced that Göbel had been murdered. When he had taken the doctor's breakfast in that morning, he had found him lying motionless in his bed, the sheets around his head soaked with blood.

Uhl had run all the way from Göbel's billet at Le Vieux Clos, a large, attractive house opposite the old island mill, to Le Manoir, where Company HQ was located. He arrived out of breath and clearly shocked by what he had seen – so much so that the company sergeant major couldn't get much sense out of him. He despatched one of the medics, Corporal Rudolph Metz, to the scene of the crime to confirm the batman's report, as well as to establish whether the doctor's pistol had been fired, so as to rule out the possibility of suicide.

Metz was a short, bespectacled man whose natural awkwardness stood in stark contrast to the easy confidence of his late colleague. After a brief visit to Le Vieux Clos, he reported back that he had inspected the pistol and could confirm that it hadn't been fired. Lying on the floor by the doctor's bed was a bloodstained golf club, which appeared to have been used to bludgeon him over the head in his sleep.

A few hours later, the official investigative team arrived on the island: a military judge called Dr Weiss, along with some detectives from the Geheime Feldpolizei, the plain-clothes police force that struck such terror into the Channel Islanders that many believed they were actually part of the Gestapo.

The murder had already sent shockwaves through Sark, a sleepy, close-knit community that had suffered little crime of any kind in living memory, let alone something as serious as murder. The islanders were convinced that the guilty party must be one of the German soldiers, but the investigators thought it far more likely that a local person was responsible – perhaps the aggrieved husband of one of Dr Göbel's many female acquaintances. Unsurprisingly, the friendly, trusting relationship that had existed between the troops and the islanders grew increasingly strained. The fact was that someone among the 650 men and women on the island was a murderer.

The Field Police began by shutting down the island's tiny harbour so that the guilty party couldn't escape. Male islanders were instructed to report to the authorities daily, bringing their identity cards with them to ensure that no one was able to quietly disappear. One by one, every home was thoroughly searched, beds upended and cupboards emptied onto floors in the hunt for incriminating evidence. At the Grand Dixcart guesthouse, Julia Tremaine's daughter Norah was terrified that they might stumble across her mother's secret diary and begged her to throw it on the fire, but she refused. 'I have found a safe cubbyhole where even she cannot find it,' Mrs Tremaine wrote that evening. 'As shooting seems to be the penalty for most things I must make my cubbyhole very safe.'

Although the bloodstained golf club appeared to be the obvious murder weapon, a post-mortem on Göbel's body suggested that a sharper object had in fact been used to strike the fatal blow. Suspicion immediately fell on the first man known to have been on the scene, the doctor's batman Uhl. The young man occupied the room next door to Göbel, giving him the opportunity to creep in and murder him in his sleep without fear of being discovered. Although popular with the locals, the doctor was known to have been something of a slave driver to his subordinates, giving Uhl a potential motive as well. Perhaps, the detectives speculated, he had killed his master with a German Army axe or cleaver, and then bloodied the golf club to mislead them into looking for a civilian suspect.

Uhl was hauled in for an interrogation that would have made the real Gestapo proud, questioned day and night in his dead master's room by one investigator after another. Most intimidating was a sergeant by the name of Karl Wölfle, who was rather proud of his (somewhat inaccurate) local nickname, 'The Wolf of the Gestapo'. By the time Uhl was released several days later, he was a shadow of his former self, having been driven to the verge of madness by the incessant questioning, threats and sleep deprivation. He had protested his innocence throughout, but the Field Police seemed to have already made up their minds. Uhl was well aware that, in the absence of any other suspects, they might decide to pin the crime on him just for the sake of closing the case.

In time, though, a second suspect did emerge: the company

armourer, Corporal Lankmann. He had begged Dr Göbel for a referral to a specialist to treat his recurring tuberculosis, which he hoped would see him discharged from the Army, but Göbel had refused. Clearly there was no love lost between the two men. Shortly after the doctor's murder, Lankmann had sent a letter to his wife in Germany – intercepted by the postal censorship office in Guernsey – in which he wrote, 'The island, and myself especially, have been freed from a monster. Perhaps I will soon be back home.'

A search of Lankmann's workshop turned up a scrap of newspaper stained with blood of the same type that had been found on Göbel's golf club. Corporal Metz, who had been assisting with the investigation, pointed out that when Göbel's clubs had been damaged in the past he would get Uhl to take them to Lankmann for repair.

The Field Police sent for Uhl, now no longer their prime suspect, to see if he could shed any light on the whereabouts of the golf club in the period leading up to his master's death. But the batman was nowhere to be found, even after an exhaustive search of the island. With the harbour closed, he couldn't possibly have got away by boat. He had, it seemed, disappeared into thin air.

Eventually, after the best part of a week, the mystery of the missing batman was solved. Uhl had not gone far. His body was hauled from the 80-foot depths of the Vieux Clos well, in which he had apparently drowned himself, traumatised by his treatment at the hands of the Field Police and convinced that – innocent or not – they intended to execute him for the crime.

As a suicide, Uhl was buried without ceremony, in an unmarked grave dug on the Eperquerie, a vast, empty meadow at the northernmost tip of the island, bounded by the crashing waves 300 feet below. Corporal Metz was despatched to Germany to break the news to Uhl's family, returning just in time to attend Lankmann's official court martial.

The accused insisted that he was innocent of the crime, and that his cheerful reaction to Göbel's death was not, in itself, evidence that he had murdered him. How the bloodstained newspaper had found its way into his workshop he was unable to explain, but – with a shrewd knowledge of the German Army legal system – he demanded what was known as the *Führergesuch*, a direct petition to Hitler for civilian detectives to investigate charges against an accused serviceman.

The petition was granted, and a pair of detectives from the murder squad of the *Kriminalpolizei* (or 'Kripo') in Berlin, Bernd Wehner and Heinrich Philipps, were ordered to Sark to begin their own investigation. It took them many days of travel to reach the small island, and they arrived already fully briefed on the particulars of the case and eager to see the crime scene for themselves. Corporal Metz accompanied the two investigators to Le Vieux Clos, showing them where he had found Göbel's body and following them around the house and gardens.

There was still no sign of the real murder weapon, but as the men stood outside going over the details of the case, a sudden thought occurred to Wehner. Metz was standing on a large square manhole cover, underneath which was the cesspit for the house. Wehner ordered the pit to be searched – a miserable task but one that proved worthwhile. The next day, a metal German Army cleaver was discovered among the sewage, and once the filth had been carefully wiped away, the tell-tale spatters of dried blood underneath were plain to see.

When Metz was shown the metal cleaver he announced that he had seen it before – in fact, he himself had sent it to Lankmann for repair after the handle had broken. The noose around the armourer's neck appeared to be growing ever tighter. But when Wehner and Philipps interrogated Lankmann, who by now was in about as rough a state as Uhl had been before – stubbly and red-eyed, he had developed an anxious facial twitch – they were unable to ignore a gut feeling that the man sitting before them was innocent.

Wehner decided to re-interview everyone with a connection to the case, painstakingly going over the evidence they had given before. The suspects and witnesses were held in a waiting room on the floor below until they were called, and were enjoined not to speak to each other. It was a lengthy process, and after a while they began to grow restless. At one point during an interrogation, Wehner thought he heard a sound outside the door and flung it open to reveal Corporal Metz standing outside. 'Excuse me,' the corporal stammered, 'I came upstairs to look for the toilet.'

Wehner was furious at this breach of protocol and asked the company commander to impress upon Metz that it was crucial none of the witnesses left the waiting room. 'If you don't stay with the others you'll have to be locked up on your own,' Metz was told. Chastened, the corporal returned downstairs to wait with the other witnesses.

It was another nine hours before Metz was finally called in to give his evidence. He talked Wehner and Philipps through his actions on the morning of the murder – how he had been sent by the company sergeant major to verify Göbel's death and to check if the doctor's pistol had been fired so that the possibility of suicide could be ruled out.

Wehner took out his own weapon and handed it to the corporal. 'Check if I have fired it since the last time it was cleaned,' he told him. It was a long shot, but perhaps the re-enactment would reveal something that had been missed before.

Metz took the gun over to the window, holding the muzzle up to the light and peering inside. 'You haven't fired it,' he declared confidently, handing the weapon back.

As Metz passed him the gun, a flash of inspiration suddenly struck the chief investigator. On the day of the murder, Dr Göbel's bedroom had been thoroughly searched for fingerprints, but none had been found – either on the golf club or on the doctor's pistol. Yet if Metz had checked the weapon as he claimed, his prints should have appeared on the handle.

There was only one explanation: despite his orders, Metz hadn't bothered to check the gun. And the obvious reason was that he already knew it hadn't been fired.

'Lankmann is free!' Wehner exclaimed, watching with satisfaction as a look of panic spread across Metz's face. 'It was you who killed the doctor.'

'You will have to prove it!' Metz yelled, his face suddenly contorted with rage.

Corporal Metz was taken to Berlin for interrogation at Alexanderplatz police station. It was several weeks before he cracked, but eventually the whole story came flooding out. The short, socially awkward corporal had always been jealous of Dr Göbel, with his good looks, easy charm and numerous female admirers. Somehow Metz had got into the habit of opening the letters Göbel received from his lady friends, and had even started writing his own replies. When Dr Göbel discovered Metz's obsessive behaviour he had threatened to have him demoted back to private.

Metz knew a black mark against his name could see him lose his idyllic posting on Sark, and there was every chance that he might receive a transfer to the Eastern Front, from which a million men had already failed to return. He decided to murder the doctor before he could follow through on his threat, creeping into Göbel's bedroom in the dead of night and striking him over the head with the metal cleaver, before dipping the golf club in the pool of blood and disposing of the real murder weapon in the cesspit. All the while, the unfortunate batman Uhl had slept soundly in the room next door.

When the investigation had been launched the following day, Metz had played the role of the ever-helpful witness, looking on with satisfaction as Uhl was fingered for the crime. Then he had planted the blood-soaked newspaper in Lankmann's workshop, throwing suspicion on a second innocent man. Again and again he had offered his assistance to the detectives, maintaining his position close to the heart of the investigation. But during the final series of interviews, his anxiety and frustration had got the better of him and he had been unable to resist the urge to slip out of the waiting room and eavesdrop on the latest line of questioning, his ear pressed to the door of the interrogation room, where he had been discovered by the incensed Inspector Wehner.

When they had finished gathering their evidence, Wehner and Philipps brought Metz back to Guernsey to face a court martial. He was found guilty and taken to a field in Torteval, where a firing squad carried out the sentence of execution. The body was buried without ceremony in St Saviour's Churchyard.

CHAPTER NINETEEN

NO NEWS IS BAD NEWS

Almost two years had passed since the departure of the last evacuation boat had cut the Channel Islands off from the rest of the British Isles. In that time, the occasional twenty-five-word messages that arrived via the Red Cross bureaus had served as the only link with family and friends on the mainland. But there was one other connection to the world outside that provided great solace: the BBC.

Aside from a brief period in the wake of the Nicolle and Symes affair when radios had been temporarily confiscated, the islanders had always enjoyed full and regular access to the latest broadcasts from London, and with them an ongoing source of information on the war. Although the BBC almost never mentioned the Channel Islands explicitly – the fact that British territory remained in German hands was not something they were keen to dwell on – the daily reminders that a free life was still going on elsewhere offered hope for the future.

On 6 June 1942, the Germans announced that this precious umbilical cord was to be cut. All wireless receiving sets were to be handed in immediately, and this time the confiscation would be permanent. Following protests from the island bailiffs they published a notice in the papers declaring that the decision had been taken, 'not as a reprisal or due to bad behaviour on the part of the civilian population, but for purely military reasons'. What exactly those reasons were they never explained, but in recent days a BBC broadcast from London to Occupied France had caused a group of people to evacuate a given area prior to RAF bombing, proof that such radio communications could prompt meaningful action on the ground.

Within a fortnight, tens of thousands of sets had been collected, but for many islanders the unwelcome order represented a new dilemma, and an opportunity to rebel against their rulers. Those who owned more than one radio were tempted to hold a set back, keeping it hidden and listening to the BBC in secret. The Dame of Sark kept a wireless set in a trunk in a small upstairs storage room. Every night she and her husband, along with a couple of friends, would tune into the nine o'clock news, ready to bundle the radio back into its hiding place if they heard her two poodles barking to signal an unexpected visitor at the Seigneurie.

For those with less space, concealing a large and cumbersome wireless was no simple matter, but some islanders came up with ingenious solutions. Bill Green successfully hid two sets: one between the springs of his armchair (he fitted connections in the casters under the feet so that the chair itself could be discreetly plugged into the mains) and another at his shop in town, suspended on a cork float inside a half-filled oil drum. Eric Snelling, the impresario of the Lyric No. 1 Company, hid his own radio in plain sight, built into the console of the Compton organ that rose up from the stage of the Regal Cinema between performances. Every day, the illegal set would appear on stage, in full view of hundreds of German soldiers sitting in the auditorium, but none of them ever realised what they were looking at.

Some islanders who had given up their own sets were invited to share in the 'black wireless' activities of their neighbours. Apprentice carpenter Roy Burton was surprised to be invited in to hear the news at a house in Albecq, Guernsey, where he had been fixing a door. His colleague Albert was thrilled, and persuaded Roy to string the work out over several days, offering to do various other odd jobs around the house, so that they could carry on listening to the BBC.

The Germans were well aware that not everyone had done as they were ordered. Aside from the radios that were discovered during random house searches, there was the evidence provided by the electricity generating stations. Rex Kirby worked at a power station in Jersey, where a couple of German sentries were posted to see off potential saboteurs. Every night, at a few minutes to ten – nine o'clock in mainland Britain – there would be a sharp spike in the demand for electricity. 'A-ha,' one of the Germans remarked the first time he witnessed the dial flicker. 'Your friends must be listening to Mr Churchill.'

More than two hundred islanders were convicted for possessing illegal radios. There was generally little warning before a house was raided, not even a knock on the door – although the officer in charge would usually offer his hand for a peremptory shake before turning a residence upside down. Some people were lucky enough to be tipped off by their neighbours when the search parties were on their way. One woman hastily grabbed a tea-cosy and plonked it over her little set, carrying it around in her arms as the Germans ransacked her home. Another was forced to sacrifice her precious equipment by hurling it into a bucketful of soap suds in which she had been doing the week's laundry.

Jersey hairdresser Hermann Rentsch had a wireless set stashed away in his house on Roseville Street, St Helier. One day, his wife called him at the salon to say that the Germans were conducting a house-to-house search in their neighbourhood. Hermann raced home, leaving several customers under the dryers, whisked the set out of its hiding place and bundled it into his son Tony's pram, which contained a secret compartment designed for just such a purpose. Then he lay Tony down on top of it and wheeled him off down the street, heading for the farm of a friend who had offered to hide the set if Hermann ever needed to get rid of it. When he arrived, Hermann was directed to a large barn in the yard. He pulled aside a pile of hay, only to find dozens of sets underneath it already, of every make and model imaginable. He hastily added his own radio to the collection before replacing the hay and dashing back to his customers.

Being caught with a contraband wireless was an offence that could have serious consequences. The authorities published a notice in the island papers announcing an amnesty until the end of the year but threatening severe punishments once the period of grace had elapsed. 'Contraventions of the above-mentioned order after 1st January 1943 will be punished by imprisonment, with or without hard labour, or fines, or in serious cases by the death penalty,' it warned.

Despite such threats, islanders continued to hold on to their contraband wirelesses, and unsurprisingly there were a number of close calls. Jerseyman Arthur Rabet had kept an old Pye radio, rigging it up in the loft above the scullery at his farm in St Lawrence. After the Germans began searching adjacent properties, he took the set and hid it under an old lorry in one of his outbuildings. Unfortunately, Arthur's four-year-old son Alan was fascinated by the rusty old vehicle, and devoted much of his time to enthusiastically exploring its every nook and cranny. One day, while Arthur was showing a German inspector around the yard, the boy ran up to him, tugged on the leg of his trousers and said excitedly, 'Dad! I've just found a wireless under the old lorry.' Arthur went white, but the German didn't seem to react. Evidently, he hadn't caught the meaning of the boy's words. 'You tell me about it later,' Arthur told his son, nudging him away rather forcefully and giving the inspector his full attention.

At Les Pieux Hotel in Guernsey, Mr Smith kept a radio hidden in the cellar. One evening, a young soldier who was billeted at the hotel unexpectedly wandered through the back door into the kitchen. Rather than heading up to his room, he decided to rest his feet in the family's kitchen, drawing up a chair by the dining table and attempting to engage Mrs Smith in conversation. It was a few minutes before seven – six o'clock in London – and her husband had just disappeared through a trap door in the floor of the family linen cupboard to the cellar down below, to tune into the latest news broadcast.

When she heard the muffled but unmistakable bongs of Big Ben floating up through the floorboards, Mrs Smith was horrified. She began chattering wildly, raising her voice a few notches, and tapping her foot on the floor as subtly as possible. Picking up on what was happening, Pearl and Gwen joined in too, improvising a furious argument. Their screams and shouts drew a look of perplexed embarrassment from the German. 'Perhaps it is a bad time,' he said as he headed for the lounge.

Mrs Smith said nothing until the young man was out of earshot. Then she declared furiously, 'You wait till I get hold of your father! That stupid radio will be the death of us!'

In fact, some Germans took a rather lackadaisical approach to the search for illegal radios. One local policeman was paired up with a feldgendarme from Austria. Whenever the two of them were sent to investigate a suspected black wireless, the Austrian man would open the front door, poke his head inside briefly and ask, 'Do you see a wireless set?' When his local partner shook his head he would conclude cheerfully, 'No more do I,' and the two of them would go on their way.

Bob Le Sueur's mother Lizzie had always been a hoarder, but when the call came for islanders to hand in their radios her habit was finally vindicated. Her husband was furious at the idea of giving up their wireless, which had only been installed a few years earlier when the house was connected to mains electricity. Fortunately, though, Lizzie had kept their old battery-powered Pye radio up in the loft – the perfect sacrificial offering to satisfy the Germans while the family continued listening to the newer set.

In time, though, the unthinkable happened: the wireless suddenly stopped working. Unwilling to give up their precious link to the outside world, Bob found a sympathetic repairman who was prepared to deal in illegal goods. On the man's instructions, he carefully smuggled the set out of the house – transporting it on a trailer attached to his bike, buried under a pile of firewood in a hessian sack – and brought it to the back entrance of the repair shop, keeping his eyes peeled for any German customers. Before long, he was on his way back home with a fully functional radio. But when he reached his parents' house, he found a German soldier resting his weight on the sea wall across the road, taking in the view of the water.

Bob knew that loitering outside the house would look suspicious. He would just have to get the radio in quickly and pray the German didn't turn around. He rested his bike against the wall, hooked open the gate and quietly unlocked the front door. Then he made his way back to the bike and, checking that the German was still facing away from him, grabbed the hessian sack from under the pile of firewood and hurried up the garden path.

A couple of seconds later, Bob was over the threshold. But as he stepped further into the hall, he was suddenly halted: the sack seemed to be tugging him in the opposite direction. Confused, Bob looked down and saw that the long electrical flex had fallen out and was running all the way down the garden path. He gave it a yank, but it wouldn't give. The plug had got caught between the spokes of his bicycle wheel.

Bob raced through the garden and onto the street, wrestling to free the plug and casting anxious glances across the road to the German, who still appeared to be lost in his reverie. Finally, he disentangled it from the wheel, racing up to the house again and slipping through the door. He hurled the flex inside and pulled the door to, before heading back to the bike to collect the firewood.

As he gathered the wood up in his arms, the German casually turned to face him, and the two of them locked eyes for a moment. Bob couldn't be sure, but he thought the other man was smiling at him. Then he turned away and resumed his perusal of the seascape.

Some Germans did more than simply turn a blind eye and actually participated in black-wireless activities themselves. Although listening to 'enemy' broadcasts was strictly forbidden, a number of soldiers took the risk, getting hold of their own contraband sets and secretly tuning in to the BBC. Mrs Le Bideau was surprised to find her lodger Maiya staggering upstairs under the weight of a bulky wireless, which he intended to set up in his bedroom. 'I don't want to be sent to prison if that gets found in my house!' she announced. The young man reassured her that he would take full responsibility if the set was discovered, and would tell his superiors that his landlady knew nothing about it.

Ever since the start of the Occupation, wild rumours and tall tales had circulated freely around the islands, and with less reliable information than ever thanks to the confiscation of wireless sets, the speculation, anticipation and exaggeration had only increased. Mrs Le Bideau was distinctly unimpressed by what increasingly passed for news on the island. 'We hear that in Herm (uninhabited) the people are expected to talk German,' she wrote sarcastically. 'The rabbits (the only occupants, and hitherto speechless) find great difficulty in pronouncing the syllable "ich".' But joking aside, the islanders were finding it increasingly hard to distinguish between fact and fiction. One Guernseyman was convinced that he had seen Hitler landing at the airport, accompanied by twenty-three fighter planes.

The black wireless offered access to reliable news, something that was enormously valuable to both German and local audiences, since even the military reports published in the English-language newspapers were supplied by the German censors. (Their spelling and grammar was often left uncorrected by the sub-editors so as to make their provenance obvious to readers.) Many islanders regarded the international news pages as little more than cheap toilet paper. 'The papers are getting more and more flamboyant,' wrote Mrs Le Bideau. 'The Germans appear to be marching through Russia without losing so much as a pocket handkerchief. According to black wireless, the boot is on the other foot and how we hope it is, for our only hope is in some unknown catastrophe – some expected unexpected.' Most members of the Army of Occupation were equally sceptical about the reports placed in their own rags, *Deutsche Inselzeitung* and *Deutsche Guernsey Zeitung* – and, with the RAF bombing towns all over Germany, those with family and friends in the line of fire were desperate to know what was really going on.

In August 1942, when six thousand Allied troops landed at Dieppe, the rumour mill went into overdrive. If the raid signalled the start of a second front in the war, the islanders speculated, then liberation could be just round the corner. It didn't take long for such hopes to be dashed, however. The raid was a catastrophic failure: more than half of the men who took part were either killed, wounded or captured, and over a hundred RAF planes were destroyed, along with more than thirty landing craft.

As news of the defeat spread through the islands, it was met with disbelief, followed by resignation. With no end to the Occupation in sight, the islanders realised they would be spending another winter under the jackboot. Morale fell to an all-time low, and for once it was hard to entirely discount the German version of events splashed over the front pages of the newspapers.

For those who had already given up their wireless sets but wanted to keep abreast of the latest news, there was another option. Soon the same ingenious spirit that had seen bulky appliances elaborately concealed within ordinary household objects was employed in a new task: building makeshift radios from scratch. These 'crystal sets' required no power, simply a long coil of wire to pick up the signal and a 'cat's whisker' (a thin strip of copper) attached to a lump of semiconducting mineral. They were thus much smaller and lighter than the traditional bulky wirelesses and could be concealed within a large box of matches, or built into a light fitting. The Guernsey physician Dr Rose incorporated his set into an ornate oak clock that sat on his mantelpiece, carefully building the radio around the existing mechanism so that the clock would continue to function. Much to his frustration, when he attempted to camouflage the new parts with gold leaf, the metal coating interfered with the conductive properties of the wire, rendering the radio useless. But after scraping the connections clean again he was left with a functional, and almost entirely invisible, piece of equipment.

Constructing a crystal set was a relatively simple matter, especially since the BBC broadcast detailed instructions on how to do it. Even a child could master the technique, and many did – among them young Rollo Sherwill, the son of Guernsey's former attorney general, who kept up quite a production line supplying his schoolfriends with illicit home-made radios. The hardest part was sourcing the eponymous crystal. Some people searched endlessly for the right bit of mineral – a lump of coal with a streak of gold was thought to be the best conductor – but others discovered that this too could be manu-factured with a bit of effort. Guernsey schoolboy Bryan Vandertang produced his own crystals by shaving a few scraps off an old lead pipe and mixing them with some flowers of brimstone – a bright yellow powder used extensively in agriculture, and thus readily available on the island. The mixture would then be stuffed inside a used cartridge case – there was certainly no shortage of these, given the German Army's frequent military exercises – and heated over a naked flame. When it was properly cooked, the case would split open, releasing a noxious gas, and the bits of crystal could then be carefully removed and put to use.

For many people, the hardest bit of equipment to get hold of was a pair of headphones, without which the crystal sets, which produced a very faint signal compared to traditional wirelesses, were essentially useless. Leo Harris managed to acquire a pair from another boy at school in exchange for some marbles. But with increased demand as more and more people got their hands on their own crystal sets, the islands began to experience a supply problem. Public telephone booths were plundered for their old-fashioned handheld earpieces, which proved a serviceable alternative to proper headphones. When Mr Le Vosgeur, a senior engineer with the Jersey telephone company, realised the reason behind the spate of thefts, he began replacing them in double-quick time. He felt no ill will towards the thieves who were taking the earpieces – in fact, as far as he was concerned, he was involved in a supply chain that was enabling islanders to tune into the broadcasts from the mainland. In his own small way, Mr Le Vosgeur was helping with the war effort.

As well as being readily available, the telephone earpieces were less conspicuous than the larger pairs of headphones – and more easily passed off as old junk in the event of a house being searched. Since the only reason for an islander to possess a pair of headphones was for use with a crystal set, they were a dead giveaway that one would be found somewhere on the premises. One Guernseyman was caught off guard by a patrol bursting into his house as he was listening to the news in the kitchen. He hurled his crystal set into a pan of soup that was simmering on the stove before calmly going to greet the Germans.

'We have been informed you have a wireless set,' one of them declared. 'Where is it?'

'I'm afraid you have been misinformed,' the man replied calmly.

'If you have no radio,' the German asked him, 'then why are you wearing headphones?'

For most islanders, the black wireless was first and foremost a source of news, but the BBC did more than just educate and inform. For some it was the entertainment provided by the illegal sets that was most precious of all. Pearl and Gwen Smith had a crystal set hidden beneath the floorboards in their bedroom, and every night they would tune in to catch the latest popular songs. Pearl would transcribe the lyrics, while Gwen noted down the melody. The girls' performances at the Lyric always included recent hits, and from the reactions of the audience whenever they played a new number, it was clear that they weren't the only ones listening. One week, the sisters performed the latest Vera Lynn song and were met with thunderous applause from the auditorium, not to mention some very confused looks from the Germans who were watching the show along with the locals.

John Harris warned his son Leo never to whistle any tunes he had heard on the radio out in public, let alone talk about the latest news from the BBC. But it was a case of do what I say, not what I do. Whenever an interesting news story was broadcast on the evening news, Mr Harris would be on his bike the next morning, stopping off at a number of friends' houses to share the latest developments over the garden gate.

As far as the Germans were concerned, spreading information in this way was a serious crime, much worse than simply listening privately. Canon Clifford Cohu, who served voluntarily as chaplain at Jersey's General Hospital, spent much of his time touring the wards and passing on the latest news. He had no radio himself but relied on information from a local cemetery worker, Joseph Tierney, who in turn knew a third man, John Nicolle, who was actually tuning into the BBC broadcasts.

Following a tip-off from an informant, all three men were arrested, charged with 'disseminating anti-German news', and sentenced to imprisonment on the Continent. Canon Cohu was moved from one prison to another until finally he arrived at Spergau/Zöschen labour camp, three stone lighter than when he left Jersey. It was an awful place, where the prisoners slept thirty men to a tent, with only straw on the ground beneath them for warmth. As a British clergyman, Cohu was immediately singled out. The SS guards subjected him to relentless beatings, speculating that he wouldn't last a week at the camp. Sure enough, exactly seven days after his arrival, Cohu was dead, having fallen prey to a bout of dysentery from which his weakened body couldn't recover.

The outcome for his co-conspirators was no better. Joe Tierney, who had supplied Cohu with the latest news reports, died on a forced march near Celle, and his own source, John Nicolle, perished from exhaustion at a camp in Dortmund. For something as simple as passing on the latest news, the three men joined the growing list of islanders whose refusal to submit to the Occupation had ultimately cost them their lives.

The BBC broadcasts weren't the only source of news in the Channel Islands. During their regular sorties, the RAF dropped large numbers of leaflets headed 'News from England'. Printed to look like a traditional English newspaper, complete with satirical cartoons, they soon became highly prized souvenirs. In a rarely used upstairs bathroom at Les Pieux Hotel in Cobo, Gwen and Pearl Smith kept an impressive stash hidden behind one of the wooden panels that surrounded the bath.

For schoolchildren, meanwhile, the RAF publications were a valuable trading commodity. Defying their teachers, boys and girls who weren't afraid to trespass across fields, crawl under hedges or climb up into the branches of tall trees would arrive in their classrooms proudly clutching the latest issues. On one miserable rainy day, Peter Girard, the Guernsey farmer turned headmaster, arrived to find dozens of leaflets hung up to dry in his classroom. They were hastily confiscated and destroyed.

While collecting illegal leaflets was a punishable offence, far more dangerous was actually creating them. But despite the potential penalties, a number of islanders published underground news-sheets so that those without access to the black wireless could keep abreast of the latest events. In Jersey, one of Bob Le Sueur's schoolfriends, Norman Le Brocq, the son of a florist who had attended Victoria College on a scholarship, founded the Jersey Communist Party in 1942, along with an older trade-union activist, Leslie Huelin. They had only a handful of members, but between them managed to produce a monthly news bulletin right through to the end of the war.

Another Jersey news-sheet, the 'Bulletin of British Patriots', was less successful, however. The authorities found out about it almost immediately, and after ten islanders were arrested and held as hostages, the two brothers who were behind the publication handed themselves in.

Most significant was the Guernsey Underground News Service (or GUNS), which produced a daily one-sheet including the verbatim text of the previous night's BBC news broadcast. It was founded by a linotype operator at the *Star* newspaper, Charles Machon, who relied on associates with their own illegal wireless sets to provide the transcriptions, which were then typed onto tomato-packing paper. Passed from hand to hand, GUNS was believed to reach around three hundred people. Among them was the island's bailiff, Victor Carey, who arrived at work every morning to find a copy lying on his desk. Shrewdly, he never asked who had put it there, or what happened to it once he had finished reading it, but at the top of each edition – underneath a giant V-sign – was the instruction, 'Burn after reading'.

For almost two years, GUNS provided islanders with a daily dose of accurate and unbiased news, right under the nose of the Germans. There were a few close calls – one reader forgot to dispose of his copy, leaving it within the pages of a book he had borrowed from the library. Fortunately the next person to take out the book was discreet enough to destroy it straightaway.

In the end, it was a friend of Charles Machon, an Irishman called Peter Doyle, who betrayed him to the authorities. An unscrupulous black-marketeer, Doyle was already on the German payroll as a 'V-Mann' (a paid informant). When the time came, he not only provided his police contacts with a copy of the news-sheet, but led them directly to Machon's house. There they found a typewriter already loaded with GUNS headed paper, ready for the next day's edition.

Over the next few weeks, Machon was subjected to a gruelling interrogation. He suffered from a stomach ulcer, for which he required a special diet, but even when his elderly mother arrived at the prison with a tin of his food, the Germans refused to allow him to eat it. When they threatened to arrest her as well, he finally cracked. She was seventy-four, and it was an ordeal he wasn't sure she would survive. To save his mother, Machon gave up the names of his transcribers: Cecil Duquemin, a baker, Ernest Legg, a carpenter, Legg's brother-in-law Joseph Gillingham, a stoker at the Guernsey Brewery, and one of Machon's colleagues at the *Star*, the reporter Frank Falla.

The five men were tried at the Royal Court, where a huge swastika flag completely covered the island coat of arms, and were refused any kind of legal counsel. It didn't take long for the German judge to find them guilty. Machon was sentenced to two and a half years in prison on the Continent, and his conspirators to gaol terms ranging from ten months to just under two years.

Of the five, only Cecil Duquemin survived the experience in relatively good health. Frank Falla lost more than three stone and developed a severe case of pneumonia, while Ernest Legg very nearly died of dropsy. Charles Machon, whose health had never been good, lasted only five months before he perished in a camp near Hamelin. Joseph Gillingham, meanwhile, simply vanished from the face of the earth. To this day, his final resting place has never been found.

Not all illegal publications were targeted at the islanders. As well as producing their own monthly newsletter in English, the Jersey Communist Party was committed to reaching the Organisation Todt workers. One day, Bob Le Sueur was asked by his old schoolfriend Norman Le Brocq if he would help translate the latest BBC news broadcast for the benefit of the island's two thousand Spanish forced labourers. Bob, who had passed School Certificate Spanish, replied that he would be delighted to help. Before long, his translation was flying off the JCP's Gestetner machine, ready to be smuggled into the OT camps during the next visit of the delousing teams.

One of the most remarkable instances of anti-German propaganda was directed at the soldiers themselves, thanks to two middle-aged French women who had moved to Jersey only a couple of years before the war. Lucy Schwob and Suzanne Malherbe, who both came from Jewish families, had been lovers ever since they met in Nantes as teenagers. They had spent most of their adult lives in Paris at the centre of a set of left-wing surrealist artists, hosting salons in their apartment on the Rue de Grenelle, a stone's throw from the Left Bank of the Seine. Lucy was known for her imaginative photographic self-portraits, which displayed a distinctly fluid approach to gender: she shaved her head, frequently wore men's clothes, and described herself as neither male nor female. Since her early twenties she had gone by the pseudonym 'Claude Cahun', while Suzanne – who was her artistic collaborator as well as her lover – styled herself as 'Marcel Moore'.

The couple were, in other words, about as far from the Nazi ideal as possible, and the feeling of intense disgust was mutual. Throughout the Occupation, Lucy and Suzanne did their bit to subvert German authority and morale with a unique brand of resistance that stood somewhere between propaganda and performance art. Suzanne would take down BBC news stories via the black wireless, which Lucy would then work into little rhyming couplets, written and illustrated in a variety of coloured inks and enigmatically signed *'der Soldat ohne Namen'* ('the Soldier with No Name'). The two women would slip these little notes into soldiers' pockets, or tuck them under the windscreen wipers of officers' requisitioned cars, employing a variety of wigs and disguises that weren't a million miles away from the personas Lucy had adopted in their photographic collaborations.

The authorities were certainly aware of the women's activities – more than 350 of their leaflets were collected by the German Field Police – but it took several years before they were able to identify the culprits. Finally, caught and interrogated by menacing plain-clothes detectives, Lucy and Suzanne were found guilty of inciting rebellion and sentenced to death. Their house was raided, and their priceless collection of 'degenerate' art, including works by Miró and Picasso, was burned to a cinder. Baron von Aufsess was evidently disgusted by what he found there. In his diary he describes a hoard of 'ugly cubist paintings' and 'pornographic material of an especially revolting nature', including images of Lucy 'photographed in the nude from every angle' and 'practising sexual perversion, exhibitionism and flagellation'. But his revulsion didn't stop him from making the most of the women's extensive library. 'I have found more reading material than I shall be likely to get through,' he commented cheerfully, helping himself to a copy of André Gide's *Pages de Journal*.

The two women's death sentences, meanwhile, fast became a cause of controversy. The Jersey bailiff, Alexander Coutanche, wrote to the authorities to object to the proposed execution, pointing out that the crimes of which they been found guilty were acts of subversion not violence. 'The knowledge that such a sentence has been pronounced is causing anxiety and distress among the population,' he explained, 'not because of any particular acquaintance with or sympathy for the condemned persons, but because of a feeling of repugnance against the carrying out of a sentence of death on women.'

In the end, the authorities backed down and the capital sentences were commuted to life imprisonment.

CHAPTER TWENTY

SENT PACKING

When the German sociologist Professor Karl Pfeffer had visited the Channel Islands at the behest of the Führer, he had returned to Berlin with a number of recommendations. As well as suggesting that the islanders should be viewed as potential 'hostages', he also proposed a way of weakening their resolve for the war. As Pfeffer saw it, the Army of Occupation should attempt to drive a wedge between the native, born-and-bred islanders and the large British population living alongside them, which was composed primarily of wealthy expatriates.

The islanders, Pfeffer had observed, 'regard themselves as Jersey or Guernsey folk, but not as English'. He suggested 'promoting as far as possible the independence of the inhabitants' by means of 'appealing very strongly to the Norman heritage, treating the islands like little Germanic States, which only stood in an accidental personal union with England'. If this was achieved, he predicted, the English residents would simply up sticks and leave of their own accord, and then the islanders' loyalty to Britain would begin to diminish.

For some time, British-born residents of the Channel Islands had been aware of a subtle difference in the way they were treated compared to their native neighbours. 'The Germans certainly like the Sark folk better than the English,' wrote Julia Tremaine, an Englishwoman who had been running a guesthouse on the island for more than two decades. 'If they ask you, "Are you Sark?" and you say, "No, English," they look at you in quite an evil way.'

In September 1942, Pfeffer's proposed policy reached its logical conclusion. A notice was published announcing that British subjects and their families were to be deported to internment camps in Germany. The news was as unexpected as it was unwelcome. 'The bolt has come straight out of the blue,' wrote Mrs Le Bideau, 'and those to whom it applies are half stunned by it.'

For children of British parents, who had grown up on the islands, and in some cases had never even visited the mainland, it was a shock suddenly being classed as outsiders deserving of exile. Jersey teenager Michael Ginns was on his way into St Helier with his mother when they were stopped by a family friend, Mrs Ross. The poor woman's face was as white as a sheet. 'We're all being sent to Germany,' she told them. 'It's up in the *Evening Post* window.'

Michael and his mother hurried along to the newspaper's offices, where a huge crowd was gathered in the street outside, staring at the window display. Sure enough, there was the notice from the newly appointed feldkommandant, Colonel Friedrich Knackfuss, announcing the 'evacuation' – the Germans never used the word 'deportation' – of those islanders 'who belong to the English people'.

All that remained was for the deportees to be given their marching orders. In Jersey this was the subject of some controversy. Colonel Knackfuss instructed the island constables to perform the unpleasant task, but the bailiff, Alexander Coutanche, was adamant: if the Germans were going to insist on 'evacuating' British-born residents, they would have to do the dirty work themselves. In the meantime, the States passed a motion censuring the authorities for their new policy, and drawing their attention to the terms of surrender issued two years earlier, which had 'solemnly guaranteed' the 'lives, property and liberty' of the inhabitants of the Channel Islands.

The protests fell on deaf ears. Personally, Knackfuss agreed with the bailiff and his colleagues, but his orders came direct from the Führer. The same night that the notice was published in the island newspapers, German troops began going from door to door, delivering the deportation notices, and twenty-four hours later the first boatload of deportees were on their way to the Continent.

Michael's family were lucky that their papers weren't served until the following day, so they had more time to prepare than some of their neighbours. Nonetheless, Mrs Ginns worked frantically, stuffing suitcases full of warm winter clothes, as advised in the official instructions, and readying the house for sudden abandonment. On Friday morning, the day the family were due to depart, a van arrived from the animal shelter to pick up their little terrier, Bill. 'Keep him in over the weekend,' Mrs Ginns told the driver, still hoping there might be a last-minute reprieve. 'But if you don't hear from us by Monday morning you'll have to put him down.'

Bill wasn't the only animal in the family whose days were numbered thanks to the unexpected evacuation. As well as warm clothes, they had been advised to pack 'provisions' for the journey. For a while now the family had been breeding rabbits for the dinner table, but the mother of these broods, a black floppy-eared bunny called Sooty, had always been treated as a pet. There was no way they could take her to Germany, though. Mrs Ginns summoned a butcher to carry out the deed, and soon a small parcel of what Michael called 'Sooty sandwiches' was added to the family's luggage.

While Mrs Ginns was busy preparing for her family's departure, other islanders were attempting to get their names off the deportation lists. There were several grounds for exemption, but the most straightforward was medical infirmity. A panel of doctors – both local and German – would examine doubtful cases and decide whether they were well enough to travel. John Harris, who despite hailing from Edinburgh was 'English' as far as the Germans were concerned, persuaded his family physician, Dr Gow, to fabricate a fictitious medical history for his wife Anne, claiming that she had come to live in Jersey because her poor health required a warmer climate than Scotland could provide, and that to transport her to Germany would be dangerous. Thanks to the doctor's strongly worded recommendation, the whole family were struck off the list.

Others were saved by friends in high places. At Les Pieux Hotel in Guernsey, Gwen and Pearl Smith had already packed their belongings when a telephone call came through demanding that their father report to German headquarters. There he was met by a family friend, Sister Young, an Irish nurse who had arrived in Guernsey around the time that war was declared, and who, as a citizen of a neutral country, had found herself much in favour with the German regime. Mr Smith was astonished when she marched him into the commandant's office and began a conversation – in fluent German – with the man himself.

When they had finished talking, the commandant addressed Mr Smith in English. 'You and your family are exempt from leaving,' he told him.

The terms that Sister Young had negotiated required Mr Smith to take a job with the German authorities, so that he could be considered indispensable to the functioning of the island. He was ordered to report to the Rockmount Hotel the following morning to help prepare food for the Organisation Todt workers.

Mr Smith couldn't believe his good fortune, but on his way home he began to question how the Irish nurse had managed to work such magic on the commandant. A worrying thought occurred to him: was it more than just a coincidence that Sister Young, with her excellent command of German, had arrived in Guernsey just as war was declared? Had she in fact been a fifth columnist all along, paving the way for the German invasion?

Either way, the Smiths weren't the only family saved from exile on the whim of the authorities. Many islanders wrote desperate letters begging to be allowed to stay, and some of them were successful. Reverend Edwin Foley, a Baptist minister in Guernsey, penned an impassioned apology for his own country's conduct going back almost thirty years. 'Though I am English born, I am very, very sorry for all the wrong which I believe England has done to Germany,' he wrote. 'I was not in favour of England declaring war on Germany in 1914 and got into some trouble for saying so. I believe the Treaty of Versailles was iniquitous and did much wrong to Germany. And I was not in favour of England declaring war on Germany in 1939.' Having established his position on international relations, the reverend tried a more personal approach. 'Sometimes good German Baptists come to our services and I always give them a warm welcome in the name of our common Lord,' he wrote. 'I try to say to them in my perhaps broken German, "Wie sind Bruder in Christ" – "We are all brothers in Christ."' Reverend Foley and his wife were allowed to remain on the island indefinitely.

On Sark, Dame Sybil intervened to attempt to prevent the deportation of a handful of residents. With the help of her Jewish friend Annie Wranowsky, she composed a letter in German addressed to the Guernsey Feldkommandantur. 'Please free the following men and declare them as absolutely indispensable and necessary for existence and administration,' she wrote confidently, providing a list of four names. Among them was that of her husband, Bob Hathaway, who as an American national was considered as much persona non grata as if he had been born in England. 'The parliament could not sit without him, and the whole civil administration is illegal without his presence,' Sybil wrote. 'Our ancient feudal system does not allow me, as a married woman, to have special rights in the absence of my husband.'

Thanks to his wife's intervention, Bob was given leave to remain, as was the island priest, Reverend Phillips, without whom, the Dame declared, 'no marriage could be pronounced valid as we recognise no other ceremony than the religious'. But her attempts to save two other men – the island miller, Mr Bishop, and a retired army major, John Skelton – were unsuccessful. They were ordered to board a boat for Guernsey, from where they would travel on to France, and eventually Germany, with the rest of the deportees.

On the morning of Saturday 26 September, the Dame walked down to the harbour to see the boat off. There was a nasty storm brewing and one of the biggest tides the island had seen for decades, but the British stiff upper lip was out in force and a mood of defiant good humour pervaded the sad occasion. One by one the deportees boarded the little boat, clutching suitcases stuffed with clothes and belongings. But as the vessel was about to depart, the Germans realised that two people were missing: Major Skelton and his wife Madge had failed to report as ordered.

The boat was forced to go without them, while the soldiers began a search of the island. It was inconceivable that the Skeltons could have escaped on their own, particularly in such bad weather. Nonetheless, by nightfall there was still no sign of the AWOL deportees.

Early the following morning, Sybil was roused from her bed by a German soldier. Madge Skelton had been found and was asking to see her. It was the couple's dog, roaming the island in a state of distress, that had led the search parties to its owners, lying on the common at La Rondellerie. Major Skelton was already dead, having slashed his wrists, but Madge, who had intended to join him in a suicide pact, had vomited up the poison she had swallowed. She had stabbed herself no less than sixteen times, but had failed to inflict a fatal wound, merely giving herself a number of horrific injuries.

Sybil sat on the ground holding Madge's hand while they waited for the ambulance to arrive. When it did, she was checked over by the German Army doctors before being put on the next boat to Guernsey. She was, at least, spared the trauma of being deported as planned, instead finding herself admitted for an indefinite stay at the island's civilian hospital.

Far from driving a wedge between the native islanders and their neighbours from the mainland, the deportations actually forged a stronger bond between them. As the boats were loaded, crowds of locals lined the roads nearby to support the departing families. Up on Jersey's Mount Bingham, overlooking the harbour, a group of schoolboys belted out 'There'll Always Be an England'. Down below, the St John Ambulance Association offered free bread and jam to the queues of people waiting by the weighbridge. They had even put together a generous ration pack for every deportee, including a loaf of bread, milk, chocolate and cigarettes. Several unscrupulous local lads sidled into the queues, hoping to grab their own goody-bags, and narrowly avoided being deported themselves.

Many of the soldiers charged with carrying out the 'evacuations' were privately appalled at their orders, quietly apologising to the deportees even as they herded them onto the boats. But the noisy crowds who had turned out to see the English off were dangerously close to an organised protest. Unsurprisingly, the Army soon clamped down on the troublemakers. In Jersey, more than a dozen teenage boys ended up spending a night in the cells for shouting at soldiers and kicking around a German helmet in the streets.

In Guernsey too, the departure of the ships was a politically charged event, with the crowds of deportees met by spontaneous displays of solidarity, much to the irritation of the authorities. The journalists at the *Star* had already laid out a full page on the emotional scenes at the White Rock, complete with poignant personal stories and heavily illustrated with photographs, when they received a notice from the Feldkommandantur ordering them not to publish any of it. An early page proof had already been run off, however, and soon found its way into circulation as an unofficial tribute to the deportees.

In the ensuing days speculation was rife, both as to the final destination of those who had departed – 'there is a rumour about Madagascar but nothing is definite', wrote Mrs Le Bideau, for once without irony – and as to the reason for their sudden exile. Was the move a reprisal for the recent bombing of German towns by the RAF, or the ill-fated raid on Dieppe? No one could be sure.

There was, in fact, a rationale behind the deportations, although it was a somewhat obscure one. A year earlier, when British forces in Iran had begun interning German citizens, Hitler had issued an order: for every German held there, ten British citizens should be taken from the Channel Islands to the Pripet Marshes in Ukraine. At the time, his military commanders had been far from enthusiastic at the prospect of moving thousands of civilians into an operational area, so they had stalled. Sure enough, the Führer's attention had soon turned to other matters, not least his obsession with fortifying the islands against naval assault.

It was only in September 1942 that a Swiss official working on a prisoner-exchange proposal inadvertently drew Hitler's attention to the fact that the deportations had never been carried out. Enraged, the Führer sent his order through again, and this time there was no getting around it.

The islanders might not have known the full story behind the deportations, but they certainly knew how they felt about them. Once again, it seemed, the Germans had shown that their word was not to be trusted. The impromptu demonstrations as the boats left the islands spoke to a barely suppressed well of resentment, and occasionally those feelings spilled out into the open. Pearl and Gwen Smith were sad to learn that the parents of their friend Douglas Luckie, the charismatic baritone from the Lyric No. 1 Company, were among those who had been forced to quit the island. As a young adult who had been born in Guernsey, Douglas himself was exempt, but his parents' departure left him homeless. Fortunately, Mr and Mrs Smith were more than willing to take him in. He moved into a little room at the top of the hotel, and was immediately accepted as a member of the family.

Douglas was a sensitive young man, and the loss of his parents hit him hard. The night they left, the Lyric company were reviving one of their staples, *Café Continental*, and he was down to perform the final song, 'Absent Friends'. Pearl and Gwen watched from one of the little café tables that littered the stage as he walked slowly down to the footlights with a glass of wine in his hand and began to sing. His normally smooth voice had a crack in it, and he struggled to get through to the end of the song.

When he reached the final line, Douglas raised his glass in the air. 'The toast is absent friends,' he sang, downing the wine as the curtain fell.

For a moment there was total silence in the theatre. Then from somewhere at the back of the auditorium a voice called out, 'Don't worry, Doug, they'll be home again soon!'

Suddenly, the crowd erupted in applause, and the noise of five hundred stamping feet filled the theatre, along with whoops and cries of 'Encore!' The Germans in the audience were confused, and more than a little concerned at the sudden outburst.

As the curtain rose and the orchestra struck up again for a reprise, the applause continued unabated. Douglas was overcome with emotion, and this time when he tried to sing he just couldn't get the words out. The rest of the cast rose from their tables and performed the song for him, choking back their own tears until they reached the final lines. Then they stepped down to the front of the stage and took their bows.

With the curfew looming, there was no time for the audience to hang around. Obediently, they began filing out of the theatre, returning to the quiet solitude of their homes and the daily drudgery of life under Occupation. But they left in the knowledge that they had shared something precious together, an electrifying moment of solidarity.

CHAPTER TWENTY-ONE

UNHAPPY CAMPERS

It was more than two years since Hubert Nicolle and James Symes had begun their ill-fated undercover operation in Guernsey, and in that time the Channel Islanders could be forgiven for thinking that the British government had more or less forgotten about them. So when a team of twelve commandos from the Special Operations Executive landed on Sark in October 1942 they certainly had the element of surprise.

The principal goal of the raid was to capture a German soldier for interrogation by MI19, the section of military intelligence responsible for extracting information from enemy prisoners. Aside from aerial reconnaissance, the British had little information on what was happening in the Channel Islands – even the deportation of two thousand islanders the previous month had so far gone unnoticed. If there was any possibility of an armed invasion at some future date, they would need reliable information on the strength of the new Atlantic Wall fortifications, not to mention the disposition of the twenty-five-thousand-odd German soldiers currently stationed there.

But for Churchill, there was a more emotional rationale as well. He didn't like the thought of German soldiers relaxing and sunning themselves in British territory as if they were on vacation, and was determined to make their stay on the islands an unpleasant one.

At 11.30 p.m. on 3 October, the commandos landed at Point Chateau, climbing up the 'Hog's Back' to the island plateau, 300 feet above sea level. Then they set off inland, heading first for Petit Dixcart, a rather grand house where they hoped they might find some sleeping Germans (it turned out to be unoccupied) and then on to the next large dwelling, La Jaspellerie. Here they encountered Frances Pittard, a widow in her early forties whose husband had died only a few months before, leaving her alone in the house.

Despite her shock at being roused by tough-looking men with blackened faces, armed with guns and knives, Mrs Pittard rendered valuable assistance. Once she had put on a dressing gown, she produced a map of the island and began directing the leader of the commandos, Major Geoffrey Appleyard, to the nearest German billet, in an annexe of the Dixcart Hotel. She also filled him in on the recent deportations, producing a copy of the *Guernsey Evening Press* for him to take back to London as evidence.

The commandos pressed on to the hotel, where they spotted a sentry on guard duty. One of the men crept up behind him and drew his knife, plunging it down between the German's shoulders. Then he dragged the body behind a bush, and rejoined the rest of the team as they entered the hotel.

Inside, they found five German soldiers, asleep and snoring loudly. Rousing them at knifepoint, they manhandled them out of their beds, bound their hands, and led them outside in their nightshirts to begin the trek back to Point Chateau, where the boat was waiting to take them to England.

Suddenly, one of the prisoners bolted, knocking his captor to the ground and disappearing into the darkness. Spurred on by his example, the other Germans attempted to escape as well, and in the ensuing chaos, one more prisoner struggled free.

'If they try to get away, shoot them!' shouted Major Appleyard. Several shots rang out, and two of the German men were hit.

The commandos were left with just one prisoner. They rushed back with him to the waiting boat, making their escape from Sark before reinforcements could arrive on the scene. A little after half past six that morning, they were back on English soil.

All in all, the mission had been a qualified success. Despite the chaotic scene outside the hotel, the commandos had succeeded in their objective. They had captured a German prisoner and gathered valuable intelligence as well, thanks to Mrs Pittard and her newspaper.

In the long run, however, the raid did more harm than good. Hitler was incensed at the fact that his men had been bound by the British commandos, not to mention that three of them were now dead. The Führer's office released an angry statement on the 'disgraceful' incident, damning the 'terrorist and sabotage parties of the British and their confederates, who do not act like soldiers but like bandits'. Two weeks later, a special 'Commando Order' was issued, instructing German soldiers to execute Allied agents without trial, even if they were captured in uniform. In Sark, the curfew was extended from 7 p.m. to 7 a.m. as punishment for Mrs Pittard's actions – she herself was sent to prison in Guernsey – and the island was reinforced with additional barbed wire and landmines. 'It seemed a heavy price to pay for the capture of one prisoner and a copy of the *Guernsey Evening Press*,' the Dame commented wryly.

Still reeling from the deportation of the British citizens a couple of weeks earlier, the local people waited anxiously to see what further punishments might be in store. In the meantime, there was another wartime Christmas to prepare for. For the Germans, it was always an important time, and they went to considerable effort to make it as special as possible, turning the island hall into a grotto filled with pine trees and inviting the local children to come and collect presents crafted by the soldiers during their off-hours.

In Guernsey, eleven-year-old Doris Lihou had learned to expect little in the way of Christmas presents, but before the family's meagre decorations were even packed away for the new year, she received a gift far in excess of anything she had dreamed of. After many months behind bars in France, her father Stanley was granted an early release and sent back home to his family.

Given the circumstances, it was a sombre celebration. The last time Stanley had seen his wife and children was during his brief visit to attend his son John's funeral. Doris noticed that her father never spoke of his time behind bars, and it seemed to have forged a new distance between him and her mother. But she was just delighted to have him back again. Perhaps finally the family could begin to heal.

The Germans, though, had something else in mind. Hitler was still smarting from the humiliation of the British raid on Sark, and in February a new punishment was imposed on the islanders, with the announcement of a second round of deportations. This time the targets were 'undesirables' – including anyone who had served a prison sentence for crimes against the regime. Mr Lihou, along with his whole family, were earmarked for 'evacuation'.

There was an exemption for children over the age of seventeen, which meant Doris's elder sister Blanche was entitled to stay in Guernsey. But her parents were anxious about leaving her alone on an island full of young German soldiers. Since her brother Richard's seventeenth birthday would be coming up in May, Mrs Lihou went to the Kommandantur and pleaded for him to be allowed to remain as well. Much to her relief, the request was granted.

The Lihou family weren't the only ones seeking special dispensation from the Germans. For his part in the Nicolle and Symes affair, Ambrose Sherwill's name had been added to the list, but he wrote personally to Baron von Aufsess, begging that his wife and sons should be allowed to stay in Guernsey. Against his own better judgement – not to mention his orders from Berlin – the baron agreed to the request.

Some pleas, however, fell on deaf ears. The Dame of Sark, who had saved both her husband Bob and the island vicar, Reverend Phillips, from exile during the previous round of deportations, was unable to repeat the trick a second time. Despite her vehement protestations, she was told that both men would have to go. Also beyond reprieve was Pearl and Gwen's Jewish aunt Betty, who had been lucky enough to escape the purge which had caught her friends Therese and Gusti the previous year. This time, Betty and her husband Harry, along with their baby daughter, were forced to leave the island after all. So too were the Jewish men and women in Jersey, whose names had been gathered the previous year. And, of course, the cause of all the trouble: Mrs Pittard.

With the paperwork signed, sealed and delivered, the deportees set about the frantic preparation for departure. Once again the islands were thrown into chaos as cases were packed, houses boarded up, and beloved pets sent off to the vet for the final time. On the allotted day, the reluctant travellers hauled their belongings with them into town and waited to be herded onto the boats.

On 12 February 1943, those from Guernsey and Sark gathered at the Gaumont Cinema in St Peter Port, where they sat patiently in the auditorium awaiting instructions. It was a foul day to set sail, and the voyage was delayed for many hours, but eventually the weary troop were ushered down to the White Rock, soaked through by the driving rain. One by one they piled onto the little coal boat that was to take them across to St Malo.

Once on board, the men and women were ushered into separate dining areas and given a bowl each of watery swede soup. Despite the weather, some were looking forward to the voyage, especially the younger deportees, for whom a trip to the Continent smacked more of adventure than punishment. Many had never left their island homes before, and taking a journey to France – let alone Germany – was exciting, whatever the circumstances. Fifteen-year-old Nellie Galliene from Sark was thrilled to board the boat at St Peter Port Harbour, and looked forward to the new camp life that awaited her.

It didn't take long for her enthusiasm to wear off, however. The boat had not been out at sea long before most of the passengers began feeling seasick. As they were tossed up and down on the waves, one by one they brought up the disgusting soup they had just eaten.

Doris Lihou was one of only a handful of islanders who was spared the ordeal of seasickness, but her mother Amy wasn't so lucky. After she disappeared to the toilet for a worryingly long time, Doris went to look for her, only to find her knelt down on the deck outside the cubicle, with a metal bucket clutched between her knees. She was plunging her hands into the liquid inside, searching for the set of false teeth she had accidentally vomited up along with her meal.

All in all, it was a hellish journey, and by the time they reached the ancient walled city of St Malo three hours later, the islanders were desperate to set foot on dry land. But they were forced to wait – still lurching a little with every movement of the sea – until a group of dockers arrived to unload their luggage. One woman from Sark, Gladys Falle, was still so ill that she had to be carried ashore.

In St Malo, the travellers were bundled onto a waiting train to begin the long journey to Germany. Once again, the men were kept in a separate carriage from the women, but Doris consoled herself with the thought that she would see her father again soon, when they arrived at their final destination.

They were not long into the journey when the train suddenly ground to a halt and everyone was ordered to disembark. A British air raid was in progress, and there were fears that the train could be hit. Fortunately, the danger soon passed, and the men and women returned to their allotted carriages. What they didn't realise, how-ever, was that during their stop the train had been uncoupled. The women and children went on their way, while the men's carriage remained behind, waiting for a second locomotive.

It was only when Doris and her mother arrived in Compiègne, about fifty miles north-east of Paris, that they realised Stanley was no longer travelling with them. The men were being sent straight on to Laufen, a camp in Germany, while the women and children would be held in France indefinitely. Mrs Lihou asked the guards repeatedly how long the separation would last, but no one seemed able or willing to provide an answer.

By the time they finally disembarked at Compiègne Station, most of the deportees wanted nothing more than to lie down on something that wasn't moving, but instead they found themselves bundled into rickety horse-drawn carts for the three-mile trip to Front Stalag Z122.

For Nellie Galliene, the journey had well and truly lost its sheen of excitement. As she listened to the the horses' hooves clattering on the cobblestoned streets, all she could think about were the final journeys of French prisoners on their way to the guillotine.

The little cart Nellie was travelling in arrived in front of the looming gates of the camp, where huge searchlights beamed down on the new arrivals. The prisoners were led inside for processing – first their fingerprints were taken, then they were each assigned a prisoner number, printed on a small metal disk. At last, when the formalities were concluded, the exhausted travellers were offered a mug of disgusting mint tea before being taken to their beds.

There were over a hundred women and children staying at the camp, plus a handful of elderly men who had been deemed unsuitable for transport with the younger males. Most slept in large dormitories, kept warm – just about – thanks to a tiny stove in the corner. The straw-filled palliasses were infested with bed bugs, but most of the deportees were too shattered to care. Nellie slumped onto her mattress and closed her eyes, trying to ignore the feeling that the room was swaying as if she was still on the sea.

The next morning, the deportees got a better look at their new home, and it wasn't encouraging. The only washing facilities were a trough of cold water, and the toilets were no more than holes in the ground. To add to the islanders' humiliations, the authorities seemed to be on a fanatical hunt for nits. Infested women and girls had their hair cut very short and their scalps daubed with a noxious black substance. One of the youngest to undergo the unpleasant treatment was one-year-old Janet Duquemin, Pearl and Gwen Smith's baby cousin.

Janet's mother Betty, meanwhile, soon found that her fluent German meant she was seen as a useful asset in the camp. She was given the role of camp leader, charged with negotiating between her fellow islanders and the German guards. It was a difficult position for Betty, already separated from her husband and living among largely unfamiliar faces. Many of the islanders instinctively distrusted her, assuming that a woman who spoke the language of the enemy must be guilty of fraternisation. Little did they realise that as a Jew the last thing she wanted was to draw the attention of the Germans.

At least Betty wasn't the only internee on the receiving end of such distrust and opprobrium. Among the hundred-odd residents of the camp were the wives of the Guernsey policemen who had been caught stealing from the island's food stores. Even nine months later, the matter was still a raw one for many islanders, and the women who had benefited from their husbands' crimes were generally treated as co-conspirators. Amy Lihou was furious to learn that she would be forced to share a dormitory with some of them, anxious that she might be tarred by association. It was bad enough that her own husband had been caught up in a criminal enterprise, but at least Stanley hadn't betrayed his own countryfolk the way the bent coppers had.

While Mrs Lihou got to grips with the politics of the camp, her daughter Doris was already making new friends. In another complex adjacent to the one that held the islanders, a group of American servicemen were being held prisoner. When they learned that the Channel Island deportees had received no parcels of goods from the Red Cross – since they were being held temporarily, rather than permanently, they were not yet entitled to them – the Yanks generously shared some of their own stash, tossing tins of salmon and packets of cigarettes over the tall barbed-wire fence.

Doris's twelfth birthday was approaching, and the Americans were determined that she should celebrate in style. 'How about we give you a concert?' one of them suggested. She had told them that she had a passion for tap-dancing. In fact, before leaving Guernsey she had been taking lessons with Gwen Smith in the mirrored hut at the back of Les Pieux Hotel, and had dreamed of one day joining her teacher on the stage. 'You dance,' the Americans told her, 'and we'll take care of the music.'

Somehow, the word made its way around the islanders' camp, and soon everyone was preparing for the big day. Doris collected up the paper labels attached to the Red Cross salmon tins, until she had a pile of colourful little fishes to decorate her dress with. The Yanks, meanwhile, went a step further, stripping the straw out of their palliasses to make their own Hawaiian-style grass skirts, and hauling an upright piano out into the yard to provide the soundtrack to the party.

When they discovered how much their neighbours enjoyed the

American tunes, Doris's friends had the German guards bring their gramophone over to the islanders' camp, along with a recording of 'When It's Springtime in the Rockies'. For the next three days the song was on hard rotation in the main hallway of the barracks, until every one of the deportees knew the lyrics by heart.

The cheery goodwill of the Americans was enough to lift anyone's spirits, but on the other side of the camp was a grim reminder of the cruelty of the Nazi regime. A third complex at Compiègne housed a mixture of French Jews and political prisoners, many of whom had served with the Resistance. It was a transit camp, and every so often, in the dead of night – when the latest batch of prisoners was marched out of the gates to board one of the trains to Auschwitz – the islanders would be woken by the defiant strains of the Marseillaise being sung with full gusto.

It was a wonder the French prisoners could muster the energy to sing. They were pitifully undernourished, and would often resort to eating scraps off the floor. Sometimes, during their thrice-daily roll calls, the Channel Island deportees would see them pulling up clumps of grass and stuffing them into their mouths.

Several of the islanders – Mrs Lihou among them – began throwing their own food over the wire for the poor Frenchmen. But when the Germans realised what was happening, they clamped down on such acts of generosity, fixing their powerful searchlights on the barrier between the two camps to catch any good Samaritans in the act.

Like the Frenchmen, the islanders held at Compiègne were technically still in transit, but what had started off as a stop of perhaps a few days had grown to weeks, and then months, with no sign of the long-awaited departure. Finally, though, it came, and once again the deportees were ordered to pack up their belongings and prepare themselves for an arduous journey. This time they would be travelling to Ilag V-B Biberach, one of half a dozen camps in Germany now playing host to 'evacuated' Channel Islanders. There they would be joining the first batch of deportees who had left the islands the previous autumn.

Before leaving Compiègne, Doris made sure to visit her American friends to say goodbye. She brought with her a little autograph book, which they passed around the group, signing their names along with messages of support and friendship. Among many pages of doggerel poetry – not to mention the odd pencil sketch – was a touchingly simple note written by a man from Texas: 'Pleased to meet. Sorry to part. Hope to meet again.'

It was over four hundred miles from Compiègne to the small German town of Biberach, but at least the long rail journey offered some attractive scenery along the way. The deportees' new home was a large camp on the top of a hill, with picturesque views over the timber-framed houses of the town below, nestled in the crook of the River Riss. To the west were the pine trees of the Black Forest and to the south the jutting peaks of the Bavarian Alps.

Compared to the French transit camp, Ilag V-B Biberach was a significant improvement. Eight months earlier, when the first islanders had arrived at the camp, it had been as rough and ready as Compiègne, but by the time Doris and her fellow travellers turned up, conditions had improved immeasurably, and the thousand-odd residents were living in relative comfort, all things considered. There were proper, flushing toilets and electric lights in every barrack block, real mattresses on the wooden bunkbeds, and even a communal hot-water shower room – as the deportees discovered shortly after their arrival, when they were ordered to strip off for a much-needed wash, and to hand over the clothes they had been wearing for delousing.

The regime in the camp was distinctly hands-off. The German Army had yielded responsibility for the prisoners to the local police, and they in turn had allowed a committee of islanders, headed by a 'camp captain', a Guernsey architect called Garfield Garland, to take care of most day-to-day business. Garland was a slightly aloof figure, but respected by deportees and Germans alike, and his strict-but-fair approach to discipline was certainly preferable to appealing to the guards to resolve disputes. His private living quarters generated a degree of resentment – most internees at the camp were housed in eighty-four-person barracks, with up to eighteen people per room – but he had managed to get the camp running smoothly, appealed judiciously to the Germans for specific improvements to be made – for example, persuading them to fit proper doors on the women's toilets – and through a mixture of tact and the threat of minor punishments, brought almost every member of his thousand-strong community more or less in line.

This was no small matter given the broad composition of the population. If the regime was to be seen as a fair one, it was important that everyone contributed equally, taking on tasks such as cleaning the latrines, tilling the vegetable plots and serving up food in the canteen. But for those deportees who had arrived still dressed in their finest fur coats and high-heeled shoes, such a suggestion had been tantamount to revolution.

To help maintain order, Garland had his own camp police force, with fourteen constables alternating on a daily rota system, and their own headquarters (Barrack 16, alias 'Bow Street'), which was open twenty-four hours a day and functioned, somewhat bizarrely, as a prison-within-a-prison. In practice, the long arm of the law didn't extend much further than keeping the camp's younger residents out of trouble. Almost 150 of the deportees at Biberach were children and, just as on the islands, pranking the Germans was a popular pastime.

For the most part, the inmates behaved remarkably well, and any minor disagreements were resolved via a camp tribunal. Sometimes, though, delicacy and tact were required of those in authority. Fifteen miles away from Biberach was Ilag V-C Wurzach, where more than six hundred Jersey people were housed – and where the camp captain, Major F. A. Ray, found himself smoothing over an unpleasant family dispute.

With her good looks and raven-black hair, Joan Ingram had been cast as a gypsy princess in an am-dram production for the camp theatre, starring opposite a man called Len Grubb. But unfortunately for Joan's husband Cliff, the romantic spark kindled between the two performers soon spilled over into a backstage affair. When Joan left him for Len, Cliff took it on the chin, keen to avoid an awkward scene in a community from which there was literally no escape. But his father, who was in charge of the camp soup queue, was less willing to forgive and forget. Every day, when he saw Len approaching, he would bellow, 'There he is, Grubb by name and Grubb by nature!' In the end, the camp captain was forced to intervene and persuade the old man to drop his vendetta.

In many respects, the standard of life in the camps was no worse than it had been back home. In fact, since the Red Cross provided every inmate with a generous parcel every twelve days, containing such treats as sugar, cocoa and chocolate as well as the more essential foodstuffs, they were better fed than some of their compatriots on the islands. So popular were the Red Cross handouts that the camp's official meals – meagre portions of soup and stale bread – often went uneaten, and those who had more food than they needed entered into an elaborate bartering system. Others, meanwhile, put their crafting skills to good use on the packing materials. Mr Davidson was the acknowledged master of this particular art, working the little metal tins into everything from makeshift crockery to children's toys. He soon acquired a new nickname: 'Can-Can'.

Such activities were an important part of life at Biberach, where the greatest hardship was perpetual boredom. Many inmates threw themselves into creative pursuits, producing prodigious quantities of clothes, toys and assorted nick-nacks out of all manner of unlikely materials. Young boys and girls would fly handcrafted kites over the parade ground – that is, when the adults weren't using it for games of football, cricket and hockey. There was a well-stocked library – all books having been deemed suitable by the German authorities and officially stamped 'Approved' – and the numerous instruments provided by the Red Cross ensured a busy repertoire of musical performances.

For those who felt the urge to stretch their legs, meanwhile, guided (and guarded) walks would depart three times a week, with a German sergeant and his trusty Alsatian leading the inmates out

into the surrounding forest – often with a brief stop-off at one of
the town's charming inns on the way home for a cheeky mug or two
of local ale. Unsurprisingly, these outings were massively oversub-
scribed, so access was on a ticketed basis, adding another valuable
commodity to the unofficial barter economy.

Of all the camp activities, none was more popular than the shows
performed weekly in an old barrack hut that had been converted into
a theatre, complete with a stage, lighting, scenery and even numbered
seating. The box office would release tickets for each evening's show
at ten o'clock in the morning, but to stand a chance of getting in,
prisoners would have to be in the queue soon after seven. Groups of
friends would drag their chairs out to the yard and sit in line, taking
it in turns to nip off to the canteen and scoff their breakfast.

A camp repertory company performed a new play every Sunday
evening, while two rival variety outfits, run by Guernseymen Tony
Chubb and Len Teel, vied to provide the ultimate evening's entertainment. Like their counterparts in the Channel Islands, the two
impresarios were always on the look-out for new talent. Doris
Lihou's reputation as a tap-dancer must have preceded her since after
only a few days at Biberach, she was asked to try out for Mr Chubb's
company. In Doris's case, the audition was little more than a formality, but it did offer her the chance to watch a few other hopefuls
showing what they could do. Among them was Betty Duquemin, the
Jewish interpreter, who gave a moving rendition of 'One Day When
We Were Young'. From a technical standpoint her voice was far
from strong, and she spoke at least as many words as she sang, but
there was something mesmerising about the performance, a tragic
intensity that made it impossible to look away. By the time she hit
the final note there were tears streaming down her face.

'That was lovely, but do you know anything a bit more cheerful?'
Mr Chubb asked her uncertainly. Betty tried her best to belt out a
few lighter numbers, but it soon became clear that her talent only
extended to sad songs.

Before long, Doris was hard at work on rehearsals for the next
big production: the old Guernsey stalwart *Café Continental*. Mr

Chubb's producer was a man called Fred Williams, who had been involved in the Lyric No. 1 Company before he was deported. In Biberach, Fred was determined to recreate some of the highlights of the Lyric repertoire, and he had done a remarkable job of sourcing local costumes and props that were not far off the originals. The age range of the cast was quite different – at twelve years old, Doris was by no means the youngest of the trio of dancing girls, whose short polka-dot skirts and bikini tops seemed rather old for their years – but the scenery and props, down to a comedy rubber chicken, were virtually identical to those that had been used at the Lyric. The audience reaction, meanwhile, was more than equal to the rapturous applause the original company received in Guernsey. During her first performance, Doris was surprised to spot the camp's German commandant sitting in the front row, cheering enthusiastically at the end of each number.

There was, of course, one big difference between the Biberach staging of *Café Continental* and the original Guernsey production: this show featured performers from Jersey as well. Although the majority of the larger island's deportees had been moved on to the camp at Bad Wurzach, Jersey folk still represented a sizeable minority in the camp, making up around a fifth of the total number of inmates.

The two islands had always enjoyed a good-natured rivalry, and even had disparaging pet names for each other: in Jersey, the Guernsey folk were known as Donkeys (or *Ânes* in the old Norman French patois), while in Guernsey the men and women of Jersey were called *Crapauds*, or Toads. Every year, the top sportsmen of the two islands would compete in a football competition known as the Muratti Vase. Biberach hosted its own version of the contest, although predictably, given the numbers, the Guernsey team always came out on top.

In any case, the community in the camps was constantly evolving, as new groups of prisoners arrived and departed. In August, three months after she had arrived at Biberach, and almost half a year since they had become separated on the train to Compiègne, Doris

Lihou heard a rumour that her father would be coming to join the rest of the family. Her mother, Amy, insisted on staying in her room, worried that the sight of her husband after such a long separation might be more than she could cope with, so Doris went down to the gates alone to await the new arrivals. One by one she scanned the faces of the men in the crowd until she found her father, looking a little thinner and more dishevelled than she remembered him but otherwise fit and healthy.

'Dad!' she called.

Stanley raced over and swept her up into a hug. A few moments later, though, he was shepherded off for processing, along with the other men who had recently arrived from Laufen. 'I'll see you in the morning,' he promised, squeezing his daughter's hand before he was led away.

Doris rushed back to tell her mother the good news. Mrs Lihou was not normally one to show her emotions in public, but the joy and relief she felt was plain to see.

Although married couples were forced to sleep in separate barracks, in daylight hours they were able to spend most of their time together. Since the dormitories were crowded at the best of times, the residents came up with an unofficial rota system, whereby each couple would alternate between days when the husband visited his wife and vice versa. In any case, Mr Lihou chose not to spend much time in his wife and daughter's crowded room. More often, he would take them off for walks around the camp and, when they could get the necessary tickets, out into the countryside.

An internment camp was certainly an unusual place to grow up, but the islanders went to great lengths to build a functioning community in exile. Doris attended the camp's senior school in the 'Big House', an attractive two-storey building with a terrace where the Germans and Captain Garland had their rooms. She was taught by a group of former teachers, largely from Jersey, who between them did their best to provide the children with as rounded an education as possible.

In the camps, life gradually settled into a relatively comfortable routine. The islanders enjoyed a relaxed regime, plenty of food thanks to the Red Cross parcels – not to mention the odd apple thrown over the fence by the local villagers – and a surprisingly broad repertoire of leisure activities. Back at home, meanwhile, conditions only continued to deteriorate as the Occupation bit harder and harder.

They weren't to know it at the time, but in many respects the deportees were the lucky ones.

CHAPTER TWENTY-TWO

CRUEL AND UNUSUAL

In the German internment camp at Laufen, Ambrose Sherwill had finally returned to high office, serving as camp captain to his own little community of displaced Channel Islanders. But in the two years since his spectacular fall from power in Guernsey, his Jersey counterpart, Alexander Coutanche, had remained firmly in place.

As president of the Controlling Committee, Sherwill had seen himself as a 'buffer' between the Germans and the islanders, although he himself had been forced to conclude that he was never a very good one. Coutanche pursued a similar policy, but far more effectively. A shrewd and calculating man with many years of political experience, his cool, aloof manner had earned him the respect of the Germans, even as his clever manoeuvring continued to infuriate them. 'He is our sworn opponent,' wrote Baron von Aufsess, 'not so much because he hates us – he's too wily an old lawyer for that – as because he understandably chafes against the restriction to his authority and feels wounded in his self-esteem.' After one particularly frustrating encounter with Coutanche, von Aufsess was forced to admit defeat, writing, with a mixture of respect and resentment, 'The bailiff, cold and vulpine-visaged, departed as justified victor of the day.'

In spring of 1943, Coutanche faced a particularly knotty challenge. On 27 April, a number of supply boats on their way to the islands from France came under attack by the RAF, and a substantial quantity of food ended up at the bottom of the Channel. Three days later, the Jersey feldkommandant, Colonel Knackfuss, published a notice announcing that as a result the bread, meat and cheese rations of the civilian populations would be reduced.

In the years since the Germans had arrived on the islands, Coutanche had never spoken to the bailiff of Guernsey, the elderly Victor Carey. But on the morning of Saturday 1 May, he received a message that Carey would like to talk to him, so he paid a visit to the Feldkommandantur and asked to use their phone.

'What are you going to do about this cutting of the food rations?' Carey asked Coutanche, once the call had been connected.

'Well, in the first place we are going to protest,' Coutanche told him. 'All other things apart, this is a reprisal, which goes against the Hague Convention.'

Suddenly, the line went dead. The German operator had cut off the conversation.

In the past, Coutanche and his colleagues on the island's Superior Council had registered their objection to new German laws by writing to the Feldkommandantur, but this situation seemed to call for something more. Having consulted with his colleagues, Coutanche hatched a plan to write to the Swiss ambassador in Berlin. Switzerland was the 'protecting power' for the islands, and their only official diplomatic link with Germany.

Coutanche penned an eloquent letter to the Swiss ambassador, arguing that as a reprisal the German response was illegal under international law. When it was finished he delivered it to Colonel Knackfuss, requesting he send it on to Berlin.

Before long, the bailiff found himself summoned to the colonel's office. Knackfuss was deeply unhappy. 'I do not like this word reprisal,' he said, brandishing the letter, which he obviously hadn't yet posted. 'The reduction in food rations is not a reprisal at all. Food was lost due to the actions of the British planes, and that loss must be made good.'

Ever the political poker player, Coutanche remained stony-faced.

'A letter to the protecting power is a very serious matter,' the colonel continued. 'I must request that you withdraw it.'

Coutanche, however, was resolute. 'I'm sorry, but I must insist that you send it,' he told the colonel. The diplomatic stand-off continued until Knackfuss made it clear that the meeting was at an end.

As it turned out, however, Knackfuss wasn't the only German big-wig with an interest in the outcome of the case. General von Schmettow had learned of Coutanche's letter and was equally keen that it should never leave the island. On Sunday morning, Coutanche's right-hand man, the attorney general Charles Duret Aubin, told him that he had been approached in the street by an interpreter working for Major von Helldorf, von Schmettow's number two, requesting that he and Coutanche come in to see him as soon as possible.

Von Schmettow could easily have sent his message through official channels, but he evidently didn't want Knackfuss to find out about the meeting. Puzzled, Coutanche and Duret Aubin drove over to the commandant's headquarters at the Metropole Hotel, where an officious German sergeant insisted they park their cars on the street rather than in the courtyard, which was reserved for German officers.

The two men obliged, but seeing von Helldorf approach them, Coutanche couldn't resist pushing back against the affront. 'I don't know what the commander-in-chief would like,' he remarked casually, 'but perhaps this is a rather secret meeting? It is twelve o'clock on a Sunday morning, when all the faithful will soon be returning from church. If they see two motor-cars standing outside your office, one of which is mine and the other that of the attorney general, they will begin to wonder what's happening.' To Coutanche's satisfaction, von Helldorf angrily ordered the sergeant to move the two vehicles inside.

The second meeting was no more decisive than the first. What von Schmettow wanted was apparently a blow-by-blow account of everything that had occurred in Knackfuss's office. Once this was provided, Coutanche and Duret Aubin were dismissed.

By the time he left, Coutanche was none the wiser about the commandant's plans, but one thing was clear: von Schmettow didn't trust Knackfuss. The Germans were obviously far from united on the question of reprisals – and that, he reasoned, could only be a good thing.

The next Coutanche heard, Colonel Knackfuss was climbing down from his position. There would be a temporary 20 per cent reduction in the bread ration, but the quantities of all other food-stuffs were to remain unchanged. More importantly, the colonel reluctantly acknowledged that cutting food supplies in response to military action, and where there was no genuine shortage, was a clear violation of the Hague Convention.

With these points agreed, Coutanche consented to withdrawing his letter to the Swiss embassy. But to push his victory home, he had the Jersey newspaper print a notice explaining that the reduced ration of bread was 'dictated by the existing war situation and is in no sense a punishment against the civilian population'. The 'vulpine-visaged' bailiff had won another round against the Germans.

Coutanche might have been an effective advocate for his own people, but that was about as far as his influence went. He had not, for example, made any effort to protect the island's Jewish population, beyond a symbolic protest at forcing them to wear the Star of David. By now, the Jews had been largely forgotten in the Channel Islands, and after a brief period of unease surrounding the two waves of mass deportations, the regimes in Jersey, Guernsey and Sark had returned to a relatively peaceable equilibrium. But on the long-abandoned island of Alderney, whose rulers had spent the last three years living in exile on the mainland, sinister activities were afoot.

Codenamed 'Adolf' in official German communications, Alderney was the most remote of the Channel Islands, closer to the coast of occupied France than it was to the rest of the archipelago. For several years now, rumours of atrocities taking place there had filtered over to the larger islands, but in the absence of any concrete evidence, most people had dismissed them as anti-German propaganda. In fact, those responsible had simply managed to keep the worst abuses of the Occupation hidden from view. In Alderney, a stark and windswept place with no civilian population to speak of, they had found the perfect place for acts of the most outrageous brutality to go unnoticed by the wider population.

Four camps had been quietly built on the island by the notorious Organisation Todt, and the workers housed in them – a mixture of Russian POWs, French Jews, Spanish republicans and more – were treated with even less compassion than the forced labourers on the larger islands. But in March 1943, the situation on Alderney grew even worse, as one of the camps, Lager Sylt (named after a tiny German island in the Frisian Archipelago), was transferred to the authority of the SS, as an extension of the Neuengamme concentration camp just outside Hamburg. With the new guards came new prisoners in blue-and-white striped pyjamas, along with orders signed by Himmler himself stating that in the event of an Allied assault on the island the troops were to carry out a mass execution rather than allow any of the inmates to be rescued.

Those who endured the camps on Alderney and lived to tell the tale described a catalogue of brutality that ranked with the worst atrocities of the Third Reich. John Dalmau, who as a Spaniard was spared the worst abuses, later wrote about the horrors he witnessed: prisoners so starved of food that they would fight over scraps of rotting food and gobble down raw octopuses and conger eels straight from the sea; men who collapsed from exhaustion being thrown off the cliffs to their deaths; others shot through the head for stooping to tie their shoelaces; sadistic rituals in which prisoners were forced to 'dance' while the guards fired their guns at the ground beneath their feet. Other survivors told of prisoners crucified on the camp gates, their bodies left hanging there for days as a warning to others.

At Lager Norderney, on the far side of the island from Sylt, a barber who plied his trade in the room next door to the camp commandant's office witnessed the daily cleaning of blood off the walls there. On at least four occasions the mess was so bad that they had to be repainted.

In all four camps, prisoners endured appalling conditions, working sixteen-hour days on pathetically meagre rations, in clothes that were riddled with lice. When the outfits they had brought with them fell to pieces, they would cut holes in the corners of cement bags and wear them instead. There were no toilet breaks during working hours – if a prisoner needed to defecate, a supervisor would simply hold out a spade – and the men and boys (some as young as fourteen) worked through the most atrocious weather, soaked through with rain and buffeted by the blasting sea wind.

When they retired to their 120-bed barracks in the evenings, the exhausted prisoners would fall asleep almost immediately. No one was surprised when they woke up the next morning to find a corpse in the bed next to their own, sometimes already attracting the attention of rats. All the while, the SS officers lived a life of relative luxury, with plenty of food, raucous parties, and their own comfort women shipped in from France – forced labourers, all under the age of twenty-five, who would be spared any manual work other than a little cleaning, as long as they agreed to share the Germans' beds.

The depravity of the men in charge of the camps knew no bounds. When workers collapsed into the concrete they were mixing, the supervisors would allow them to be buried alive rather than stop the machines. When they were caught scrounging through the rubbish bins for scraps, the Germans would set the dogs on them. When they collapsed and died from overwork, they would be unceremoniously hurled into the sea, or buried at low tide in hastily dug pits in the wet sand.

Sometimes, when they wanted to get rid of a batch of unproductive workers, the guards would arrange a pretext for cold-blooded murder, pulling aside a section of fencing and herding the prisoners over the line with their Alsatians so that they could shoot them in the act of 'escaping'. Exactly how many prisoners died on Alderney is hard to ascertain, but some estimates run into the thousands. It was, in the words of one historian, 'the greatest mass murder which has ever occurred on British soil'.

The British government knew of the existence of the camps from aerial reconnaissance, and the Channel Islanders were certainly aware that they were there too. But while a few whispered accounts made their way back to the larger islands, most people had no idea of the cruelty being meted out just a few dozen kilometres from their shores. They were aware only that Alderney was a hub of activity. 'Amongst other queer workmen over there are German criminals who wear pyjama-like suits of white and black stripes,' wrote Mrs Le Bideau. 'Roads are being made and houses are being demolished. Electric light is being installed everywhere. The poor Alderney people, who evacuated to a man, will find the island vastly improved when they come back.'

On the larger islands, the slave workers might have been spared the most brutal cruelties that took place on Alderney, but nonetheless they were in a parlous state. By 1943 there were more then 15,000 OT workers in the Channel Islands, and the amount of food that was made available to them was woefully inadequate. As they grew increasingly desperate, thefts from the civilian population increased. Rather than provide the workers with sufficient nourishment, their guards often allowed them to escape from their camps at night to search for food. So it was that locals awoke to find that the vegetables they had carefully tended had been ripped out of the soil, or that the rabbits they had been breeding in their yards had been snatched.

The thefts hardened the hearts of some against the starving slave workers, and the locals began to grow fearful of unexpected visitors, anxiously locking their doors at night and putting heavy wooden shutters on their windows. In one particularly shocking incident, an elderly Jersey shopkeeper, Ernest Le Gresley, was killed and his sister badly injured when a robbery unexpectedly turned violent.

Many farmers saw the slave workers as a menace against which they were entitled to defend themselves. In Jersey, Osmund Simon and his brothers set up a makeshift burglar alarm in their yard, with a bucket attached to a long trip-rope that would yank it to the ground if anyone touched it. One night they were woken by the sound of the bucket clattering to the floor and rushed outside to find one of their windows already broken and a pair of slave workers fleeing in the direction of the neighbouring farm.

One of the men got away, but Osmund managed to grab hold of the other and threw him to the ground, beating him repeatedly with a wooden truncheon his father had given him. By the time his brothers arrived to help haul the young thief back to their farm, the slave worker was covered in blood. Osmund's father placed a call to the local police station, and a little while later a Black Maria drew up outside. Osmund could only hope that the policemen stopped off at the hospital to have the battered young man patched up before they returned him to his camp.

Other slave workers went further than just sneaking out of their camps at night to steal food, making concerted attempts to escape the OT altogether. The fugitives would hide out in empty haylofts or abandoned properties, doing their best to avoid detection by the authorities. Tina Du Feu found out the hard way that a group of Russians had spent the night in her hayloft when she climbed up the ladder and felt something sticky under her hands. The escapees, who had been surviving on a diet of raw mangolds and turnips, suffered from perpetual diarrhoea, and had evidently made it no further than the edge of the loft before relieving themselves. Mrs Du Feu was livid when she realised what was on her hands. The family had long since used up their last bar of soap, and it was several days before she could get rid of the smell.

Some islanders, however, acted with surprising magnanimity when they discovered they had uninvited guests. Arthur Rabet was puzzled when an enamel milk jug went missing from his house over-night. Next, he discovered that his cows, which had previously been very productive, were dry as a bone every morning. The mystery was solved when he found a group of escaped Russians, who had been living in his barn and milking the cows late at night. But far from reporting the squatters, Mr Rabet couldn't help feeling sorry for them. He even agreed to take two of the men into his home: a young Red Army lieutenant by the name of Grigori Koslov who had been taken prisoner by the German forces at Smolensk, and an older man the family nicknamed 'John', whose emaciated body was covered in chickenpox scars.

The Russians were treated as extra members of the family. They even attended Mr and Mrs Rabet's frequent parties, where they and the neighbouring farmers – some of whom were sheltering escapees of their own – would stay up late drinking cider and singing around the piano. One time, all the escaped slave workers living in the neighbourhood came along and performed a traditional Russian dance for their local benefactors.

For the Rabets, the fact that their neighbours were also sheltering Russians provided a degree of security – they were unlikely to be informed on by someone who was in the same boat, and since their farms were in a fairly isolated part of the island, the likelihood of a chance discovery was slim. But the Germans were doing their best to persuade local people to report suspicious characters, even publishing a notice in the paper reassuring hesitant informers that any slave workers who were recaptured would be treated fairly.

By this point, most locals were deeply sceptical about promises that issued from the authorities. They had seen how the Russians and other forced labourers were treated by their OT masters, and it was pretty clear that they would receive the full force of Nazi brutality on their return to the camps. As a result, over a hundred islanders found themselves sheltering slave workers on their properties – and in some cases even going further. Dennis Le Flem was fifteen years old when he saw a group of escapees staggering across the fields towards his parents' farm. They were dressed in rags, with bleeding feet wrapped in snatches of cloth, and their bodies were covered in sores and scabs from the beatings they had endured. Dennis's parents took the lads in for a couple of days, offering them a hot bath and a change of clothes, not to mention as much food as they could rustle up, before sending them on their way.

A little while later, one of the men returned, begging the family to let him stay with them. Although the house next door had a German soldier in it, they didn't have the heart to send him away.

The whole family soon learned the young man's story. His name was Piotr Bokatenko and he was only a year or two older than Dennis. When the Germans had overrun his village in Ukraine, they had demanded a certain number of young men be handed over as labourers, on pain of death. Piotr had been rounded up and put on a train to France. A month later he was in Jersey, working for the Organisation Todt.

Piotr had already picked up a little bit of English, and during the weeks he spent with the Le Flems, he became almost an older brother to Dennis. The two lads were both keen boxers and often sparred together. When the time came for Piotr to move on, Dennis gave the young Ukrainian his ID card, telling the authorities that he had lost it and requesting that they issue a replacement. A sympathetic local photographer, A. J. Laurens of York Street, took Piotr's photograph, and it was carefully stuck into place on top of Dennis's own.

The ID card was a valuable gift, giving Piotr the freedom to go about in public. It was far from foolproof, however. One day he was stopped on the road by a German corporal who was having an affair with a local woman. Having spent quite a bit of time in the neighbourhood, the German recognised Dennis's name at once, and he knew that the man in front of him was not who he claimed to be.

Sensing the game was up, Piotr dealt the German a knock-out blow, before disappearing once more into the countryside. Before long, Dennis was summoned to the Feldkommandantur to account for his ID card. He was interrogated for what felt like hours by a German who spoke impeccable English, having studied at Oxford before the war. Throughout the lengthy questioning, the teenager resolutely stuck to his story: the card had been lost, as he had already told the authorities, and what had happened to it after that was nothing to do with him. Dennis could tell the German didn't believe a word of it but in the end he sent him home, with vague threats about imprisonment in France ringing in his ears.

Piotr, meanwhile, continued to evade the authorities. Clearly it wouldn't be safe for him to stay with the Le Flem family again, but every so often they would find a handwritten note on their doormat, providing his latest address and asking if they could spare any food. Of course, they always sent as much as they could, and although destroying them would have been much more prudent, they kept

Piotr's little notes of thanks, written in broken English, as a keepsake of the bond that had been forged between them.

'Many, many thanks to you for your's kindnness to me,' he wrote to them one time. 'I shall never not forget obout it. And if I be olive I pay you back for what have you do for me . . . I cannot nor write, nor tele, how I'm pleased, and thankfull to you.' At the bottom of the note he added, 'Excuse me if I have any mistakes and also for my writing.'

CHAPTER TWENTY-THREE

RESISTANCE

In most cases, sheltering an escaped slave worker required more than just the generosity of a given homeowner. In the small, close-knit communities of rural Jersey, a degree of silent support from friends and neighbours was generally necessary as well. Some good-hearted souls, however, went further than just turning a blind eye. One day, Bob Le Sueur, the former office boy who was now running the Jersey branch of the General Accident insurance company, had cycled from St Helier to the rural parish of St Ouen to visit a lady called Louisa Gould. She was a widow who ran the local village shop, Millais Stores, and had put in a claim for a hearth-rug that had been damaged by a stray spark falling from her fireplace. Before paying out on the company's policies, Bob always liked to inspect the damage personally to be sure that the claim was legitimate. In Mrs Gould's case, there was no question of fraud concerning the rug – he observed the damage with his own eyes. Less convincing, however, was the widow's assertion that the young man Bob found drinking tea in her living room was a French lodger. When they exchanged pleasantries – the guest apparently spoke at least a little conversational English – he couldn't help noticing that the accent was all wrong. If anything, it sounded Russian.

It didn't take long for Mrs Gould to tell Bob the truth. The young man was a member of the Russian Air Force who had been shot down during the German invasion of his homeland and subsequently captured. His name was Feodor Buryi, although Mrs Gould knew him as 'Bill'. Escaped Russians were typically given anglicised names by their local associates, partly for ease of pronunciation, but also to avoid arousing suspicion if they were spoken about in public.

Bill had been brought to Jersey as a slave labourer in the summer of 1942, and since then he had already escaped twice from his camp in the parish of St Peter. After he was recaptured the first time, he had been stripped naked, soaked with cold water and forced to wheel a barrow full of stones around the camp until he was ready to drop with exhaustion, before being left outside all night. But the ordeal – which he was lucky to survive – had only galvanised him for a second escape attempt, and this time he had been determined to make a success of it. Bill had been working at a local quarry when, claiming that he needed to relieve himself, he had seized the opportunity to slip away onto a nearby roadway, crawling along on his hands and knees to avoid being spotted. It wasn't long before a local baker's van came along the road and pulled up beside him. Bill stared in disbelief as the driver got out, came round and opened the back door, gesturing for him to get inside.

The baker had dropped Bill off a quarter of a mile down the road, well out of sight of the OT supervisors at the quarry. There was a hillside covered in gorse on one side, and the young Russian immediately set off in that direction. As he reached the top of the hill and arrived at the edge of a large farm, he found a wooden hut with the door hanging ajar. It seemed as good a place as any to hide and wait for darkness to fall, so he pushed the door open and stepped inside. But before his eyes could adjust to the dark, Bill felt a pair of hands around his throat. Someone was trying to strangle him.

'*Pomogite!*' Bill cried, instinctively calling for help in his native language. The hands slackened their grip. Bill turned and looked into the face of one of his own countrymen who had obviously mistaken him for a German.

From the other Russian, Bill learned that he had reached the land of a sympathetic local farmer, René Le Mottée. Between the little hut Bill had stumbled upon, a large store building and the hayloft of his barn, Le Mottée already had a number of Russians hiding out on his farm, and despite having five children of his own, he was doing his best to feed and shelter all of them.

It was Le Mottée who had introduced Bill to Louisa Gould. The Germans had begun searching farms in his neighbourhood following the theft of some railway sleepers that had been taken for firewood, and knowing that his Russian guests would no longer be safe there Le Mottée had set about placing them with friends. For the lonely widow, the timing was eerily appropriate. She had recently received word that her son Edward had been killed while serving in the Royal Navy in the Mediterranean. His younger brother Ralph, meanwhile, was at university in Oxford. 'You are coming with me,' Mrs Gould told Bill decisively. 'I have lost one of my boys in this war and the other is away, and I'll try and make up for it by looking after you.'

Mrs Gould dressed Bill in Edward's clothes and gave him his old bicycle so they could ride into town together. With the help of a local doctor, Noel McKinstry, he was provided with false papers and even a ration card, and as his English improved thanks to regular lessons with his new adoptive 'mother', the young man felt increasingly confident going out on his own.

Bob listened to the story with amazement. He couldn't help feeling that Mrs Gould was taking quite a risk sheltering Bill, but when he tried to broach the subject, she replied simply, 'I had to do something for another mother's son.' In time, though, his concern turned out to be justified. Mrs Gould was betrayed by a pair of elderly ladies who lived nearby and knew she had been sheltering a Russian fugitive. Fortunately, the letter they wrote denouncing her was incorrectly addressed: instead of arriving at Victoria College House, a boarding facility which had been requisitioned for the Jersey Feldkommandantur, it was delivered to the college itself, and opened by the acting headmaster Pat Tatam.

Tatam felt he had no choice but to forward the letter on to the Germans, but before doing so he despatched a messenger to Mrs Gould, warning her that it was on its way and would reach the Feldkommandantur the following morning. That night, she and Bill worked frantically to destroy any evidence of his stay with her, and at 6 a.m. the next day he set off on his bike.

A few days later, on Saturday morning, Bob was working alone at the insurance company offices in St Helier when someone came to the door with a message: Mrs Gould's sister, Ivy Foster, would like to see him at his earliest convenience.

That afternoon, Bob closed up the office and cycled over to Mrs Foster's house, where he found Bill waiting in the living room. Mrs Foster explained the situation, and asked if he might be able to help. She and her husband were not in a position to keep Bill with them, she told him. They already had another Russian staying in an upstairs bedroom – Grigori Koslov, the Red Army lieutenant who had been caught milking Mr Rabet's cows – and could scarcely run the risk of taking on a second, especially since once the police were done raiding Louisa's house there was every chance they would begin looking into her family and friends.

Bob understood completely. 'He can stay at my office for the rest of the weekend,' he replied. The following Monday was a bank holiday, so it would be deserted for the next couple of days. Hopefully that would be enough time to find Bill somewhere more permanent to stay.

The two young men set off at once on their bicycles, Bill carefully tracing Bob's route while making sure to stay about fifty yards behind him to avoid attracting attention. When they arrived at the office, Bob led him up to the filing room, which was to be his home for the next two days. He had access to a bathroom, and the farmer René Le Mottée, who had heard about the letter of denunciation, soon arrived on his own bike, with bags of food hanging off the handlebars to keep him going during his confinement.

With Bill hidden away in the filing room, Bob applied himself to the task of finding him somewhere else to stay, but Monday came and went without any success. The Russian could scarcely remain in the office with customers coming and going all day – not to mention the other members of staff, who might need to do their own filing – so a little before curfew Bob moved him out again, first to a nearby shed, and then a few days later to a lock-up garage. In the meantime, he continued to make discreet enquiries about accommodation.

Finally, Bob found what he thought was the perfect solution, at least for a couple of weeks. He had become friendly with a pair of English conscientious objectors who had come to the island in 1940 to dig potatoes and had been caught out by the evacuation crisis. One of the men, Michael Frowd, had subsequently injured his back while working as a tree feller, and despite being largely bedbound had managed to set up a magazine, the *Jersey Forum* (or, as Bob privately termed it, 'The Jersey Boredom'), which offered a mixture of am-dram theatre reviews and political musings on Jersey's post-war future that had somehow escaped the attentions of the German censors. The other man, René Franoux, earned a meagre living offering French and German lessons, and was currently in hospital having his appendix removed – which meant there was a spare bed in their little flat on Grosvenor Street.

Michael agreed that Bill could stay with him until René was discharged, but when his flatmate returned from hospital he insisted that the Russian should remain. The three young men all slept together in the flat's single bedroom – Michael and René on a pair of twin beds and Bill on a blow-up mattress on the floor.

Bob was relieved that at last Bill had a permanent place to stay, and he couldn't help feeling rather impressed at his friends' attitude. They might not have been willing to take a life in the name of their country, but they were more than willing to risk their own for the sake of a stranger.

While Bill settled into his new home, Louisa Gould was adjusting to life behind bars. The Germans had arrived to search her house shortly after the young Russian had left, and despite her best efforts to destroy any evidence of his stay with her they had found enough to corroborate their informants' story. The Russian-English dictionary on her bookshelf was not in itself conclusive evidence, but when coupled with some discarded scraps of paper on which Bill had been practising his English, it was enough to see Mrs Gould placed under arrest for 'aiding and abetting a breach of the working peace'.

A week later, the Fosters' home was targeted. Fortunately, the Russian Grigori was out at the time, and Mr Foster was at work, but his wife was taken in for questioning and charged alongside her sister. Before long, a third sibling, Harold Le Druillenec, was brought in as well. He had never sheltered any Russians himself, although he had given Bill some English lessons while he was staying with Mrs Gould. As far as the Germans were concerned, though, Harold was guilty by association, even if the only crime they could actually pin on him was listening to his sister's illegal wireless.

The three siblings were sentenced to lengthy prison terms on the Continent – five months each for Harold and Ivy, and two years for Louisa. Ivy managed to avoid being sent away with the help of a trainee doctor who visited her in prison. By falsifying her medical records and swapping a sputum sample with one from a different patient, he was able to convince the Germans that she was suffering from tuberculosis, and had her transferred instead to the General Hospital. Nothing, however, could be done for Louisa and Harold, who were shipped off to St Malo, and from there to a prison in Rennes.

It wasn't until after the war that anyone on the islands found out what happened to them next. Harold was taken to the concentration camp at Bergen-Belsen, an ordeal he was lucky to survive. He saw fellow prisoners drop dead from exhaustion, and in some cases even resort to cannibalism. Louisa, meanwhile, was sent to Ravensbrück, a concentration camp exclusively for women. A detachment of SS personnel had recently arrived there from Auschwitz and begun work on a new building, about thirty feet in length, which was adjacent to the camp crematorium. Every day at the 2 p.m. roll call 150 women would be selected by the deputy commandant and led inside. One cold February afternoon, Louisa was one of the women he picked. None of them ever came out again.

Meanwhile, back in Jersey, Bob Le Sueur had discovered a new vocation. Thanks to his job, he had reason to travel widely around the island, cycling off to visit customers in remote rural areas. Bit by bit, he became a kind of unofficial letting agent for escaped slave workers in search of safe places to hide. Each time he heard of a new escapee, he would find a pretext to travel from farm to farm, sharing the poor man's story and attempting to find somewhere to place him.

In this way, Bob managed to find homes for around a dozen former slave workers, some of them little more than teenagers. Most of the time, however, his efforts on the young men's behalf came to nothing. Everyone he spoke to was sympathetic to their plight, but the majority were unwilling to stick their necks out and run the risk of harbouring a fugitive. 'I quite understand,' Bob would reply kindly, in the face of the latest hand-wringing apology. 'Would you do just one thing for me though? Please don't mention that I spoke to you about this.'

As far as he knew, nobody ever did, and Bob was able to continue his good-Samaritan work without attracting the attention of the authorities. There was only one occasion when he thought he had come close to denunciation. A woman on the outskirts of St Helier had found a slave worker in the fields behind her house, desperately pulling up root vegetables with his bare hands. The man's face was ashen grey and, struck with a sudden pang of pity, she impulsively ushered him over the little fence into her garden, and from there to her husband's lock-up garage, where she brought him some food.

When the woman's husband came home, he was sympathetic, but he insisted there was no way the visitor could stay. They had small children in the house, and he was afraid that if one of them caught a glimpse of the man in the garage they might unthinkingly let slip what they had seen to the wrong person.

Bob was tasked with finding alternative accommodation for the young labourer. He remembered hearing that the physiotherapist Albert Bedane was sympathetic to the escapees and promptly booked himself an appointment for a massage, waiting his turn alongside the other paying customers. But when he shut the door behind him and began to tell Mr Bedane what it was that he wanted, the other man suddenly grew angry. 'You've got a cheek coming to me with a proposition like that!' he exploded. 'Don't you realise that the commandant's office is only up the road? I have Germans coming in here every day for treatment.' Ushering Bob towards the door, he muttered furiously, 'You're lucky I don't report you for this, young man.'

Bob was shaken by the encounter, and anxious that Bedane might change his mind and report him to the authorities after all. Little did he know that the other man's outrage was no more than an act. He was merely exercising due caution – for all he knew, Bob could have been an informant, or even a German spy. In fact, the physiotherapist already had two Russians hiding in his basement, along with the Jewish woman Mary Richardson.

Secrecy was key to the success of such risky endeavours. Bob knew he wasn't the only one involved in the kind of work he was doing, but there was no centralised organisation, and certainly no leadership structure – nothing that would exactly merit the traditional label of a resistance group. There were simply people who knew people, sympathetic and willing do to their bit when asked.

As well as placing escaped slave labourers, Bob developed a sideline in producing fake ID cards for them. One of his associates had a contact who worked in the office where the blank cards were printed – Bob never asked who it was, preferring to know as little as possible about matters that didn't concern him – and whenever a recently escaped Russian required a new identity, he or she would slip one of them out and it would be passed on to Bob. He would then take the blank card, along with a passport photo of the escapee in question, provided by another sympathetic individual, to a friend called Alan who worked at the records office in town. Bob always visited during the lunch hour, when the manager and his secretary were out. Alan's contribution was simply to leave Bob alone for a few minutes in the room where the ink pad and the little swastika stamp were located, on the pretext that he needed something from the back office. Of course he knew perfectly well what Bob was doing, but he had no desire to actually witness it. Alan would never have considered himself a *résistant*, and yet in his own small, silent way he was helping to subvert the regime.

Bob never spoke of his clandestine activities to anyone, not even his parents. That way, as he saw it, they would have nothing to confess to if they should find themselves hauled in for questioning. He also did his best to find out as little as possible about what his associates were up to – he had no desire to partake of valuable information that he knew could be extracted under torture. He merely got on with his own small part of the puzzle, reassured by the thought that he was one of many who were quietly doing good work for a greater cause.

Since Bill was now living permanently with his friends Michael and René, Bob continued to see him regularly. The more he got to know the young Russian, the more he felt like he belonged in a Chekhov play. Bill was a dreamer, prone to eloquent flights of fancy, and rarely entirely present in the here and now. His mood veered wildly, from the depths of depression to the heights of ecstatic joy. In short, he was not the easiest person to live with, although the two conscientious objectors never complained. In fact, they soon grew fond of their eccentric new flatmate, and in time Bob too came to see Bill as a friend.

Fortunately for Michael and René, some of the practical strains of sheltering an escaped slave worker were eased by the fact that Bill had other friends on the island who were willing to help. The young man's food was still being provided by his original benefactor, the farmer René Le Mottée. Every Saturday, without fail, he would arrive at Bob's office by way of the back roads, his handlebars heavy with bags of fresh produce, ready for delivery by Bob to the little flat on Grosvenor Street.

In time, Bill even began bringing in an income of his own. He was a skilled draughtsman, and could produce beautiful pen-and-ink copies of any image he was given. It was Bob who realised that the Russian's talent could be turned to financial advantage. One day he brought Bill an image of Jesus to copy. As a good communist citizen, Bill was a committed atheist, but he applied himself to the task diligently, producing an impeccable re-creation of the original artwork.

Bob took Bill's picture down to a small Christian bookshop in St Helier, and showed it to the manageress. 'It was drawn by a friend of mine, Oscar Le Breuilly,' he told her. (This was the name given on Bill's fake ID card.) 'Unfortunately, he's too ill to leave his bed, so he asked me to bring it to show you.'

The woman was evidently touched by Bob's story. 'To think that a man in such great misery could produce such a spiritual picture!' she exclaimed. She insisted on displaying the drawing prominently in the shop window, and made Bob promise to return with more works by the talented young artist.

With Bob as his agent, Bill's career flourished. His religious pictures flew off the shelves of the little Christian shop, and soon he began branching out. One of Bob's old schoolfriends, an RAF pilot called Victor Hamon, had been killed when his plane was shot down over Holland in August 1942. Bob visited Victor's mother and asked if she had a photograph of him that he could borrow for a few days. He returned, much to Mrs Hamon's delight, with a beautiful pen-and-ink portrait – drawn, he told her, by the local artist Oscar Le Breuilly.

Mrs Hamon was delighted at the gift, and as sympathetic to the bedridden fellow who had produced it as the woman in the Christian shop had been. 'Oh, that poor young man!' she cried when Bob told her the story. Then she thought for a moment. 'You know,' she said, 'if you put this up in a window somewhere, along with Victor's photograph, I think people would want to get their own done.'

It was an inspired suggestion, and Bob knew just where to advertise the service. He had a friend, Mrs Osbourne, who worked at a hairdressing salon on Colomberie and he was sure she would be happy for him to use their window. Sure enough, she agreed, and a notice went up advertising bespoke portraits for £5 a pop. The commissions came flooding in, and before long Bill was struggling to keep up with demand. The Russian fugitive had become the main breadwinner of the little flat on Grosvenor Street.

Bob continued to act as Bill's professional link to the outside world, but in time the young artist began venturing out into town himself, in the persona of Oscar Le Breuilly. The disguise he employed was a bizarre one: he wore a long trenchcoat, whatever the weather, and a dark trilby hat, along with a pair of plain-glass spectacles that Bob had borrowed from a friend in the local am-dram group. If anything, Bill looked like he had wandered out of a bad spy movie, but miraculously the authorities never stopped him. Occasionally, this peculiarly dressed character would be seen lurking around Waterloo Street, peering through the window of the little Christian bookshop at the pictures that had brought him an odd kind of fame.

On Bob's twenty-first birthday, Michael and René presented him with a gift: a beautiful pen-and-ink portrait, which had been signed not 'Oscar Le Breuilly' but 'Bill'. The two men had visited Bob's mother to borrow a photograph for the young Russian to copy. Lizzie Le Sueur had been a little surprised at the request, but she had long since decided not to ask too many questions about Bob's associates or their activities.

Bob was touched at the present his three friends had given him. 'You know, one of these days you'll have to sign this again with your real name,' he told Bill. In the meantime, he would just have to be the only person in Jersey who knew they had an authentic Feodor Buryi hanging on their wall.

CHAPTER TWENTY-FOUR

SUMMER IN SARK

In the Channel Islands, winter was always a time of foreboding. For young German men used to a crisper climate, the cold damp air and the misty shores blasted day and night by crashing waves were enough to induce a distinct feeling of gloom. One chilly afternoon, Mrs Le Bideau was out in St Saviour's Churchyard, gathering wood for her fire, when she came across a rather miserable looking soldier. 'I made a few remarks about the weather, and he said that the German winter with thick snow and 30 degrees of frost was preferable to ours,' she wrote. 'I certainly agreed with him.'

For those who had already seen the seasons come and go on the islands, there was at least the reassurance that the bad weather was only temporary. Soon, the long, magical summer would return, and the dreary, windswept islands would be transformed once more into a balmy paradise.

Werner Rang was still counting his blessings that he had managed to escape a transfer to the Russian Front. The death of his friend Fritz, who had killed himself rather than face the horrors of that frozen battlefield, haunted him. But in May 1943, Werner received a new posting to the one place in the world that he would have chosen above all others: Sark.

Since his brief visit to the island the previous year, the 'little paradise', as his friend Karl had called it, had never been far from Werner's thoughts. His company was stationed at Pleinmont, on Guernsey's western coast, where a series of giant new concrete fortifications faced across the Channel towards England. It was an impressive outlook, with miles of unbroken sea stretching out in a grand panorama, but Werner much preferred the more peaceful view from St Peter Port, on the other side of the island. There, on a good day, Sark and Herm were clearly visible atop the glistening blue of the sea.

Now he and his comrades were being transferred to Sark for a six-month tour of duty, just as the weather was growing milder. Two days on the island had felt like a glorious holiday, and soon he would be spending an entire summer there.

The short voyage from St Peter Port to the little Creux Harbour was as pleasant as Werner's previous trip had been. Of the 180 men of his company who were travelling that day, he was one of the few who had been to the island before. When the troops disembarked and marched through the little swastika-emblazoned tunnel chiselled through the sheer rock of the cliff face, and then up the steep hill to the village, he enjoyed watching the looks of amazement spread over the other men's faces.

It didn't take long for Werner to settle into his new routine on the island. He was one of two orderlies assigned to handle Sark's medical needs, under the supervision of a middle-aged German physician, Dr Willbaeker. 'Now I don't want to hear any complaints,' the doctor warned him. 'If you behave in an improper manner to any of the local girls, there will be consequences.' More than a few mildly flirtatious friendships between soldiers and civilians on Sark had already crossed the line into illicit liaisons.

'Don't worry, sir,' Werner reassured him. 'My parents brought me up well.'

Every morning, the medical team would open a surgery in the island's junior school. Between 8 and 9 a.m., they would see military patients, and from 9 to 10 they would deal with civilians. After that, they would go off on their rounds, attending to anyone who required a house call.

When the day's work was done, Werner would return to his billet, a charming room in the Junior School building. It had previously been occupied by the schoolmistress, Miss Howard, who had suffered a mental collapse during the deportation crisis and been sent to a hospital in Guernsey. Compared to the usual sparse army accommodation, the little room had a lived-in air, and Werner appreciated the feminine touch that the previous tenant had applied to the decor.

On closer acquaintance, Sark proved even more idyllic than Werner had realised on his previous trip. Then he had been more or less confined to the area around his friend Karl's billet, but now he had the run of the whole island. Werner had brought his bike over with him on the boat from Guernsey, and he made the most of the freedom it offered, riding along the quiet dirt lanes and admiring the serene beauty everywhere he went.

One of his first patients was Mr Baker, an elderly gentleman who lived on Little Sark, the large triangular peninsula that stood on the far side of La Coupée. On the approach to the steep winding crossing, with its precipitous slope down to the beach at La Grande Grève on one side and a sheer eighty-metre drop to the surf on the other, he stopped for a moment to fully appreciate the landscape that surrounded him. The glistening blue sea seemed to stretch out to infinity all around, while the glowing sun painted the island's broad, sweeping fields in a wash of gold. From this vantage point, at one of the island's highest spots, Werner felt like he was standing on top of the world.

Tearing his eyes away from the view, he set off on the alarming ride across La Coupée, and on to Mr Baker's farm. The old man was suffering from a nasty eye infection, and required treatment twice a week. Whenever Werner returned to administer the latest dose, Mrs Baker would ply him with a glass of fresh milk from their cows, and later, when the Bakers began to attend Werner's surgeries at the Junior School, they always arrived with a gift in hand – some homegrown vegetables, or a couple of eggs wrapped in a red-and-white check handkerchief. Werner soon came to realise that payment in kind was an accepted tradition on the island. The locals wouldn't dream of offering the German medical personnel money, but neither were they entirely comfortable accepting their services for free. As a result, the young medics enjoyed a life of plenty, their army rations supplemented by generous quantities of local produce: milk, butter, fish, and even the occasional wild rabbit.

Werner's responsibility for the health of the civilian population extended all the way to the top, and it wasn't long before he was asked to attend the Seigneurie for a house call with the Dame of Sark herself. Sybil Hathaway was suffering from a debilitating tooth-ache, and when Werner and his colleague examined the cause of her misery, it was clear that an extraction would be necessary.

The Dame took the unpleasant news in her stride, calmly leading the two men to the nearest bathroom with all the authoritative dig-nity of a formal procession. There they injected the offending area with a syringe of novocaine before setting to work with some pliers. As Werner yanked furiously, Dame Sybil remained as unflappable as ever. Once the procedure was completed she thanked the two men, and gave them each a bottle of wine to take home with them.

There was one strange feature to the visit, which Werner found rather amusing. He had been told – per the gossip on the island – that the Dame was a fluent German speaker, with a masterful command of the language that ensured she maintained the best possible rela-tionship with the local commandant and his officers. True, he was hardly meeting her at her best, but as far as Werner could see such claims were wildly exaggerated. The Dame spoke some conversa-tional German, but it was little more than Werner's own schoolboy English. In her official dealings with the authorities, she relied heavily on the translation skills of her friend Annie Wranowsky, the Czech Jew who had avoided deportation by insisting on her 'Aryan' bloodline.

Evidently, Werner realised, the myth of the ferociously capable linguist had been absorbed as part of the larger-than-life character of 'La Dame'. To most of her people, whose command of the language was extremely limited, Sybil's basic competence had been conven-iently recast as a gift.

Although the Dame purposely cultivated an air of awe among her subjects, she was at least generally liked by them. The same could scarcely be said for her opposite number among the Germans, the island commandant Captain Johann Hinkel. A strict authoritarian, he was an odd choice to head up the distinctly laid-back Occupation of Sark and was disliked by both his own men and the local people.

Rightly or wrongly, many of the Sarkese blamed Hinkel for the deportations earlier in the year. He might have been just following orders from Berlin, but he had, it was felt, carried them out with the merciless zeal of a true Nazi. He had also overseen a massive fortification of the island, laying over thirteen thousand mines, blocking access to some of the most popular beaches, and installing additional anti-tank and anti-aircraft guns.

One Sunday afternoon, a car pulled up outside the Junior School, one of a handful the German Army had imported into the previously vehicle-free island. Werner was ordered to get in, and soon found himself being driven to the Eperquerie, the broad, windswept headland at the northern tip of Sark, where a terrible accident had just taken place.

The commandant and two of his subordinates had been directing some men in a boat down below, who were attempting to move a sea-mine that had drifted into shore. In doing so they had, somewhat ironically, wandered into a minefield themselves. Hinkel was convinced that he knew the precise locations of all the mines, and had ordered the other two men to follow him. But his hubris had proved his undoing. When a mine he was standing on suddenly exploded, the commandant was decapitated instantly, quite literally hoist with his own petard.

By the time Werner arrived on the scene, all that was left of Hinkel was a headless corpse. The corporal who had been walking directly behind him was badly injured too, lying on the ground with blood gushing from one of his boots. The third man, a private, was rooted to the spot in sheer terror.

Without waiting for the pioneers to arrive, Werner set off through the minefield, heading straight for the injured man. The blood was still pouring out of his boot and the young medic had a job to staunch the flow. He applied a rough-and-ready tourniquet to the leg and with his knife began cutting the boot away from the mangled flesh underneath, until the wound to the foot was clearly exposed. It was a nasty injury, but before long Werner had managed to stem the bleeding.

The poor corporal was screaming in agony as Werner carried him back out of the minefield. He bundled him into the waiting staff car, and told the driver to head back to the Junior School.

Dosed up on morphine, the patient's spirits improved a great deal, and Werner was able to return to the scene of the accident to attend to the other two men. By this point, the pioneers had cleared a safe route through the minefield, and the terrified private had been brought out of harm's way. All that remained was to recover Captain Hinkel's body. The corpse was loaded onto a stretcher, and taken by a horse and cart to the island's makeshift hospital. But the dead man's head was still nowhere to be seen.

The job of preparing the body for burial fell to Werner. He removed Hinkel's watch and rings, and packaged them up to be sent off to his wife in Germany. More troubling, though, was the question of the officer's missing head. Even if the corpse were wrapped in a shroud, its absence would be obvious up until the point when the coffin was screwed shut.

Werner puzzled over the matter for some time before he finally came up with a solution. He found a stash of old newspapers and began scrunching the sheets up in little balls, as if he were laying a fire. Then he took a long sheet of bandage and gathered the paper together into a football-sized clump, before taping it down to the raw stump of the commandant's neck. With the application of enough bandages, he managed to produce a fairly respectable-looking – if incongruously mummified – human body, which was shipped off on the next boat for Guernsey and buried in the cemetery at Fort George.

How Hinkel's wife in Germany took the news of his death, Werner and his colleagues could only guess, but one thing was certain: there were few tears shed for him on Sark. Julia Tremaine was positively gleeful at the thought of the German mines killing their own men. 'They are surely falling into the nets they have laid for themselves,' she wrote cheerfully in her diary.

In Hinkel's place, the islanders were assigned a new commandant, the much more popular Captain Karl Müller. A former school-teacher, with a passion for playing the violin, Müller soon endeared himself to everyone, not least since – at least as far as the local grapevine had it – one of his first acts on assuming command was to cancel the deportation orders of a further forty islanders, which Hinkel had been on the point of signing off.

One of those allegedly saved from deportation was nineteen-year-old Phyllis Baker, who had befriended the doomed Jewish woman Therese Steiner on the beach back in 1939. Phyllis had studied German under Annie Wranowsky, and her quick grasp of the language had made her the star pupil in the class. She had even won first prize in an oral examination held in front of the military top brass. As a result, she had begun to be employed by the Army medics as a semi-official interpreter, doing her best to translate her fellow islanders' symptoms from English (or, in the case of many elderly residents, Sarkese patois) into German. She had even been gifted a medical dictionary to improve her vocabulary.

It was not, however, in this medical capacity that Phyllis first encountered Werner Rang. In fact, she was a patient at the time, suffering from a gruesome bout of tonsillitis. Dr Willbaeker had prescribed plenty of bedrest, promising to send one of his new medics to check up on her and administer some vitamin tablets.

When Werner arrived at the Baker family home, La Ville Farm, he was met at the door by Phyllis's mother and grandmother. In faltering English, he attempted to explain the purpose of his visit, but he soon found that words were superfluous. His red medical armband saw him escorted straight up the stairs to Phyllis's bedroom, where he was astonished to be greeted in his native tongue. '*Bitte, kommen Sie rein,*' Phyllis called out cheerfully. '*Nehmen Sie Platz.*'

Werner did as he was told, entering the room and sitting himself down on a small chair by the side of the bed. '*Guten Morgen*,' he replied a little awkwardly. Phyllis was propped up on at least five pillows, with a towel draped under her chin to catch the saliva dribbling out of her mouth. But even so, as he looked into her dark brown eyes, he couldn't help noticing that she was beautiful.

Werner leant forward and gently placed a thermometer in Phyllis's mouth, taking her wrist in his hand so he could measure her pulse. As the two of them sat there in silence, he felt suddenly self-conscious. Despite her pallid complexion and feverish brow, he was gripped by an almost overwhelming attraction to her.

Werner did his best to maintain a professional air as he carefully extracted the thermometer. Then he noted down the reading on a little pad, and fumbled in his bag for the bottle of vitamins. He carefully shook out a tablet, which Phyllis swallowed with a little sip of water. All the time, the young man barely spoke.

Phyllis was entirely unaware of the effect she had wrought on Werner, but from that moment on the young medic was utterly lovesick. He didn't dare tell anyone, knowing that Dr Willbaeker would be furious at the thought of one of his orderlies getting involved with a local girl. For all Werner knew he might send him back to Guernsey in disgrace. And in any case, surely a nice girl from a respectable family wouldn't dream of falling in love with an enemy soldier.

But try as he might to push Phyllis from the back of his mind, as the days and weeks went on Werner's feelings for her only seemed to grow. When her father, Jack, suffered a thumb injury that required frequent visits to change the dressing, he was secretly thrilled at the opportunity to see her again. Mr Baker was a veteran of the First World War who had been taken prisoner at the Battle of Cambrai, spending two years in a POW camp. Although he always treated Werner with politeness, the idea of a German soldier having romantic aspirations towards his daughter would no doubt have appalled him.

Fortunately, the female inhabitants of La Ville Farm were more welcoming. Whenever Werner called to change Jack's dressing, Mrs

Baker would give him a glass of fresh milk for his trouble, and soon Phyllis's grandmother was offering to darn his socks and make repairs to his uniform as well.

Phyllis herself, meanwhile, was beginning to enjoy Werner's company, not to mention the opportunity to practise her conversational German. After she had recovered her health, she invited him to play badminton with her in the Island Hall, along with her sister Margaret and an old schoolfriend, Jacqueline Carré.

Jacqueline was a vivacious young woman who already had a German admirer of her own. In her case, the attraction was reciprocal – although her parents had no idea about the affair, Jacqueline was head over heels in love. In fact, several times Phyllis had applied her translation skills to helping her write love letters to her soldier boyfriend.

On Sark, such relationships were a little more accepted than they were on the larger islands, especially as far as the younger generation were concerned. Nonetheless, discretion was very much the watchword, and even couples who made no secret of their romances were careful to observe the rules of decorum. Georgina Wakley, a girl around Phyllis's age, had been involved with a German lieutenant called Karl for almost two years. They spent all their free time in each other's company, going for long walks along the dusty country lanes and swimming in the sea at Dixcart Bay. But they would never have dreamed of going out for dinner together, or in any way acknowledging their relationship in public. Georgina's parents knew about her German boyfriend, but they didn't ask to be introduced to him. As far as they were concerned, it was a dalliance that would run its course once the war came to an end. They felt sure that Georgina would never agree to go and live in Germany, and it was hard to believe that Karl would be willing to stay in Sark for good either.

When the new commandant, Captain Müller, decided to hold a party at the Dixcart Hotel, Georgina and Karl were both invited, but they were seated apart from each other. Werner had been given the task of making the placecards for the dining table, and he was thrilled to find that Phyllis was also on the guest list.

It was a marvellous evening, about as luxurious as was possible under Occupation, and Werner and Phyllis both enjoyed themselves more than they had done for ages. The Pickthall family, who owned the hotel, had opened up a secret stash of spirits that had been hidden in the cellar, and for dessert Mrs Pickthall had baked some glorious brandy snaps, oozing with fresh Sark cream.

Captain Müller played his violin beautifully, and even persuaded Werner to perform a few tunes on his accordion. The festivities continued until well after curfew, which meant, of course, that the young ladies would have to be walked home. For Werner, the gentle stroll back to La Ville Farm, walking with the girl he loved across an island bathed in gentle moonlight, was the most wonderful part of the whole night.

Phyllis may not have realised the true depths of Werner's feelings, but she knew he was willing to take risks to spend time with her. Her young admirer frequently visited her at home when he was supposed to be tending to his medical duties. But Werner wasn't the only German who paid regular visits to La Ville Farm. The commandant, Captain Müller, had learned that Phyllis was an accomplished pianist, and frequently dropped in to borrow her sheet music. On one such visit he had discerned the unmistakable four notes that heralded a BBC broadcast coming from somewhere in the house. 'Be a good girl and get rid of your radio,' he had told Phyllis amiably, and there the matter had rested.

Unlike his predecessor Hinkel, Müller was a distinctly soft touch, with a relaxed attitude to discipline that was far better suited to Sark. But there were limits to how much latitude he would allow his subordinates. One afternoon, Werner was drinking tea with Phyllis in the living room when they heard the distinctive sound of the commandant's car pulling up outside.

The young medic leapt to his feet. 'Quick!' Phyllis hissed, shoving him into the kitchen. There he was met by her grandmother, who smuggled him out into the garden, from where he was able to make his way back to the Junior School.

Phyllis, meanwhile, went to the front door to welcome the

commandant. But as she led him into the living room she started. There on the floor, by the chair Werner had been sitting in, was his belt, with a holstered pistol attached, which he had removed as a mark of respect to the family.

Fortunately, Phyllis managed to kick the offending weapon under the sofa as she sat down. Captain Müller, apparently entirely oblivious, chose his music and went on his way.

Werner had always known that his summer in Sark couldn't last for ever, but when the news came that he and his company were to pack up and leave it still felt like a shock. In typical Army fashion, the long-anticipated orders were finally announced with almost no warning, and he found himself hastily gathering his belongings for the journey back to Guernsey.

There was just time for a quick visit to La Ville Farm to say his farewells to Phyllis and her family. But when he arrived, the object of his affections was nowhere to be seen. She was off on the other side of the island, he was told, helping the doctor with his rounds.

Poor Werner began the nine-mile voyage back to Guernsey without seeing the face of the girl he loved. But he was determined that somehow, however improbable it seemed, the two of them would one day be reunited.

CHAPTER TWENTY-FIVE

RUNNING LOW

At sixteen years old, Pearl Smith had grown bored of working behind the counter in Grut's photographic studio and had decided to realise a long-held ambition of going into nursing. She sent in her application to the Emergency Hospital in Castel parish, and a few days later was granted an interview with the formidable surgical matron, Ellen Hall. When Miss Hall asked her age, Pearl's answer was somewhat evasive. 'I'll soon be eighteen,' she replied carefully, without specifying just how soon that might be.

The matron scrutinised Pearl for a moment, before deciding not to enquire further. Instead, she informed her of her hours – typically, gruelling twelve-hour shifts, often working through the night by no more than candlelight – told her what kind of wage she could expect, and instructed her to report for duty on the first day of the following month, in uniform.

For some young women, finding suitable clothes was the hardest requirement of the job. Despite their best efforts to beg, borrow or steal appropriate kit, more than a few began their time on the wards in their old Girl Guide uniforms, which were at least a suitable shade of blue. Such improvisation was in keeping with the make-do-and-mend spirit that pertained in the hospital more generally, where bandages were made from recycled crepe paper and old sheets were cut up into swabs.

Predictably, as the new girl on the ward, Pearl was given all the least popular tasks: changing the bedpans, cleaning vomit off the floor, and laying out the bodies of patients who had died. But the job she found most interesting was helping out in the operating theatre. Unlike some of the nurses, Pearl never suffered from squeamishness when it came to the blood and guts of the surgical ward. She enjoyed watching the surgeon, Dr Sutcliffe, perform amputations, carefully marking the skin with a pen to ensure there was a big enough flap to cover the raw muscle and bone beneath.

One time, Pearl was surprised to see a familiar face in the theatre. Rex Priaulx, the young tenor from the Lyric No. 1 Company had become a nursing orderly with the Voluntary Aid Detachment. Rex had always been a bit of a know-it-all, and he was determined to show Pearl how much he had learned in his training. The way he was acting, anyone would have thought he was about to perform the operation.

Rex's cocky swagger didn't last long, though. When Dr Sutcliffe passed him the leg he had just sawn off and asked him to take it to the incinerator, the young man suddenly went very pale. He stood rooted to the ground for a moment before crashing to the floor, unconscious.

The leg rolled away in the direction of the corridor. 'Could someone get that, please?' Dr Sutcliffe asked laconically, without taking his eyes off what he was doing.

Rex came to a little while later to find that the operation was over and the others had left him alone in the theatre. It was the last time he ever volunteered for surgical duty.

While Pearl was settling in on the surgical ward, one floor above her another teenage girl was learning the ropes in Maternity. Margaret Chalker had left the Red Cross Bureau in downtown St Peter Port for a nursing position, imagining that she would be spending her days cooing at cute babies. But she soon found the job was more taxing than she had anticipated, juggling the bathtimes and feeding schedules of any number of wailing infants while their mothers rested up in bed.

Then there was the endless stream of dirty nappies, which had not only to be changed but also carefully sorted into individual named bags for the fathers to collect and take home to wash. Sometimes no man would appear for a child's laundry, and it would be left to the grandmother to pick it up instead. Margaret soon learned the reason: these were the babies of 'Jerrybags', whose German boyfriends were either unwilling or unable to do anything to help them.

In the popular slang of the day, women who became pregnant by the Germans were known as 'troop carriers', and generally they were looked on as the lowest of the low. In the hospital, though, they were treated no differently to any other patients, thanks to the strict instructions of the maternity matron, Miss Finch. One day, Margaret was startled to see a girl she knew from school arrive at the hospital to give birth to a German baby. The poor young mother was only fifteen. Margaret did her best to make her stay as comfortable as possible, and was relieved that none of her colleagues passed comment on her awful predicament.

Since starting work at the hospital, Pearl had grown accustomed to the sight of nasty injuries, but one day a patient arrived with a compound fracture that caused even her to draw a sharp breath. It was Jacqueline Carré, the vivacious young woman with the German boyfriend who had joined Phyllis and Werner for their games of badminton in Sark.

The night before, Jacqueline had been out late with her beloved. Sneaking home after curfew, she had been attempting to climb over a hedge when she slipped and suffered a bad fall, shattering the bones in her leg. Two of the larger fragments had burst through the skin, and the resulting wound was a gruesome, bloody mess.

Phyllis had learned of her friend's accident in the morning, when she arrived at the Junior School surgery to accompany the doctor on his rounds. The poor man had been up half the night attempting to remove all the fragments of bone from Jacqueline's leg, but after four hours of surgery, fearing that he was in danger of losing her, he had decided to call it quits and refer her to the hospital in Guernsey. Still not entirely convinced that the site was clear, he had left the wound open rather than stitching it up, covering it with a piece of plaster to prevent the spread of infection.

As soon as Phyllis heard what had happened, she rushed in to see her old schoolfriend. She found Jacqueline relatively pain free – she was already heavily dosed up on morphine – but more than a little agitated. Her concern wasn't so much for her own health, but a fear that her parents might learn the whole story surrounding the accident and find out that she had been seeing one of the Germans.

Phyllis reassured Jacqueline that there was no need for anyone to share that particular detail. She herself had always been the model of discretion where her friend's relationship was concerned, knowing the damage it could do to her family.

The boat, with a German medic onboard, was expected any time now, ready to transport Jacqueline to Guernsey. In the meantime, Phyllis had her own medical responsibilities to attend to. She set off on her rounds with the doctor, telling her friend that she would keep her in her thoughts.

When the little boat arrived at Creux Harbour, the young man who disembarked and began the trek up the hill to the village was one who knew the route better than most. Werner Rang had received orders early that morning to go and fetch a patient from Sark for an emergency medical transfer. But he hadn't been told who it was that he was supposed to be collecting, and when he walked into the Junior School and discovered that one of his own friends had been injured, he was understandably shocked.

Unfortunately, since Phyllis had already left on her rounds, Werner missed the chance to connect with her again, but Jacqueline was greatly relieved to see him. Her parents, who would also be making the nine-mile journey to Guernsey by sea, were beside themselves with worry, and a familiar face would help to keep all their spirits up.

Jacqueline was a tall girl, and the task of loading her stretcher onto the little boat wasn't an easy one, particularly with a strong tide heaving the vessel to and fro. But the sailing conditions were good, and they arrived in St Peter Port Harbour on time. There, they were met by an ambulance that would convey Jacqueline and her parents to the Castel Hospital, while Werner returned to his camp.

At the hospital, Pearl was assigned to care for Jacqueline while she waited to see the surgeon. She was feeling more lucid now, and did her best to put on a brave face as they chatted together. Pearl generally got on well with her patients, but with Jacqueline, who was around her own age, she felt an immediate connection. Before long the two young women were sharing all their hopes and dreams with each other.

Despite the instructions of the Sark doctor, Jacqueline's leg had not been x-rayed on arrival at the hospital. Instead, she had been parked on the ward to await the surgeon's decision on how to proceed. By the time he arrived, however, the wound had already begun to turn gangrenous. Pearl knew as well as anyone what that meant: it would have to be amputated, and quickly.

The operation went smoothly. The cut was made just above the joint of the knee, and soon the infected limb was on its way to the hospital incinerator. Jacqueline returned to the ward to rest, and Pearl did all she could to make her comfortable. After a little while, however, she heard a strange noise coming from the direction of the girl's bed: a regular, persistent dripping sound, as if a tap hadn't been turned off all the way.

Pearl rushed over to find a steady supply of blood dropping from Jacqueline's stump onto the floor. Clearly the amputation had been less successful than the doctors believed. They would have to try again, cutting higher this time – perhaps all the way to the hip.

Pearl wasn't around to witness the second operation. With her shift at an end, she headed home to sleep, but the next morning she returned to the hospital anxious for news of her patient. When she entered the ward, she saw that Jacqueline's bed was empty. 'The surgeon operated again,' one of the other nurses explained, 'but unfortunately she died in the night.'

The news reached Sark remarkably quickly. Phyllis heard it directly from Jacqueline's father, who had taken the first boat back to the island in order to let his own mother know. The old lady lived in a bungalow not far from La Ville Farm, and she was so distraught at the death of her only grandchild that Phyllis was asked to fetch the doctor to attend to her. She rushed off to find him, clamping down on her own emotions and focusing on doing her duty. But when she arrived at the Junior School she was as white as a sheet, and the doctor knew immediately that something was wrong. 'She's not dead, is she?' he asked anxiously.

At first, all Phyllis could do was nod, but she soon offered up the whole story, as best she understood it: the delay with the x-ray, the failed amputation and the second unsuccessful operation.

The doctor, of course, had lost patients before, but nonetheless Jacqueline's death hit him hard. And he wasn't the only one. The whole of Sark seemed to have been plunged into mourning, as if a cloud had descended over the idyllic, picture-postcard island. The bubbly young woman had been well liked by all who knew her, and the shock of losing her so suddenly was felt by everyone.

A few days later, the little boat from Guernsey returned, this time carrying the dead girl's body. Jacqueline was borne up the Harbour Hill in sombre fashion, for burial in the churchyard of St Peter's. The grave was festooned with over a hundred floral wreaths, and so many of the islanders gathered to pay their respects that it felt almost like a state occasion. Phyllis herself was too distraught to attend, but her mother and sister went in her stead, joining the throng of mourners gathered at the church.

To Jacqueline's devastated parents, the huge turnout offered a glimmer of consolation, but her death left a hole in their lives that would never be filled again. For decades, the bedroom she had slept in remained untouched, a shrine to the luminous daughter they had lost on that awful moonlit night.

Mrs and Mrs Carré never did find out the true story of what Jacqueline had been doing that evening, scrambling over a hedge well after curfew. But if they had inspected the cards attached to the flowers of remembrance closely enough, they might have discovered a clue. Among the dozens of notes from family and friends was a short message written in German. It read simply, '*Mein letzter Gruß*' ('My last greeting').

As the months rolled on and the leaves began to drop from the trees again, the Channel Islanders steeled themselves for their toughest Occupation winter yet. With rations continuing to fall, hunger had become a constant worry, particularly for those living in the towns, with no means of growing their own produce. Formerly plump islanders had begun to acquire a lean and hungry look. 'For the first time since the fun began I saw myself in a dressmaker's full-length mirror,' wrote Mrs Le Bideau. 'The sight was depressing: every rib, every vertebra, every single bone in my body was shining through my skin.'

Another Guernseywoman, Ruth Ozanne, was astonished to realise that since the war began she had dropped from a portly thirteen stone to just under eight. In her case, the change had been largely beneficial, if only because her pre-war diet had been so unhealthy. 'Nobody knows me now and I look like a scrawny old hen,' she wrote, 'but I feel very well indeed and am never tired.'

In fact, a number of islanders had seen their health improve on the Occupation diet. 'People have got rid of all sorts of diseases since they gave up meat, wine and tobacco and led, very unwillingly, this ascetic life,' observed Mrs Le Bideau, joking that she had come up with a scheme to parlay her wartime experience into a profitable post-war enterprise. The plan, she explained, was to rent a shop on Tottenham Court Road in London and advertise herself as a kind of health guru – 'Survivor of the Guernsey Occupation' – offering cures for all manner of ailments. 'I should dilate upon the joys of living on nothing, eating nothing, drinking nothing, seeing nothing and going nowhere,' the old lady wrote. 'The consultation fee would be heavy but the cost of treatment would be nil. There is nothing less expensive than living on air.'

A vicar in Guernsey must have been thinking along similar lines when he chose John 4:32 as the subject of his sermon one Sunday. But while spiritual sustenance might have been enough for Jesus, his own congregation was more cynical. When the preacher recited the famous line, 'I have meat that ye know not of,' a voice from the back of the church yelled, 'Black market!'

For those who now spent their lives trying to ignore the uncomfortable rumbling of an empty belly, the mere mention of food could be enough to induce pangs of misery. 'The authorities, one hopes, will soon pass a bylaw forbidding the mention of meals,' wrote Mrs Le Bideau. 'Most of us suffer in reading novels because the characters are always sitting down to dinner or getting up from lunch, and as for the people in books who say "No, thank you," to a course, we feel that they must be insane.'

Joking aside, the lack of adequate food was becoming a serious health problem. At the Castel Hospital, Pearl Smith began seeing more and more patients who were suffering from acute malnutrition. In some cases, it was so bad that when she took a swab from the inside of their cheeks, she had to take care not to puncture the skin. The feeble islanders were put on a regime of therapeutic milks intended to bring them back to health, but often the damage had already been done.

Jersey altar boy Leo Harris had not quite reached that stage, but he was beginning to grow increasingly tired and weak, struggling even to make a fist with his hand. One Sunday morning he was performing his duties at church when he suddenly fainted, hitting his head on the altar as he fell.

Leo's mother took him to see Dr Gow, the man who had falsified her medical records to prevent the family from being deported. This time, however, there was a limit to how much he could help. 'I'm afraid this is the best I can do,' he explained, writing out a voucher for a thin slab of Menier's chocolate. 'Make sure you eat at least one square of it every day,' he told Leo sternly.

For most thirteen-year-old boys, it would have been a hard injunction to refuse, but Leo felt terrible munching away on the chocolate bar when his brother Francis and his parents were so hungry as well.

In the end, he agreed to take his daily dose only on the condition that they each had a little bite.

It wasn't just food that was beginning to run low – fuel was in increasingly short supply too. Those who had already adjusted to slow-cooking their meals in a haybox to save on gas were now finding themselves short of coal to get their fires going in the first place, leaving them both unable to cook and struggling to heat their homes through the winter months.

A number of islanders resorted to stealing in order to keep the home fires burning. Seven-year-old Guernsey schoolgirl Gwen Trebert and her father snuck out one night after curfew, creeping into the grounds of the nearby St George Estate, which had been taken over by the Germans, and quietly sawing down a small tree. Nellie and Oswald Falla, meanwhile, organised a minor coal heist, wheeling an old garden trolley down to the local gasworks after dark and helping themselves to the open coal store. The next day, Nellie was alarmed to see a notice in the paper about the robbery, promising the stolen goods would soon be recovered. She and Oswald worked frantically to hide the coal they had taken, stashing individual lumps in little hiding places all over the house, and a whole sack down the back of their wardrobe. For the next few days, they waited anxiously to see if their crime would be discovered, but the Germans never did come calling, and gradually they grew brave enough to retrieve their secret hoard and light the fire again.

As the gas supply dwindled, temporary cut-offs became more and more common. This was enormously frustrating to anyone caught out midway through cooking a meal. One night at Les Pieux Hotel, Mrs Smith was boiling up some sugar beet when her burner suddenly sputtered and died. She threw her hands up in the air, storming out of the kitchen and off to bed. But in her exasperation she had forgotten to turn the little knob on the stove to the off position. By the time her husband came down for his breakfast the next morning – by which time the gas supply had been reconnected – the kitchen was already filled with a strong, queasy aroma, and the family's two canaries were lying dead on the floor of their cage, their legs up in the air. Mr Smith rushed over to the cooker and turned off the gas ring at once, flinging open the doors and windows to allow the poisonous air to dissipate. He was just relieved that no one had tried to relight the stove that morning, or the whole hotel could have gone up in smoke.

As time went on, the hours of the day when gas was available got shorter and shorter. After the announcement of the latest cut in Jersey, Bob Le Sueur's conscientious objector friends Michael and René decided to mark the occasion by hosting a party. There wasn't really much to celebrate, but it was as good an excuse as any to invite some people round for a knees-up, in defiance of the increasingly depressing Occupation lifestyle.

As was usual on such occasions, the guests all arrived bearing something to eat or drink. One of Bob's farmer friends had a lucrative sideline distilling home-grown cider into illegal Calvados, and he had brought with him several bottles of the stuff. But he hadn't taken into account the effect that such strong spirits might have on revellers who hadn't eaten a proper square meal for several years.

Before the party was even well underway, the Russian fugitive Bill had already downed half a bottle. He had always been prone to wild flights of emotion, trawling the depths of despair one moment and flying high the next. Now, under the influence of the apple brandy, he was thrown into a kind of bacchanalian frenzy, as if he had been transported back to the partying days of his youth in Siberia. Without warning, he marched into the centre of the room, folded his arms, squatted down on his haunches and began a traditional Cossack dance, bellowing a Russian song at the top of his lungs as he kicked his legs out in front of him.

The other guests stared at Bill in amazement, but one fellow standing by the window had a far more anxious look on his face. 'There are Germans in the street outside!' he hissed. 'Quick, someone shut him up!' He slammed closed the shutters, while someone else rushed off to the kitchen to grab an old dishcloth, which was hastily stuffed into Bill's mouth.

The Russian took the impromptu gagging remarkably well, sitting on the floor looking more bemused than angry. Now that he had stopped singing, everyone could hear the noise coming from the street below. There were Germans out there all right, but fortunately they were marching, and the sound of their own bombastic songs – not to mention their heavy, regular footfall – must have drowned out Bill's solo performance. In a few minutes the soldiers were gone, none the wiser about the illegal party that they had just passed, nor the slave worker who had been the star attraction.

As the Calvados wore off, Bill's wild mood dissolved and he grew increasingly gloomy and pensive. It was well after curfew when the revellers decided to call it a night, dispersing to different areas of the flat in search of a soft surface to rest their heads on.

Bob slept top-to-toe with René in his little single bed. On the inflatable mattress on the floor, Bill was snoring heavily. But as he tossed and turned in the night, he must have dislodged the valve, and Bob heard the distinctive hiss of air escaping.

When Bill's body sank down onto the hard wooden floor, it was enough to half-wake him from his slumber. 'Bugger this world,' he murmured in his thick Russian accent, before rolling over and drifting off to sleep again.

CHAPTER TWENTY-SIX

A GLIMMER OF HOPE

It was rare for Mrs Le Bideau to write from the heart, but in the autumn of 1943 events in the wider world punctured her usual bubble of irony. 'We are feeling dazed,' she wrote. 'It seems like the beginning of hope, as though there really was a time coming when we can breathe again.' The cause of this uncharacteristic bout of earnestness was summed up in three short words: 'Italy is kaput.'

In the Channel Islands, as around the world, the announcement on 8 September that the Italian forces had surrendered provided a much-needed boost to morale. Finally, the prospect of a German defeat seemed more real – and with it, the long-dreamed-of day when the invaders would be sent back home and life on the islands could return to normal. That is, assuming the food and fuel held out long enough for there to be any islanders left to enjoy it.

A month later, Bob Le Sueur was playing chess with a friend in St Helier when they were interrupted by yet more good news: the new Italian government had formally declared war on Germany. The two men made their way down to the town's Royal Square, where a large crowd had spontaneously gathered. The mood was that of a vigil rather than a demonstration. No one dared speak of the news, which had been heard on illegal wireless sets, but the little nods and smiles of recognition told their own story. The German soldiers on duty knew perfectly well why the people had gathered, but since no laws were being broken there was little they could do to stop them.

They merely watched, gloomily, until curfew time approached, and the mysterious, silent gathering dispersed just as suddenly as it had formed.

Of course, what was good news for the islanders was a blow to the Army of Occupation. The local people could feel that the mood of the Germans had changed. The once polite and disciplined forces seemed on edge, and they were prone to sudden outbursts of frustration and anger.

John Harris was dismayed to find a group of soldiers playing football with a rolled-up Union Jack, delighting in kicking and stomping it underfoot. When they departed, leaving the battered and muddied flag behind, he carefully scooped it up and hid it under his coat. 'When Berlin falls, I'll fly this flag!' he told Leo and Francis that evening, before stashing it away in his bedroom.

The impromptu vigil in St Helier's Royal Square wasn't the last such spontaneous gathering, although the next time it happened the circumstances were rather more sombre. On 23 October, two Royal Navy vessels, HMS *Charybdis* and HMS *Limbourne*, were sunk off the coast of France during an unsuccessful attack on a German shipping convoy. The defeat was as tragic as it was humiliating: between the two ships, 460 young men lost their lives.

Over the ensuing days and weeks, badly decomposed bodies began washing up on the beaches of the Channel Islands, a constant reminder of the grim defeat that had taken place so close to home. In Guernsey, the chief of police, Albert Lamy, reported to the island's Controlling Committee that nineteen men, wearing a mixture of naval battledress and dark-blue dungarees, had been identified thanks to their identity disks and inscribed leather belts. Their personal effects – a little sterling currency, a couple of wedding rings, photos of loved ones and a handful of good-luck charms – would be held until it was possible to return them to the dead men's families.

In the meantime, the bodies would have to be buried. The German authorities realised that they had been presented with an opportunity to both reaffirm their status as 'model' occupiers and ensure that they remained in control of a potentially incendiary situation. They announced that the nineteen sailors would be buried with full military honours, in a public ceremony orchestrated by the German Navy.

At 3 p.m. on 17 November, a chilly but bright autumn day, the Foulon Cemetery in St Peter Port paid host to this carefully choreographed event. Benediction was provided by both Protestant and Catholic representatives – the Dean of Guernsey, Reverend Agnew Giffard, and Canon Thomas Hickey, respectively – an honour guard of forty German marines fired a three-volley salute, and General von Schmettow, who had recently relocated to Guernsey, offered words of consolation and healing. 'In the death which follows and results from duty done,' he declared, 'the heart knows no frontier lines, and mourning becomes international.'

To underscore the gesture of symbolic unity, the enclosure for official mourners housed a mixture of local and German representatives, the bailiff, Victor Carey, and the jurats of the Royal Court rubbing shoulders with the top brass of the German military. What the organisers hadn't counted on, however, was the sheer number of uninvited guests. The funeral attracted the largest crowd that had been seen since the start of the Occupation as almost five thousand men, women and children flocked from the four corners of the island to pay their respects to the dead, and to prove that however benign the regime might seem, there was no doubt where their own loyalties lay.

Some expressed their patriotic fervour in a defiantly subversive manner. As instructed by their teachers, a group of forty children from the Vauxbelets School wore their red, white and blue scarves on the outside of their coats so the Germans couldn't miss them.

Pearl Smith attended the funeral in her nurse's uniform, along with the other girls from the hospital. But like many of the people who had come along that day, she found it hard to reconcile the respectful, dignified behaviour of the German officials with the fact that it was their comrades who had killed the nineteen British lads they were burying. Despite the veneer of respectability hanging over the whole affair, in her gut she couldn't help feeling that it was wrong, a kind of monstrous hypocrisy that everyone was expected to just go along with.

Pearl wasn't the only one at the cemetery who was seething with barely suppressed rage. The atmosphere was electric, as if the islanders were poised to suddenly give themselves over to outright defiance of the regime. The sham of the model occupation was hanging by a thread.

In the end, though, good old British reserve won the day – not to mention respect for the dead. A funeral was hardly the place for a spontaneous uprising, and gradually the huge crowd dispersed, leaving behind them a sea of seven hundred brightly coloured floral tributes. There were wreaths from the German Navy and the Feldkommandantur, from the island fire brigade and the amateur boxing club, and many more left by ordinary people.

Some had clearly come not just for the drowned sailors but to remember their own friends and relatives in the forces. 'In loving remembrance of two nephews who lost their lives at sea,' read one of the cards, while another was signed simply, 'From a soldier's wife.'

By the time Christmas rolled around again – the fourth under occupation – the Channel Islanders were used to a rather scaled-back celebration, with a feast that grew more and more meagre every year. Nonetheless, most people at least attempted to do something for the occasion, crafting their own handmade presents and cards for friends and family, and often sharing what little they had with those who had less. Sark resident Julia Tremaine was deeply touched to receive a parcel containing a large slab of English chocolate. It had been sent by the island's former priest, Reverend Phillips, who had been deported to the internment camp at Biberach earlier in the year. Since the deportees were entitled to Red Cross parcels, they received a regular supply of such treats, the very idea of which would make the mouths of their compatriots back home water. 'They seem to get so much,' wrote Mrs Tremaine, 'and it is kind of them to think of us poor neglected ones.'

Even those who were struggling could enjoy a great Christmas if they had friends who were willing to share with them. Leo Harris was thrilled to hear that his family had been invited to spend the festive period with his father's farmer friend Ken Richardson. Some months earlier, Mr Harris had helped Ken hide a beautiful Vauxhall 16 under some straw in one of his barns, and when he had told him he was looking for a secure hiding place for one of his own vehicles – a black 1934 Rover that was currently stashed behind a timber pile in his front yard – the farmer had told him to bring the car along too. 'Why don't you drive it over, and you and your family can all stay for the holiday,' he suggested.

So it was that, just after curfew on Christmas Eve, the Harrises eased open the large gates of the yard – carefully greased to avoid any tell-tale noises – and piled into the Rover, setting off on a distinctly illegal journey to North Lynn Farm. The car's tail lights were blacked out with shoe polish, but since the bright beams at the front were too powerful for this, Mr Harris had removed the nearside bulb completely and draped the offside one with a piece of black cloth, secured with a bit of string, which allowed just a sliver of light to shine through.

As Mr Harris had hoped, the streets were largely deserted, and the car sped past the local swimming baths and the Ommaroo Hotel without encountering a single German soldier. But as they rounded a bend on the approach to College House, where the Feldkommandantur was located, he suddenly spied trouble up ahead: a seven-man patrol, heavily armed, was marching towards them.

'Everyone stay calm,' Mr Harris said quietly, willing the corporal at the head of the patrol not to stop them. Leo's mother gave his hand a little squeeze and he realised his heart was pounding in his chest.

As they sped along, the German patrol grew closer and closer without seeming to take any notice of them. Perhaps the corporal had no interest in pulling over a random vehicle when he had plenty of other matters to be getting on with. Leo began to relax – it looked like they were going to make it.

Then suddenly the piece of cloth that was obscuring the offside headlight slipped out of place and started fluttering in the breeze. The full beam glared directly in the faces of the German patrol. Leo could see the corporal wince before turning and issuing an order to the men behind him. He held his breath, waiting for the command to halt that he was sure would be bellowed any minute.

The seven German soldiers turned in unison to face the oncoming vehicle, but then something remarkable happened: the corporal stepped forward and raised his hand in the Nazi salute.

Bewildered, Mr Harris carried on driving, passing the German patrol and then rapidly picking up speed. It wasn't until the soldiers were far away out of view that Leo finally felt himself breathe again.

The family spent the rest of the journey to St Martin parish puzzling over what had just happened. The corporal must have been blinded by the headlight and taken them for a German staff car, they decided, flashing its beams to wish them a merry Christmas. Perhaps, dazzled by the light, they had seen the patch of black fabric flapping in the wind and mistaken it for the little iron-cross flag that normally stuck out from the mudwing of the German vehicles.

Either way, it had been an extraordinarily lucky escape. When the family arrived at North Lynn Farm and told the story to Ken Richardson and his wife, the farmer laughed so hard that Leo feared he would fall off his chair.

While the Harris family enjoyed a lavish Christmas feast thanks to the Richardsons, elsewhere in the Channel Islands a dangerous mission was afoot, and the outcome was far less successful than their hair-raising drive across Jersey. Late in the evening of Christmas Day, an inter-Allied commando team comprising a mixture of British and Free French soldiers landed on Sark for a reconnaissance mission, as part of series of raids in the area known as Operation Hardtack.

Like the majority of military operations in the Channel Islands, this one was an unmitigated disaster. On their first attempt, the invaders were defeated by Sark's virtually impregnable geography, turning round and heading back to England when they found themselves unable to scale the steep cliffs. Two days later, they tried again at a different spot and this time made their way inland – only to stumble into a minefield.

In the ensuing explosions, two men, Corporal Roger Bellamy and Private André Dignac, were badly wounded. Bellamy died almost straightaway, while Dignac clung onto life. The private's comrades attempted to carry him to safety, along with the body of the deceased Bellamy, but in the process set off another two mines, this time killing Dignac outright.

By now, all but one of the men in the unit had sustained some kind of injury and their leader, Lieutenant Ambrose McGonigal, decided it was time to cut their losses. The Germans couldn't fail to have heard the explosions and it was only a matter of time before they came looking for the cause. McGonigal gave the order to abandon the two dead bodies in the minefield and make haste back to their boat.

The men hurried to the coast, setting off yet more mines as they went, but miraculously escaping serious injury. Soon they were once again at sea, heading back to England with their tails between their legs.

When the German soldiers arrived on the scene, they were in no rush to remove the two dead bodies from the minefield, but eventually the remains were taken to a little shed nearby and laid out on the cold stone floor. This time, though, there was to be no dignified military funeral. Instead the men were buried secretly at dawn, without ceremony or mourners, and no prayers were said over their graves. The Führer had decreed that the commandos were little better than gangsters, and the two dead soldiers were treated accordingly.

In time, though, the Sark people found a way to pay their own respects to Dignac and Bellamy. A small wooden cross inscribed with the two men's names was erected by the graves, and soon began to attract floral tributes. The Dame sent a pair of wreaths made from the camellias of the Seigneurie gardens, while others assembled little posies out of whatever flowers they had to hand. Many of the tiny bunches were tied together with ribbons in red, white and blue.

CHAPTER TWENTY-SEVEN

A NEW FRONT

In one sense, it was the worst-kept secret in military history. Everybody knew that the second front was coming – for more than two years now the Americans had been massing their forces in England, preparing to finally take the fight back to Europe. But while the general plan was beyond doubt, the specifics of the invasion – the where, how and perhaps most crucially when – were shrouded in mystery. Great efforts had been taken to confound German intelligence, with fake radio traffic, hollow diplomatic overtures, double agents feeding false information, and even an entirely fictitious First US Army Group comprising inflatable tanks and dummy landing craft, stationed at Dover in preparation for an imaginary attack on the Pas de Calais. The elaborate feat of misdirection, codenamed Operation Fortitude, ensured that while anticipation for D-Day was intense, very few people were entirely sure what it was they were anticipating.

For the Channel Islanders, D-Day represented more than just a potential turning point in the war. If the Allies succeeded in gaining a foothold in Europe, they assumed, surely their own liberation would be next. The prospect of a proper fight for the islands, something that had been avoided four years earlier when the British declined to defend them, was an alarming one, especially given the sheer number of troops stationed there, not to mention their intense fortification work. But if it meant freedom from German occupation it was a risk most were willing to take.

In the meantime, the only thing they could do was wait. But the islanders had been waiting for four long years now, and all the while life had got harder and harder. Many of them were beginning to grow impatient. Boys who had watched the first German troops arrive had gradually transformed into young men. In any other circumstances, they would already have paid a visit to their local recruiting office to sign up for what General Eisenhower called 'The Great Crusade'.

For many young men, the situation was deeply frustrating. Eighteen-year-old Osmund Simon dreamed of flying Spitfires and Hurricanes but, trapped in Jersey, he resorted to acts of sabotage instead. One night, Osmund crept out of the attic room he shared with his two brothers at their farm in the parish of St Peter and made his way down to the clubhouse of a local golf course, which was being used as an OT railway depot. The building was deserted, and inside he found one of the diesel locomotives that was used to cart sand and gravel up and down the coast for the fortification work. Osmund identified the engine's starting handle and in a few minutes had succeeded in removing it, hurling it into a hedge on his way home.

When he got back, his brothers had noticed his absence, but they knew better than to ask what he had been doing. Osmund would have loved to share the story, but he decided it was safer for all of them if he remained silent. The following day, from a safe distance, he observed the goings on at the depot. All morning the Germans struggled to get the locomotive working again, and it was well into the afternoon before they finally succeeded.

The OT trains were a popular target for sabotage, since the length of track involved meant it was impossible for the Germans to guard them adequately. Francis Harris, who had grown up with a passion for Western movies, attempted to derail a German train using a batch of home-made explosives made from a mixture of sodium chlorate weedkiller and sugar, tightly wrapped up in cloth cylinders. Having laid the charges, he retreated to a safe distance to watch, but what he witnessed was a far cry from the spectacular explosions he had seen at the cinema. As a train approached, the little bomb went off at just the right moment. There was a puff of smoke and a rather loud bang – loud enough, at any rate, for the driver to stop the train and get out to peer suspiciously at the track. But other than causing a delay of a few seconds, the explosion had done no real damage. Soon the train was on its way again, and the frustrated would-be saboteur was skulking off home.

What Francis lacked in bomb-making prowess, he more than made up for in burglary. He was an adept thief, and spent much of his free time robbing German storerooms with the help of a couple of schoolfriends, Donald and Dicky. Sometimes the lads would bring Leo along as well, as a look-out. While they applied themselves to the latest act of larceny, he would stand in the street outside, whistling – one tune if the coast was clear and another if he saw a sentry coming.

When the Harris boys came home clutching tins of purloined food, packets of cigarettes – even, on one occasion, a German Army field dressing – their father struggled to hide his pride. Mr Harris didn't quite encourage their hobby, but he certainly never discouraged it either. His wife was more naturally cautious, but since the family were living on the breadline she was in no position to turn down extra rations.

Mrs Harris did, however, warn her boys to be careful not to advertise their activities to potential informants. One of the neighbours, Mrs Grey, worked as a cook at Bagnoles, a large local house that had been requisitioned by the Germans. As a result, Mrs Harris never quite felt she could trust her. When the cheerful old lady popped round to offer her a bit of fish from the German kitchens, she would accept the gift gratefully, but she made sure never to let her guard down, fearful that perhaps she was under surveillance.

On 6 June 1944, Colonel Siegfried Heine, the newly appointed 'Fortress Commandant' of Jersey, posted a special proclamation at St Helier Town Hall. 'Germany's enemy is on the point of attacking French soil,' he declared. 'I expect the population of Jersey to keep its head, to remain calm and to refrain from any acts of sabotage and from hostile acts against the German Forces, even should the fighting spread to Jersey.' The notice included an ominous threat. 'At the first signs of unrest or trouble I will close the streets to every traffic and will secure hostages,' Heine warned. 'Attacks against the German Forces will be punished by death.'

By the time Heine's notice went up, most islanders were already well aware of what was going on just the other side of the Cotentin Peninsula. The Dame of Sark had been briefed unofficially over breakfast, when the island's German doctor came to call at the Seigneurie just as she was polishing off her fried potatoes and ersatz coffee. 'You must tell nobody or I will be shot,' he whispered, 'but I have news for you. The Allies have landed on the French coast.'

Others had already reached the same conclusion without the benefit of inside knowledge, having woken that morning to find the skies above their homes black with aircraft. Tens of thousands of planes flying over the Channel could mean only one thing: D-Day had finally arrived.

It was the most thrilling, and tantalising, moment that the island-ers had experienced in four years of Occupation. They could not, of course, celebrate openly but many people were determined to participate in the big day one way or another. In Guernsey, Joan Coutanche joined the crowds who flocked to Richmond Beach, just outside St Peter Port. As she sat and watched the swarms of planes flying over, listening for the heavy thud of the bombs dropping a hundred kilometres away in Normandy, she couldn't help thinking of the young British men whose lives were hanging in the balance.

While most islanders felt a thrill at the sight of the British and American planes, for Phyllis Baker they were distinctly alarming. With an appalling sense of timing, she had fallen prey to diphtheria just as the invasion was about to begin, and the German doctor on Sark had insisted on sending her to Guernsey for treatment. On the morning of D-Day, as the Allied armies fought tooth and nail for every inch of the Normandy coastline, Phyllis was at sea, making the short journey from Creux Harbour to St Peter Port in her uncle Walter's little fishing boat, the *Sunbeam*. It was flying a white flag, but with two German soldiers conspicuously standing guard on deck, he was concerned that one of the Allied bombers passing by overhead might consider it a tempting target.

When a handful of planes swooped down low, Walter unfurled a large tarpaulin. 'Tell them to get under this!' he told Phyllis.

Despite her poor health, Phyllis translated her uncle's instruction and the two soldiers obligingly hid under the sheet for the rest of the journey. When the little boat finally docked at the White Rock, everyone on board was extremely relieved to have made it in one piece.

Meanwhile, across the Channel Islands, the grapevine was buzzing with the latest news. Those who were in possession of black wireless sets threw caution to the wind, desperate for every last scrap of information. At half past ten that morning, the Harris family huddled together around the little Bush radio that was hidden in one of their kitchen cupboards, straining to hear the BBC newsreader John Snagge offer the first official confirmation that Allied forces had landed in France. When he finally spoke the words everyone had been waiting to hear, declaring portentously, 'D-Day has come,' they hugged each other ecstatically.

For many islanders, those words were all they needed to hear. The invasion was finally underway and liberation must surely be just around the corner. Union Jacks that had been hidden away for years were brought out of their hiding places, ready to be flown again in triumph.

Mr Harris, however, refused to tempt fate, keeping the flag he had rescued from a group of disgruntled Germans safely stowed until he felt sure the time had come to fly it. The invasion of France might have begun, but he knew the Occupation was far from over. 'Look out the window,' he told his sons, pointing down to the street below. It was a hive of activity, with German soldiers frantically rushing back and forth, stringing out barbed-wire barriers and bolstering their bunkers with sandbags. Several new machine-guns had suddenly appeared on the far side of the road, their barrels trained on the beach. Clearly the Germans were preparing for the fight of their lives.

All over the Channel Islands, similar activities were afoot. The beaches were closed, the telephone exchanges were shut down, and guards were posted outside the gas works and electricity stations. In the fields, huge concrete posts sprouted up to prevent glider pilots from landing. But despite the extensive preparations, the expected invasion force never came.

By midnight, all five of the Normandy beaches – Omaha, Utah, Sword, Juno and Gold – were in Allied hands, and over the ensuing days and weeks the crusading troops continued their steady progress into Europe. Leo had got hold of an old school atlas, and as each new scrap of information came through from the BBC, he and Francis excitedly plotted the latest front lines on its pages. But as the relentless advance eastwards continued, one thing gradually became clear: the Channel Islands were not part of General Eisenhower's invasion plan.

It wasn't that the islands had been forgotten about altogether. In fact, the decision to bypass them and press onward to Berlin had been debated at the highest levels. Set against the symbolic value of liberating them were more practical considerations. The extensive fortifications in Jersey and Guernsey meant that it could take up to three Army divisions to recapture them, and given the proximity between soldiers and civilians, the collateral damage would likely be considerable. The American top brass, in particular, were alarmed at the prospect of their troops inadvertently killing British subjects. As far as they were concerned, it made far more sense to leave the islands out of the equation. The Army of Occupation would presumably surrender sooner or later, when they realised that the war was a lost cause.

Even the Germans could see the logic behind the decision. 'It is now pretty obvious that the British do not intend to take the islands by force, but to spare them and let them fall into their hands like ripe fruit at the end of the war,' wrote Baron von Aufsess. 'If the British are wise, they will continue to refrain from any premature demand for the surrender of the islands, through which they might be forced into an attack upon, and the senseless destruction of, territory which to all intents and purposes is already theirs.'

But despite such rationalisations, for the sixty thousand-odd people who had already endured four years of occupation, the realisation that they were not part of the grand march to freedom came as a crushing blow. The islanders' disillusionment was summed up by one simple, depressing thought: 'They've left us behind.' Some of them had never really forgiven Churchill for demilitarising the islands four years earlier, and being left out of the fight for a second time felt like another betrayal.

As the days and weeks went by and the reality of the situation sank in, the victory flags were returned to their hiding places, and the mood of buoyant optimism that had spontaneously erupted on D-Day gave way to a more familiar resignation. Now, once again, the islanders could do nothing more than wait.

This time, however, the siege mentality was shared by occupiers and occupied alike. On 17 August, the ancient Breton town of St Malo fell to the Allies. As its picturesque medieval buildings burned to the ground, groups of young Jersey lads cycled up to the clifftops to get a better view of the raging fires, which were clearly visible across less than fifty miles of water.

With the French coast in Allied hands, the twenty-five thousand German troops in the Channel Islands were cut off from their supply lines, and their mood took an appreciable turn for the worse. Suddenly, their idyllic seaside posting didn't seem quite so cushy after all. Baron von Aufsess was typically blunt in his assessment. 'The front is now some hundreds of miles away from us,' he wrote. 'We are deep in Anglo-American territory.'

The new circumstances meant an adjustment for everyone. 'It is a strange situation revealing itself,' wrote Julia Tremaine, 'for although the Germans are cornered here and are English prisoners, we are still German prisoners, and we know it.'

Prisoners the islanders remained, but there was at least a limited changing of the guard. In preparation for the anticipated invasion, vast underground hospitals had been built in both Jersey and Guernsey – thanks to the unstinting labour of the abused OT workers, the majority of whom had subsequently been shipped off to the Continent. In the wake of the Allied landings in France, the new facilities were put to good use, treating injured German servicemen who had fled to the Channel Islands to avoid being captured. The influx of new arrivals pushed the ratio of Germans to local people closer than ever. In Guernsey, the soldiers made up a third of the total population, and with the fall of St Malo several hundred more servicemen, a mixture of ground forces and sailors, were soon living on the islands as well.

Among the new arrivals that summer was Kriegsmarine admiral Friedrich Hüffmeier, a committed National Socialist who made little effort to hide his disdain for Count von Schmettow's soft approach to Occupation. The Nazis in the Channel Islands had always been in the minority, held in check by their more moderate, aristocratic superiors. Now, though, they had a high-ranking ally working behind the scenes, determined to undermine von Schmettow's regime.

If anything, the worse the war went for the Germans, the more the hardline Nazis asserted themselves. On 24 July, four days after the failed bomb plot against the Führer, the Hitler salute was made mandatory throughout the armed forces. In Guernsey, Admiral Hüffmeier even attempted to impose it on the local police force, if in a rather roundabout way. He summoned the chief of police, Albert Lamy, to a meeting, telling him that he found the traditional military salutes his men offered too stiff. Perhaps they could just raise their right hands in front of them instead, the admiral suggested. Lamy saw through the ruse immediately and tactfully declined the proposal. The British policemen took their saluting very seriously, he insisted, and couldn't possibly offer such an informal gesture.

Unsurprisingly, Hüffmeier soon made enemies among the more moderate German leaders on the islands. Baron von Aufsess was typically snobbish, dismissing him as an unsophisticated bigot. Unlike the highly educated aristocrats who had headed the Channel Islands regime from the beginning, the admiral struggled to understand even basic English, but this was hardly surprising, since his formal education had ended by the age of sixteen, when he had joined the Navy.

Over his thirty years with the Kriegsmarine, Hüffmeier's ascent through the ranks had been something of a mystery to those who served under him. Most regarded him as little more than a liability, more likely to scupper a vessel than to distinguish himself in command. During his brief tenure as captain of the battlecruiser *Scharnhorst*, he had run the ship aground, collided with a submarine, and got his starboard propeller so badly tangled up in a buoy wire that he was forced to return to dock for repairs. His promotion to admiral by the head of the Kriegsmarine, Karl Dönitz, with whom he was on friendly terms, had perhaps been born out of a desire to see him 'kicked upstairs' to a position where he could do relatively little harm. Hüffmeier had traded the bridge of a battleship for an office job, leading a new department charged with instilling 'military-ideological leadership' in naval officers.

Baron von Aufsess saw the admiral as a military lightweight whose career had been built on the back of his ideological convictions more than his ability – a man as hopelessly ineffectual as he was physically, and morally, unattractive. 'Hüffmeier himself, podgy and inelegant, is an unimpressive figure,' he wrote after their first proper meeting. 'As he sat there, with bowed shoulders, I thought the desk might be his more proper sphere of action. But on second thoughts, surveying his snub nose and fat cheeks, I decided he might well have been a one-time roistering student who, on inheriting his father's prosperous business, settled down to hard work and a successful career, thus acquiring a not unpleasing but still not quite convincing self-confidence of expression.'

Underestimating the admiral would prove to be an error, however. Bureaucratically minded he might be, but Hüffmeier was more ambitious than von Aufsess realised, and in the Channel Islands his star was in the ascendant.

CHAPTER TWENTY-EIGHT

OVERTURES

Whatever the local people thought, the British hadn't forgotten about the Channel Islands altogether. Just over a week after the German withdrawal from St Malo, Free French forces were parading down the Champs-Élysées. The war was going badly for Germany, and intelligence received in London suggested that morale among the Army of Occupation was at an all-time low. A little nudge – it was hoped – might be enough to crush their fighting spirit for good and secure a bloodless surrender.

The result was a full-on assault, not of military personnel but of words. The German forces on the islands, who relied for their news on their ludicrously unconvincing propaganda papers, were suddenly deluged with copies of something called *Nachrichten für die Truppe* (News for the Troops). The leaflets, dropped by passing RAF aircraft, not only offered a more reliable account of the war raging across Europe, but included frequent enjoinders to surrender. For almost two weeks a nightly delivery was made, with tens of thousands of news-sheets falling from the skies.

At 11 p.m. on 1 September, the RAF delivered a different kind of mail. A pair of cylinders were dropped by parachute, each one containing a copy of a letter written on the headed notepaper of SHAEF (Supreme Headquarters, Allied Expeditionary Force) and addressed personally to General von Schmettow. The commandant was requested to reconnect the telephone line to the French mainland, where a captured Luftwaffe officer, Major General Gerhard Bassenge, was ready to discuss the possibility of surrender.

The British officer in charge of the operation, Major Alan Chambers, waited patiently for a reply, but von Schmettow greeted his overture with a stony silence. Reluctant to take no for an answer, Chambers tried again three weeks later, this time declaring that, under the white flag of truce, he intended to sail to a neutral position four miles off the coast of Guernsey, and requesting that the general meet him there for a parley.

The following morning, Chambers and Bassenge departed from the French port of Carteret, reaching the rendezvous co-ordinates by lunchtime. But there was no sign of General von Schmettow.

Chambers was not a man to give up easily, however. He decided to press on towards the shore, but before long, he was stopped by a German patrol boat. The major explained that he had come to speak with von Schmettow. A little surprised, the German patrol relayed the message to shore by signal lamp, and a few minutes later they received a rather guarded response: 'Specifically what matter does Major Chambers want to discuss?'

'Tell him I want to talk about the military situation in general,' the exasperated major replied.

The message was relayed, and Chambers waited patiently for an answer. It was more than half an hour before it finally came: 'General von Schmettow is fully informed as to the military situation and therefore declines any discussion.'

For Major Chambers, who had put so much effort into arranging a conversation, von Schmettow's refusal to talk felt like a slap in the face. But there was nothing he could do about it now. Reluctantly, he informed the patrol boat that he would be going about and heading back to France.

Once he reached dry land – having narrowly avoided being sunk by a belligerent coastal battery on Alderney – Chambers prepared a report for his superiors in London, offering two possible explanations for von Schmettow's behaviour. Either the general's family back home in Germany were being used as hostages against him, the major suggested, or his control over the islands had been compromised by fanatical Nazi underlings.

The German authorities might not have been ready to surrender, but the ordinary soldiers were growing twitchier than ever. When Phyllis Baker returned to Sark after her hospital stay in Guernsey, she was surprised to find that even the sleepy, bucolic island was more on edge than at any time she could remember. The curfew, which had always been rather laxly enforced, was now rigidly adhered to, and whenever Phyllis was asked to accompany the doctor to see a patient outside the permitted hours she was given a password, which was changed every day, and escorted at all times by a pair of German guards.

In Guernsey, meanwhile, Phyllis's devoted secret admirer Werner Rang had also noticed that tensions were rising. He was called out late one night to attend to an incident at the Imperial Hotel, arriving a little after 1 a.m. to find that his patient, a young soldier who had only recently been transferred to the island, was already dead. Werner always found it upsetting when there was nothing he could do to save a life, but when he learned the circumstances of the incident he was more troubled than usual. The man had been out on sentry duty when he had encountered a fellow soldier in the dark, who had anxiously demanded the latest password. In the heat of the moment, the word had gone right out of his head, and his hesitation had been enough to seal his fate. The other soldier had fired his gun and the young man had dropped to the ground, mortally wounded. But the worst thing about the story was the fact that the shooter had failed to recognise his victim. Only when he rushed over to inspect the body had he realised that the man he had shot was his own brother.

Trigger-happy soldiers were, of course, not just a threat to their own comrades. Leo and Francis Harris had heard plenty of stories about a pair of American officers from the Sixth Armored Division, Captain Edward Clark and Lieutenant George Haas, who had been taken captive by the Germans and were being held in Jersey. The men were regarded as war heroes, having helped capture the town of Granville in Normandy, and as a result were treated as local celebrities.

One day, the Harris boys were standing on the pavement with their father when they spotted one of the Americans being led along by a German patrol. Mr Harris rushed inside and grabbed what remained of his tobacco ration. 'See if you can slip that to the Yank,' he told Francis, pressing it into his hand.

Francis accepted the challenge, crossing the road and tailing the group of soldiers at a couple of metres' distance, hoping that something might distract them long enough for him to pass the tobacco to the American. But no such opportunity presented itself, and in the end, rather than give up altogether, he decided to take a more direct approach, darting in between the German soldiers until he was face to face with the GI. He held out his hand, offering up the little foil package.

The American, though, wanted nothing to do with it. 'No, son,' he said, taking a step backwards and holding his own hands up in the air. He was evidently trying to show his captors that he was a compliant and co-operative prisoner, but his reaction left Francis high and dry. As the German guards turned to face him, he bolted out from their midst and began running at full pelt down the road again.

Leo and his father watched in horror as the corporal at the head of the German patrol gave chase, rifle in hand. 'Halt!' he bellowed, but Francis didn't heed him. Instead he careened into a side street and disappeared from view.

The corporal, however, was still in pursuit. A few seconds later he reached the junction where Francis had turned off the road. He stopped, carefully planting his feet and raising the gun to his shoulder. For Leo, time seemed to slow down as he watched the German slide the bolt of the rifle and take aim. He was waiting for the terrible crack of the gun being fired.

But the sound never came. After a few seconds, the corporal lowered the gun again and stomped back to the rest of the patrol, muttering German expletives under his breath. Francis had obviously been too quick for him to get a clear shot.

A few hours later, Francis returned home, still clutching his father's tobacco. Mr Harris was mortified to think that his rash act of generosity had almost cost his son his life. But it wasn't the last dangerous encounter between him and the German authorities.

During one of his raids on the nearby army storerooms with his schoolfriends Donald and Dickie, Francis had acquired quite a trophy: a genuine Wehrmacht-issue Mauser rifle. When he showed it to his father, Mr Harris's pride was clear to see. He had not entirely given up hope of an Allied invasion of Jersey, and if the Tommies did come calling, he had every intention of joining the fight. Francis might be only sixteen, but as a veteran of the First World War, Mr Harris had known plenty of boys his age who had lied to get into the services, and if his son wanted to do his bit for king and country, he certainly wasn't going to stop him. In the meantime, however, he told Francis to take the rifle upstairs and hide it well.

One chilly autumn morning, after Leo had already left for school on his bike, Francis was woken by his father. 'Come here, quickly,' Mr Harris whispered, ushering him over to the window.

They looked down on the street outside, where a German Army lorry was parked. A mixture of soldiers and plain-clothes police were standing in the road, along with a couple of teenage boys who appeared to be under arrest. 'Do you know those lads?' Mr Harris asked.

'Yes, Dad,' Francis replied nervously. 'I know one of them, and I think the other one might be someone from school.'

'Do they know about the rifle?' his father asked him.

Francis nodded.

Mr Harris didn't waste any time. He took the rifle out from its hiding place, bundled it into a sack, and calmly gave Francis his orders. The family owned a cottage in town that he didn't think the Germans were aware of. It was the best place he could think of to stash an illegal weapon.

Mr Harris pressed the key into his son's hand. 'Hide this in the brickwork when you're done,' he told him. 'Don't bring it back here with you.' He gave him an encouraging squeeze on the shoulder. 'Now be quick!'

Francis didn't need telling twice. He raced downstairs, with the sack over his shoulder, and made his way out of the back door to the yard outside, securing the heavy load around the handlebars of his bicycle. Then he set off along the promenade, heading into town. To his relief, no one seemed to be following.

It felt like the longest journey of his life. Whether because of his nerves or the extra weight on the bicycle, he soon found himself struggling to go on, and as he reached the slight incline of Green Street he was forced to get off and push.

Francis wheeled the bike past the Snow Hill bus station and onto Colomberie, then down through Bath Street to the little road where the cottage was located. Fumbling in his pocket for the key, he let himself inside, removed the rifle from its sack and stowed it safely. Then he locked up, hid the key as his father had instructed him, and got back on his bike again. As he whizzed along the roads towards home, it felt at least fifty pounds lighter.

Francis rounded the corner onto Havre des Pas, when he heard someone calling his name. He squeezed hard on the brakes and came to a stop outside La Plage Hotel, where Mrs Grey – the neighbour who had taken a job with the Germans – was standing on the pavement wringing her hands. 'Don't go home!' she told Francis. 'The Gestapo are there. I think they must have gone to arrest your father.'

Francis felt a lump form in his throat. 'Thank you,' he told the old woman, although he had no intention of heeding her advice. If his family were in trouble because of him, it was only right that they should all face the music together.

Francis pedalled on until he reached the courtyard outside the Harris residence. There he was met by a feldgendarme who ushered him inside, before giving him a little shove into the kitchen.

Francis found his parents in the company of some distinctly sinister house guests. Two plain-clothes policemen were sitting casually at the table as if they had just called round for tea. One of them, wearing a smart suit, waistcoat and trilby hat, he recognised as Karl Wölfle, the infamous 'Wolf of the Gestapo'. The other was dressed in a full-length leather coat and introduced himself as Willi.

'Please take a seat,' Wölfle told Francis, pulling out an old wooden chair.

Francis sat obediently, clocking his mother's anxious expression. 'So, Francis,' Wölfle said casually, 'some of your friends tell me you have a rifle.' His eyes narrowed as he took in the young lad's face. Then after what felt like an age, he asked, 'Is this so?'

Francis returned the German's gaze as confidently as he could. 'No,' he replied.

Wölfle smiled patiently. 'Oh, I think you do have a rifle,' he said. 'Why don't you show it to me now and we can settle this little matter?'

The man's words sounded as sweet as honey, but Francis was resolute. 'I haven't got a rifle,' he insisted.

The detective rose from his chair and began to idly walk around the room. Mrs Harris started, struck with a sudden realisation. In a pot on the stove was a tinful of bully-beef rations that Francis had stolen, which she had been heating up for lunch. The smell was quite distinctive and she was sure that sooner or later the Germans would notice it. She marched over to the cooker, grabbed the handle of the pot and swiftly poured the contents down the sink.

Wölfle regarded her suspiciously.

'It was spoiled,' Mrs Harris lied. Given the dire food shortages, this explanation was a little hard to swallow, but the policeman let it go and continued his casual stalking around the kitchen, peering in the odd cupboard as he went with an air of detached curiosity.

When he came to the tall wooden dresser on which the family kept their crockery, Wölfle stretched up his arm to feel along the top. About halfway along, he stopped and a flicker of satisfaction spread across his face. 'Ah,' he said cheerfully, pulling down a little unfinished crystal set that Francis had been working on the night before. He walked over and placed it gently on the table. 'So, you are making radios,' he remarked calmly.

Francis said nothing, but Wölfle's words had clearly not been intended as a question. 'This is very serious, you know,' he said gravely. 'I think perhaps you had better come with us.' He gestured to a gendarme standing outside the room.

The soldier entered and immediately laid hands on Francis, pulling him out of his chair and leading him roughly to an Austin saloon car parked outside. He was bundled in, and the driver set off for Gloucester Street prison.

Wölfle and Willi, meanwhile, remained behind at the house. A little while later, when Leo arrived home from school for lunch, he found them sitting in the kitchen with his parents, along with two more of their colleagues.

Leo caught his father's eye, and his terror must have been obvious. 'It's all right,' said Mr Harris, in a soothing voice that he normally used when one of his children had hurt themselves. 'They just want to ask us a few questions.' Mrs Harris smiled encouragingly, but her face was as white as a sheet.

It was Wölfle who finally broke the silence. 'Bernard, take the boy upstairs,' he barked at one of the other policemen. 'Willi and I must have a few more words with the parents.'

Leo accompanied the policeman up to the first floor, where he watched as one by one every drawer and cupboard was comprehensively ransacked. Despite Bernard's best efforts, there was, of course, no sign of the missing rifle, but it didn't take him long to find something else that was rather hard to explain: the green field dressing – emblazed with the distinctive Wehrmacht eagle – that Leo and Francis had stolen several months earlier.

Leo's breath caught in his throat as he watched the German carefully unwrap the dressing and inspect the cotton-wool inside. He seemed to think for a moment, as if wrestling with a dilemma. Then he looked up at Leo and said, 'Get rid of this, quickly.'

Leo didn't need telling twice. He took the dressing from Bernard's outstretched hand and raced to the nearest window, hurling it across the road and over the sea wall, and watching with satisfaction as the little green pouch was taken by the tide.

'Come,' Bernard told Leo, leading him back down into the kitchen, where his colleagues were also performing a thorough search. The policeman called Willi was gazing suspiciously at the light fitting in the ceiling – or more precisely at the little two-way electrical junction that split the current between the bulb and a wire passing down into the large plywood wardrobe where the family kept their radio hidden. It had been rigged so that the set would come on along with the light, to save anyone having to faff around in the depths of the cupboard when they wanted to turn it on or off.

Willi had obviously seen such set-ups before. He walked over to the switch and flicked it to the 'on' position, peering suspiciously into the wardrobe. But aside from the mountains of old coats and scarves piled up inside, there didn't seem to be anything amiss. He flicked the switch back off again and Leo breathed a sigh of relief. What he knew, and the German evidently didn't, was that the radio took several seconds to warm up. If he had waited a few seconds longer, he might have heard the incriminating sound of a BBC news broadcast.

The tension in the room was almost unbearable. Mr Harris was in no doubt that his family's safety was hanging by a thread. With one son already on his way to prison, the least he could do was try to get the other out of the fray. 'Leo!' he barked, assuming the unfamiliar tone of a Victorian patriarch. 'Get yourself off to school before you're late for the afternoon's lessons.'

Leo was dumbfounded. The last thing he wanted to do was to leave his parents alone at a time like this, knowing that he might never see them again. And in any case, surely the Germans wouldn't allow him to leave just like that.

But to his surprise, Wölfle gave a little nod. 'Do as your father says,' he instructed.

Leo made his way to the door, stopping to offer his mother and father a brief kiss on the cheek. When he reached the yard and went to pick up his bicycle, a feldgendarme grabbed him by the arm and pushed him out of the gate on foot instead. He walked all the way to school, arriving late for lessons but already well past caring about getting in trouble. After all, a ticking off from one of his teachers was nothing after a lunchbreak spent in the company of the Gestapo.

The afternoon passed by in a daze, and Leo had never been more relieved to go home at the end of a schoolday. He half-ran most of the way, hardly daring to think about what he would find there. When he arrived, his mother was still in the kitchen where he had left her, but his father was nowhere to be seen. 'They took him away too,' she told Leo quietly, drawing him into a tight embrace.

Mrs Harris put the kettle on and brewed up a pot of carrot tea. For once, Leo didn't notice the unpleasant flavour, and the warm drink helped to soothe his nerves a little.

When their cups were empty, his mother told him she would have to go out for a little while to see about some things before dinner. Leo nodded. 'All right, Mum,' he said, doing his best to put on a brave face.

But when he heard the door shut behind her, he felt like the strength had drained out of him. He curled up on an armchair and began sobbing uncontrollably. At thirteen years old, he had never felt more alone in his life.

CHAPTER TWENTY-NINE

STARVATION

It was probably fortunate for Francis that his arrest had taken place when it did. Six months earlier he would most likely have been shipped off to France, where he could easily have met the same fate as young Peter Painter, the patrol leader of the 11th Jersey Scout Troop who had perished in a German labour camp. As it was, with the sea link to the Continent severed, the Germans could do little more than hold him in prison indefinitely. So far, at least, they had refrained from shooting civilian criminals, and it was unlikely that they were about to change their policy by executing a sixteen-year-old boy.

Instead, Francis was confined to a cell at Gloucester Street prison, along with three political prisoners – a Dutchman, a Ukrainian and a fellow islander by the name of Frank Keiller. But he didn't get to spend much time there – several times a day, and often in the middle of the night as well, he would be hauled away to the headquarters of the Geheime Feldpolizei for interrogation.

In the absence of physical violence, the plain-clothes detectives employed every trick they could think of to break him psychologically. With no way of telling the time, Francis soon became disorientated, a typical Gestapo strategy to induce a feeling of helplessness in their prisoners. The interviews were conducted with a light shined in the young man's face, by an interrogator, Major Bodie, who ostentatiously placed his pistol on the table between them before every bout of questioning.

It soon became clear that Francis' father was being held more as a hostage than a suspect in his own right, as a way of exerting leverage. The Germans threatened to shoot him as a *résistant* if Francis didn't give up the hidden rifle. It was obvious, they claimed, that it had been stolen on his father's orders.

In between interrogation sessions, Francis got to know his cellmates better. The Jerseyman Frank Keiller was a forthright chap only a couple of years older than himself, with a shock of bright red hair that suited his fiery personality. Frank had been arrested following a failed attempt to escape from the island by boat. Since the nearby French coast had fallen into Allied hands, reaching the British forces had become a much more achievable proposition, a crossing of less than fifteen miles at sea. With food stocks on the islands running low, more than fifty young men decided to seize the opportunity, most intending to sign up when they got there, as well as to pass on valuable intelligence. Assuming they made it to open water, the success rate was relatively high – while half a dozen islanders lost their lives in the attempt, forty-seven reached their destination safely. Among them were the two Americans, Ed Clark and George Haas, who survived a gruelling fourteen-hour crossing in a stolen rowing boat.

Although Frank and his comrades never made it to France, they were lucky to survive the attempt. They were already far from the shore when their canoe began taking on water and they were forced to abandon it, stripping off their clothes and jumping into the bitterly cold sea. The craggy outcroppings along the Jersey coastline proved to be their saving grace. For two hours they swam from rock to rock, moving on every time the encroaching tide enveloped their latest safe spot. By the time dawn broke they were exhausted, almost at the point of physical collapse, and the nearest beach was still a long way off.

The young men had little choice but to call for help, bellowing at the top of their lungs until they caught the attention of a couple of islanders. The good Samaritans set out to rescue them, but unfortunately their cries had also attracted the attention of the local German patrol, and they returned to dry land under the glare of a pair of searchlights.

After a brief stop at the local OT hospital, Frank was taken away for interrogation. He was slapped and kicked repeatedly, and had his head slammed against a bookshelf by a German policeman – and this was before the questions had even begun. After ten minutes or so, the 'bad cop' disappeared and a 'good cop' took over. Frank was offered a blanket and a bowl of soup, and gently talked through the circumstances of his escape attempt.

When the interrogator was satisfied that he had got enough for the time being, Frank was transferred to Gloucester Street prison. He had already been there for a couple of months by the time Francis arrived, and the young lad soon found a friend in the failed escapee. When the Germans moved Francis from the shared cell to a solitary, damp dungeon in the basement, it was Frank who persuaded them to change their minds, pointing out that German victory in the war was far from certain and if they turned out to be on the losing side, they might easily find themselves imprisoned for mistreating an under-age inmate. The other prisoners also did their best to look out for Francis, always offering him the largest chunk of the bread they were given to share. One of them even taught him to play chess, and they whiled away many quiet hours hunched over the little wooden board.

Frank Keiller, meanwhile, had other things on his mind. He was a man of action, not content to sit back and accept unfortunate circumstances, and in time this attitude reached its logical conclusion. With the help of a screwdriver and chisel stolen from the prison workshop, Frank succeeded in escaping from Gloucester Street, dropping thirty feet from the roof of the prison to the street below and twisting his ankle in the process.

Frank was hidden by a couple of friends, with false papers and a brand-new ration book provided by the ever-helpful Dr McKinstry. There was just one problem: his bright red hair was extremely recognisable, whatever the name on his ID card. First he tried rubbing it with coffee grains, but the ginger resolutely shone through. In desperation, Frank turned to Bob Le Sueur, who was friendly with the staff of a local hair salon – the same one, in fact, where the Russian Bill's bespoke drawings were advertised in the window. With their help, Bob was able to source some black dye without anyone asking too many questions about what it was for.

Unfortunately, Bob was far from an experienced stylist, and managed to dye not only Frank's hair but most of his neck black as well, meaning that for several months he was obliged to wear turtleneck sweaters whenever he left the house. It was just as well that Bob didn't attempt to smear the noxious substance on his friend's ginger eyebrows. Instead, Frank applied a daily coating of black mascara. 'I felt a complete nonker putting it on,' he joked, but it was a small price to pay for his freedom.

Francis, meanwhile, remained behind bars for the forseeable future. His father was released and allowed to return home to the family, but the teenager was offered no such reprieve. As far as the Germans were concerned, he would remain in Gloucester Street until their link to the French coast was restored and they could have him sent away to an internment camp. Or alternatively, as was beginning to look increasingly likely, until they were forced to surrender the island altogether.

It wasn't just the military links to the Continent that had been severed by the Allied invasion. The islanders, who depended on the trading post in Granville for much of their food, had been left with a rapidly dwindling stockpile of rations on which to survive. Clearly, the situation was unsustainable. The islands had never been self-sufficient, relying on imports to supplement the limited supply of locally produced meat and veg. Now they were effectively under siege.

The first cut to civilian rations came three months after D-Day, but the authorities knew that they were staring down a potential disaster. On 19 September, the Guernsey Controlling Committee received a report from the island's medical services officer, Dr Symons. 'It is my considered opinion,' he wrote, 'that should relief not be forthcoming in some form or another, the condition of the inhabitants of the Island will become one of great danger in the near future.' Mid-November, the doctor predicted, would be the point of no return, when 'life here will become unbearable for the population as a whole'. With no flour, sugar, gas, electricity or coal to get them through the winter, it was a toss-up whether the population would starve or freeze to death first. 'The lucky ones will be those who die quickly,' Dr Symons predicted ominously.

The islands were in an unfortunate position, stuck between two warring countries, neither of which accepted responsibility for their welfare. General von Schmettow soon fell out with the bailiff of Guernsey, Victor Carey, over their varying interpretations of the Hague Convention. The way Carey saw it, the Germans had a responsibility as an occupying force to ensure the survival of the civilian population. If they were no longer able to do so, they should pull out of the islands altogether. Von Schmettow, however, was adamant: the responsibility lay with the British government. 'The besiegers are the Allied forces, and we the besieged,' he wrote. 'Now the islands are cut off, I can no longer provide for the population.'

When Carey refused to hand over sixty tonnes of dried beans that were owed to the Germans, hoping to use them as a bargaining chip, the general responded with uncharacteristic vehemence. The islanders, he told him, didn't know the meaning of war. 'They are unable to realise its effects as felt by the German towns, the whole of France, London and South England, nor the sacrifices and sufferings which the affected countries have to live through,' von Schmettow wrote. 'Compared to these, the islands have not even felt a breath of it.' In other words, they should count themselves lucky, and be grateful for whatever they got.

Finally, in case the bailiff was in any doubt as to his resolve, von Schmettow declared threateningly, 'The German Army does not build fortifications of such strength without holding them with the greatest bitterness and until the exhaustion of its powers of resistance. Even the advent of a calamity for the population after some time, for which the besieger alone will be responsible, will change nothing to the fact.'

If the general was bluffing, he was making a pretty good fist of it. In fact, though, the question of whether or not to let the civilian population starve was the subject of intense debate at the highest levels of the administration. Baron von Aufsess found the idea morally repugnant. 'Never must the German soldier be made the instrument of so hideous a crime,' he wrote in his diary. 'We could not in all conscience carry out orders to this effect.' After tossing and turning all night worrying about the issue, he summoned his senior colleagues to let them know that he had reached a decision: he would rather die, he told them, than 'serve as hangman's assistant in the annihilation of the population'.

It was hard to believe that von Schmettow, in his heart of hearts, felt all that differently to von Aufsess, but his own power as commander in chief of the Channel Islands was increasingly compromised. On orders from Berlin, his chief of staff, the moderate Hans von Helldorf, had been replaced – against von Schmettow's strong objections – by the fanatical Admiral Hüffmeier. The admiral was a man with few qualms about the humanitarian consequences of his actions. When Baron von Aufsess asked one of his naval colleagues about Hüffmeier's views on the food crisis, the response he received wasn't encouraging. 'All he cared about,' the baron wrote, 'was holding out until the bitter end, irrespective of whether the civilian population was wiped out.'

The way von Aufsess saw it, the only thing standing in the way of a catastrophic humanitarian crisis was von Schmettow's ability to keep Hüffmeier at bay. It was, he wrote, 'a trial of strength' between the two men, and he wasn't at all sure who would come out on top.

General von Schmettow was well aware that his position was vulnerable, and a direct conflict with his fanatical second in command was the last thing he needed. Hence his insistence to the Guernsey bailiff that it was the British who would have to solve the problem. But Admiral Hüffmeier wasn't the only pugnacious character taking an interest in the affair – on the other side was none other than Winston Churchill.

As far as the prime minister was concerned, the Channel Islanders had been personae non gratae ever since Ambrose Sherwill's ill-thought-out radio broadcast four years earlier, in which his rose-tinted description of the Occupation had seen him written off in London as a quisling. When a plan to isolate the German troops on the islands and wait for them to surrender landed on Churchill's desk, he wrote cheerfully in the margin, 'Let 'em starve. No fighting. They can rot at their leisure.'

Churchill meant, of course, the German soldiers rather than the local people, but the sentiment, in a broader sense, captured his attitude to the islands overall. The fact was that he didn't much care for them. When his home secretary, Herbert Morrison, requested he insert a line in a speech recognising the suffering that the islanders had endured, he flatly refused to do so. When he was asked to send food, he also declined, on the grounds that it might be appropriated by the Germans.

The island leaders were growing increasingly desperate. The bailiff of Jersey, Alexander Coutanche, was convinced that he could make the British government see sense, if only he were allowed to speak to them directly. He proposed to sail to London on a kind of parole, make his case in person, and then return obediently to Jersey. But however honest the bailiff's intentions were, there was no way von Schmettow could agree to his plan. What was to stop Coutanche from changing his mind once he was safely ensconced on the mainland, where his detailed knowledge of the military situation on the islands would no doubt be of great interest to his hosts?

In Guernsey, meanwhile, Victor Carey asked for permission to write directly to the 'protecting power', Switzerland, which again the general strenuously refused. 'The request', he wrote bluntly, 'is physically impossible and in any case could not be permitted.'

Finally, the bailiff sent a telegram to the secretary general of the Red Cross in Geneva, begging them to provide humanitarian relief. 'Conditions rapidly deteriorating here,' he wrote. 'Will soon become impossible.' He urged an immediate visit from Red Cross representatives to assess the situation for themselves.

Carey must have known, though, that they could never agree to send aid against the express wishes of the British prime minister. If Churchill didn't change his mind, the situation was hopeless.

While the anguished messages flew back and forth, life for ordinary islanders – particularly those living in the towns – was becoming increasingly difficult. When the gas supply finally failed altogether, people were left without the means of cooking their own meals. Instead, each family was allocated to a communal oven, generally at their local bakery. Space was limited, with only a single one-foot-square tin allowed per family, and the arrangement relied on trust, since it required people to leave their most precious commodity – food – in the hands of a stranger for several hours at a time.

Predictably, there was some scope for working the system. One Guernsey baker was so surprised at the generous dollop of fat he found floating in a customer's bean jar that he skimmed it off and transferred it to his brother's dish instead. When the lucky beneficiary arrived to collect it, he didn't recognise his own food. 'I don't think this is ours,' he protested. 'Just get home, will you!' the baker replied, practically shoving his brother out of the shop.

It wasn't just mealtimes that were affected by the cuts. Since few islanders had mains electricity, no gas meant no artificial light either. Candles and matches became priceless black-market commodities, changing hands for exorbitant prices. For those without the means to pay, much of that autumn was spent sitting around in the dark. And with electricity running low as well, the cinema was put out of action too. Eventually, the electric grid was formally taken over by the Germans, meaning that those islanders who had previously been connected to the mains were suddenly cut off altogether.

At the Castel Hospital, where Pearl Smith was still nursing, the situation was increasingly grim. The scalpels were blunt, rubber gloves worn through, cotton-wool virtually non-existent, and supplies of catgut so low that all but the most essential life-saving operations were being postponed indefinitely. Even basic medicines such as aspirin had run out completely.

As the nights got longer – and colder – the shortage of fuel became increasingly serious. Previously, the islanders had kept their houses warm thanks to imports of French briquettes made from compressed coal dust. Now they were reliant on what they could scavenge, and the well-heeled gentlewomen of St Helier and St Peter Port began to be spotted snatching stray twigs from the side of the road.

In desperation, many people resorted to illegal tree-felling. On one particularly cold day in Jersey, a mob descended on the row of ancient, wind-bent oaks that lined the esplanade between St Helier and St Aubin, and began mercilessly hacking them down. Baron von Aufsess was appalled. 'The local people are curiously insensitive to the beauty of their island,' he wrote in his diary, apparently without irony. 'It will be fifty years at least before the trees can again reach the stature and fantastic shape which lent the Avenue its special charm.'

Enraged at what he saw as wanton vandalism, the baron set out to put a stop to the amateur lumberjacks. One by one, he confiscated their axes and saws, and took down the names on their ID cards. But after a while, the sheer number of desperate souls waiting in line to be processed began to affect him, and he let the rest of the criminals go on their way. 'Humanly speaking,' he concluded, 'it is painful to have to check the famished, freezing people in their search for fuel, especially as the cold is abnormal for these parts; tonight it registered 6 degrees below freezing.'

For most islanders, the only thing worse than the lack of fuel was the food shortage. Some had already resorted to desperate measures to put meals on the table. One woman was surprised to come home and find her father tucking into a plate full of sparrows he had caught with a home-made trap. Many others had reluctantly steeled themselves to kill rabbits that had once been considered pets. For the Le Tissier family in Guernsey, the idea of eating their beloved white bunny Fluffy was so distressing that Mrs Le Tissier struck a deal with the butcher, trading him for a stringy little guinea fowl which she felt no compunction about serving for dinner. Bob Le Sueur, meanwhile, initiated an exchange with his next-door neighbour in which each of them ate the other's former pet.

As time went on, the islanders were growing increasingly desperate, something which hadn't escaped the attention of the Germans.

Twelve-year-old Molly Finigan was out collecting sawdust shavings to throw on her parents' fire one day when a soldier approached her with a loaf of bread in his hands. The little girl stared at it in wonder, but she soon realised that the man wasn't offering it freely. Molly didn't know much German, but the word '*Bett*' ('bed'), coupled with the soldier's gesticulations, gave her a pretty good idea of what he was after. '*Nein!*' she shrieked emphatically, turning tail and running home as fast as she could.

Others were driven to distraction by a combination of gnawing hunger and worry. Jersey estate agent Alec Podger had been eating nothing but swedes for three weeks when he was visited by an elderly neighbour. The poor woman was in a state of confusion and had spent the morning going from door to door distributing what little food she had left.

'You're going to want this!' Alec protested when the old lady offered him a slice of crusty bread.

'It's all right,' she replied. 'Elijah is coming this afternoon to take me to heaven.'

Alec accepted the offering and the woman went on her way, but the next morning he went round and left the bread on her doorstep. He was relieved to see that many other local people had already done the same thing. Elijah could come for her when he pleased, but in the meantime her neighbours weren't about to hurry her into the grave.

It was children and the elderly, of course, who were most vulnerable to malnutrition. One seventy-year-old woman died of heart failure weighing only three stone. In some families the dire food shortage led to terrible dilemmas. Kaye Le Cheminant's grandmother was ninety years old and already suffering from mild dementia when her poor diet saw her confined to her bed. Her daughter, fearing that she was at death's door, began giving her Kaye's extra milk ration, but when the family doctor found out he wasn't impressed. 'Kaye has her life before her,' he told Mrs Le Cheminant. 'Your mother has already had hers.' On the doctor's orders, the milk ration was returned to its rightful recipient, and the grandmother died a few months later.

As the death rate soared to almost three times the average, morale on the islands was in freefall. 'We are living like animals, feeding on roots,' wrote Sark hotelier Julia Tremaine. 'It's not living, it's just a bare existence from day to day.' Mrs Tremaine's daughter Norah was succumbing to a fatalistic depression: 'she says we ought to order our coffins and be done with it,' wrote her mother sadly. To make matters worse, the Sarkese were already reeling from a sudden, and horrific, loss. On 2 October, four-year-old Nanette Hamon had been playing with a couple of friends when she accidentally wandered into a minefield. The explosion that killed her was heard all over the island, and the death of the sweet little girl cast a shadow of gloom over locals and Germans alike.

There seemed no end to the cruelties of that interminable winter, as the islanders were pinched by chill winds and battered by torrential storms. Their very existence had become an ordeal, and for once the big-wigs in London couldn't claim ignorance of what they were going through. Over two hundred letters sent by islanders to relatives in the German internment camps had been intercepted, with extracts forwarded on to Whitehall. 'We are starving here,' they read. 'Life is not worth living ... it is more than human nature can endure.' In December *The Times* invoked the ire of the Home Office by publishing a letter from a Jerseywoman which detailed the grim reality of living below the breadline. 'We all feel that we have been abandoned by the Mother Country,' the author wrote bitterly. 'We are thoroughly neglected.'

The mood among Churchill's war cabinet was fast turning against him. Four years earlier, they had talked him into abandoning the islands without a fight, something which had never sat easily with the naturally pugnacious leader. Now, they were determined to convince him to soften his stance once again. 'We have not unlimited time to come to the relief of our fellow countrymen,' warned the home secretary, Herbert Morrison. The minister of labour, Ernest Bevin, produced a letter written by his counterpart in Jersey, Edward Le Quesne. 'The condition of the poorer section of the population is getting near the breaking point,' Le Quesne wrote. 'We have no gas, no coal, sometimes one hundredweight of wood fuel per month. Medical supplies and anaesthetics are practically non-existent. There is no soap, no sugar, no tea or coffee. The meat ration is 4oz per head once a fortnight.' There was no explicit criticism of British military policy in the letter, but the implication was clear. 'Things are getting desperate,' Le Quesne wrote. 'We are all waiting anxiously for the day of release from our island prison.'

Finally, Churchill relented, agreeing that the Red Cross should be allowed to provide food parcels for the islanders. But it took another two weeks to secure the agreement of the authorities in Berlin, and even then there was no guarantee that the aid would arrive quickly. As ever, there was little the islanders could do but wait – and do their best to prepare for the most miserable and meagre Christmas of their lives.

It wasn't just the local people who were hit hard by the siege conditions. The German Army, too, had seen a dramatic reduction in their rations. In this respect, at least, Churchill had been correct – it was only a matter of time before they would be starved into submission. From their home in St Jacques, on the outskirts of St Peter Port, Joan and Harry Coutanche would watch the local unit of marines parading up the hill to their billet at the Colinette Hotel. As the months went by and their own belts got tighter and tighter, the Germans too seemed to be gradually wasting away – the company of hearty, smartly dressed young men replaced by a weary group of thin and sallow-looking creatures, whose oversized uniforms hung awkwardly off their shrunken frames.

But while the ordinary soldiers were beginning to feel the pangs of hunger that the islanders had known for several years now – a malady all the more painful in their case because it had manifested so suddenly – their officers continued to enjoy a life of relative luxury. On 29 November, Baron von Aufsess shared a roast goose with a friend who had just been promoted to captain, departing at the end of the evening well wined and dined, and drifting into a state of blissful reverie. 'On the way back I noticed how the sky had cleared of all but a few drifting tatters of cloud,' he wrote in his diary. 'It was a lovely mild moonlit night with air as fresh as a cool wine. I had a sense of rediscovery of the vast vault of heaven, of the infinity of stars shining so remotely and peacefully above a war-torn world.'

The baron was aware that his fellow countrymen were suffering. During a tour of the island's Field Police stations, he noted that they seemed to be 'short of everything': 'no light, little heating, poor food, insufficient clothing, no petrol, no tyres for their vehicles, et cetera.' Nonetheless, as his own troops struggled, and the local people starved, von Aufsess continued to enjoy the fruits of Occupation, taking day trips to the tiny island of Herm to go pheasant-shooting, and flirting with local girls.

For most islanders, Christmas of 1944 was a sombre occasion. Unless the food situation improved quickly, there was every chance that it could be their last. Nonetheless, they made the best they could of a bad situation, sitting down to the traditional festive meal, however ludicrously meagre it might be. Kaye Le Cheminant's Christmas dinner was fairly typical: everyone got a slice of pork about the size of the bottom of a teacup, along with a share of a single roast cauliflower and a solitary swede, both of which had to be divided between six people.

There was precious little to celebrate. 'No presents this year,' commented Julia Tremaine. 'We talk and wonder if the shops are lit up in England and what there is to buy, and we ache to be there, even with no money to spend.' On Boxing Day she wrote, 'I am pleased it is over because there is nothing to make merry about.'

It wasn't long, however, before the islanders received a delivery that would have put Santa to shame. On 27 December, the residents of St Peter Port spotted a vessel docking at the White Rock that hadn't been seen for four and a half years. It was the SS *Vega*, a Swedish steamer that had previously brought hay to the islands, and which was now under charter to the Red Cross. On board were more than a hundred thousand food parcels containing a mouth-watering array of goods brought all the way from Canada and New Zealand.

Guernsey civil servant Ken Lewis recorded the cornucopia of delights he discovered on opening his own family's parcels:

5 ozs. Lowney's Canadian Vanilla sweet chocolate.
2 × 5 ozs. Neilson's chocolate made expressly for Canadian Red X Society.
3 × 10½ ozs. 'Kam' – an all pork product.
3 × 1 oz. Pepper and salt – mixed.
1 lb. 'Zest' Orange, Lemon & Grapefruit Marmalade.
1 lb. 'Zest' Apple and Peach Jam – added Pectin and colour.
12 fluid ozs. Aylmer Pure Seville Orange Marmalade.
12 ozs. Fray Bentos Corned Beef.
12 ozs. Helmet Corned Beef.
12 ozs. Exeter Corned Beef.
7¾ ozs. Astra Canadian Salmon – Medium Red Cohoe.
7¾ ozs. Sergeant Dan Salmon – Fancy Red Cohoe.
7¾ ozs. Paramount Fancy Pink Salmon.
3 × 1 lb. Maple Leaf 'Creamery' Butter.
1 × ¼ lb. Lyons Red Cross Tea.
1 × ¼ lb. Tea.
1 × ¼ lb. Coffee.
3 × 7 ozs. Atlas Prunes.
1 × 3½ ozs. Brunswick Canadian Sardines in oil.
2 × 3½ ozs. Fairhaven Canadian Sardines – Tiny fish in cotton seed oil.
2 × 1 lb. 'Klim' Powdered Whole Milk.
1 lb. 'Cowbell' Cow and Gate Whole Milk Powder.
3 × 1 lb. Paulin's Biscuits. (2 more without name)
2 × 3 ozs. Crest Canadian Soap.

The distribution of the parcels was organised with Teutonic efficiency, but it wasn't a particularly swift process. Once the large cardboard boxes were unloaded from the boat, under the strict supervision of Red Cross personnel, they were taken by train to St George's Hall, a former music venue about a mile out of town that had been used as a furniture store throughout the Occupation. From here, they were sent on to local shops around the island, where customers would present their ration cards as usual and sign for their family's allocation.

It was four days after the boat had first docked in St Peter Port before the parcels were ready for collection, but the islanders were used to waiting by now, and the long queues of hungry, expectant customers buzzed with excitement more than frustration. Even the normally downbeat Julia Tremaine found it hard to conceal her joy. 'We were all like schoolchildren going down to collect our parcels,' she wrote later that day. 'It gives us a new hope of life.'

Christmas might have come late this year, but every man, woman and child had received what they most wanted in the world, and the opening of the presents was treated with the same reverence as the usual festive unwrapping. Ken Lewis made a point of visiting an elderly neighbour to mark the big occasion. 'As she is living all alone,' he wrote, 'it would have been no pleasure to open hers on her own.' Like a child anxiously counting the sleeps up to Christmas, he confessed that the mere thought of the Red Cross packages had been keeping him awake at night. Clearly Julia Tremaine wasn't the only one who had regressed to a state of youthful enthusiasm.

From Guernsey, the *Vega* sailed on to Jersey, where the same ecstatic scenes were repeated. Leo Harris brought a wheelbarrow down to the local shop to pick up his family's parcels, including one to be taken to Francis at Gloucester Street prison. When he got home, he and his parents unpacked the boxes excitedly, marvelling at all the exotic foreign labels. Some of the products were unlike anything the family had seen before: tins of chicken-meat and heavy blocks of chocolate, not to mention several packets of a powder labelled as 'KLIM'. (Its name spelled backwards told you what you'd get when you mixed it with water.)

For some younger islanders, even common goods could seem like a novelty. Jersey schoolgirl Christine Du Feu could scarcely remember a time when her family had drunk real tea. She had grown up on the ersatz Occupation variety, a sweet and noxious mixture made by dissolving little cubes of baked sugar beet in boiling water. Christine had lost count of the number of times her mother had commented sadly, after one disappointment or another, 'Oh, if only we could have a proper cup of tea.' So when they collected the family's parcel from Godfrey the grocers and discovered a generous packet of tea-leaves among its contents, she felt instinctively that all the problems of the last few years were about to be solved. Mrs Du Feu could barely contain her excitement as she brewed up a pot, setting a cup down in front of Christine as if she had just produced a gourmet meal. But while her mother found the drink as delicious as she remembered, Christine spat it out in disgust. As far as she was concerned, real tea was made from sugar beet.

Some islanders had even stronger reactions to the sudden transformation of their diet. One man was so excited at the array of rich delights in his Red Cross parcel that he ate the whole lot in four days. But his stomach couldn't cope with the sudden influx of sweet, fatty foods, and on the fifth day he was found dead from gorging.

In fact, the foreign supermarket fare that made up the contents of the Red Cross parcels was the least of the luxuries the SS *Vega* had on board. On 29 December, the captain hosted a lavish meal for the top brass of the Army of Occupation. (He had initially extended the invitation to the island's civilian leaders as well, but was told that – however good relations were between the two sides – there was no way they could sit down to eat together.) Even Baron von Aufsess, whose tastes were far from modest, was astounded by the feast, which was served in a beautifully furnished cabin of gleaming polished wood and burnished brass. 'The meal was out of this world,' he wrote ecstatically, 'French piquance supplemented by Swedish liberality: first hors d'oeuvre, 10 sorts, with white bread and mountains of butter. Then fried frankfurters with omelette, then asparagus with butter sauce. And then, after an hour and a half, the meal proper began, with six courses, champagne and real coffee and liqueurs to finish up with.' The German officers hadn't eaten so well in years, and when they were invited back for a second feast four days later, they certainly didn't need to be asked twice.

Meanwhile, the ordinary men of the Wehrmacht – who had, rather tactlessly, been forced to handle the distribution of the Red Cross parcels – were settling down to their usual meagre fare. For the first time since the Occupation began, they were significantly worse off than the locals. By now most longed for nothing more than a swift end to the war – whether defeat or victory – so that they could finally go home.

Some allowed their resentment to spill over into outright hostility. One night, during the hours of darkness, over a thousand civilian houses were smeared with black tar in the shape of swastikas, in an act that the Kriegsmarine sailors responsible claimed was a gesture of 'political protest'. By now, though, the islanders were beyond such provocation. In response, they began their own cheerful graffiti campaign: one man captioned his swastika with the words, 'England for ever', while another – somewhat surreally – dug out an old picture frame and hung it on the wall around the offensive symbol. But despite the good-natured reaction, Baron von Aufsess was furious. He ordered an immediate clean-up operation, and within a few days the last traces of the thousand-odd swastikas had been painstakingly wiped away, thanks to the efficiency of the OT slave workers.

For the Channel Islanders, the Red Cross parcels had brought more than just sustenance – they had brought hope for the future. No one could say for certain what the year 1945 would hold. The recent German counter-offensive in the Ardennes Forest, and the bloody 'Battle of the Bulge' that was raging as a result, had cast doubt on the idea that the march from Normandy to Berlin would be a straightforward one. But at least, with new Red Cross parcels promised every few weeks, the islanders were not about to starve any time soon.

At Guernsey's Lyric Theatre, the New Year was marked with an unprecedented theatrical gesture. For the finale to the No. 1 Company's Christmas show, the troupe's wily impresario Peter Campbell had ordered an extension to be added to the set: a pair of ramps leading down into the auditorium, with handrails on either side for safety. As the cast took their final bow during the curtain call, the orchestra struck up unexpectedly with the opening bars of 'Auld Lang Syne'. The line of performers began to spread out as those on the ends stepped down the ramps into the audience, extending their arms to the German officers seated in the front row.

A little taken aback, the soldiers stood and took their hands, and one by one the entire audience followed suit, standing and linking crossed arms until they had formed one long, unbroken chain.

When the vast choir launched into the chorus – the Germans mostly humming along, since they didn't know the words – the feeling in the room was indescribable. Pearl sang like she had never sung before, and so, it seemed, did everyone else in the theatre.

For those few moments, the war was left outside. The men and women from opposite sides were as one – just people, cast adrift and clinging together for comfort, on an island battered by the winter storms.

CHAPTER THIRTY

THE TABLES ARE TURNED

It had been the toughest winter in living memory, but in time the bitter chill air lost its bite. Thanks to the timely arrival of the SS *Vega,* the civilian food crisis had been averted. There was, however, one crucial item that had so far been absent from the vessel's cargo: flour. According to international law, the Red Cross parcels were intended to supplement the basic diet, not replace it, and therefore weren't really supposed to include essential foodstuffs.

As a result of the lack of flour, the bread supply continued to diminish – 'I am glad I have a magnifying glass to be sure of seeing my bread ration,' joked Mrs Le Bideau. Eventually the bakers were forced to shut up shop altogether. For David Le Poidevin, who ran the Perelle Bakery in Guernsey, the whole experience was profoundly upsetting. The responsibility of feeding the local population with increasingly meagre amounts of rough, scratchy flour weighed so heavily on his shoulders that it ultimately drove him to a breakdown.

When the *Vega* finally docked in St Peter Port bearing a special shipment of pure white flour, it was a moment of the most profound relief and joy. In Perelle, the local people gathered to watch the delivery van arrive, their eyes wet with tears, and enthusiastically helped to unload the solid paper bags. The light, fluffy bread was unlike anything they had tasted for years – although, having grown used to baking stodgy Occupation loaves, Mr Le Poidevin had forgotten to leave enough space between the new ones, so several of them came out of the oven stuck together.

After a month of bitter fighting, the German counter-attack in the Ardennes Forest had finally been repulsed, and the Allied troops were once again making good headway towards Berlin. The only question was who would get there first: the Anglo-American forces who had landed on D-Day, or the Russians who were closing in from the East.

But while the German Army faced the prospect of annihilation on two fronts, the dark days of the Occupation were far from over. In fact, the winter's frost had scarcely begun to thaw on the ground when an alarming notice appeared in the German-language newspaper *Deutsche Inselzeitung*, signed by none other than Admiral Friedrich Hüffmeier.

Guernsey civil servant Ken Lewis provided a translation:

On 28 February 1945, at 12 o'clock noon, I have taken over from Generalleutnant Graf von Schmettow, who has been recalled to the Fatherland for reasons of health, the duties of Commander in Chief of the Channel islands and Commandant of the Fortress of Guernsey. I know only one aim: to hold out until final victory. I believe in the mission of our Führer and of our people. I will serve them with unflinching faithfulness.

Hail to our beloved Führer!

The story about von Schmettow's supposed health crisis wasn't exactly convincing. Those who had seen the general in the preceding days knew he was as fit as a fiddle. 'The whole business smacks of a putsch or coup d'état,' wrote Baron von Aufsess. 'What lies behind it all is as yet by no means clear, but I suspect it is a move long since carefully planned.'

Von Aufsess himself was deeply troubled by the change of leadership, which he described as 'shattering news'. As an ally of both von Schmettow and his former chief of staff, von Helldorf – who was now awaiting court martial on a spurious charge of failing to follow orders from Berlin – he felt certain that his own days in the Channel Islands were numbered.

Several months earlier, the Jersey bailiff, Alexander Coutanche, had been alarmed when the baron told him he was on a list of men Hüffmeier considered personae non gratae, along with von Schmettow, von Helldorf, and von Aufsess himself. 'We shall not all be taken at once,' the baron had told him. 'You have in your language a story about the ten little nigger boys? Well, this is different. There are only four little nigger boys in this – the general, the major, myself and you. One day I will telephone and say that we are now only three. Later I will say that we are now only two. When I telephone and say that we are now only one, that will be the time for you to look out.'

Now von Aufsess's prediction appeared to be coming true. First von Helldorf and then von Schmettow had been toppled. The baron was sure that his own turn was coming next.

That evening, von Aufsess received a summons to a meeting in Guernsey: apparently Hüffmeier wanted to see him to discuss his future. He arrived to find the admiral already waiting for him on the White Rock, his arm raised in front of him in the traditional Nazi salute. Von Aufsess raised his own arm and barked, 'Heil Hitler!', doing his best to sound as if he meant it.

The official interview took place in the admiral's quarters. He began by saying that it had come to his attention that von Aufsess was not much of a National Socialist. He had read an essay the baron had written entitled 'The Gentle Exercise of Power', and had formed the opinion that it was little more than idealistic hogwash. However, he declared, he was willing to put up with differences of opinion from his subordinates as long as he could be sure of their loyalty – both to himself and, more importantly, to the Führer. Having made his point, Hüffmeier leapt out of his chair, extending a hand with what seemed like genuine warmth. Von Aufsess left the meeting feeling utterly bewildered.

Before returning to Jersey, the baron paid a brief visit to the outgoing commander-in-chief, General von Schmettow. He found him a broken man, hunched over his old desk and surrounded by photographs and mementos of his loved ones back home. The prospect of returning to the Fatherland was far from a happy one, however, with Russian troops storming through the country, leaving a trail of destruction and misery in their wake. 'He is returning to a Germany where he will not have a roof over his head,' wrote von Aufsess sadly, 'where his homeland has been overrun by the enemy and where his family must be on the road somewhere as refugees.'

Von Aufsess accompanied the general to the nearby German Army stables, where von Schmettow gently stroked the mane of his favourite horse, reminiscing about the happy years he had spent in his idyllic island posting. The baron sent him on his way with a bottle of port to comfort him on the perilous flight back to Germany. Then he returned to Hüffmeier's quarters to spend a long and painful evening listening to wildly exaggerated tales of the admiral's exploits at sea, and trying to look like he was enjoying himself.

Admiral Hüffmeier had assumed command of the Channel Islands on the basis of his willingness to fight on to the bitter end. 'We shall never surrender,' he had told Bailiff Coutanche. 'In the end you and I will be eating nothing but grass.' But in reality the only battle he was likely to find himself waging was for the hearts and minds of his own beleaguered men. The combination of their increasingly poor diet and the depressing news coming from home had led to a catastrophic breakdown in morale. Despite the relentless propaganda they were officially subjected to, most now had alternative, more reliable sources of information, not least the 'black wireless' sets that they were supposed to be confiscating from civilians. They were well aware of the devastation being meted out on German cities such as Dresden and Berlin. If anything, the admiral's vehement denialism only made them feel more despondent. Those, like von Aufsess, who were high-ranking enough to have Hüffmeier's ear, didn't dare speak their minds for fear of being thought disloyal defeatists. The ordinary men, meanwhile – a handful of ardent Nazis excepted – deduced correctly that they were being led by a maniac, whose ideological zeal blinded him to the reality of their situation.

Already, there had been at least one high-profile case of desertion: a young soldier called Nicholas Schmitz who had thrown away his uniform and gone to live with his Jersey girlfriend, Alice Thareaux. Initially, the young lovers had been sentenced to die together, but the bailiff had succeeded in having Alice's sentence commuted to ten years in prison. ('A young woman in love does not always weigh the consequences of her deeds,' Coutanche had written sagely.)

The star-crossed lovers were held in separate blocks at Gloucester Street prison, but on the day of the execution, Nicholas was brought in chains within sight of Alice's cell. 'Nicki, Nicki!' she shouted, as her fellow prisoners lifted her up to the little grate so she could get a last glimpse of her beloved. A few hours later, he was taken to Fort Regent and shot.

As far as Hüffmeier was concerned, the deserter's girlfriend had got off lightly, but he understood that such emotionally charged cases did little to help troop morale. What most of his men wanted – an end to the war and a ticket back home to Germany – was neither within his gift nor his inclination, but he could offer them the next best thing: a small taste of victory to assuage the overwhelming feeling of defeat.

A few months earlier, General von Schmettow had begun planning a raid on the French port of Granville, which was now in the hands of the Americans. The proposed sortie had been called off thanks to the unfavourable winter weather, but within a fortnight in his new job, Admiral Hüffmeier had revived it.

Seven hundred and fifty men participated in the attack, arriving at Granville Harbour a little after 1 a.m. on 9 March in a flotilla of heavily armed ships. It was practically a textbook operation. By flashing the signal station a nonsensical message, a pair of minesweepers were able to bamboozle them long enough to pull up alongside the quays before the Americans even knew what was happening. Minutes later, the landing parties were on shore and had taken up strategic positions.

The Americans retaliated bravely, but for an hour and a half the Germans had full command of the area, and were able to do considerable damage, crippling three large Allied ships with the use of depth charges and destroying the port's numerous cranes, wagons and fuel dumps. By the time they set sail for the return journey to St Helier, they had rescued more than fifty German prisoners, captured several dozen Americans, and commandeered a 1,200-ton coal carrier, the SS *Eskwood*, which they brought back to Jersey as a trophy. They had lost only one motor torpedo boat, which ran aground and had to be scuttled, and their casualties stood at one dead and five wounded.

All in all, the raid had been a blistering success – the high point, in fact, of Admiral Hüffmeier's chequered military career. But an army could not live on victories alone, and the brief boost to morale could do little to assuage the gnawing hunger that was gradually destroying his men's spirit. The bronzed, muscular soldiers who had arrived on the islands four years earlier, looking resplendent in their trim uniforms and gleaming black boots, now resembled little more than a rabble: unwashed, unshaven and unkempt – not to mention unnourished.

Some islanders were moved to pity at the sight of the German soldiers, while others made the most of the opportunity to settle old scores. Bill Finigan couldn't help feeling a rush of exhilaration when an emaciated Wehrmacht officer knocked on his door, offering to trade a pair of high-grade Army binoculars for a small bar of chocolate. The man was clearly desperate, and Mr Finigan saw his chance to haggle. 'I'll give you half a bar,' he told the German, savouring the feeling of superiority as the wretched man all too willingly accepted his offer. In truth, he could probably have got the binoculars for a single square.

Guernsey schoolgirl Betty Jagou, meanwhile, couldn't resist playing a cruel prank. She and a group of schoolfriends carefully saved the empty tins from their Red Cross parcels, filling them up with soil and then packing them back in the cardboard box again. Then they left the box in a field near a local German gun emplacement and waited, peering through a little gap in a wall to see what would happen next. Before long, one of the soldiers chanced upon the box, his eyes lighting up as he felt the weight of it and assumed that he had stumbled upon a priceless bounty. But as he tore off the lid and began opening up the tins inside, the look of joy on his face was replaced by tragic confusion. The children tried to stifle their laughs at the pathetic sight. As far as they were concerned, though, pranking the enemy was very much fair game.

For the most part, the German soldiers never so much as touched the Red Cross deliveries, even when the locals did their best to provoke them, ostentatiously munching away on the latest delights from Canada or New Zealand right in front of the starving men. When the *Vega* brought special deliveries of flour, desperate soldiers were spotted following the trolleys to the Red Cross depot with little spoons to scoop up any wastage, but even then they never attempted to steal any that wasn't legitimate windfall.

In this respect, at least, military discipline remained intact. However, there were situations in which parcels could fall into German hands. The plain-clothes policemen of the Geheime Feldpolizei were more than capable of extorting the occasional tin of food in exchange for lenient treatment, and Leo Harris was not in the least surprised to discover a large pile of discarded Red Cross packaging on a deserted part of the beach near to their Jersey head-quarters, an attractive seaside villa known as Silvertide.

Pearl and Gwen Smith found themselves on the receiving end of just such an extortion racket when a German soldier barged into their room at Les Pieux Hotel – they had, unfortunately, forgot-ten to lock the door – and found them lying on the floor glued to their crystal set, listening intently to the latest popular songs from England in preparation for the following week's show at the Lyric Theatre. 'So,' the German remarked triumphantly, 'this is what you do up here in your room?'

Pearl was too petrified to speak, and it was left to Gwen to reply. 'You're not going to report us, are you?' she asked.

The soldier considered for a moment. 'I will do a deal with you,' he suggested. 'Next time your Red Cross parcels come through, you will share the contents with me, and I won't say a word about what I've seen.'

Pearl's heart sank, but she could see no way out of the arrangement. 'Is it a deal?' the German man prompted.

She nodded her head weakly, and Gwen whispered, 'Yes, it's a deal.'

That night, Pearl could hardly sleep for worry. She had put herself in a compromising position and allowed herself to be blackmailed by the enemy. The thought of all the delicious food she would have to share kept running through her mind, and she struggled to hold back the tears. From the tossing and turning she could hear on the other side of the room, it was clear that Gwen wasn't getting much sleep either.

The following week was a torment for the two girls. They didn't dare tell their parents what had happened, fearing that they would be angry. Pearl kept her eyes peeled for the young German soldier. She was terrified that she would run into him on the stairs and he would make some remark that would give the game away, but oddly there seemed to be no sign of him.

The anxiety of the situation continued to take a toll on the girls, and eventually their mother confronted them. 'Let's have it,' she demanded. 'There's something wrong with you both. Tell me what the trouble is.'

Pearl could hold her tongue no longer. She poured out the whole sorry story, not looking up from the table in front of her until she had finished. When she did, she was surprised to see a smile on her mother's face. 'Which German was it?' Mrs Smith asked her.

'The one in Room 5,' interjected Gwen.

The mother's smile broadened further. 'I'm pretty sure he was teasing you,' she told the two girls. 'He was transferred off the island two days ago. He came to see me before he left and asked me to give you some advice – to make sure you lock your bedroom door in future!'

As the Germans grew increasingly hungry, their remaining scruples were worn down, and soon theft and looting were widespread. The once hale and hearty Army of Occupation had come to resemble the wretched forced labourers of the OT. Now, instead of Russian slaves it was young German soldiers who were spotted in the fields, pulling raw stumps of broccoli out of the ground and stuffing them straight into their mouths, or scavenging for the tiniest scraps in local people's bins.

On Sark, Dame Sybil was shocked at the sudden spate of looting. 'You haven't got an army,' she told the island commandant, Captain Heiner Magsam. 'You've only got a pack of thieves and beggars.' The German officers, at least, did seem to take such lawless acts fairly seriously. When the Hamon family lost half a dozen geese from their farm in Little Sark, they reported the theft to the authorities. A day later, the guilty party – a skinny lad who couldn't have been more than eighteen – was hauled down to the farm by his commanding officer. He was practically in tears as he told Mrs Hamon how embarrassed his parents back home in Germany would be if they ever found out what he had done. She was moved by the young man's obvious contrition, and told him that she accepted his apology. As far as she was concerned, the matter was over. She just hoped that, given the circumstances, the lad's officer would be equally lenient.

Certainly, in some cases, such crimes would be punished severely. When Guernsey grower Oswald Falla started suffering nightly thefts of his grapes, he decided to take matters into his own hands. As darkness fell, he made his way to his greenhouse, the 'Titanic' – it had been built in 1912, the same year as the ill-fated vessel, and its long, hulking shape somewhat resembled its namesake – and waited patiently for the thief to put in an appearance.

After a few hours, Oswald began to doze off, but he was awoken by the sound of glass shattering, and as he peered around in the dark, he could see that one of the panes was missing. Stealthily, he made his way over to the hole – just in time to see a head popping through it.

Without thinking, Oswald brought his arm down hard on the

back of the intruder's neck. The thief was momentarily dazed, but as he came to his senses, he slid back out of the hole in the glass wall, and began running away into the darkness. It was several seconds before Oswald realised he had left something behind him: his Army-issue cap.

The next morning, soon after curfew, Oswald set off for the local German camp, brandishing his valuable piece of evidence. It didn't take long for the guilty party to be identified, and – presumably for Oswald's benefit – subjected to a bit of exemplary punishment. Oswald watched in astonishment as a tub full of clinkers, still smouldering from the camp boiler, was poured out on the ground to make a pathway, and the unfortunate thief was forced to crawl on his hands and knees from one end to the other.

Despite the threat of punishment, hunger pushed the German soldiers to commit increasingly serious crimes. With hardly any meat left in their rations, they began to supplement their diet with what they could catch, plucking snails from the hedgerows and shooting seagulls out of the sky, against the express orders of their superiors, who had outlawed the practice on the grounds of public safety. It was in any case deeply taboo to kill a seagull, particularly for the men of the Kriegsmarine, among whom there was an old superstition that the birds held the souls of drowned sailors. But desperate times called for desperate measures.

Werner Rang had always been relatively slim, and having lost more than three stone in a matter of months he was now looking distinctly emaciated. He knew that others were even worse off, though. The authorities had instituted a two-hour nap every afternoon, but even so it could be hard to make it through the day. One afternoon, Werner found a soldier collapsed by the side of a hedge, drifting in and out of consciousness. He was too weak to carry the man by himself, but he managed to get him onto the seat of his bicycle and gently pushed him the short distance to the nearest casualty station. By the time they arrived, the man was already dead, and he was far from the first German soldier to perish from a lack of adequate nutrition.

Werner and his friends were determined not to go the same way, and set about supplementing their rations any way they could. One night, they crept into a nearby field and stole some carrots that belonged to a local farmer, hiding them at the bottom of a large pile of stacking crates in their storeroom. The military police came to investigate, but they too were exhausted and hungry, and just as Werner had predicted, they gave up searching the boxes long before they reached the hidden cache.

As time went on, Werner and his friends grew increasingly ingenious, setting traps for blackbirds and shooting their fair share of seagulls too. The meat, boiled up into a stew, was tough and stringy, but welcome nonetheless. Finally, they set their sights on a more ambitious endeavour. They might be stuck on an island, but there were worse places to be marooned – there were, after all, plenty of fish in the sea. The only problem was how to go about catching them.

Along with two of his friends, Werner began constructing a rudimentary boat out of some old tent poles, strapped together and covered with a tarpaulin. After two weeks, the jerry-built craft was just about seaworthy, and the trio of foolhardy adventurers set sail, armed with half a dozen grenades and a net on a stick. They pushed off from Portelet Harbour at high tide and rowed out for about half a mile before they began setting off the depth charges, watching with satisfaction as a handful of fish rose to the surface after each muffled explosion. By the time they had scooped up the full haul, they had about twenty to divide up between them.

The three men began paddling back towards the shore, but the tide was now against them and it was almost nine o'clock at night before they finally reached land again. As they dragged their battered and bedraggled craft up the slipway, they suddenly realised they were no longer alone. Standing there waiting for them was Lieutenant Müller, a brusque and business-like officer in his late thirties who was known as something of a stickler for the rules.

Werner saw the lieutenant in good time, and managed to hide a couple of fish in his pockets before he reached the top of the slip-way. It was just as well, since Müller soon confiscated the rest of the catch. Then, after a somewhat half-hearted ear-bashing on the dangers of risking their lives at sea, he told the men they were free to go on their way.

Werner and his friends repaired to their camp, where they smoked their two purloined fish in the chimney. It was the most glorious meal that any of them had tasted for months.

As time went on, the extent of German looting only increased, until it reached epidemic proportions. 'The theft everywhere is terrible,' wrote Guernseywoman Ruth Ozanne. 'Nobody can keep fowls, goats, pigs, cows or any livestock.' But it wasn't just farm animals that were being taken. Five-year-old Kath Lloyd was heartbroken when her cat Tortie suddenly went missing. She was devoted to the animal, and loved nothing better than dressing her up in a little dress and bonnet. A few days after Tortie's disappearance, Kath and her parents were coming home from church when they saw something hanging on the washing line of the German troops who lived down the road. It looked like a kind of furry ginger scarf. Suddenly, Kath recoiled as she realised what she was seeing: it was Tortie's skin, hung up in the sun to dry.

Understandably, not all German soldiers were comfortable with the idea of eating domestic animals. One man, Hans Glauber, played a rather cruel trick on a comrade who told him he could never eat a cat. Having captured and killed a local moggy, he boiled up the meat for a couple of hours, adding nettles and a few stolen potatoes until he had a fairly serviceable stew. By the time it was cooked, there was no way of telling what kind of meat was in the pot, so he told his squeamish friend that it was rabbit.

The other man wolfed down the meal, and only after he had finished did Hans reveal the truth: 'You've just eaten a nice big tomcat,' he told him gleefully. At first his friend thought he was winding him up, but when Hans produced the animal's skin, all doubt was dispelled from his mind. He ran outside and promptly threw up the whole meal.

It wasn't just cats that were in the Germans' sights – in fact, if anything, pet dogs were more vulnerable to being taken. Their size meant that the meat would go a lot further, and they were generally easier to catch. Guernseywoman Ruth Ozanne knew several people whose animals had vanished in suspicious circumstances, and was terrified that her own little terrier could be next. 'I dare not let Gary out of my sight,' she wrote in her diary. 'The Germans look at him with hungry eyes.'

At Les Pieux Hotel in Cobo, Pearl Smith and her family kept a close eye on their Alsatian, Risky. It was hard to believe that any of the Germans staying at the hotel would harm her – they loved the dog and spent hours happily petting her. But things being what they were, you couldn't be too careful. Pearl's cousin Eileen had gone out to fetch her dog Sally one morning and found the lock on the kennel had been forced. With no sign of Sally anywhere, she and her family had begun a frantic search of the area, aided by a friendly German man who lived in the house next door. But after a whole day traipsing across fields calling her name, they could find no sign of Sally anywhere, and in the end – much to Eileen's disappointment – the search was called off.

The next day, the German neighbour arrived at the door. In his hand was a small package wrapped up in newspaper. 'This is for you,' he told Eileen's mother, placing it down on the kitchen table. 'Something to give your children tonight.'

She opened the newspaper parcel and was amazed to find a joint of meat inside. 'Oh, how lovely!' she exclaimed, her eyes lighting up at the sight. But Eileen leapt from the stool where she was sitting, tears already streaming down her face. 'No!' she screamed. 'Take it away! We don't want it.'

The girl's mother couldn't understand what had got into her. 'Eileen!' she scolded her angrily.

'Can't you see, Mum?' Eileen whispered between sobs. 'It's my dog. It's Sally.'

Understandably, such incidents did little to foster good relations between the local people and the Germans. Occasionally, when the circumstances allowed, the islanders would even fight back – a nation of animal lovers wasn't going to let its pets be taken by the enemy without putting up a little resistance. Guernsey teenager Esme Ingrouille was astonished to see a German soldier run past the front door of her house in L'Islet carrying a sack which was writhing furiously. She could hear muffled miaowing coming from inside, and sure enough, moments later an angry woman appeared, shouting at the German to bring back her cat as she pursued him down the road.

Esme's father leapt up to give chase as well, but got no further than the front steps of his house before he slipped and twisted his ankle. 'You go, love!' he shouted to his daughter. 'See if you can catch him!'

Esme darted off as fast as her young legs would carry her, overtaking the elderly lady and soon gaining ground on the German soldier. He was terribly thin, and the wriggling sack was slowing him down. As she reached the end of the road and began pursuing him into a nearby field, she realised that she wasn't alone. Several of her neighbours had also joined the chase, and soon a whole host of them were charging across the field together in pursuit of the German soldier.

The German reached the far side of the field, where a little stream ran alongside some woodland. He had to slow down to cross it, and the rabble were rapidly gaining on him. Esme saw him turn around and stare at the mob in terror. Then he opened the bag, upended it over the stream, and bolted into the wood.

Esme and her comrades arrived to find the cat scowling as it dragged itself out of the muddy water. Soon, it was back in its owner's arms, safe – for now at least – from being made into anyone's dinner.

The German soldier had learnt his lesson: he wouldn't dare show his face in that neighbourhood again. But his hunger clearly hadn't abated. The following day, one of the nearby farmers reported that his dog had gone missing in the night.

CHAPTER THIRTY-ONE

MUTINY

With his forces in such dire straits, Admiral Hüffmeier knew that the battle for hearts and minds was going to be a tough one, but he wasn't a man to give up easily. He had only been in the top job on the islands less than a month when he embarked on a kind of speaking tour that wouldn't have been out of place in a political campaign.

On 25 March, Werner Rang and his friends were summoned to a speech at Guernsey's Regal Cinema, which had been specially bedecked with huge swastika banners. The admiral marched onto the stage, taking up a central position under a bright white spotlight. 'Heil Hitler!' he bellowed, raising his right arm.

'Heil Hitler,' Werner called in response, with a distinct lack of enthusiasm. Of the two hundred-odd men standing alongside him, he was sure that no more than a handful could have put any real feeling into the words. Most of them were probably as jaded as he was. But while everyone knew that the war was about to be lost, they didn't dare say it in public. No one wanted to be the one to stand up and declare that the emperor was wearing no clothes.

Hüffmeier, at least, was clearly giving it his all. 'I intend to hold out here with you until the Fatherland has won back its lost ground and the final victory is wrested,' he intoned gravely. 'From our present pain, and with the certainty of German victory, as commander of the defences of the Channel Islands I will carry out plainly and without compromise, strictly but justly, the mandate given to me by the Führer.'

It was hard to imagine that the admiral himself believed the words he was speaking. The whole performance felt like a sham. But his power as an orator was undeniable – and, of course, when he finally stopped speaking and the orchestra in the pit struck up a rousing tune, the crowd erupted into their usual deafening applause.

A month later, as the Channel Islands were blooming into their usual rainbow of spring flowers, those with access to a radio were subjected to the most shocking news broadcast of the war. On 19 April, the BBC broadcast a report from their correspondent Richard Dimbleby, who had joined British troops liberating the concentration camp at Bergen-Belsen. They arrived to find more than thirteen thousand unburied corpses littered around the camp, just a fraction of the tens of thousands of men, women and children who had died there in the last two years. Those prisoners who were still alive were in a desperate state. Among them was Louisa Gould's brother Harold Le Druillenec, the only British survivor of the camp, who now weighed just five stone.

The horrors Dimbleby saw at Belsen made such a strong impact on him that he had to stop his recording five times because he was unable to control his own tears. It was, he said, the worst day of his life, and the twelve-minute report – with its vivid descriptions of moaning, skeletal prisoners, naked, lice-infested women, and tiny babies who had died from a lack of milk – was not easily forgotten by those who heard it. For anyone who still doubted the true depravity of the Nazi regime, this was surely the final straw.

The morning after the BBC broadcast, Adolf Hitler celebrated his fifty-sixth birthday in what was left of the Chancellery gardens, pinning medals to the boys of the Hitler Youth – some as young as twelve – who were still fighting to save Berlin from the Russian advance. When the ceremony was over, he returned to his underground bunker, for what he must have known would be the final time. The great and the good of the Nazi Party – Göring, Goebbels, Himmler, Bormann, von Ribbentrop and Speer – along with the man who would soon be appointed as Hitler's successor, Admiral

Karl Dönitz, had all come to pay homage to their Führer. Given the circumstances, however, the celebrations were distinctly muted.

In the Channel Islands, meanwhile, the big day was marked as bombastically as ever. There were military parades through the streets, and swastika flags hoisted far and wide. At the RealKino cinema in Guernsey, Admiral Hüffmeier gave another of his barnstorming performances, complete with enormous flags, dramatic floodlights and a full orchestra to play him onto the stage. When he reached the rostrum, he stood there in silence for at least thirty seconds, milking the moment for all it was worth. Then he launched into the performance of his life.

Even Baron von Aufsess, who was no fan of Hüffmeier's, couldn't help being impressed. 'This scion of a family of Protestant pastors began his National Socialist sermon,' he wrote sardonically, 'speaking with evangelical fervour but on behalf of Adolf instead of God. He spoke, too, with consummate skill, first engaging the common sentiments of his listeners, then speaking frankly, glossing nothing over, the more compellingly to carry them away in a final surge of emotion.' The admiral, von Aufsess was forced to concede, was not just one of Hitler's most devoted disciples – he was also a pretty convincing surrogate for the Führer's unparalleled rhetorical style.

Indeed, so persuasive was Hüffmeier's performance that von Aufsess was almost drawn in by it himself. 'What German could resist this heady mixture?' he wrote. 'I was not myself altogether immune to its appeal.' The admiral had offered him not only a glimpse at his rhetorical skill, but a reminder of how dangerous that skill could be in the hands of a man impervious to reason.

As far as Baron von Aufsess was concerned, the time was coming when matters might have to be taken out of Hüffmeier's hands. He had long regarded the admiral as a potential threat to his own safety, not least since his wife – to whom he had written a number of dangerously frank letters – was currently languishing in a German prison cell as an 'enemy of the state', having been overheard lamenting the failure of the July bomb plot.

Four days earlier, Hüffmeier had summoned von Aufsess to take up a new position in Guernsey. The baron had been convinced it was a trap, so much so that he had begun to put in motion a plan to escape by boat to France. He had a small vessel ready and waiting in Gorey Harbour, along with a week's worth of field rations and a set of fake identity documents proclaiming him to be a French OT worker. He had even begun writing some farewell letters, before the news had come through – from one of his most trusted sources in Guernsey – that the admiral simply wanted to reassign him, and he was in no immediate danger of arrest. At the last minute, the baron had cancelled the escape attempt and packed his bags for the new posting instead.

It was only after speaking to the admiral that von Aufsess had deduced the real reason for his reassignment. Hüffmeier had become embroiled in a bitter dispute with Bailiff Coutanche, who had threatened him with legal action after the war if he did anything to increase the suffering of the island population. The admiral was livid, and determined to put the bailiff in his place. Knowing that Coutanche had always seen von Aufsess as a political moderate, if not quite an ally, the admiral had removed him from the Feldkommandantur to signal that the policy of moderation had come to an end. In its place, he intended to institute a much tougher regime, with stricter discipline, exemplary punishment of potential *résistants*, and displays of military power that would scare the people into submission.

Hüffmeier's bombastic performance at the RealKino had only confirmed the baron's opinion that he was a dangerous man – a mini-Hitler, equally unbending and equally capable of bringing his own people to the point of destruction in order to feed his wild fanaticism. When von Aufsess tentatively suggested the Germans might one day have to rely on the goodwill of the islanders, the admiral could barely suppress his rage.

The baron paid a visit to General von Schmettow's former chief of staff, Colonel von Helldorf, who was still awaiting court martial proceedings for supposedly failing to carry out orders. Unsurprisingly, he too had a very low opinion of Hüffmeier – who had, after all, stolen his job before he had taken von Schmettow's – and he was determined to do something about it. 'We are close on the time when the admiral will have to be put out of action,' von Helldorf declared. 'And one of us will have to do it.'

That night, over several glasses of port, the two conspirators worked out the details of their plan, sneaking across to the door every now and then to check that no one was listening. Von Helldorf volunteered to carry out the assassination himself, with von Aufsess – who had, it seemed, managed to gain the admiral's trust – obtaining as much information as possible about his routine and security arrangements, to give them the best chance of success.

It was late by the time von Aufsess finally retired to his own quarters, feeling distinctly tipsy thanks to the heady mixture of fortified wine and dastardly plotting. There was no doubt in his mind that the course they had chosen was the right one. 'What had happened to our moral scruples in thus planning to kill in cold blood?' he wrote in his diary, which was now carefully hidden away behind a loose panel of wallpaper. 'They had been disposed of in the long sleepless nights which inexorably led us to decide on this act of deliverance. In the past few months I have felt a hardening of resolve which will permit no further compromise with or concession to these enemies of humanity.'

All that remained was to find the right opportunity, but in this respect Admiral Hüffmeier appeared to be playing right into his would-be assassins' hands. Three days later, von Aufsess reported in his diary that the commander-in-chief had developed a new obsession: the conversion of a ten-bedroom mock-gothic mansion, Carey Castle – briefly mentioned in Victor Hugo's novel *Toilers of the Sea* – into a grand officers' club. Von Aufsess volunteered to take an active role in the project, enthusiastically moving furniture and rearranging paintings as a pretext to spend more time around Hüffmeier. 'The club is the admiral's current hobby and preoccupation,' he wrote, 'and thus provides an innocuous ground on which to establish closer relations with him for a far from innocuous purpose.' He soon had some valuable information to pass on to von Helldorf: every morning at 9 a.m. precisely, Hüffmeier would walk through the castle grounds on his way to inspect the latest renovations. His obsessive routine, as regular as clockwork, made him a sitting duck for an ambush.

As the days went by, von Aufsess was beginning to have qualms about his role in the assassination plot. The more time he spent with Hüffmeier debating trivial questions of interior design, the more guilty he felt about planning his murder. The two men were never going to become friends, but in Carey Castle they had found a joint project, and an area in which – ostensibly at least – they were on the same side. 'I can scarcely credit my own duplicity,' von Aufsess wrote in his diary. 'Should I not rather be warning him?' In his heart, though, he knew there was only one solution to the current predicament, and if that meant the admiral's death it was a price he was willing to pay. The latest talk among Hüffmeier and his cronies was of holding the islands for another two years, even if Germany itself was forced to surrender. And the baron was under no illusion that his own safety was assured. 'It only needs a radio message from Berlin and I am finished,' he wrote tersely.

Von Aufsess waited anxiously for von Helldorf to act on his intelligence, but the next morning the admiral appeared at Carey Castle alive and well, knocking back his daily glass of Guernsey milk as he cheerfully surveyed the renovation work. The day after, to the baron's dismay, he once again arrived bang on time, and in apparently perfect health.

It didn't take long for von Aufsess to find out what had happened. Von Helldorf had been despatched unexpectedly to the tiny island of Herm, supposedly to report on its suitability for agricultural development. But for anyone familiar with the bad blood between him and the admiral, it was clear that he had essentially been banished.

The alarming question now preoccupying Baron von Aufsess was whether the timing had been just a coincidence. The other alternative didn't bear thinking about. 'Had Helldorf, out of his unbridled hatred for the admiral, let slip some compromising information?' he wondered. 'Had one of his undercover connections been brought to light?' With no information to go on, and his own escape route from the islands far away in Jersey, there was little the baron could do other than continue to play house with Hüffmeier and keep his ears open for more information.

As it happened, von Helldorf and von Aufsess weren't the only ones who had been plotting against Admiral Hüffmeier. In fact, within the ranks of his own forces a mutiny was already simmering. For several months now, seditious notes had been appearing, encouraging disaffected troops to wrest control from the admiral and sue for peace. 'Hitler's promises were nothing but pie-crust,' read one. 'How long do you intend to take part in this, the biggest deception of all time? How long do you want to stay here and starve?' The proposition was clear: 'The war is lost,' the note concluded. 'Through stubborn holding out we are spoiling our chances of an assured future. We call upon you to surrender.'

Some men, at least, appeared to be listening. On 7 March, a fire had gutted the Palace Hotel in Jersey – a popular hang-out for Wehrmacht officers – in what was widely assumed to have been an act of sabotage. Less than a fortnight later, General Rudolf Wulf, the commanding officer of 319 Infantry Division, was lucky to survive a bomb attack on his staff car by one of his own men, who was promptly arrested and executed. Now new notices began to appear, suggesting an uprising was imminent. 'When the signal is given for the rebellion, tie a white handkerchief around your left arm and follow the orders of your leaders,' one of them read. 'All officers are to be arrested, and on resistance shot immediately.'

Jersey insurance agent Bob Le Sueur had continued to do odd jobs for associates involved in the civilian resistance movement. As well as translating the local Communist Party's leaflets into Spanish, he had recently provided some blond hair dye courtesy of his friend Mrs Osbourne at the salon on Colomberie, and had even sourced an entire outfit for his old schoolfriend Norman Le Brocq, who had told him he needed it for an escaped Russian.

The latter task had been particularly challenging. After five years of Occupation, decent clothes were hard to come by, and Bob had been forced to appeal to the mother of his friend Victor Hamon, who had been shot down over Holland while serving in the RAF. The poor lady had already given away most of her dead son's clothes, saving only one smart navy-blue suit for sentimental reasons. 'I'm sure Victor would be happy to think it was being used to save another man's life,' she told Bob resolutely.

It was well known among those involved in resistance activities that Bob was in contact with a number of escaped Russian slave workers. One day he was approached by a man called Paul Casimir, who worked in Berger's antiquarian bookshop in St Helier, to see if he could arrange for a particularly subversive leaflet to be translated and written out in Cyrillic script. The intention was to circulate it among the members of the Russian Liberation Army, a group of anti-communist defectors who had joined the Wehrmacht hoping to help topple Stalin from power, but who in recent months had started to wonder if they had backed the wrong side. These Russian troops controlled a section of the north-eastern coast of Jersey and were easily identified by the white-and-blue patches that they wore on the shoulders of their German Army uniforms. The hope, Casimir explained to Bob, was that with a little provocation, the whole unit could be persuaded to turn against the authorities.

Bob told Casimir he knew the perfect man for the job: Feodor Buryi, aka 'Bill', the escaped Russian who was living with his friends Michael and René. He was sure Bill would leap at the chance to do anything to help the Allied cause, but he wasn't convinced that it was fair on the two young men sheltering him – who were, after all, conscientious objectors – to involve their illegal flatmate in a plot that if discovered would almost certainly get all of them shot.

Bob decided that it was only right to ask his friends whether they were happy for him to approach Bill. After some deliberation they agreed, but on one condition: they first wanted Bob to reassure them that the mutiny had a decent chance of success. They had seen the subversive notes littering the streets in recent weeks, calling on troops to commit acts of sabotage and troublemaking, but they weren't sure whether these were the work of serious revolutionaries, or simply a bunch of young hotheads who had no real idea what they were doing.

Bob's approach to his resistance activities had always been one of calculated inattentiveness as far as the activities of his comrades was concerned. The way he saw it, the less he knew about who else was involved, and what exactly they were planning, the better. He was perfectly happy to source a bottle of hair dye here, or a change of civilian clothes there, without ever seeking to know who they were for, or why they wanted them. But his friends had made a compelling argument, and he promised them that he would do what he could to find out more about the people they would all be working with.

Bob returned to the antiquarian bookshop and explained the situation to Paul Casimir. The other man thought for a moment. 'Someone will meet you,' he told Bob a little guardedly. 'Wait outside the sports hall on Victoria Road this evening, opposite the allotments. He'll be humming *Eine Kleine Nachtmusik*.'

That evening, Bob cycled to the appointed spot and waited, trying not to let his nerves get the better of him. Compared to his own previous resistance activities, this was proper cloak-and-dagger stuff. Who was the mysterious contact, he wondered, and what exactly were they planning to do with him? Loitering by the side of the road, he couldn't help feeling exposed. What if someone saw him and wondered what he was doing there?

No sooner had the thought crossed his mind than he spotted his old schoolfriend Norman Le Brocq cycling along the road. 'Hello, Bob!' he called out, coming to a halt on the pavement beside him.

Bob felt panicked. This wasn't part of the plan. If his mysterious contact saw him chatting with Norman, they might abandon the rendezvous altogether. But then, he could hardly tell his friend to get lost without explaining what he was doing there.

'Hello, Norman,' he replied weakly, hoping that he wasn't planning to stay and chat.

But his old friend seemed to be in a convivial mood. 'It's a dreary evening, isn't it?' he remarked chattily. Then he began, ever so quietly, to hum. 'Dum, da-dum, da-dum-dum dum-dum-dah ...'

Bob's eyes widened. 'Oh,' he said, momentarily lost for words.

'Come on!' Norman told him, hopping back on his bike and pedalling away at speed.

Bob followed him along Victoria Road, and then onto the Rue des Pres. They rode on for several minutes in silence. As they approached the junction with Longueville Road, Norman dismounted in front of a little wooden door, which led into the back garden of one of the nearby houses. He pulled a silver key out of his pocket, opened the door, and ushered Bob inside.

They propped their bikes up against the wall and headed across the garden in silence. Entering by the house's back door, Norman led Bob up a little flight of stairs to a room that was lit by an oil lamp. Sitting at a table was a man of about thirty. His hair was a striking shade of blond, and he was wearing a smart navy-blue suit. Bob did his best not to smile.

The man stood and extended a hand to Bob. 'Hello,' he said. 'My name is Paul Mülbach.'

Bob's blood froze in his veins. This was no Russian, he realised. The man had spoken with an unmistakable German accent. For the first time in the whole bizarre evening, he felt he might have just walked into a trap.

It was left to his old schoolfriend to reassure him. The man in the blue suit was indeed a German, Norman explained, but he was a deserter, and a passionate anti-Nazi. Mülbach was a socialist who had fought with the International Brigade during the Spanish Civil War. When he was captured and repatriated to Germany, he was given a choice between joining the Army or being sent to the concentration camp at Dachau, where his father, a somewhat troublesome trade unionist, had been imprisoned prior to his death. Unsurprisingly, Mülbach had chosen the former, but his time in uniform had only made him more committed to bringing about an end to Nazism once and for all.

Since arriving in Jersey the previous year, Mülbach had been working to bring other soldiers around to his cause. It was he who had been behind the leaflets calling on the German soldiers to

mutiny, which had been printed by Bob's old friend Norman on the
Jersey Communist Party duplicator. When Mülbach had been forced
to go underground, Norman and his associates had sheltered him,
providing him with the outfit and hair dye sourced by Bob in order
to disguise his appearance. Now, the German man explained, he
believed he could count on a number of senior officers to rally their
units to mutiny as soon as he gave the signal.

Bob could scarcely believe what he was hearing. This was a much
more serious business than anything he had been involved in before.
But he was, at least, reassured on one count. Whatever his chances
of success, Mülbach was no fool. With the help of Norman and
his fellow communist *résistants*, he had managed to evade capture
ever since his desertion, and now he had a plan that could end the
Occupation for good. Bob had no qualms about returning to Michael
and René and telling them that his contacts had met their require-
ments. He felt sure that, if they had met Mülbach themselves, they
would be more than willing to risk their lives for his scheme.

Bob told the German mutineer that he would supply the translation he wanted. But that wasn't quite the end of his role in the
rebellion. The mutiny had been planned for the morning of Tuesday
1 May, a date rich in symbolism for Mülbach and his communist
associates. The signal for the uprising to begin would be a cannon
fired at Elizabeth Castle at 10 a.m. exactly. The officers in the know
had all been briefed, and the civilians supporting the operation had
their parts to play as well. Several of them had been assigned to the
various schools within earshot of the cannon. When they heard it
go off, they were to rush inside and tell the headteachers what was
happening, instructing them to get the children home as quickly as
possible. Bob was given responsibility for a school near his parents'
house at First Tower.

While the schoolchildren were herded to safety, other volunteers
would spend the morning distributing leaflets addressed to the citizens of St Helier, informing them about the mutiny and letting them
know what they could do to help. 'As you read this, German troops
wearing white armbands are converging on St Helier,' the leaflets

announced. 'It is here in the town that the affair will be decided. It is in YOUR interest that this mutiny should succeed.'

The general public were asked to do three things to give the mutineers the best chance of success: 'Keep off the streets', 'Do not harbour Nazis' and 'Carry out any requests made by troops wearing white armbands'. The leaflet ended with a rousing call to victory: 'You have been longing for the end of this Nazi occupation. Follow these instructions and so ensure that end. Down with the Nazis!'

The morning of 1 May was unseasonably cold. Standing in the street outside the school building at First Tower, Bob shivered as he watched a few solitary snowflakes flutter to the ground. His ears strained to hear the sound of the cannon, but ten o'clock came and went and nothing happened.

Bob waited for another hour but still there was no signal, so he set off on his bike towards St Helier. On the way he stopped at the flat of one of Norman's communist associates, Leslie Huelin, who had been standing ready to seize control of the island government once the uprising began. When Bob arrived, he found Leslie and his friends in a state of stupefaction. Their bold plans had seemingly come to nothing.

In fact, events abroad had overtaken them. Later that day, the first reports began coming in from Berlin that Adolf Hitler had committed suicide in his bunker.

CHAPTER THIRTY-TWO

LIBERATION

It was another couple of days before the news was officially published in the Channel Islands, but by Thursday evening, when the *Jersey Evening Post* finally ran the headline 'Adolf Hitler Falls at his Post', there wasn't a man, woman or child who didn't already know the full story. Nonetheless, the newsstands were swamped: everyone wanted their own souvenir edition. No matter that the heavily censored reporting was deliberately vague about the circumstances of the Führer's demise, nor that it presented him as a brave warrior who had 'met a hero's death', rather than a tyrant who had chosen to take his own life instead of answering for his crimes. The simple headline was enough on its own.

For Baron von Aufsess, the best part of the news was the naming of Hitler's successor. The head of the Kriegsmarine, Admiral Dönitz, had been made the new president of Germany. If there was anyone who could persuade Hüffmeier to surrender the Channel Islands rather than hold out until the last man was dead, it was his old friend and superior officer. And for Dönitz himself, the clock was clearly ticking. A day earlier, the garrison defending Berlin had surrendered to the Russians, after a bloody battle that had seen many of the city's historic buildings destroyed and a combined military and civilian death toll in the hundreds of thousands. Meanwhile, the formal capitulation of German troops in Italy had also come into effect, taking around a million soldiers out of the war.

But Dönitz was continuing to hold out, hoping to negotiate an armistice that would protect German interests in the East, and Hüffmeier was not going to do anything without a direct order from his superior officer. He had, in fact, publicly said as much at a rally on the day of the aborted mutiny, declaring that he would refuse to recognise any Allied puppet government that was set up in Berlin. 'I receive my orders from Adolf Hitler or his successor,' he had proclaimed. 'It is to this that I have sworn allegiance and I shall stick to it even if he lives no longer.'

The following day, the admiral proved as good as his word. In the early hours of the morning, the troops in Alderney received a message in Morse code sent by signal lamp from the Cotentin Peninsula in France, requesting that they begin negotiations for surrender. Hüffmeier ordered his men to transmit a one-word reply: 'Superfluous.'

Once again, it seemed, all the islanders could do was wait until events reached their inevitable conclusion. In the meantime, they would remain in a strange limbo between war and peace. The shops were already selling Union Jacks for the big celebration to come, but no one was quite sure when to start flying them. The German troops were still notionally in control, but they had never looked less commanding. Nearly all of them now wanted the same thing as the islanders: for the war to end quickly so that they could go home and try to rebuild what was left of their lives. In the meantime, causing trouble was the last thing on their minds – they knew that soon, their own fates would be in the hands of the Allies, and this was no time to blot their copybooks with bad behaviour.

In dealing with civilians, the mood was one of moderation and restraint – even, in some cases, of negotiation. For almost two years now, Leo Harris's father had been holding onto the Union Jack he had rescued from a group of German soldiers. At the time, he had promised to fly it on the day that Berlin fell, and now that this momentous occasion had come to pass he was as good as his word, proudly hoisting the giant standard up a pole that stood on the third-floor balcony overlooking the seafront. As far as he knew, it was the first Union Jack to fly in the Channel Islands since the Occupation had begun five years earlier.

The flag soon began attracting attention. A few hours later, a German staff car pulled up on the street outside, and a rather elegant Wehrmacht officer got out and knocked on the door. 'Are you the owner of this house?' he asked Mr Harris.

'I am,' Leo's father replied.

'Then may I ask you, sir, as one gentleman to another, to take down your flag,' begged the officer. 'The ordinary soldiers do not know how near the war is to ending, and I'm afraid it may lead to bloodshed on the streets.' He bowed his head in a deferential gesture and added, 'Please.'

For Mr Harris, the moral victory of the encounter was worth far more than the symbolism of the flag. Here was a German officer treating him as an equal, making a request instead of issuing an order. He had no wish to be the cause of violent unrest so close to the end of the war – and he was sure it would only be a matter of days before he was fully entitled to hoist the flag again in victory. 'Certainly,' he told the officer with a smile.

The German extended a hand, which Mr Harris shook warmly. Then he took a step backwards and offered a respectful salute. 'Perhaps this war will end very soon,' he remarked cheerfully, 'and then we can all go back to our families.'

A few moments later, the staff car was speeding off along the road again. As Mr Harris climbed the stairs to the balcony, he realised that the officer hadn't even waited to see the flag come down. The word of one gentleman to another had been enough for him.

In the Channel Islands, the longed-for moment of liberation might not have arrived just yet, but those islanders who had been deported to internment camps in Germany were already savouring their first taste of freedom. The first of the camps to be liberated had been Biberach – appropriately enough on St George's Day. It was not, however, the British Tommies who arrived to greet the prisoners but the Free French Army, under the leadership of General Leclerc.

It had been a chaotic and frightening experience. From their vantage point at the top of the hill, the inmates had witnessed the Allied bombing of the village below, in which a number of local people had been killed or buried alive. But even after the bulk of the German forces had withdrawn, small pockets of resistance had remained to harass the advancing French forces. The camp captain, Garfield Garland, had sent a messenger to inform General Leclerc of the location of the camp, assuming that this would ensure the inmates' safety. But even so, the battle came alarmingly close. As shells flew by overhead, exploding just outside the barbed-wire fences, it was a miracle that no one was harmed.

When the first French soldiers arrived at the gates to declare that the fighting was over, they were greeted by a mob of greatly relieved Channel Islanders. In time, the camp residents were handed over to the care of the Americans, who arrived to keep an eye on them until it was time to fly them to England. The GIs had been in Biberach only a few days before they threw a grand celebratory party, which was held in the big hall. There was a live band, plenty of dancing – everything from the foxtrot to jive – and more champagne than the islanders knew what to do with.

At fourteen years old, Doris Lihou had never touched a drop of alcohol before, and the bubbles went straight to her head. The night was still young when her legs gave out beneath her on the dance floor, and a couple of friends had to carry her back to her billet. She was sad to miss the rest of the party, but nothing could wipe the smile off her face at the thought that she and her family were finally free again.

The camp at Bad Wurzach, which housed around six hundred inmates from Jersey, was liberated five days after Biberach, and this time it was an even closer shave for the inmates. Around noon on 28 April, a French tank entered the village – long since abandoned by the German Army – and made its way towards the camp, targeting the large building in which the Channel Islanders were held, which they assumed must be the local Nazi headquarters. They were stopped in the nick of time by a group of old men from the village, who ran out of their houses waving white flags and explained in broken French that the camp housed only English prisoners. A few minutes later, the French soldiers were at the gates, smashing the locks and setting the inmates free.

When they ventured into the town, the islanders were soon able to return the favour. Five of their former German guards had been lined up against a wall in the town square, in preparation for a summary execution. The French, having heard of the atrocities committed in the concentration camps, had decided to exact a little vigilante justice. The islanders rushed up to the soldiers and explained that the guards were just ordinary policemen, not SS, and had always behaved decently towards the prisoners. The impromptu death sentences were commuted, and the men were taken off for official processing instead.

Like their fellow islanders in Biberach, the Wurzach internees would have a while to wait before they were sent to England. Some of them, however, had already made the journey thanks to a series of early repatriations. Jersey teenager Michael Ginns was more than a little disappointed when his father's chronic poor health saw the whole family earmarked to leave. For a start, he was a passionate military enthusiast, and the thought of missing out on the liberation of the camp seemed like a terrible shame. But there was another reason too: at seventeen years old, Michael was a mainstay of the camp's theatre scene, and had just been cast as the romantic lead opposite a young woman nine years his senior with whom he was more than a little besotted. Midway through rehearsals, Michael received the news that he was to be packed off to England, and his role – lengthy kissing scene and all – was passed on to another young actor.

There was only one islander in Michael's repatriation group whose health was so bad that she couldn't have stayed in the camp any longer – a woman called Mrs Berry, who was slowly dying of stomach cancer and constantly complained of feeling cold. Throughout the five-hour journey to Munich, she was tended to by Michael's mother Emma, a former nurse, with the help of a German medical orderly called Karl. The young man didn't speak much English, but Michael had picked up enough German at Wurzach to get to know him pretty well en route.

When they pulled up at Munich goods yard alongside a coal train, Karl began handing out buckets to Michael and the other reasonably healthy-looking islanders. 'Fill these up,' he told them in German, gesturing towards the other vehicle. 'And look out for the railway police.'

It was a bitterly cold evening, and the ground around the train was thick with snow. Inside the carriage, Mrs Berry was shivering miserably. Michael shovelled as much coal as he could fit into his bucket, and then returned to the train, where Karl lit the little furnace in their carriage. Gradually, the small compartment began to warm up, but the stove was giving off a lot of smoke. Mrs Berry began coughing and wheezing.

From a little cupboard at the end of the carriage, Karl extracted a long flue brush. Then he opened the door of the train and disappeared outside. A few moments later, Michael could hear footsteps on the roof, right above the chimney of the stove. Then suddenly, a flash of light lit up the sky outside the window, and a loud bang made everyone in the carriage flinch. It was followed by a muffled crash on the far side of the train.

Michael rushed out of the door to find Karl slumped motionless in the snow, the charred flue-brush still gripped tightly in his hand. He had forgotten that the wires above the train were electrified, and the error had cost him his life.

When Karl's colleagues came out to take up the body, Michael asked if they could pass on a message to the young man's family. 'Just to tell them how sorry we all are,' he explained. 'And that we're grateful for everything he did to help us.'

But the other German men were unmoved. 'No,' one of them told him. 'This is war. When someone dies you just have to forget about it.' Within an hour or so, a new orderly had been assigned to Michael's carriage, and the train was on its way again.

They travelled all through the night, passing just to the west of

Berlin and up into Occupied Denmark, and arriving at Helsingør shortly before dawn. Four kilometres away, across the strait of Øresund, Michael could see the coast of Sweden. The neutral country observed no blackout regulations, and the twinkling lights of Helsingborg looked like a fairyland.

That morning, the deportees boarded the little Red Cross ferry for the short journey to the Swedish side of the strait. At last, after almost five years, they were out of the clutches of the Germans. But the long journey wasn't over yet. It was another two hundred kilometres by train to Gothenburg, where the cruise liner SS *Drottningholm* was waiting to set sail.

When they finally arrived in Liverpool, the weary travellers were met by a delegation of British Intelligence officers. The last thing Michael felt like doing was explaining why he and his fellow islanders had no valid identity papers, and he was enormously relieved when the suspicious interrogators decided to accept that he must be who he said he was, and allowed him to go on his way.

Michael's godparents lived near Epsom Downs in Surrey, and it was here that he and his parents would be staying for the remainder of the war. On 1 May, when he heard the news of Hitler's death, he knew that it wouldn't be long before the whole family would be able to go home again.

Six days later, Michael was walking along the chalky uplands near the local railway line when a train shot past blasting an unusual set of notes on its whistle. Pricking his ears, he realised that the pattern was a familiar one: three short blasts, followed by one long one.

It was the Morse code for the letter 'V'. 'V' for Victory.

When news of the German surrender reached the Channel Islands that evening there was scarcely a man, woman or child – save, perhaps, Admiral Hüffmeier himself – who greeted it with anything other than relief. Even the vanquished German Army viewed the end of the war less as a defeat than a deliverance. Werner Rang and his friends sat around glued to a little radio set, and when they heard that Admiral Dönitz had finally capitulated they felt it was time for an impromptu celebration. The young men lit a large bonfire and began setting light to their swastika flags.

That evening, the front page of the *Guernsey Evening Press* appeared uncensored for the first time in nearly five years. With the signature of the surrender document, Dönitz had issued a command to all German fighting units around the world to lay down their arms, and all U-boats still out at sea were recalled to their ports. Surely, here was an order that Admiral Hüffmeier would be forced to obey.

The following morning, on what had been designated VE Day, the islanders awoke confident that the Occupation was finally over. In Jersey, Bailiff Coutanche had reached an agreement with Admiral Hüffmeier that loudspeakers could be erected in the Royal Square to broadcast Winston Churchill's speech to the nation that afternoon. In return he had promised that no Union Jacks would be flown until the prime minister had finished his broadcast. Already, a pair of British destroyers were en route from Plymouth to accept the admiral's surrender. He had signalled that he would send a representative to meet them at 2 p.m. local time (noon GMT) at Les Hanois, a mile off the westernmost tip of Guernsey.

Yet even at the eleventh hour, and with express orders from his own commanding officer to surrender, Hüffmeier couldn't quite bring himself to co-operate. 'I often have the impression that he is torn by some inner conflict of conscience amounting to a frenzy,' Baron von Aufsess had noted in his diary the night before – and the day's events certainly seemed to prove him right. When the two British vessels arrived at the designated co-ordinates, they were met by a young naval officer, Lieutenant-Commander Arnim Zimmerman, who greeted them with arm outstretched and a cry of 'Heil Hitler!'

Baron von Aufsess was incredulous when he heard about this extraordinary gesture. 'One can only guess at the feelings of the astounded British officer,' he commented bitterly. 'With one foolish gesture of defiance, all the goodwill earned by the troops in years of exemplary behaviour has been destroyed.'

To make matters worse, Zimmerman insisted that he had come

to discuss terms for an armistice, not to sign an unconditional surrender. The British representative, Brigadier A. E. Snow, informed him hotly that this was out of the question.

Zimmerman left in something of a huff, warning the brigadier that he would be well advised to retreat to a safe distance or his ships might find themselves fired upon by Guernsey's coastal batteries. Although the German surrender had already been signed, he pointed out slyly, the ceasefire didn't become legally binding until midnight. In the meantime, Admiral Hüffmeier was entitled to view the presence of British ships in his waters as an act of provocation.

Brigadier Snow was furious. If Hüffmeier ordered his men to fire on a British ship now, he told Zimmerman, he would personally see him hanged the next day. Nonetheless, rather than risk calling the bluff of a madman, he decided to exercise the better part of valour. After Zimmerman had returned to his minesweeper and set off for St Peter Port Harbour, the brigadier gave the order to withdraw.

Once the British ships were out of range of the coastal batteries, Hüffmeier sent a new signal announcing that his second in command, General Major Heine, would come to meet them at midnight to sign the necessary paperwork. As a point of principle, it seemed – and regardless of clear instructions from Berlin – he was determined to hold onto his island prizes until the very last minute.

The defiant gesture was somewhat lost on the bemused Channel Islanders. They were a little surprised when the boatloads of Tommies failed to materialise as expected on VE Day, but by now unanticipated delays had become a way of life, and waiting almost as commonplace as breathing. In the meantime, however, there was one appointment that everyone intended to keep: Winston Churchill's official public broadcast at five o'clock that afternoon.

Those within easy walking distance of St Helier and St Peter Port made their way into town to listen over the newly installed loudspeaker systems. Others further afield made sure to find a friend or relative with a wireless set of their own – the authorities had announced a complete amnesty on the 'black' radios, promising that from now on nobody would be prosecuted for using them. Bob

Le Sueur's mother Lizzie insisted that their set should be placed on a table next to the open bay windows, with the volume turned up to the maximum, so that their neighbours on either side would be able to hear the speech as well. But when Bob set off on his bike to attend the public broadcast in town, he realised that his mother's act of generosity had been quite unnecessary since every homeowner on the street had come up with the same idea. Bob smiled as he cycled past a row of open bay windows, with a motley array of old radios lined up behind them.

By the time he arrived in town, the square was already heaving, but one of his work colleagues had a friend who worked in an adjoining building, and who was able to let them up onto a parapet. Looking down at the scene below, he was struck not just by the cheerful excitement of the crowd – so different from the modulated restraint that had become second nature to the islanders in the past few years – but by the relative absence of Germans. Aside from a handful of soldiers dotted around the town, the troops seemed to have quietly gone to ground.

At 5 p.m. precisely, the chimes of Big Ben rang out, and moments later Churchill's broadcast began, coming live from his office in Downing Street, and broadcast simultaneously around the world. In Trafalgar Square, the heaving throng of several thousand Londoners fell so silent that you could have heard a pin drop, and at the same moment, the smaller crowds in St Peter Port and St Helier's town squares were listening with equally rapt attention as the prime minister calmly detailed the exact terms, and the precise timeline, of the surrender.

But there was one line that sent an electric shock through the crowds in the island capitals, not to mention the tens of thousands of men and women glued to radio sets in houses from coast to coast. 'Hostilities will end officially at one minute after midnight tonight,' Churchill growled triumphantly, 'but in the interests of saving lives, the ceasefire began yesterday to be sounded all along the front, and our dear Channel Islands are also to be freed today.'

At these words, the crowds erupted in a frenzy of cheers and applause, and those who had brought little Union Jacks with them began waving them wildly in the air. Across the islands, people reacted with unrestrained emotion. In Guernsey's St Sampson parish, Nellie Falla was so overwhelmed with excitement that she leapt with a yelp through the open window and began running around in circles in her garden. In Jersey, meanwhile, John Harris led the rapturous applause among a gaggle of local people who had gathered in the street to hear the set he kept hidden in the kitchen cupboard, which he had hooked up to a loudspeaker outside.

But not everyone was quite so enchanted with the prime minister's warm words about the Channel Islands. After all, in five years, this was the first time he had so much as deigned to mention them. 'Our *dear* Channel Islands?' Pearl Smith repeated sarcastically, as she and her sister Gwen huddled around their little crystal set. 'What a nerve! He couldn't have cared less if we'd all been shot!'

Churchill ended his speech with a rousing plea to defeat the Japanese once and for all, and bring the war to a speedy conclusion. 'We must now devote all our strength and resources to the completion of our task,' he declared. 'Advance, Britannia! Long live the cause of freedom! God Save the King!'

It was a rousing performance, and not one that many men would have dared to follow, but for the Jersey bailiff, Alexander Coutanche, who had listened to the broadcast from a commanding position on the balcony of the Court House, the opportunity was too tempting to resist. The applause for the prime minister had scarcely begun to die down before he had seized a conveniently placed microphone and started, for the first time in five years, to address his people directly.

He began by offering a prayer of thanks for the island's deliverance, before proceeding to provide some details of what was to come. The British Tommies, he told the crowd, were already on their way, and would be arriving on the islands very soon, along with no less than a squadron of naval cruisers and destroyers. As the Union Jack and the flag of Jersey were hoisted up the twin flagposts of the Royal Court, the people erupted in yet more rapturous applause and cheering.

'I want you all to feel that I am amongst you,' the bailiff told the assembled masses, laying down his microphone with a theatrical flourish and disappearing from view, only to re-emerge moments later in the square itself. Here he mingled cheerfully among the ecstatic revellers, pressing hands and offering joyful platitudes wherever he went. 'God Save the King!' he bellowed – and several hundred voices echoed the words back at him.

'And now,' the bailiff shouted triumphantly, 'I will ask you to join me in singing the national anthem.' Coutanche had never been a particularly strong singer, but he threw himself into the performance with all the verve of a seasoned professional, leading the crowd in a confident, heartfelt rendition of the song.

Within an hour, the whole town was festooned with flags and bunting, and church bells were ringing out in celebration. But thanks to Admiral Hüffmeier's perverse intransigence, the British vessels that had been earmarked for liberation remained lying off Guernsey's waters. The German soldiers appeared to have mostly vanished, and yet the Tommies were nowhere to be seen.

In the absence of any authority figures, it didn't take much for the atmosphere of unchecked revelry to spill over into a kind of lawless chaos. Jersey teenager Don Dolbel was thrown into the air by some of his friends in order to grab the huge swastika flag that hung from the Pomme d'Or Hotel. Once he had ripped it free from the flagpole, the lads set about trampling it into the ground with relish.

Don had already participated in a bit of vigilante justice that afternoon, smashing the window of a known collaborator and throwing a bucket of tar into their living room. But that evening in town he caught a glimpse of a more brutal form of punishment. As he rounded a corner, he encountered a gang of lads struggling with a young woman, who was thrashing about wildly as they hacked away at her hair with a large pair of scissors. She must be a Jerrybag, Don realised, and this was her punishment for sleeping with the enemy. The men had intended to humiliate rather than harm her, but as she struggled to get free the blade of the scissors sliced through her ear and the lads left her shaking and bleeding on the ground.

She wasn't the only young woman in St Helier to suffer rough justice from an angry mob that evening. Joe Miere witnessed a girl of about sixteen, with her head shaved and bleeding, running down the road completely naked. Moved by the plight of the poor young woman, who was shaking with terror and crying hysterically, he rushed over and offered her his raincoat, telling her, 'It's all right, my love.' The girl was so traumatised that she instinctively recoiled, raising a hand to protect herself from the blow she expected to fall. 'Where do you live?' Joe asked her gently. She pointed in the direction of La Motte Street, and he helped her up and accompanied her home.

All over Jersey, women were being subjected to the same kind of cruel treatment. For the island's angry young men, they had somehow become the embodiment of Occupation resentment. Denied a chance to fight for their country, and not quite willing to take the risk of attacking the Germans, they channelled their rage into an assault on the girls they felt had betrayed them.

Jersey teenager Osmund Simon joined a group of lads in St Peter parish lying in wait outside a local woman's house. When she emerged, a bucket of tar was thrown over her head, and the lads scarpered before she could see who had attacked her. It was an unpleasant business, but Osmund felt it was his duty to teach the Jerrybags a lesson. As he put it, 'They're the enemy too.'

At midnight that evening, the British destroyers *Bulldog* and *Beagle* returned for their second rendezvous with the Germans. This time, Lieutenant Commander Zimmerman was accompanied by a more august representative – not Admiral Hüffmeier himself but the next best thing, his chief of staff, Major General Siegfried Heine, who was empowered to sign the document that would formally turn the islands over to the British.

The two Germans disembarked from their minesweeper and came over to the *Bulldog*, where they were formally piped aboard. When Heine was asked if he was willing to accept unconditional surrender, he replied tersely, '*Ja*.'

Brigadier Snow gave the order to proceed to The Roads, a strait of water just outside St Peter Port Harbour, having first checked with the German representatives that they would not encounter any mines along the way. There the representatives of the two warring nations spent the hours until dawn locked in a series of tedious meetings.

Finally, at 7.14 a.m., General Heine was led out onto the quarterdeck, where the surrender document was laid out, in fine naval tradition, on an upturned rum barrel. Once he had made his inky mark on the piece of paper, he returned to shore, followed shortly afterwards by a small party led by Lieutenant Colonel Stoneman, who set up his headquarters at the Royal Hotel, just as Major Albrecht Lanz had done almost five years earlier.

Brigadier Snow, meanwhile, was transferred to the other destroyer, HMS *Beagle*, to pay a visit to the island commandant for Jersey, Major General Rudolf Wulf. Although Heine's surrender was legally binding across the Channel Islands, Snow was keen to dot all his 'i's and cross all his 't's.

The ship rounded Noirmont Point a little before 10 a.m., to cheers of 'There she is!' from the gathering crowds. But when they weighed anchor in St Aubin's Bay, Wulf appeared to be a no-show.

Brigadier Snow sent a couple of officers ashore to find Wulf and bring him on board at once. It was more than two hours later when the recalcitrant commandant finally put in a sulky appearance on board ship. The brigadier was furious, and tore him off such a strip that he signed the surrender document on the verge of tears.

Alongside Wulf was the Jersey bailiff, Alexander Coutanche, with his advisers Charles Duret Aubin and Cecil Harrison. The bailiff had, in fact, been partially responsible for the commandant's late arrival. When a naval rating had called that morning to request his attendance at the official surrender, Coutanche had readily agreed. 'I have never in my life received an order with which I shall have greater pleasure in complying,' he had replied cheerfully. But at the Pomme d'Or Hotel, where he had arrived to meet the commandant at noon, the bailiff's infuriating pedantry – so long a thorn in the side of the

German authorities – had once again reared its ugly head. 'I had understood that you and I were going alone,' he had told Wulf, who was accompanied by a couple of German officers. 'If you are taking members of your staff with you then I should like to be accompanied by mine.' Coutanche had insisted that the party could not depart for the *Beagle* until Duret Aubin and Harrison were summoned to form his own entourage.

With the surrender document signed, the German representatives were led away, and the bailiff joined the British landing party on the trip back to shore, looking on with paternal satisfaction as the Tommies were embraced by the crowd on the pier. One woman pushed her child into the arms of a soldier. 'Kiss him!' she begged the young man. 'Make him clean.' Coutanche couldn't fail to be moved. 'It was', he later wrote, 'the most memorable and fantastic occasion of my life.'

In Guernsey, meanwhile, the first encounter between the British forces and the locals had not quite gone according to plan. At 9 a.m., HMS *Bulldog* was still anchored in the straits outside St Peter Port, when a little fishing boat came out to greet it. On board were thirteen local people from the parish of St Sampson, who had come to pass on their thanks and best wishes to the British servicemen. They pulled up alongside, and were welcomed on board with open arms, toasting the liberation with a gaggle of friendly Tommies on the deck and swapping Occupation newspapers and souvenir Reichsmarks for cigarettes, chocolate and sweets. But before long an officer came down from the bridge to tell the visitors that they would have to leave: the bailiff and his official reception party were on their way. Victor Carey, it was feared, would be rather put out to think that he had been pipped to the post by a random group of locals.

The visitors replied that they understood completely and made their way back to shore, accompanied by cheers from the sailors. They dispersed to their various homes for some lunch, before meeting up again, this time on their bicycles, for the five-kilometre ride into town. The only question was which side of the road to cycle on. One man who set off on the left narrowly avoided a head-on collision. 'We're liberated now, it's changed back!' he bellowed angrily at the other cyclist, as they whizzed past within inches of each other. 'I've heard nothing yet!' the other man shouted, obstinately sticking to the right.

It was a dangerous business, since there were more bikes on the road that day than ever before – not to mention quite a few cars in the hands of people who hadn't driven for half a decade. Bob Le Sueur was cycling with a group of friends that included René Franoux and his Russian lodger 'Bill', who was finally able to safely go out in public without his disguise. They had decided to pick out a spot on one of the piers, from where they hoped to get a good view of the Tommies arriving in St Helier.

The shortest route, they realised, was to take the German tunnel that had been bored through the rock beneath Fort Regent, an imposing nineteenth-century fortress that overlooked the town. Although most of the soldiers were now keeping a distinctly low profile, the tunnel – which was also used as a storage depot – was still guarded by a pair of sentries, armed with rifles.

Bob had fallen back a little, and by the time he reached the tunnel entrance, his friends were almost out the other side. Suddenly, he heard a noise that made him start. It was the sound of the wire clip which held the hosepipe wrapped around his bicycle wheel snapping open – but in the echoey confines of the tunnel, it bore a distinct resemblance to a gunshot. He brought the bike to a halt, just in time to see one of the sentries – a young man of no more than eighteen – turn around to face him, instinctively raising his rifle.

If I die now, Bob thought, I might be the last casualty of the war.

For a moment the two men stared at each other, frozen to the spot. Then the German realised what had happened, and he broke into a broad grin. Bob felt a strong urge to walk up and shake the young man by the hand, but he didn't do it. Instead, he fixed the clip back onto his bike wheel, climbed onto the saddle, and pedalled off in search of his friends.

All around the harbour, a crowd of thousands had gathered – so many people that it seemed as if the entire population had come out to greet the Tommies. Most of the islanders were laughing and cheering, but a few were in a more thoughtful mood. Twenty-three-year-old estate agent Alec Podger had tears of joy streaming down his face. For five long years, he had felt perpetually on guard, always watching what he said and did for fear that a German informer might be observing him. It wasn't the curfew that had bothered him most about the Occupation, or the strict rules and regulations, or even the fear of strict military discipline. It was the feeling that his authentic self had to somehow stay hidden – the soul-crushing misery of day-to-day life in a totalitarian regime. Now at last, Alec was free of the mental prison he had been living in. He felt truly liberated, not just in body but in spirit as well.

Francis Harris, meanwhile, was still confined in a more literal cell in Gloucester Street prison. His father had attempted to get him out the day before, but had been told that there was no way a prisoner who was awaiting trial could be released to anyone but the British military authorities. On Liberation Day, however, Mr Harris wasn't going to take no for an answer, and in case his powers of persuasion failed him, this time he had brought a gun as well. When the German guard on duty once again refused to grant his request, he raised the barrel and pointed it straight at the man's head. After five years of living under the jackboot, it felt good to be the one making the threats.

Just as Mr Harris had expected, his bluff did the trick. A few minutes later, Francis was free, and on his way home to rejoin the rest of the family.

That afternoon, the British troops began to disembark, around two hundred each in St Peter Port and St Helier. The remaining six thousand men earmarked for the islands under what was known as Operation Nestegg would not set sail from England for another two days. But what they lacked in numbers, the early arrivals more than made up for in symbolism. To those islanders who remembered the departure of the Tommies in the summer of 1940, the mere sight of their khaki uniforms was enough to raise a smile.

To the youngsters who had only ever known German soldiers, the showers of treats the Tommies hurled into the crowds guaranteed them a warm welcome. Jersey boy Tony Rentsch had been born during the first year of the Occupation, and to him the English boiled sweets were an exotic novelty. Other children his age were puzzled by the sight of oranges tossed out by the troops. Some tried to bite right through the skin without peeling them first, while others mistook them for toy balls, not realising that they were even edible.

Some of the older boys were thrilled to be given an official role in the liberation. The members of Jersey's 11th Scout Troop, which had operated undercover throughout the Occupation, had relished the opportunity to finally don their uniforms again, marching down to St Helier en masse. It didn't take long for them to catch the attention of one of the British officers. 'We could do with your help,' the man told them, ordering them to report to the Pomme d'Or Hotel, where they were assigned, one or two to each unit, to lead the troops to their various billets around the town.

They weren't the only locals doing all they could for the Tommies. In Guernsey, Joan and Harry Coutanche watched with excitement as the British troops took over the German signal centre near their home in St Jacques. As soon as the building had been secured, they popped over to introduce themselves, keeping the soldiers supplied with cups of tea and coffee all afternoon.

Once the troops had drunk their fill, Joan and Harry set off on a friend's tractor, waving a Union Jack as they toured around the island. Then they returned to St Peter Port and partied all night long, staying up until well after daybreak the following morning.

For every islander, it was a night to remember, wherever – and however – they chose to celebrate it. Nellie and Oswald Falla walked home from town that evening and conceived a 'Liberation Baby' – one of a large number of children born in a local 'boom' nine months later. Others found themselves marking the big day in surprising company. Ambrose Sherwill was still in England, awaiting passage back to Guernsey, but his wife and sons joined the German soldiers who were living in their attic for an impromptu party, cracking open several bottles of wine and drinking a toast to the end of the war. It was a moment of solidarity that her exiled husband would have been proud of.

On Sark, too, Germans and local people celebrated together, dancing in the Island Hall – which had been decorated with paper bunting and flowers – until the early hours of the morning. There was plenty of booze on offer, and more than a few of the revellers ended up being carried home by their friends.

In Guernsey, Pearl and Gwen Smith set off from Cobo to Saumarez Park, where a special Liberation Day dance was being held in the hall. All the way there, the two girls sang at the top of their lungs: 'God Save the King', 'Rule, Britannia!', and Guernsey's unofficial national anthem, 'Sarnia Cherie'. There were tears in their eyes by the time they arrived at the party and made their way onto the wooden dance floor.

As they twirled around the room to the lively sound of the latest tunes from England, Pearl felt that she had never been happier. For the first time in five years, nine o'clock came and went and nobody took a blind bit of notice. There was no curfew any more, no more rules and regulations. No more German soldiers telling you where to go and what to do.

After several hours on the dance floor, Pearl's feet had been rubbed raw by her wooden-soled shoes. But she didn't care. She had tasted freedom, and it was enough to keep her going until dawn.

CHAPTER THIRTY-THREE

EVER AFTER

It was another few days before the rest of the Tommies arrived, but wherever they landed they were treated to the same enthusiastic welcome. At Pembroke Bay on the north-eastern tip of Guernsey, the islanders were astounded at the sight of huge landing craft hauling themselves up onto the sand and disgorging their preloaded lorries, while amphibious DUKWs (aka 'ducks') drove out of the water and up the slipway to the edge of L'Ancresse Common. Even after five years of German Occupation, the military spectacle was quite extraordinary, like a second D-Day landing but without the bloody battle that had followed. The crowds who had gathered to watch clapped and cheered from beginning to end.

In Jersey and Guernsey the troops rapidly spread out according to a carefully orchestrated plan, seizing dozens of key locations within a matter of hours. It wasn't all work and no play, however. Soon the Tommies were getting to know the appreciative local folk – and unsurprisingly, a number of romances resulted. Sergeant Major Bill Neely took the prize for the swiftest courtship, proposing to his new girlfriend less than forty-eight hours after their first kiss.

While the Tommies were making themselves at home, most of the German soldiers – almost twelve thousand on each of the two biggest islands – were busy setting sail for England. One of the first to go was Admiral Hüffmeier himself, who finally surrendered to Brigadier Snow during a meeting at St Peter Port's Crown Hotel.

Obstinate as ever, the admiral refused to salute, and even told Snow that he could not hand over his sword, as was required by military protocol, since he had already broken it in two.

It was Snow who had the last laugh, however. The naval destroyer HMS *Faulknor* was lying in St Peter Port Harbour, ready to bear the former commandant to a POW camp in England, but when Hüffmeier stepped towards the staff car waiting outside the hotel, assuming that it had come to take him to the end of the pier, the brigadier stopped him and announced he would be going on foot instead. This uncharacteristically petty move won applause from the crowds outside, and they gleefully jeered the former commandant every step of the way, revelling in his humiliating walk of shame.

Werner Rang's company was shipped off a couple of days later, having been marched ten kilometres across the island and ordered to strip naked while their uniforms were dusted down with disinfectant powder. By the time they finally arrived at the White Rock and were loaded, forty at a time, onto landing craft, the prospect of life in a British POW camp was looking increasingly appealing.

The little boats brought the men out of the harbour to The Roads, where a large troop ship was waiting to take them to England. Dozens of seemingly helpful young sailors reached over the side and helped haul the German soldiers onto the deck. Only later did several of Werner's comrades realise that their watches had been pinched in the process.

Within a week, nearly 90 per cent of the former German garrison had arrived at POW camps in England, joining almost half a million of their countrymen who had been captured in the course of the war. Around three thousand men, however, were left behind to help clean up the mess of the Occupation – clearing minefields, rolling up barbed wire and making safe the bunkers and fortifications that had formed such an important part of Hitler's Atlantic Wall.

It was, at times, a risky business, as the Dame of Sark discovered to her dismay. When the tiny island was officially liberated on 10 May, the British commander, Lieutenant Colonel Allen, explained that the cohort of troops earmarked for Sark were unfortunately yet to depart from Plymouth. 'Would you mind being left for a few days?' he asked Sybil apologetically.

'I have been left for five years,' the Dame replied. 'I can stand a few more days.'

The truth was she was rather excited about the prospect of being left in charge of the 275 German troops on the island, and wasted no time dictating their new orders: 'First, to remove the mines from the harbour; second, to remove the anti-glider posts from among the crops; and third, to hand back our wireless sets.' When she reached the end of the list of instructions, the Dame was most gratified to hear the reply, '*Zu Befehl, gnädige Frau*' ('At your command, ma'am).

But when the former commandant, Captain Magsam, called to inform her that two of his men had been killed attempting to remove the roll-bombs hanging over the harbour, Sybil was taken aback. Suddenly the thrill of commanding a unit of soldiers had lost its appeal. The Dame arranged for the men to be buried in the island cemetery, and even secured Brigadier Snow's permission for a volley to be fired over the graves.

Captain Magsam and his troops left Sark a few days later, and the task of clearing the remaining mines was passed onto a team of Royal Engineers, with the assistance of more German POWs brought over from Guernsey. While they were there, they also took the opportunity of strengthening La Coupée, the narrow isthmus which connected the bulk of the island to the peninsula of Little Sark, and which was sorely in need of repair. Before long, though, they too had departed, along with the handful of vehicles the Army of Occupation had brought over from Guernsey. In the end, Sark was returned to its natural, peaceful state, but with a few German horses, distributed among the local farmers, in addition to their pre-Occupation complement.

Dame Sybil, meanwhile, was invited onboard HMS *Bulldog* for a lavish celebratory meal. When the captain asked her what she had missed most during the Occupation she told him, 'Hot baths and the smell of frying bacon.' It wasn't like the Dame to show her emotions in public, but when a plate of cooked bacon was set down in front of her, it was all she could do to hold back her tears.

On the larger islands, the job of undoing the damage wrought by the German war machine was extensive. Over the next three months, a hundred thousand metres of barbed wire was removed, along with more than sixty-five thousand mines. Unsurprisingly, the two casualties on Sark were only the first of many. But some of the more solid fortifications proved surprisingly resistant to removal. The dozens of bunkers that lined the coasts of Jersey and Guernsey proved almost as impervious to dynamite as their original designers had hoped, and in the end it was decided that blasting them out of the shoreline was simply more trouble than it was worth.

At the end of August, British military control of the islands was turned over once again to the lieutenant-governors, the Crown representatives who had been forced to evacuate when they were demilitarised five years earlier. And as the weeks and months went by, gradually the islanders who had left around the same time began to come home too.

One of the first to return was a young naval officer who turned up unexpectedly in Alexander Coutanche's chambers while he was in the middle of a meeting. As the lad saluted and stood to attention in the shadowy doorway, the bailiff glanced up with irritation. 'What do you want?' he barked impatiently.

'Don't you know me?' the officer replied. Then he stepped forward into the light and exclaimed, '*Dad!*'

The bailiff looked up into the face of his son John. After five years at sea, he barely recognised him.

It wasn't until several months after liberation that the majority of displaced Channel Islanders returned home. Some of the earliest to begin the journey were those who were still living in the German internment camps, albeit under Allied rather than enemy supervision. One day in the first week of June, Doris Lihou and her parents were bundled into a Free French lorry and driven the short distance to the US Air Force base at Mengen, where they remained under canvas for a couple of days waiting to board a Dakota to England. The plane was still fitted out in its wartime configuration, with benches along the sides of the fuselage and a space in the middle for the travellers' luggage. It was a bumpy ride, and Doris was extremely relieved when they finally touched down at Hendon Aerodrome.

From there, they made their way to Ash in Surrey, where they stayed with Doris's aunt Alice while they waited for a boat to take them home again. In the meantime, Mr Lihou took a job on the railway, and Doris made the most of her time on the mainland, popping up to London by train to see a show and visit the zoo. It wasn't until late in the summer that the family finally arrived back in Guernsey.

They were met at the White Rock by Doris's elder siblings Richard and Blanche. For Amy Lihou, the emotional reunion was almost too much to bear. The sight of her two adult children, both looking so much thinner than she remembered them, sent her into fresh paroxysms of worry. She couldn't help thinking of the son she had lost only a couple of years earlier, and how fragile the thread of life had been throughout those difficult years of Occupation.

Of course, Mrs Lihou had known something of the struggles Blanche and Richard had endured in Guernsey, although – thanks to the plentiful supply of food in the internment camps – she had been spared that last bitterly hungry winter. Many of the returning island-ers, however, had no idea what their compatriots had been through. Those who had evacuated in the summer of 1940 came home to an island very different to the one they remembered. The picturesque beaches had been sullied by ugly concrete fortifications. Their houses had been ransacked for furniture and firewood – in some cases even the floorboards and banisters had been ripped out. The community into which they were attempting to reintegrate knew little of their war – struggling to survive in a strange land, under constant threat of German bombing – and the feeling of confusion and mistrust was mutual. Many of those who had stayed saw the evacuees as little more than cowards who had been spared the worst privations of the Occupation. The evacuees, meanwhile, who had never even seen a

German, much less spoken to one, often suspected those who had stayed behind of something approaching collaboration.

The split in society was mirrored on a more personal level by painful rifts within families. Esme Ingrouille found her own brother virtually unintelligible thanks to the broad Cheshire accent he had picked up in England. Jim Bishop, meanwhile, who had evacuated with just two out of his ten siblings, returned to a family that no longer felt like his own. His brothers and sisters who had stayed in Guernsey were like strangers, and he couldn't shake the feeling that for the five long years he had spent away from home, his mother had simply forgotten about him. In the end, Jim found his old home too hard to readjust to. At the first opportunity, he ran off and joined the Navy, forsaking the island he no longer knew for a life at sea.

Many of those who returned to the islands had been profoundly changed by their experiences abroad. For four-year-old Janet Duquemin, whose earliest memories were of life in an internment camp, the twenty-five square miles of Guernsey felt terrifyingly vast. She had never slept in a room on her own before, and the idea of taking a bus to school appalled her. Janet had become entirely institutionalised by camp life, and adapting to the real world was traumatic. Her mother Betty, meanwhile, never quite returned to the cheerful, outgoing woman she had been before the war. Not only had she lost her closest friends in Guernsey to the gas chambers, but many of her family back home in Vienna had been taken from her as well. Once a talented and passionate musician, now she rarely sang or played the piano, and then only under duress. She turned in on herself, living for her family but withdrawing from the wider community, and she almost never spoke about the war.

Harold Le Druillenec had been lucky to survive incarceration at Bergen-Belsen, but he too was never quite the same again. After giving evidence at the Belsen trials, a precursor to the inquests held at Nuremberg, he went on to a successful career as a teacher, although the horrors he had seen in the camp were seldom far from his thoughts and the trauma continued to plague him for the rest of his life.

And then there were the islanders who never came home at all. Harold's sister Louisa Gould, who had sheltered the Russian 'Bill' after her own son had died, and paid for it with her life in the gas chamber. The Jersey scout leader Peter Painter and his father Clarence, who had perished as prisoners in Germany. Louis Symes, father of the brave commando Jim, who had taken his own life in Cherche-Midi prison only days before his son's death sentence was commuted. Not to mention the scores of islanders who might never have died if it weren't for the Occupation, beginning with the forty-four killed during the German bombing raids of June 1940, and ending with those who had perished in the last terrible winter.

One way or another, the Occupation had taken well over a hundred lives. On Sark, the twin losses of the bubbly twenty-year-old Jacqueline Carré and the sweet toddler Nanette Hamon would haunt the small island community for years. And in Guernsey, those who had known the three Jewish women sent off to Auschwitz in the spring of 1942 would find it hard to comprehend that their own government, and their own police force, had not just allowed it to happen but had actually assisted in the process.

In the months that followed, the islands attempted to heal the wounds left by the war years. Ambrose Sherwill returned to Guernsey and formally took over from Victor Carey as bailiff in 1946, holding the office for the next thirteen years. His counterpart in Jersey, Alexander Coutanche, remained in the top job even longer, finally retiring in 1962. Despite concerns in London over the behaviour of the island governments during the Occupation, both men were knighted in the first post-war honours list. Some years later, Sybil Hathaway was recognised with a DBE – making her, she joked, a 'double Dame'.

Meanwhile, ordinary people were just trying to get on with their lives. Leo Harris and his family had never intended to spend half a decade in Jersey. When they had arrived on the island in 1939, it had been for a long summer holiday, at the end of which the two boys were looking forward to returning to their old school in Edinburgh. Five years later, the time had finally come to go home. The Harrises loaded up one of their many cars – a Clement-Talbot 101 – with as much luggage as they could take with them (including a couple of small cases stashed under the mudwings on either side of the bonnet) and made their way down to the harbour.

Thanks to his various local contacts, Mr Harris had got hold of enough petrol for the four hundred-mile journey from Southampton to Edinburgh. There was just one problem: all vehicles travelling to the mainland were supposed to arrive empty, as the import of fuel was forbidden. But he knew that obtaining a full tank's worth in England would be almost impossible, so – ingenious and impetuous as ever – he came up with a solution, soldering a false bottom into the fuel tank and covering it with a small layer of rusty old gasoline to divert suspicion.

The scam worked a treat. When a man from the AA came to inspect the vehicle before it was loaded onto the mailboat, his dipstick came out suitably dry, and the car was soon being hauled aboard by a team of dockers. As the *Isle of Sark* made its way out of St Helier Harbour, Leo looked back at the island that had been his home for a third of his life. But before long he turned his attention to the view ahead of him instead. For five years, Jersey had been the family's prison. In a sense, this was their true moment of liberation.

Leo knew Southampton well, and as the boat approached from a distance, the town looked pretty much the same as ever. But the closer they drew to the harbour, the more the devastation wrought by the blitz became evident. The little arcade where he and his brother Francis had played five years earlier had been obliterated, just one of the hundreds of bombed-out husks that now littered the city. Driving through the shattered streets on their way to the London Road, the extent of the destruction they saw was horrifying. Beautiful Victorian buildings had been reduced to rubble, and ancient churches burned to the ground. As he took in the scenes of devastation, Leo began to wonder if being stuck in Jersey hadn't really been so bad after all.

Mr Harris drove on through the night, reaching the outskirts of Edinburgh shortly before dawn. After five years of blackout, the twinkling lights of the city were a joy to behold. When the family pulled up outside their house in Morningside, it was with a peculiar feeling of déjà vu – aside from the old railings, which had been taken away and melted down for the war effort, everything was just as they had left it. But as Leo went inside and began rummaging through his belongings, suddenly their time away seemed more real again. What he found were the toys of a nine-year-old, not a lad of fifteen. The Occupation had seen him grow up.

With the war over, Bob Le Sueur's resistance activities had also come to an end, but his day job was still keeping him busy. As islanders returned from the mainland to find the damage that had been wrought in their absence, the number of insurance claims skyrocketed. There was, though, still no sign of the elusive branch manager, Mr Barnes, who had unceremoniously departed back in 1940. For the time being, it seemed, Bob would continue to call the shots at General Accident.

In November, he was invited to a meeting at the Grosvenor Hotel in London. The head of the company was over from America and wanted to meet his youngest manager. He was obviously impressed at Bob's ability to keep the business ticking over with virtually no help from outside, and asked him where he saw his future with General Accident. Bob replied that after five years cooped up on a small island, what he longed for more than anything was to travel. 'I'm sure that can be arranged,' the other man told him.

There was just one aspect of Bob's management of the Jersey office that the boss was struggling to get his head around. It was standard practice for insurance companies to spread their risk around, reinsuring high-value policies with other providers to guard against the danger of an unexpected claim imposing a crippling financial burden. This was, in a sense, the insurer's own insurance, and all that stood between them and potential bankruptcy. Without it, the whole business was little more than a gamble.

But with the link to the mainland severed, Bob had not had access to the usual trading channels. 'What did you do about reinsurance?' the head of the company asked him.

Bob took a deep breath before answering. 'I'm afraid, sir, there was none,' he said. 'It was either that or shut up shop, so I decided to just hope for the best.'

The look on the old man's face was one he would remember for the rest of his life.

Early in 1946, Phyllis Baker received an unexpected letter. It was from prisoner D 254397, alias Werner Rang, who was currently serving time at a POW camp in Hampshire. Since he had arrived at the camp the previous year, Werner had been practising his English, and he had finally plucked up the courage to write to the young woman who had captured his heart on Sark almost three years earlier.

So began a long correspondence between the two young people, which gradually grew into a mutual love affair, as Werner's beautifully illustrated missives won their way into Phyllis's heart. The fact that her father initially forbade her from replying, if anything, probably only fanned the flames.

That Christmas, some of the men from Werner's camp were invited to a festive meal at the home of a local aristocrat, Lady Gower. The older woman took an instant liking to Werner, and when he told her the story about his summer in Sark, and the beautiful young woman he had met there, she was determined to do her bit as a matchmaker. With Werner's approval, Lady Gower telephoned Phyllis and asked if she would like to come and visit Hampshire for a couple of weeks. The invitation was readily accepted.

By the time Phyllis arrived, Werner's wealthy patroness had fitted him out in a smart navy-blue suit and trilby hat, which was guaranteed to make a much better impression than his frayed prisoner's garb. She had even arranged a day out for the young couple in London, taking on the role of chaperone herself.

Once they reached the capital, Werner was instructed to keep his mouth shut so as not to attract attention. They took a tour of Westminster Abbey, admired the waxworks at Madame Tussauds, and enjoyed a lavish afternoon tea in the café at Harrods, where their fellow diners never suspected for a moment that the young man in the smart blue suit was actually a German prisoner of war.

That evening, back at Lady Gower's grand house, The Oaks, Werner and Phyllis were briefly left alone in the drawing room. It was here that they shared their first kiss, and Werner declared his love for her. The strength of his feelings came as little surprise to Phyllis – she had deduced as much from his letters – but what caught her off guard was the fact that she was beginning to feel the same way. By the time she returned to Sark, she was convinced that she had met her soulmate.

The next problem, though, was what to do about it. The war might be over, but Werner was still a German. Her father hadn't even wanted her to write to him. As the letters continued coming thick and fast – sometimes as many as two a day – Phyllis was racked with anxiety. Her weight dropped to just seven and a half stone from the stress, and the combined teasing from her grandmother and the local postman, both of whom had noticed the prodigious amount of mail she received, didn't help.

In the end, Phyllis decided to confide in her sister, but the response wasn't quite what she had hoped for. 'You must be mad!' the other girl told her.

By spring 1948, three years after liberation, the situation had come to a head. With the Olympic Games about to arrive in London, the German prisoners were finally being repatriated. Werner was informed that come 14 May, he would be sent back home, like it or not. Since his parents' house was now in the Russian Zone of Germany, this was not an appealing prospect – and if he did go, there was little hope that he would ever see Phyllis again.

Once again, Lady Gower telephoned Phyllis to ask if she would like to come and visit. On 8 May, less than a week before the deadline, she arrived at The Oaks, still not sure what she was going to do. But a few hours later, when Werner went down on one knee and proposed to her, there was no longer any doubt in her mind. The young lovers toasted their engagement with a bottle of Lady Gower's finest champagne.

At twenty-three, Phyllis was old enough to make her own decision about who she wanted to marry, but as a matter of courtesy Werner insisted that she telephone her father. Mr Baker didn't exactly take the news well, though. 'If all you have to tell me is you're marrying a German then you needn't bother to come home!' he told her angrily.

'Very well then, I won't!' Phyllis replied, slamming down the receiver.

Five days later, she and Werner were married, in a small ceremony at the Methodist church in Fareham. There were no family members present, just Lady Gower and a POW friend of Werner's called George. Their honeymoon was a day out on the Isle of Wight. It rained the whole time they were there, but the weather did nothing to dampen their spirits.

Phyllis returned to Sark soon after the wedding, but it was another six weeks before Werner was able to join her. By the time he arrived, her father had come round to the idea of his new son-in-law, and gradually they developed a good relationship. Werner began working on the family farm, and in time, after he and Phyllis discovered they were expecting a baby, they moved into a cottage of their own.

Almost seventy years later, Werner and Phyllis are still happily married, and still living in the 'little paradise' he first fell in love with in the summer of 1943.

In mainland Britain, the Occupation of the Channel Islands is generally seen as a minor sideshow when it comes to the broader Second World War experience – if, that is, it is ever even mentioned at all. Generations of British schoolchildren have learned about the rise of Hitler and the Nazis, about the occupations in France and the other European countries, but the subject of the Channel Islands rarely comes up. A key part of our own national experience of the war – not to mention a chilling insight into a counterfactual history that so easily could have been – has simply been swept under the carpet.

In part, this may be connected to Britain's anxieties about the Occupation story. In the months after liberation, teams of investigators arrived in Jersey and Guernsey to look into allegations of collaboration, but the issue went away again almost as quickly as it was raised. The mood of the government in London was perhaps best summed up in the promise of Home Secretary Herbert Morrison that he had enough 'whitewash' to cover the islands – the unspoken dual assumption being that the islanders had something to be ashamed of, and that it was a subject best avoided.

Over the years, perhaps Winston Churchill's unsympathetic view of the Channel Island experience – an experience that, however it turned out, would have undermined his soaring rhetoric about Britain's unique role in the war, uncompromising and never defeated – has fed into this collective desire to forget. Ask most mainland Brits today what they know about the Channel Islands and they are more likely to talk about tax breaks than German soldiers.

On the islands themselves, the situation couldn't be more different. Every year, on the anniversary of Liberation Day, huge crowds gather to watch the parades through St Peter Port and St Helier. For the local newspapers and radio stations, tales of the Occupation are a mainstay of discussion and debate. The high-street bookshops overflow with locally published memoirs and diaries, offering hundreds of individual perspectives on the most significant five years of the islands' collective history. An entire tourist industry has been built around the relics of the war – the bunkers and fortifications, the abandoned weaponry and uniforms, even the empty hospitals left behind by the Army of Occupation. The islanders can no more escape the Occupation now than they could escape the islands themselves during the war years. The legacies of that complex period are quite literally a part of the landscape – the concrete bunkers jutting out onto almost every stretch of sand and the huge observation towers still looming on the clifftops.

To those who lived through it, the Occupation was the defining moment in their lives – not just for the islanders, but for many of the Germans as well. In the decades following the Allied victory, as their nation was brought back into the European fold, many former enemies chose to return to the islands as friends. Some came to visit the houses they had stayed in, others to see the stunning natural landscape again. A number of former soldiers stayed in touch for the rest of their lives with islanders they had befriended across the divide of patriotic loyalty.

Some men, meanwhile, returned to exorcise old demons. In 1995, on the fiftieth anniversary of liberation, Judith Le Tissier arrived for a service of remembrance at her local church in Guernsey. As she parked her car outside, she was surprised to spot a vehicle with a German licence plate. He must be brave, she thought to herself.

Judith was a member of the church choir, which gave her a good vantage point to survey the congregation during the service. Sitting in the back row was an elderly man who she was sure must be the owner of the German vehicle. There was something about him that gave her the shivers.

She cast her mind back fifty years to the Occupation, when she had attended the same church as a child. Suddenly an image flashed into her mind of a German soldier who would stand at the back to prevent any troublemaking, his hand never far from the pistol on his belt. As a little girl, she had always been terrified of him.

At the end of the service, the man in the back row stood up and began walking down the aisle towards the altar. Judith could see that his cheeks were flecked with tears. When she caught his eye, he muttered something in broken English. It was three words: 'My liberation too.'

ACKNOWLEDGEMENTS

No man is an island, and this book would certainly never have been written without the generous assistance, support and patience of a great many people. First and foremost, I am grateful to the hundred-odd Channel Islanders who were willing to share their own Occupation memories with me during my three-month visit to Jersey, Guernsey and Sark in the summer of 2016: Jennifer Baker, Joyce Balleine, Alan Balleine, Vera Bearder, Betty Bishop, Jim Bishop, Kath Bisson, Mack Bisson, Brenda Bisson, Laura Bisson, Mazel Boleat, Doris Bougourd, Pauline Bown, Marcelle Burrows, Roy Burton, Jean-Claude Cadot, Vernon Cavey, Rex Champion, Yvonne Coleman, Joan Coutanche, Harry Coutanche, Margaret De Bourgos, Janet De Santos, Christine Delahay, Don Dolbel, Heather Duggan, Wynne Eker, Nellie Falla, Marie Ferbrache, Daphne Froulx, Olive Gaudion, Michael Ginns, Francis Girard, Joyce Girard, Ruth Gorvel, George Guille, Georgina Guille, Leo Harris, Tony Hobbs, Claire Jehan, Brenda Langlois, Marjorie Lawrence, Gwen Le Bideau, Jeff Le Caudy, Nellie Le Feuvre, Dennis Le Flem, Judy Le Flem, Joan Le Grand, Roger Le Gros, John Le Page, Joan Le Page, Lloyd Le Poidevin, Bob Le Sueur, Marion Le Tissier, Roy Le Tissier, Len Le Tissier, Frank Le Tissier, Mick Le Tissier, Judith Le Tissier, Michael Le Tissier, Eileen Lerche-Thomsen, Cyril John Lievre, Kath Lloyd, Eric Mace, Rosemary Mace, Daphne Macready, Miriam Mahy, Irene Mallet, Frank Marquis, Esme Marquis, George Martel, Gladys Martel, Liz Ogier, David O'Meara, Lilian Pardeau,

Brian Penaluna, Esther Peree, Alec Podger, Margaret Pringent, David Rabet, Phyllis Rang, Werner Rang, Tom Remfrey, Tony Rentsch, Yvonne Rounault, Arthur Ruez, Jolyon Sherwill, Osmund Simon, Margaret Smith, Margaret Stacey, Robin Stevens, Myrtle Tabel, Dorothy Taylor, Marion Torode, Marion Totsevin, Pat Troy, Michael Trubuil, Bryan Vandertang, Joan Vandertang, Tom Waterman, Eileen Watson, Pearl White-Regan, Adriana Wilcox, Ethel Wolley and a handful of others who wished to remain anonymous.

Many of my interviewees have been sharing their Occupation memories for years, and some have written their own books on the subject. For anyone interested in reading more of their stories, I cannot recommend these highly enough. Leo Harris's two volumes, *A Boy Remembers* and *Boys Remember More,* include not only dozens of fascinating anecdotes that I didn't have room for here, but also beautiful pen-and-ink illustrations by Leo himself. *Excuse Me, I'm Occupied* by Pearl White-Regan (née Smith) includes a number of wonderful poems written between performances at the Lyric, and Werner and Phyllis Rang's joint biography, *Island Destiny*, written by Richard Le Tissier, goes far beyond the scope of my book, telling the story of their lives together right up to the twenty-first century.

In my research I have drawn extensively on the published memoirs of Alexander Coutanche, Ambrose Sherwill and Sybil Hathaway, and on the diary of Baron von Aufsess, all of them, sadly, long gone and unavailable for interview. Major Lanz's account of the early months of occupation was kindly provided by Simon Hamon, from his own private collection, and Dr Alistair Rose's 'Impressions of the Occupation of Guernsey' by his son Michael. The diary of 'Mrs Le Bideau' – an unpublished, anonymous manuscript – was very generously given to me by Jackie de Carteret. In the absence of any biographical information on its author beyond the odd stray allusion in the text, I chose what I thought was an appealing and characteristically Guernsey name for the sharp and witty old lady who wrote it, but if any readers can shed light on her real identity I would be delighted to hear from them.

Many local people assisted with my search for interviewees,

helping to get the word out about my research and encouraging friends and family members to come forward. In particular, I am grateful to Maureen Bougeard, Andy Bown, Kaye Char, Simon Crowcroft, Peter Falla, David Gorvel, Angelika Harms-Stentiford, Michelle Johansen, Eileen Jones, Sonya Lavery, Nigel Lewis, Helen O'Meara, Mandy Regan, Chris Robillard and Janet Williams. Others provided me with invaluable research materials or shared second-hand stories from their own families – thanks to Sue Collins, Jeff Falla, Yvonne Gettings, Justin Joanknecht, Matthew Mauger, Chrysta Rang, Gail Shearer and Maurice Troy.

For helping to cast the net wider, I am grateful to print journalists Aaron Carpenter, Gill Kay and Nick Le Messurier, and to broadcasters Tony Gillham, Oliver Guillou and Jenny Kendall-Tobias. Jenny invited me onto her BBC Radio show only days after I arrived in Guernsey, and in the course of our interview I'm pretty sure I learned more from her than she learned from me. Thanks also to Adam Bayfield at the Guille-Alles Library for organising a public event about my research, as well as for hosting me on his excellent podcast.

I am grateful, too, to those who helped accommodate me and my family in the Channel Islands during our three-month visit and assisted with some of the practical challenges of adapting to a new home. In particular, thanks to Louise Harwood, Lynn, Gary and Anais De Carteret, Sally Hutchins, Carolyn McCormick, Emmy McMorrow, Paul and Ryan Neuvel, Isabel Picornell and Val Rowland.

The Occupation is a dense and complicated subject, and at times one particularly hard for a mainlander to get his head around. Fortunately a number of local experts were willing to lend a hand. I am grateful to Geraint Jennings of the Société Jersiaise, Richard Heaume of the Guernsey Occupation Museum, Danny Wakley of the Sark Museum, Phil Marrett of Jersey War Tours, Colin Isherwood and Matthew Costard of the Channel Islands Occupation Society, Amanda Bennet of Guernsey's Priaulx Library, Jason Monaghan of Guernsey Museums, Anna Baghiani and Bronwyn Matthews of the Lord Coutanche Library in Jersey, and fellow authors Gilly Carr and Gillian Mawson.

Aside from my own interviews, I also relied on information gleaned from more than forty published books, both historical accounts and personal memoirs. Among the most enlightening were *The German Occupation of the Channel Islands* by Charles Cruikshank, *Islands in Danger* by Alan and Mary Wood, *Channel Islands Invaded* by Simon Hamon, *Outpost of Occupation* by Barry Turner and *The Model Occupation* by Madeleine Bunting (the historian obliquely referred to on page 253). I am, of course, aware that Bunting's book is far from popular in the Channel Islands. Although my own approach is very different to hers, and I sympathise with those who feel her account did the islanders a disservice, I nonetheless have a lot of admiration for her work and the extraordinary stories she uncovered.

This book is not only the longest but by far the hardest I've written. For their generous support, practical and/or emotional, I am grateful to Michèle Barrett, Kristof Fabry, Christine Langhoff and Darren Rugg. For transcription of interviews I relied on the services of Rachel Lee, Becky Macnaughton, Isabelle Schoelcher and the indefatigable Gemma Edwards. Several people kindly volunteered to read all or part of the manuscript in search of errors, and I am grateful in particular to Linda King, Anna and Andy Le Page, Ben Spink and Fiona Waldispühl. My editor Iain MacGregor and my agent Jon Elek have offered confidence and encouragement throughout the process, and my copy-editor John English brought a sharp and sympathetic eye to the manuscript. Melissa Bond, Judith Long and Kaiya Shang expertly shepherded it through production. It was a conversation with Sandy King about his own family history in Jersey that first piqued my interest in the subject of the Occupation many years ago, and I am grateful to him for nudging me towards what has been a very long but rewarding journey.

Finally, this book is dedicated to my partner Nuala Calvi. Without her incredible support and patience while I was 'otherwise occupied', it would never have been finished, and her insightful advice on my messy first draft made an incalculable difference to the manuscript. I hope too that it stands as a memorial to all those who lived through the Occupation, in particular those who passed away before seeing the stories they told me in print.

Doris Bougourd (née Lihou)
4 April 1931–7 November 2017

Harry Coutanche
14 May 1922–6 July 2017

Nellie Falla (née Prince)
12 August 1919–21 September 2017

Michael Ginns
16 December 1927–2 February 2017

Gwen Le Bideau (née Trebert)
5 June 1936–14 April 2017

Dennis Le Flem
6 April 1926–1 November 2016

Miriam Mahy
12 January 1914–26 December 2017

Phyllis Rang (née Baker)
1 November 1924–29 November 2017

Werner Rang
18 March 1920–15 March 2018

INDEX